D1546257

LOLLARDS OF COVENTRY
1486–1522

LOLLARDS OF COVENTRY
1486–1522

Edited and translated by
SHANNON McSHEFFREY and NORMAN TANNER

CAMDEN FIFTH SERIES
Volume 23

CAMBRIDGE
UNIVERSITY PRESS

For the Royal Historical Society
University College London, Queen Street, London WC1 6BT
2003

BX
4901.3
.L655
2003

Published by the Press Syndicate of the University of Cambridge
The Edinburgh Building, Cambridge CB2 2RU, United Kingdom
40 West 20th Street, New York, NY 10011–4211, USA
477 Williamstown Road, Port Melbourne, VIC 3207, Australia

First published 2003

A catalogue record for this book is available from the British Library

Library of Congress Cataloging-in-Publication Data applied for

ISBN 0 521 83083 4 hardback

SUBSCRIPTIONS. The serial publications of the Royal Historical Society, *Royal Historical Society Transactions* (ISSN 0080–4401) and Camden Fifth Series (ISSN 0960–1163), volumes may be purchased together on annual subscription. The 2003 subscription price, which includes print and electronic access (but not VAT), is £67 (US$108 in the USA, Canada and Mexico) and includes Camden Fifth Series, volumes 22 and 23 (published in July and December) and Transactions Sixth Series, volume 13 (published in December). Japanese prices are available from Kinokuniya Company Ltd, P.O. Box 55, Chitose, Tokyo 156, Japan. EU subscribers (outside the UK) who are not registered for VAT should add VAT at their country's rate. VAT registered subscribers should provide their VAT registration number. Prices include delivery by air.

Subscription orders, which must be accompanied by payment, may be sent to a bookseller, subscription agent or direct to the publisher: Cambridge University Press, The Edinburgh Building, Shaftesbury Road, Cambridge CB2 2RU, UK; or in the USA, Canada and Mexico; Cambridge University Press, Journals Fulfillment Department, 110 Midland Avenue, Port Chester, NY 10573–4930, USA.

SINGLE VOLUMES AND BACK VOLUMES. A list of Royal Historical Society volumes available from Cambridge University Press may be obtained from the Humanities Marketing Department at the address above.

Printed and bound in the United Kingdom by Butler & Tanner Ltd, Frome and London

CONTENTS

Acknowledgements   vii
Editorial procedure   viii
Abbreviations   ix

INTRODUCTION   1
    The prosecution of heresy in the diocese of Coventry and
      Lichfield, 1486–1522   3
    The charges and the defendants' beliefs   14
    The defendants and the practice of Lollardy   23
    The documents   47

CHRONOLOGY OF EXAMINATIONS OF COVENTRY
LOLLARD SUSPECTS, 1486–1522   57

PROSECUTION OF THE COVENTRY LOLLARDS IN
THE ECCLESIASTICAL RECORDS, 1486–1522   61
    1486–1503   63
    1511–1512   102
    Abjurations, 1511–1512   259
    Undated fragments, c. 1511–1512   278
    1515–1522   280
    Explanatory notes   286

PROSECUTION OF THE COVENTRY LOLLARDS IN
FOXE'S MARTYROLOGIES AND IN THE COVENTRY
CIVIC ANNALS   293
    Explanatory notes   319

APPENDIX 1: Suspects named in the Coventry heresy
    prosecutions, 1486–1522   321

APPENDIX 2: Books named in the records of Coventry heresy
    prosecutions, 1486–1522   343

APPENDIX 3: Clerics and others present at Coventry heresy
    prosecutions, 1486–1522   345

INDEX   349

ACKNOWLEDGEMENTS

We thank Lichfield Joint Record Office for permission to publish the Court Book of Bishop Geoffrey Blyth, MS B/C/13, which constitutes the principal document edited here. We are especially grateful to the Archivist and staff of the Record Office for their help and consideration. We thank Andrew Pettegree, Literary Director of the Royal Historical Society, and Mrs J.N. McCarthy, Executive Secretary of the Society, for their assistance with publication.

We acknowledge our debt to many scholars who have earlier worked on the relevant material, especially in recent times John Fines, J.A.F. Thomson, Imogen Luxton, and Anne Hudson.

Our thanks are due to many people: Anne Hudson and Margaret Aston for encouragement and advice; Bob Tittler, John A.W. Lock, and Dave Postles for help with place names, and to Bob also for comments about civic annals; Andrew Larsen and Kellie Robertson for suggestions about branding; John Arnold for permission to cite an unpublished paper and P.J.P. Goldberg for allowing a paper to be read ahead of time; David Gormley for suggestions about Chaucer; Thomas Freeman and David Loades for invaluable help with John Foxe; David Bishop of Birmingham City Library for checking the transcription of the Birmingham Annal; Melanie Fishbane for research assistance; and Eric Reiter, Shannon's husband, for reading the entire typescript.

The division of work has been roughly as follows. Norman Tanner initiated the project, made an initial transcription of most of the manuscript material, and is mainly responsible for the English translation. The rest of the work – including the ordering of the material and its final presentation, the introduction, notes, and appendices – has been done largely by Shannon McSheffrey. We have worked together with pleasure and harmony – albeit with sadness at the nature of the trials – and regard the edition as a joint work.

Shannon McSheffrey
Concordia University, Montreal
Norman Tanner
Campion Hall, Oxford University

EDITORIAL PROCEDURE

Under each heading below, the transcription of the original manuscript is followed by the modern English translation. In the transcription of the original manuscript documents, punctuation and the use of capitals have been modernized and paragraphs have been introduced. The division of words has been modernized (e.g. *before* not *be fore*, *the same* not *thesame*). The forms *i* and *j*, *u* and *v* have been rationalized and the form *ff* has been reduced to *F* or *f* as appropriate. Abbreviations have been expanded except where the contrary is noted by an abbreviation mark ('). Frequently, however, there is an element of conjecture in the expansions. Names of persons in the headings, translation, and indices reflect a common modern English spelling of the forename (usually rendered in Latin in the document) and the most commonly used spelling of the surname in cases where there are multiple spellings. In transcriptions from early printed books, spelling of the original has been maintained (i.e. *u* and *v* have not been rationalized, and superscripts have been reproduced, e.g. y^e and w^t), but abbreviations have been expanded. The translations of both the original Latin and the early sixteenth-century English are into modern English, although to a great extent the flavour of the vernacular passages has been maintained (spelling has been modernized and some archaic words translated with modern ones).

All material in italics, bold type, and within square brackets has been supplied. Points in square brackets – [...] – indicate either that the script is illegible or that there is a hole in the document. There are two types of notes to the texts: the footnotes, indicated by a superscript letter ([a]), are textual notes, indicating for instance marginal notes made by the scribe. The endnotes, indicated by a superscript number ([32]), offer explanatory material.

ABBREVIATIONS

A&M (1563)	John Foxe, *Actes & monuments of these latter & perillous dayes, touching matters of the church* (London, 1563; STC 11222).
A&M (1570)	John Foxe, *The first (second) volume of the ecclesiasticall history contaynyng the Actes and Monumentes, newly recognised and inlarged*, 2 vols continuously paginated (London, 1570; STC 11223).
A&M (1843)	John Foxe, *Acts and Monuments*, 8 vols, George Townsend (ed.) (London, 1843).
Bishop Blythe's Visitations	Peter Heath (ed.), *Bishop Geoffrey Blythe's Visitations c. 1515–1525*, Collections for a History of Staffordshire, Staffordshire Record Society, 4th series, 7 (1973).
Blyth's visitation book	Lichfield, Lichfield Record Office, MS B/V/1/1, Bishop Geoffrey Blyth's visitation book, 1515–1525.
BRUC	A.B. Emden, *Biographical Register of the University of Cambridge to 1500* (Cambridge, 1963).
BRUO to 1500	A.B. Emden, *Biographical Register of the University of Oxford to 1500*, 3 vols (Oxford, 1957–1959).
Coventry Leet Book	*Coventry Leet Book, 1420–1555*, 4 pts, M.D. Harris (ed.), Early English Text Society, Original Series, 134, 135, 138, 146 (1907–1913).
DNB	*Dictionary of National Biography*, Leslie Stephen (ed.) (London, 1886).
Fines, 'Heresy trials'	John Fines, 'Heresy trials in the diocese of Coventry and Lichfield, 1511–1512', *Journal of Ecclesiastical History*, 44 (1963), pp. 160–174.
Greatrex	Joan Greatrex, *Biographical Register of the English Cathedral Priories of the Province of Canterbury, c. 1066–1540* (Oxford and New York, 1997).
Hudson, *Premature Reformation*	Anne Hudson, *The Premature Reformation: Wycliffite Texts and Lollard History* (Oxford, 1988).
Kent Heresy Proceedings	Norman P. Tanner (ed.), *Kent Heresy Proceedings 1511–12*, Kent Records 26 (Maidstone, 1997).
Latham	R.E. Latham, *Revised Medieval Latin Word-List from British and Irish Sources* (London, 1965).

LCB	Lichfield, Lichfield Record Office, MS B/C/13, Court Book of Bishop Geoffrey Blyth of Coventry and Lichfield, 1511–1512.
Le Neve, *Cov. & Lich.*	John Le Neve, *Fasti Ecclesiae Anglicanae, 1300–1541*, 12 vols (London, 1962–1967), X, *Coventry and Lichfield Diocese.*
Luxton, 'Postscript'	Imogen Luxton, 'The Lichfield Court Book: a postscript', *Bulletin of the Institute of Historical Research*, 44 (1971), pp. 120–125.
McSheffrey, *Gender*	Shannon McSheffrey, *Gender and Heresy: Women and Men in Lollard Communities, 1420–1530* (Philadelphia PA, 1995).
Norwich Trials	Norman P. Tanner (ed.), *Heresy Trials in the Diocese of Norwich, 1428–31*, Camden Society, 4th series, XX (Cambridge, 1977).
OED	*Oxford English Dictionary Online* <http://dictionary.oed.com> (Oxford, 1992–2001).
PCC	Prerogative Court of Canterbury.
Phythian-Adams, *Desolation*	Charles Phythian-Adams, *Desolation of a City: Coventry and the Urban Crisis of the Late Middle Ages* (Cambridge, 1979).
PRO	London, Public Record Office.
REED Coventry	R.W. Ingram (ed.), *Records of Early English Drama: Coventry* (Toronto, 1981).
Reg. Blyth	Lichfield, Lichfield Record Office, MS. B/A/1/14i, Register of Bishop Geoffrey Blyth of Coventry and Lichfield (1503–1531).
Reg. Hales	Lichfield, Lichfield Record Office, MS. B/A/1/12, Register of Bishop John Hales of Coventry and Lichfield (1459–1490).
STC	A.W. Pollard and G.R. Redgrave (eds), *A Short Title Catalogue of Books printed in England, Scotland and Ireland and of English Books printed abroad 1475–1640*, revised W.A. Jackson, F.S. Ferguson and K.F. Panzer, 2 vols (London, 1976 and 1986).
Thomson, *Later Lollards*	John A.F. Thomson, *The Later Lollards, 1414–1520* (London, 1965).
VCH Warws.	H. Arthur Doubleday and William Page (eds), *The Victoria History of the County of Warwick*, 8 vols (London, 1904–1969).

INTRODUCTION

The Lollard community of the Midlands city of Coventry, active between at least the 1480s and the early 1520s, is among the most well-documented of English heretical communities of the late Middle Ages.[1] This is especially owing to the survival of the Lichfield Court Book, a detailed record of the examinations, depositions, abjurations, and sentences in a series of proceedings against the city's heretical community in 1511–1512. The present volume offers both the Latin original and an English translation of this fascinating document, together with all other known evidence for heretical activities in Coventry in the late fifteenth and early sixteenth centuries. These documents (including the Lichfield Court Book itself) derive mostly from the administrative records of the bishops of the diocese of Coventry and Lichfield, but we have also included accounts of heresy prosecutions from the Protestant martyrologist, John Foxe, and from Coventry's civic annals. The largest part of this material has hitherto been available only in manuscript and, in the case of the Lichfield Court Book, a manuscript difficult to read. Easy access to the original Latin texts, along with an English translation, will help bring these intriguing materials to a wider audience of scholars and students.

Lollardy was the only popular heretical movement to flourish in England during the Middle Ages. Following the inspiration, and perhaps the leadership, of fourteenth-century Oxford theologian, John Wyclif (d. 1384), a religious movement developed in the late fourteenth and early fifteenth centuries. The Lollards, as Wyclif's followers came to be known, were dedicated to an emphasis on access to vernacular scripture and denial of the efficacy of many late medieval Catholic teachings and practices (such as the sacrament of the Eucharist and the cult of saints). Until the second decade of the fifteenth century, the main strength of the movement was in the support it found among the Oxford academic community (from which a significant corpus of Lollard writings emerged) and some gentry adherents. The 1410s, however, saw both a purge of those suspected of heresy at Oxford and an abortive Lollard-associated revolt against the crown, led by Sir John Oldcastle. These events robbed the movement of its academic and aristocratic

---

[1] The Lollards of Coventry have been studied previously by Fines, 'Heresy trials'; Thomson, *Later Lollards*, pp. 104–116; Luxton, 'Postscript'; and McSheffrey, *Gender*, pp. 22–46.

support, and from about 1420 onward Lollardy was associated primarily with lay believers of lower socio-economic station. Although there were a number of prosecutions in the 1420s, in the middle decades of the fifteenth century there was either little Lollard activity, or little official interest in uncovering it. From the mid-1480s until the 1530s there is greater evidence for communities of Lollard adherents in most dioceses in the southern half of the kingdom of England. Lollards are unlikely to have been ever more than a tiny minority in late medieval England as a whole, but in some villages and towns they constituted a sizeable and sometimes influential minority. The extent of Lollard influence on the subsequent development of English Protestantism is much debated; in any case it seems certain that when Protestant reformers began to spread similar ideas in England in the 1520s and 1530s, most Lollards were absorbed into the various streams of sixteenth-century Protestantism as they developed.[2]

Coventry was a large and important city, at least in contemporary English terms, during the late Middle Ages. It was, however, undergoing a serious economic decline in the late fifteenth and early sixteenth centuries, the precise period during which a community of Lollards flourished within its confines. Heresy – or at least evidence for it – had apparently been dormant in Coventry, as in other areas of the Midlands, in the middle years of the fifteenth century, in contrast to its strength in the early years of the Lollard movement and for some time after Oldcastle's uprising in 1414.[3] A revival of official interest in Lollard activity – and thus any surviving evidence for a heretical community – came in the 1480s. In 1486, Bishop John Hales of the diocese of Coventry and Lichfield prosecuted eight Coventry men for heresy. In 1488 one woman from Derbyshire and in 1490 another man from Coventry (neither of whom apparently had connections with the 1486 suspects) were similarly forced to abjure. Despite the bishop's efforts, at least some of the Coventry men whom Hales had prosecuted in 1486 continued to practise their faith clandestinely, and it seems likely that in the last decade of the fifteenth and first decade of the sixteenth centuries a considerable group of heretics developed in the city. Like John Hales, Geoffrey Blyth, bishop from 1503 to 1531, also intermittently pursued Lollards in the largest city in his diocese in the early years of the sixteenth century. Finally, in the autumn of 1511 (at the same time

---

[2] The standard work on Lollardy is Hudson, *Premature Reformation*. A thorough and up-to-date bibliography of Lollard studies is maintained by Derrick G. Pitard for the Lollard Society at the Society website: Derrick G. Pitard, 'Bibliographies for Lollard studies', 24 February 2001, <http://home.att.net/~lollard/bibhome.html> (accessed 9 August 2001).

[3] Thomson, *Later Lollards*, pp. 95–104.

as prosecutions of Lollards were launched in other dioceses of the province of Canterbury),[4] Blyth began a more systematic attempt to eradicate the heretics of his diocese. Over the following five months, he brought sixty-seven suspects before him or his deputies and sentenced one woman to be burned. But, like the prosecutions of 1486, his attempts did not dissuade all those he prosecuted from heresy, and there is evidence that, at least in 1515, some attempts were made by episcopal officials to observe those who had previously been involved in the movement. In 1520, seven of those who had abjured in 1511 and 1512 were prosecuted once more and burned as relapsed heretics, with another man who had fled being recaptured and likewise executed in late 1521 or early 1522.

The story of the Coventry Lollards as revealed in the records is dramatic enough in itself. In addition, the evidence that the prosecutors left gives us detailed pictures both of the inner workings of an urban Lollard community in the early sixteenth century and of episcopal strategies of prosecution. Through the examinations and depositions recorded in the Lichfield Court Book, we learn a great deal about how the bishop and his representatives attempted to uncover and deal with the heretics in the diocese, how Lollards were recruited, how they gathered together, how they practised their faith, how the participation of men and women differed and how books and reading were central to their observance of their religious ideas.

The prosecution of heresy in the diocese of Coventry and Lichfield, 1486–1522

The trials

In March 1486, eight men from Coventry were brought before Bishop Hales, in St Michael's parish church in the city, accused of various heretical doctrines. All of them admitted the charges brought against them, abjured in the customary manner, were absolved and were given penances. A woman from Derbyshire and a man from Coventry were also later tried by Bishop Hales, at his manor at Beaudesert in 1488 and in his palace at Lichfield in 1490 respectively. The bishop was supported by a large and influential group of witnesses to the abjurations in March 1486: the prior of the cathedral priory of Coventry, twelve clerics (in all cases with university degrees mentioned, six with doctorates

---

[4] See Fines, 'Heresy trials,' p. 160.

in theology or in canon or civil law), two notaries and 'very many others'. Besides those whose names appear in Hales's register there may have been others who were examined and abjured in the 1486 proceedings. Matthew Markelond, for instance, claimed in 1511 that, around the time that John Smyth and the others had abjured, he expressly renounced each and every one of the heretical opinions that he had held, and that he had not fallen back into heresy since. His 'abjuration' may not have been an official one, though, as he abjured again in 1511, with no sign that he was then regarded as relapsed.[5]

We have evidence, some direct and some indirect, that the bishops of Coventry and Lichfield sporadically pursued the heresy problem in the decades on either side of 1500. At least one isolated case of heresy was heard by Bishop Geoffrey Blyth soon after he became bishop: the case of John Shepherde in 1503.[6] Shepherde likely had no connection with the Coventry Lollards, though – he neither named any of them nor was named by them in the subsequent proceedings, and he came from a town in Lancashire, some distance from Coventry. There are also two suggestions in the Lichfield Court Book that there were other proceedings, now lost, in the years between 1490 and 1511, and these cases were more closely related to the main Lollard community in the city of Coventry itself. Thomas Warde told the court in 1511, for instance, that he had entirely renounced heresy and submitted himself to the judgement of the church twelve years before, that is about 1499 (when the bishop was John Arundel, 1496–1502). Alice Rowley admitted that she had been forced to purge herself of the suspicion of heresy (which she did with sixteen compurgators, including the wives of several prominent men) about 1506.[7] These were almost certainly not part of a large-scale heresy prosecution such as was launched in 1511, since memories of that would have made their way into the depositions recorded in the Lichfield Court Book, if nowhere else. Rather they seem to have been ad hoc reactions, perhaps resulting from individual confessions or particular notoriety.

The trials of 1511–1512 were much more extensive. Blyth, like his fellow bishops in the dioceses of Canterbury, London, and Lincoln, was likely to have been prompted to investigate the Lollards in his diocese by the 1511 convocation of bishops of the province of Canterbury, which identified heresy as a serious problem.[8] We do not know precisely what led to the late October arrests of a number of key members of the community, but it seems likely from various reports in

---

[5] See below, pp. 152, 169, 266.
[6] See below, p. 97.
[7] See below, pp. 122, 155.
[8] Fines, 'Heresy trials,' p. 160.

the court book that preachers made announcements from the pulpits warning about the dangers of heresy and erroneous books, and fulminating sentences of major excommunication on those who did not report heretical persons and readings.[9] In the course of the proceedings held from late October 1511 to early April 1512, forty-nine individuals confessed to charges of heresy and a considerable number of others either appeared as defendants or were mentioned as suspects.[10] There was clearly continuity between the men who had abjured heresy in 1486 and those who were brought before Bishop Blyth and his deputies twenty-five years later; three men who had been involved in the earlier trials – John Blumston *alias* Master John Physicion, Roger Brown, and John Smyth – remained active proselytizers into the early sixteenth century according to those examined in 1511–1512. They were all dead by the time of Blyth's prosecution, however, so they could not be prosecuted a second time.

The proceedings started some time before 28 October 1511 and continued through November and early December 1511, began again in mid-January and carried on through mid-March 1512. Many defendants appeared at two or more sessions. In most cases the place of the 1511–1512 trials was recorded simply as 'in the aforesaid place', but in every case in which the place was identified up to and including 16 January 1512, it was either 'at the priory at Maxstoke' or simply 'at Maxstoke': the priory of Augustinian canons at Maxstoke in Warwickshire.[11] At least some of the accused were imprisoned there, or possibly at nearby Maxstoke Castle, and they may have been kept there for several months.[12] Thereafter, from 22 January 1512, the venue of the proceedings against the Lollards moved to Coventry itself: 'at Coventry' on 22 January; in the parish church of the Holy Trinity on 13 February; in the chapter house or in the church of the cathedral priory on most other occasions.

All the trials of 1511–1512 until 26 January 1512 appear to have been conducted by the bishop in person. On several occasions, however, a sizeable group of clerics – usually eight or nine – were recorded as present with him and occasionally he was said to be acting 'on the

---

[9] See below, p. 132.

[10] See Appendix 1 below.

[11] David Knowles and R. Neville Hadcock, *Medieval Religious Houses: England and Wales* (London: Longmans, Green and Co., 1953), p. 145; *VCH Warws.*, II, pp. 91–94.

[12] Alice Rowley, for instance, was apparently arrested on 30 October 1511, first appeared before the bishop 31 October 1511, and, according to another deponent, was in Maxstoke Castle, presumably as a prisoner, in early December 1511. She may have been taken back to Coventry only in mid-January when the proceedings changed venue. See below, pp. 123, 230, 240. On Maxstoke Castle, see *VCH Warws.*, II, pp. 291–293; IV, pp. 133–137.

advice of those assisting him'.[13] Frequent attenders were William Dykons, prior of Maxstoke Priory, William Pollesworthe, prior of the cathedral priory in Coventry, two observant Franciscans, Thomas Danyell and David Jacobi, and various secular clerics: Thomas Barker, John Blyth, Ralph Cantrell, William Skelton, and William Wilton.[14]

The final trials, after 26 January 1512, were conducted by commissaries appointed by the bishop: Robert Caulyn, rector of Holy Trinity church, Chester, accompanied by, on various occasions, William Pollesworth and John Impingham, respectively prior and subprior of the cathedral priory of Coventry, and William Palden. Thomas Fitzherbert, the bishop's vicar-general in spirituals, and John Webbe, prior of the cathedral priory of Coventry, acted as the bishop's commissaries in the proceedings against Robert Silkby in 1521–1522.[15]

Two depositions taken in 1515, recorded in Bishop Blyth's visitation book, suggest both that the bishop and his staff still took some interest in the Lollard community of Coventry after the proceedings of 1511–1512, and that some of the Lollards themselves continued their activities even after abjuration. One witness was apparently a failed convert, while the other appears to have been a spy, sent by a former Coventry sheriff (although whether he was acting in his capacity as a civic official is unclear), to observe a woman who had abjured in 1511.[16] There is no evidence that the bishop or his deputies took further actions at this point.

Subsequent evidence of episcopal proceedings against Coventry Lollards comes mostly from non-ecclesiastical sources. Both John Foxe and the Coventry annals record that seven Lollards, at least six of whom had appeared before the bishop in 1511–1512, were apprehended in the spring of 1520, Foxe dating the arrest to Ash Wednesday 1519 (i.e. 22 February 1520 by modern reckoning). According to Foxe, they were first put into prison, presumably in Coventry, and then two days later taken to Maxstoke Priory. In all probability there they underwent some form of trial, although Foxe gives no details about this. As they were all relapsed heretics, they were sentenced to be burned to death, a sentence that was apparently carried out in early April 1520.[17]

Foxe also tells us that at the time the seven were arrested in the spring of 1520 Robert Silkby fled from Coventry. He was at large for almost two years, perhaps using the alias Dumbleby, but was arrested in Kent and brought to Coventry in December 1521 or mid-January

[13] See, for instance, below, pp. 81, 212, 214.
[14] For further information about the clerics present at the heresy proceedings, see below, Appendix 3.
[15] See below, pp. 250, 252, 255, 282.
[16] See below, p. 282.
[17] See below, pp. 298, 310, and 315.

1522, where he too was burned as a relapse. The record of his condemnation survives and was inserted into the Lichfield Court Book,[18] presumably because the court book itself was consulted for documentation of his relapsed status.

The sentences

The sentences, or penances, imposed on about half those found guilty at the trials are recorded. For the most part, they were directed towards public acknowledgement of the convicted person's recantation.

At the first trials, conducted by Bishop Hales in March 1486, all eight individuals convicted of heresy were punished with participation in a series of rituals. On the following Friday, they were to process in penitential garb, clad only in their undergarments (*solis liniis vestibus induti*), carrying a wooden faggot on their shoulders, from St Michael's parish church in Coventry, and there individually and publicly to acknowledge that they had voluntarily abjured their heresies; then to offer a candle and their faggot at the shrine of Our Lady in the Carmelite friary in the city, on account of their former contempt for the shrine; and finally, to repeat similar rituals on the following Sunday, when their abjurations were to be explained to the people in the parish church. In 1488 Margery Goyte was sentenced to variations on these rituals in her former home town of Ashbourne in Derbyshire, excepting the visit to the shrine of Mary; Robert Clerke similarly in Coventry in 1490. Instilling fear in others was explicitly stated to be the motive of the 1486 and 1488 penances.[19]

For the trials between 1511 and 1512, the sentence imposed on Thomas Flesshor on 3 November 1511, shortly after the beginning of the trials, acted as a model. It resembled the earlier penances in various ways. Flesshor was ordered to take part in the 'general procession' at Coventry on the Friday following his sentencing, carrying a faggot of wood on his shoulders. On the following Sunday he was to head the procession in St Michael's parish church in the city, again carrying a faggot of wood; he was to be present at the sermon there and was to listen to the preacher as he expounded the charges against him, during which time he was to raise the faggot back onto his shoulders. The rest of the penance, the sentence declared, was deferred until the bishop summoned him again.[20] Many other sentences simply said that the

---

[18] Now LCB, fo. 9r; see below, p. 283.
[19] See below, pp. 76–96.
[20] See below, pp. 134–136.

penance was to be the same as that imposed on Thomas Flesshor,[21] though in a few cases the penance, or part of it, was to take place in the person's home town or village rather than in Coventry.[22]

There were only a few variations to this more or less standard format, in contrast to the great variety of penances imposed on Kentish Lollards by Archbishop Warham about the same time.[23] Thomas Wrixham, Robert Silkby, and ten others sentenced in late November 1511, in addition to the usual penances, were forbidden to work in their shops or elsewhere, or to enter a church, before the following Sunday. Of those given penances at this time, Thomas Banbrooke was to join the others part way through the penance, presumably reflecting his claim to a lesser role in heretical activities.[24] A number of the women's penances were mitigated in various ways: Margery Goyte's penance in 1488, for instance was remitted from three days to one, in the hope that she would behave well in future.[25] Margery Locock, although apparently the first to confess her involvement in heresy at the end of October 1511, was not compelled to abjure nor was she given any public penance, for fear that her husband would repudiate her (presumably because of the public humiliation).[26] Joan Gest's punishment was less severe than that of the men who abjured along with her, presumably at least partly because of her sex; although there is no sign that her Lollard activities were less enthusiastic than those of her husband, when she, her husband, and a number of other men were given penances in early November 1511, hers was reduced as long as she behaved well towards her husband and the church in the future.[27] Rose Furnour's penance was to fast on bread and water on the vigil of the Assumption for seven years. The stated reason for the lenience of her penance was that she had confessed immediately and spontaneously and with great sorrow and contrition, but her relative youth and her dependent status may also have influenced the decision: although she was twenty-four, she was described as a girl (*puella*) and she had been a servant of Robert Hachet, a leading heretic.[28]

---

[21] See, e.g., below, pp. 163, 166, 169, 174. In some cases 'the same penance as for Robert Silkby' was ordered, although Silkby's penance was not described in detail and was said simply to be 'the same as for Landesdale, Flesshor and others' (see below, pp. 177, 190, 220).

[22] See, for example, below, p. 169 for Birmingham; p. 225 for Aston, near Birmingham.

[23] *Kent Heresy Proceedings*, pp. xv–xvii and xxv; N. Tanner, 'Penances imposed on Kentish Lollards by Archbishop Warham 1511–12', in M. Aston and C. Richmond (eds), *Lollardy and the Gentry in the Later Middle Ages* (New York, 1997), pp. 229–249.

[24] See below, pp. 189ff, 205ff.

[25] See below, p. 90.

[26] See below, p. 122.

[27] See below, pp. 166, 169.

[28] See below, pp. 221ff. Julian Yong, aged twenty, despite being even younger than

Yet, despite the evidence that Blyth was inclined to give women lesser penances, he also gave the most severe punishments to Lollards of the female sex: the only heretic to be burned in 1511–1512 was a woman, Joan Warde *alias* Wasshingburn, and apart from this execution, the harshest penance was given to Alice Rowley. Rowley was ordered to watch the burning of Joan Warde, all the time carrying her own faggot, which she was then to leave together with an offering of 12 pence at the shrine of Mary in the Carmelite friary.[29] Witnessing Warde's death matched a similar penance imposed by Archbishop Warham of Canterbury on seven convicted heretics in his diocese less than a year earlier in May 1511.[30] This was a gruesome enough punishment, although Foxe reported that in some cases in the early sixteenth century children of convicted heretics were actually compelled to light the fire that would burn their parents.[31] Alice Rowley may have been given a more severe penance than the others both because of her prominence in the group (which was not surpassed, however, by the positions of Roger Landesdale and Robert Silkby), and because, as she admitted, she had falsely purged herself of an accusation of heresy in 1506. Presumably Rowley was not technically relapsed in 1512, but she was close to it.

Of those convicted at the 1511–1512 trials, only Joan Warde *alias* Wasshingburn was condemned to death. She was the last to be tried and the proceedings against her appear to have been intended as the culmination of the trials. She was handed over as a relapsed heretic to the secular arm, in the persons of the sheriffs of Coventry, on 12 March 1512 and she was burnt three days later. (As discussed below, the Coventry annals suggest that six other people were burned with Joan Warde in 1512. It seems likely that this is an error,[32] but it is possible that the surviving ecclesiastical records omit the condemnation of the others.)

Although Warde *alias* Wasshingburn was probably the only person put to death in 1511–1512, eight others convicted then were burned in Coventry a decade later, while Blyth was still Bishop of Coventry and Lichfield: Robert Hachet, Thomas Bown, Joan Smyth, William Hawkyns, Thomas Wrixham, John Archer, and Roger (or Thomas) Landesdale. Following a stay at Maxstoke, where they presumably underwent interrogation and perhaps formal prosecution, on Palm

---

Rose Furnour, was nonetheless given a standard penance, as was John Bull, aged seventeen. See below, p. 221.

[29] See below, p. 241.

[30] *Kent Heresy Proceedings*, p. 36.

[31] Foxe, *A&M* (1570), pp. 917, 964; *A&M* (1843), IV, pp. 123, 181–182, 245 (cases from 1506 and 1522).

[32] See below, p. 56.

Sunday (1 April 1520) the seven accused were brought back to Coventry. According to Foxe's 1563 version of the story, they were at first given the penance of wearing an embroidered badge of faggots on their clothes so that all might know they were heretics (a fairly common penance),[33] but when Robert Hachet remonstrated with the bishop that they were being punished only for saying prayers in English, the bishop was persuaded by his advisors that these people were too dangerous to release, '& so [he] gaue iudgement on them all to be burned'. He excepted, however, Joan Smyth, who was at first sent home. (In the 1570 version, Foxe omits the stories of the embroidered badges and Hachet's remonstrance, saying only that they were brought back to Coventry and all except Joan Smyth were sentenced to be executed as relapses.) Foxe goes on to say that Joan Smyth was likewise condemned, however, when the summoner accompanying her home in the darkness discovered a scroll in her sleeve on which was written the Lord's Prayer, the Creed, and the Ten Commandments. All seven were thus executed on 4 April 1520 in the Little Park outside the Coventry walls. About two years later, Robert Silkby, who had fled from Coventry when the others were arrested, was likewise burned as a relapse.[34]

It is hard to know what to make of Foxe's story about the bishop's initial inclination to be lenient in his treatment of these obviously obdurate heretics; if there is truth to it, it does suggest that Blyth was somewhat reluctant to burn them, either because he was not entirely convinced their sins were so serious as to merit death, or because he did not want to create martyrs.

Appalling though any punishment of religious dissent now seems to us, the sentences imposed by Bishops Hales and Blyth were not unduly harsh by the standards of the age. The two bishops, for the most part, kept to a relatively simple and low-key format, albeit one that was humiliating for the convicted. Handing over relapsed or obdurate heretics to the secular authorities, in the knowledge that they would be burned by the latter, was a requirement of the secular law of the country, namely of the statute *De heretico comburendo* enacted by Parliament in 1401,[35] even though the church authorities obviously should not be absolved of complicity in the arrangement. Flogging, which was ordered at some other trials of Lollards, was avoided in the present ones.[36] So too was imprisonment, except briefly following conviction, though

---

[33] See Tanner, 'Penances', pp. 235–237.

[34] See below, pp. 295–315.

[35] *Statutes of the Realm*, 10 vols (London, 1810–1828; reprint London, 1963), II, pp. 125–128.

[36] For the punishment of Lollards after the suppression of Oldcastle's insurrection in 1414, see Thomson, *Later Lollards*, ch. 11; *Norwich Trials*, pp. 22–25; *Kent Heresy Proceedings*, pp. xv–xvii; Tanner, 'Penances', pp. 229–249.

several suspects were noted as having been kept in prison between their appearances in court,[37] and Bishop Blyth said ominously in a letter to the Bishop of Lincoln that suspects 'will not confesse but by payne of prisonment'.[38] Clearly, there was a fair amount of pressure to extract confessions, thought there is no explicit mention of torture.

Only occasionally is there information about the outcome of the penances, though all the death sentences appear to have been carried out. The eight persons sentenced in 1486 performed their penances, as the cleric supervising them certified, and a note said that Joan Smyth performed her penances imposed in November 1511.[39] Frequently the bishop allowed himself leeway to impose further penances at a later date, as in the sentences imposed on Thomas Flesshor and those modelled on it, mentioned above, but he does not appear usually to have exercised the option.

The investigative process

The Lichfield Court Book, the informal notebook kept by a clerk for Bishop Blyth and the other prosecutors of the Coventry community, is a record of the investigative process itself. Notes in the margins and in the depositions themselves show how the document was used in the course of the actual prosecution. They reveal in considerable detail the tactics and procedures the bishop and his deputies employed.

Like other ecclesiastical officials who investigated Lollardy, Bishop Blyth and his deputies examined few witnesses from outside the Lollard community. Only two apparently non-Lollard witnesses, John Olyver of Maxstoke and a man named Symon, gave depositions recorded in the Lichfield Court Book, while in the brief record of the testimony offered against Lollards in 1515 one of the deponents was a spy sent by Thomas Rowley, formerly sheriff of Coventry.[40] Otherwise it is remarkable how infrequently non-Lollards testified against Lollards.

Instead of relying on orthodox witnesses, the prosecutors traced the social connections among the Lollards through testimony offered by insiders. This was the tactic most likely to ferret out heretics, even if it was not wholly successful – the deposition given by William Borodall in 1515 indicates that his parents, Nicholas and Margaret Borodall, were involved in heretical circles with men such as Roger Landesdale,

---

[37] See below, pp. 75, 81, 113, 193.

[38] See below, p. 139.

[39] See below, pp. 80, 163.

[40] See below, pp. 122, 240, 282. Another example of non-Lollard testimony is that given by the orthodox neighbours of Margery Baxter of Norwich; *Norwich Trials*, pp. 43–51.

Robert Hachet, and Thomas Banbrooke from at least 1507, yet they are not mentioned in the records of 1511–1512.[41] The 1511 investigation was apparently broken open by one of the early depositions – the testimony of Robert Silkby, for instance, or possibly the deposition of John Holywod, which is no longer extant, but to which Robert Silkby and John Jonson, examined before and on 28 October, referred.[42] As in the case of Holywod's testimony, the depositions of those questioned early in the proceedings were routinely used in the interrogation of those who appeared later.[43] When Silkby was questioned at the beginning of the investigation, for instance, he noted that Alice Rowley knew more about the wife of Bromley and Mother Margaret than he did; in the margin beside this is written, '*Interrogat* Rowley' ('Ask Rowley'), and indeed Alice Rowley later provided evidence about these two women.[44] Beside the record of Thomasina Bradeley's interrogation in late November or early December 1511, it was noted that a question came *ex deposicione mariti* ('from the deposition of the husband'). Thomasina was also confronted with the testimony of another previous deponent, William Lodge.[45] William Revis, examined about the same time as Thomasina Bradeley, was clearly replying to a question drawn from Thomas Wrixham's deposition given on 25 November when he denied he had ever said that Landesdale was a good man and that he (Wrixham) regretted Landesdale's troubles.[46]

In cases where an obdurate suspect would not admit the truth of what an earlier witness had claimed, the bishop used the tactic of bringing in the first witness to confront him or her, face to face. Often these 'witnesses for the prosecution' were leading Lollards, which was no doubt demoralizing for those who had tried not to give in. During John Atkynson's examination, Robert Silkby appeared in person to repeat allegations he had made about Atkynson after the latter refused to admit any contact with heretics; Silkby's accusation and Roger Landesdale's corroboration the next day, seem to have led to Atkynson's eventual admission of guilt.[47] Similarly, Thomas Villers refused to

[41] See below, p. 280–281.

[42] See below, pp. 102, 111.

[43] Sometimes it appears that questions were asked based on testimony that was given but not recorded. For instance, Thomas Villers admitted in his deposition 'that he said to William Lodge that his mother taught him the opinion that is contained in the deposition of William Lodge' (see below, p. 201). While Lodge had indeed reported a conversation with Thomas Villers when he testified the day before (see below, p. 200), there is nothing recorded about Thomas Villers's mother, so presumably the interrogator had simply remembered this.

[44] See below, pp. 148, 158.

[45] See below, pp. 207, 194, 200.

[46] See below, pp. 184, 211.

[47] See below, pp. 115, 116, 127.

acknowledge his heresy until he was faced with Robert Silkby, Roger Landesdale, William Lodge, John Jonson, and his brothers-in-law, Richard Bradeley and Thomas Banbrooke.[48] When John Hebbis repudiated the suggestion that he had consorted with Roger Landesdale and Thomas Bown, they were apparently brought in to confirm that not only was he often in communication with them but that he more frequently sought their company than they sought his.[49] In January 1512 Agnes Jonson refused to admit that she held heretical beliefs, until she was confronted with Alice Rowley's testimony, repeated in person in front of her.[50]

Defendants were sometimes broken down by the testimony of others; on some other occasions they were willing to admit that they had once been involved in Lollardy but claimed that they had given up their heresies years before. On 5 November 1511, for instance, Thomas Acton, Robert Peg, and Matthew Markelond in various ways denied full involvement in the sect. Acton said that two years before he had renounced the sect and had confessed to a Franciscan friar, and that in any case he had never doubted the real presence in the Eucharist.[51] Peg admitted that he had been present during heretical communications given by Landesdale, Hachet, and Bown, but maintained that he had never held their views.[52] Markelond claimed that, although he had been part of the sect long ago, he had given it all up in the days of Bishop Hales when John Smyth and the others had abjured (in 1486). He had before then favoured all the opinions that Landesdale held, but he had abjured and renounced each and every one of them.[53] It is difficult to know to what extent these men were being truthful. Despite their protestations, all three of these men underwent abjuration. On the one hand, when confronted with evidence that they had been involved in the sect, it was an easy defence to claim that their days as Lollards were over (in Markelond's case had been over for more than twenty years). Robert Peg, at least, changed his testimony when confronted by Robert Hachet and Hachet's claim that Peg had learned heretical doctrines at Devizes. On the other hand, Matthew Markelond's assertion that he had abandoned Lollardy at the time of the previous prosecution is not incredible: the dangers inherent in involvement in the sect must have deterred at least some people.

Thomasina Bradeley presents another interesting case. Despite a considerable amount of evidence against her, including testimony given

---

[48] See below, p. 201.
[49] See below, p. 213.
[50] See below, p. 233. For other examples, see below, pp. 151, 217.
[51] See below, p. 150.
[52] See below, p. 151.
[53] See below, p. 152.

by her own husband, she stubbornly refused to admit most of the charges when questioned in late November or early December 1511 and indeed she called for judicial proofs to be introduced against her, offering to undergo death if the case could be proved.[54] She appeared again on 26 January 1512 and continued to deny her involvement. There is no record that the charges were pursued any further. It seems possible that she was able to escape abjuration and penance by obstinacy. Some others appearing at the end of January or early February 1512 also denied any involvement, apparently successfully. At the end of Isabel Trussell's examination in January or February 1512, it was recorded, 'Note that after the inquiry it was impossible to be certain that the said Isabel and the others – except those who had abjured etc. – had been and were suspected of heresy.'[55] The prosecutors seemingly recognized the difficulty of establishing cases against those who were utterly unwilling to admit any involvement in the sect; while the obstinate heretic who refused to admit his or her sins could theoretically be burned, the Bishop of Coventry and his commissaries did not pursue this course.

The charges and the defendants' beliefs

The evidence about Lollard beliefs among the adherents of the sect in Coventry indicates, at least at first glance, that their ideas focused largely on protests against the prevailing orthodoxy rather than on new conceptions of what it meant to be Christian. In some senses this is natural in a movement that set itself against an overwhelmingly hegemonic religious system, and we need not dismiss Lollards as constituting 'nothing but' a protest movement. Certainly the records of the prosecution indicate that the central issues in later Lollardy were rejections of fundamental late medieval Catholic belief: the cult of saints and the sacrament of the Eucharist. Yet Anne Hudson and others have argued that there was a coherent and positive core of Lollard belief, ultimately derived from John Wyclif's teachings and writings. The heart of this Lollard creed, according to Hudson, was the primacy of scripture: the belief that all Christian practice must spring from the precepts of the Bible.[56] Thus, it can be argued that the Lollards focused

---

[54] See below, p. 207; for testimony against her, see below, pp. 111, 118, 147, 156, 200.

[55] See below, p. 249. Similarly enquiries in the diocese of Norwich in the 1420s trailed off because defendants denied the charges and fellow villagers swore to their innocence; see *Norwich Trials*, p. 8.

[56] Hudson, *Premature Reformation*, pp. 278–389, esp. 389.

on the Eucharist and the cult of saints both because they were immensely important to the religious practice of the late medieval Church and because, in the Lollard view, they were unscriptural and thus falsely instituted. This view is given greater support by the evidence of the Coventry Lollards' reading matter: the overwhelming majority of their books were translations of the scripture. On the other hand, the emphasis on these issues may have been placed, not by the Lollards, but by the prosecutors precisely because of the centrality of the cults of the Eucharist and the saints to late medieval orthodox practice.[57]

In any case, the records we have of later Lollardy are not conducive to evincing any more detailed alternative conceptualizations of Christianity the Lollards might have held or developed: the ecclesiastical authorities who were responsible for the records were far more interested in the ways that Lollards threatened the orthodox religious system than in the complexities of their thought. Many scholars who have studied Lollard ideology have made the cogent argument that in order to understand Lollard thought it is necessary to study the writings left by Lollards, rather than (or at least in addition to) the records of those who prosecuted them.[58] What remains a problem is that the later Lollard communities – the social makeup of which was very different from the academically-oriented early Lollards who produced the texts – left almost no evidence, apart from the records of the prosecution, that bears on their religious tenets. Moreover, there is little sign that the writings of Lollards (almost all produced in the late fourteenth and early fifteenth centuries) were still being read in Lollard circles by the end of the fifteenth century. The evidence we have about the Coventry Lollards' reading matter – to be discussed in more detail below – indicates that it was almost exclusively scriptural, with a few other devotional works which were more likely to be orthodox works than Lollard in origin. We are left, then, with little choice but to use the registers and court books to understand late Lollard thought, although the picture we derive from those sources will necessarily be incomplete.

The records of Hales's prosecution – surviving only in his register – are less rich in many ways than those of Blyth's fascinating court book, but they show that he was more interested than Blyth in the beliefs held by the Lollards he pursued. The particulars of the defendants' beliefs are carefully set down in Hales's register, sometimes with quotations in the vernacular, and the formulaic nature of many such register entries for Lollard prosecutions is largely eschewed. Blyth's register entries are, by contrast, extremely formulaic, and the heretical

---

[57] See Paul Strohm, *England's Empty Throne: Usurpation and the Language of Legitimation, 1399–1422* (New Haven CT and London, 1998), pp. 37–38, 60–61.

[58] e.g. Hudson, *Premature Reformation*, pp. 7–9 and *passim*.

beliefs the defendants abjured are reduced to a few key entries. Even in the actual proceedings, according to the evidence of his court book, Blyth and his deputies made only perfunctory inquiry into the belief system of those being questioned, being interested only to establish that the people in question were indeed heretics. Blyth saved his persecutory energy instead for exploring the heretics' social networks in his bid to destroy the web of heresy in his diocese. Thus, if the records of Blyth's prosecution show only a small range of views, this should not be taken as evidence that the Lollards' beliefs had themselves become bastardized, restricted or formulaic, but rather that Blyth as prosecutor was far less interested in this question than some of his predecessors (including Hales).[59]

In Hales's register, the beliefs recorded for the eight men prosecuted in 1486 focus on a number of themes, almost all common Lollard ideas.[60] Most relate to objections to the various practices associated with the late medieval cult of saints. Two defendants, Roger Brown and Thomas Butler, attacked the doctrine of purgatory, the underlying basis for pilgrimages, veneration of images and invocation of saints. Richard Hegham and Thomas Butler both suggested that Christians would be saved by faith and not works. More concretely, statues of saints sculpted from stone or wood were denied any special power – in a saying that reflected common Lollard usage, the defendants almost all repeated that such statues were only dead sticks and stones and that to worship them was foolish. This point was made in various pithy ways: as Richard Hegham said, the statue of the Blessed Virgin Mary would make a good fire, while John Falkys opined that it was fatuous to offer to the image of Mary, for 'what is hit but a blok? If hyt cothe speke to me, I wolde gyfe hit an halpeni worth of ale'. Statues of the Virgin may have been of particular concern to the Coventry Lollards because of the local shrine, known as the Lady of the Tower, located in the Carmelite friary in the town wall near New Gate, by the London road.[61] Several defendants referred explicitly to this shrine, grouping it with more nationally famous pilgrimage destinations as the shrines to the Virgin at Doncaster and Walsingham, and the Holy Blood of Hailes.[62] Whether the Virgin herself should be an object of respect was

[59] Hudson, *Premature Reformation*, pp. 37–38.

[60] For the beliefs of the Coventry Lollards prosecuted in 1486 discussed in the following paragraphs, see below, pp. 64–72. For Lollard beliefs generally, see Hudson, *Premature Reformation*, pp. 278–389. The beliefs of the Coventry Lollards prosecuted in 1486 are discussed in more detail than here in Thomson, *Later Lollards*, pp. 104–106.

[61] See W.B. Stephens (ed.), *The Victoria History of the County of Warwick*, VIII, *The City of Coventry and Borough of Warwick* (London, 1969), pp. 132, 208; Phythian-Adams, *Desolation*, p. 21.

[62] See Diana Webb, *Pilgrimage in Medieval England* (London and New York, 2000), esp. pp. 96–105; Eamonn Duffy, *The Stripping of the Altars: Traditional Religion in England 1400–*

somewhat more ambiguous from the abjurations recorded in the register. Roger Brown apparently denied Mary any special place, suggesting that one should not adore the image of Mary of Walsingham, for Christ did not have a mother. Robert Crowther might have been suggesting something similar when he said that the words, 'who was conceived of the Holy Spirit and born of the Virgin Mary', be removed from the Creed, since they had only been put there deceitfully. On the other hand, while John Blumston, in one article, said that Mary had no more virtue than a herb, in another he suggested a homely image of respect for the Virgin when he said that one may venerate Mary as much by sitting by the fire in the kitchen, or by looking at one's sister or mother, as by visiting images. Parallel with that belief was Richard Gylmyn's abjuration that it was better to offer to the poor than to images (another common Lollard belief), for while images are only painted representations of God, the poor are God's own created likeness.

The Coventry Lollards prosecuted in 1486 also attacked various other elements of late medieval Catholic religion. Like many other Lollards, they exhibited a strong strain of anti-clerical and anti-ecclesiastical feeling. John Smyth said that all who believe what the Church believes, believe wrongly. John Blumston said that the power that had been given to Peter by Christ was not transmitted to his successors. Most of the defendants denied any special power to the priesthood; Crowther, Smyth, and Falkys denied priestly power to bind and loose, and Butler suggested that he always knew in advance what a preacher would say from the pulpit. There is, curiously, relatively little focus on the Eucharist, and only one outright denial of the real presence of the body of Christ in the sacrament – Richard Gylmyn's suggestion that the Eucharist is only bread and that the priests make it to blind the people. But even Gylmyn did imply that the priest had some power in the Mass: he said that a priest was only a priest during the Mass, and between services he was no more than a mere layman. Other articles do not indicate a complete rejection of orthodox eucharistic doctrines: Robert Crowther thought that those who receive the sacrament of the altar in mortal sin do not receive the true body of Christ, while John Falkys asked why the sick and infirm were brought only the body and not the blood of Christ. The abjurations in Hales's register also show a considerable interest (both by the defendants and by the prosecuting authorities) in English prayers and books. John Smyth was accused of believing that each person should know the Lord's Prayer, the Hail Mary, and the Creed in English.[63]

Altogether, the beliefs expressed in the abjurations made in 1486 reflect some fairly sophisticated understandings of late medieval Catholic doctrine (such as Blumston's denial of the Petrine succession), while others, such as Roger Brown's curious denial that Mary was Christ's mother, suggest a less rigorous scripturalism than one might expect from Lollards. Contradictions between beliefs abjured by different defendants and even by the same defendant may reflect real differences of opinion among those prosecuted, or indeed inconsistencies in individuals' belief systems. They may also reflect incomplete or inaccurate rendering by the recording clerk of the tenets expressed by the defendants. Or indeed they may mirror either an interrogative strategy on the part of the prosecutors that left important elements unsaid, or a deliberate attempt on the part of the defendants to mislead. In other words, the extent to which the abjured articles accurately reflect the defendants' beliefs – even in a case like Hales's register where the articles are less formulaic than was often the case in Lollard abjurations – remains an open question.

Hales's register also records two further prosecutions for heresy. In neither case is there evidence that the defendants were connected to the groups of Coventry Lollards prosecuted in 1486 and in 1511–1512. Margery Goyte, described as the wife of James Goyte, recently of Ashbourne, Derbyshire (it is not clear from the register where she was resident at the time of the prosecution), was brought before the bishop in 1488.[64] Given the considerable distance between Ashbourne and Coventry, and the gap of two years between the prosecutions, there is no indication that she had any direct relationship with the eight Coventry men brought before the bishop two years previously.[65] Her beliefs are not entirely congruent with those the Coventry men were accused of holding, although all except one find parallels with those expressed by Lollards elsewhere. This suggests that Goyte was a participant in Lollard activities in Derbyshire for which we otherwise have no evidence. Goyte may have been prosecuted largely because of indiscretion – she was charged with 'openly and publicly' proclaiming her beliefs. She abjured fairly common Lollard tenets about the real presence in the Eucharist, such as that Christ could not be really present in the sacrament of the altar because, if he were, the priests could not so easily break the host into three parts because they would

---

[63] For further discussion of English prayers and books, see Shannon McSheffrey, 'Heresy, orthodoxy, and English vernacular religion, 1480–1525', forthcoming.

[64] See below, pp. 87–90.

[65] Although Thomson, *Later Lollards*, pp. 106–107, assumes that she was part of the Coventry group.

be breaking flesh and bones. Less common, but still analogous with other Lollard beliefs, was her claim that a child conceived by Christian parents does not require the sacrament of baptism. She also abjured the belief that although Christ was born of Mary, she was not a virgin, because Joseph was married to her and knew her carnally many times. From Joseph's seed was Christ thus conceived, just as Margery herself had conceived a son from her husband's seed. Such denials of Christ's divinity were uncommon among Lollards; although Roger Brown explicitly, and Robert Crowther implicitly, suggested that Mary was not Christ's mother, they said nothing about Joseph's paternity. Margery's belief may have been prompted by the intersection of her proclivity to question orthodox doctrine and her own lived experience as a wife and mother.

In 1490, two years after Margery Goyte was brought before the bishop, Robert Clerke of Coventry was investigated for holding various heretical ideas.[66] Some of his views (such as that the riches of the Church should be redistributed to the poor and an unwillingness to take oaths) may have had Lollard origins, although there is nothing exclusively Lollard about such ideas. Other notions have no obvious connection to Lollardy, such as his assertion that he knew how to make men talk to God face to face, and his belief that if someone in a state of sin said the Lord's Prayer or the Hail Mary the prayers had more damnatory than salvific force. Clerke was arguably a religious eccentric rather than a participant in Coventry's Lollard community.[67]

While there are indications that other inquiries were made into Lollard activities in Coventry in the years between 1490 and 1511, the only direct records of such investigations is the abjuration of John Shepherde of Lancashire in 1503. Sheperde's beliefs were not indicated except by his general admission that he had held 'diverse articles and opynyons erroneows and agenst the fayth of the holy church and contrary to the determination of the same and evyll sowyndyng in the eris of well disposid cristen men'.[68]

Geoffrey Blyth's investigation beginning in the autumn of 1511 produced, however, some of the most extensive records we have of a Lollard prosecution. But despite the richness of the records, there is, in relative terms, little information about the tenets held by the community Blyth uncovered. Even the court book, which shows much more clearly his and his deputies' prosecutory and interrogatory strategies, shows that the judges were much more likely to probe witnesses about the

[66] See below, pp. 94–96.
[67] Thomson, *Later Lollards*, p. 107, concurs, while Hudson suggests that his views were misrepresented (*Premature Reformation*, p. 311).
[68] See below, pp. 97–99.

persons with whom they had heretical conversations than the content of those discussions.

There survive, both in the Lichfield Court Book and in Blyth's register, several lists of questions to which defendants replied.[69] They were clearly not used in the initial questioning of those accused of heresy but rather in the final stages of the prosecution, perhaps just prior to or as an integral part of the formal abjuration of heretical beliefs. All these are substantially the same both in meaning and vocabulary, and are reflected also almost exactly in the formal abjurations the defendants made. In each case, the defendant abjured the following articles: that the defendant had knowingly consorted with, had had conversations with and had been present at the readings of various suspect persons; that he or she had heard these suspect persons teach and have words against the sacrament of the altar, pilgrimages, and the veneration of images; and that the defendant had favoured, held (and, in one formulary, taught),[70] these same opinions; that he or she had held readings of forbidden books in his or her home, and that this had been concealed and not denounced to the ecclesiastical authorities; that the defendant had received those suspect of heresy in his or her home and had had conversation with them against the true doctrine of the Church; and that the defendant had been openly, publicly, and notoriously suspected and defamed of heresy in the city of Coventry and other neighbouring places.[71]

The trinity of Lollard beliefs repeated in the interrogatories and the various abjurations made by the Coventry Lollards – objections to the sacrament of the altar, to pilgrimages, and to the veneration of images – are also featured in the depositions recorded in Blyth's court book, in some cases giving some flesh to the bare bones. Indeed almost all the tenets appearing in the testimony recorded in the court book fall into one of these three categories; only rarely does there appear something that falls outside (such as Alice Rowley's admission that she believed

---

[69] There is one list of articles administered to Thomas Flesshor on 3 November (below, pp. 134–136); one administered to Joan Smyth on 5 November (below, pp. 161–163); one administered to Roger Landesdale and seven other defendants on 5 November (below, p. 165); and one administered to Balthasar Shugborow, Robert Peg, and Ralph Lye (below, p. 175).

[70] See below, p. 165.

[71] John H. Arnold has pointed out the similarity of this language of Lollard prosecution to that used in proceedings against heretics in southern France in the thirteenth and fourteenth centuries; this implies even more strongly that these phrases are formulaic and that the 'inquisitorial discourse' shaped ecclesiastical authorities' perceptions of heretical activity. 'Lollard trials and inquisitorial discourse', paper presented to the International Medieval Congress, University of Western Michigan, Kalamazoo, MI, May 2001.

that ten venial sins made one mortal sin).[72] According to the evidence
of the court book, the most commonly discussed question among the
early sixteenth-century Coventry Lollards was the sacrament of the
altar, an issue that had not been dominant in the articles with
which the 1486 Lollards were charged. While the interrogatories and
abjurations say little else than that the accused person held opinions
contrary to orthodox opinion on the Eucharist, the depositions show
that there was a range of views, showing both an anti-clerical, common-
sense scepticism about the real presence, and a notion that the Eucharist
was a memorial that deserved some reverence. In discussion, various
sayings were apparently bandied about: Thomas Abell, for instance,
testified that he had heard Roger Landesdale, Robert Hachet, and
Thomas Bown teaching, 'that God made man and not man God, as
the carpenter doith make the howse and not the howse the carpenter'.[73]
Robert Silkby apparently said, 'Whate can the preiste make of a morsell
of brede, et cetera? Shuld he make God and ete hym todaie and do
likewise tomorowe?'[74] Various members of the Coventry community
testified that they or others they knew did not believe the true body of
Christ to be present at the time of the consecration. Yet the leading
teachers in the Coventry community did apparently believe that the
sacrament of the altar could serve the purpose of focusing the Christian's
mind on his or her saviour: Alice Rowley, Roger Landesdale, and John
Blumston *alias* Phisicion were said to have taught others to believe that
at the time of the elevation they should believe that the Host was to
be offered spiritually in the memory of the passion of Christ.[75]

In common with their brethren prosecuted in the 1480s, those who
testified in 1511 and 1512 also held opinions decrying the orthodox
practices of pilgrimage and the veneration of images. Thomas Abell
said that he had been taught, by the authority of Wyclif (the only
mention of Wyclif in any of these proceedings), that one should not
make pilgrimages, and he said that he had detested the veneration of
images from that time forward.[76] Others repeated the common Lollard
saying that images are only dead blocks of wood (*trunci mortui*) and
suggested that offerings would better be given to paupers.[77] A favourite
reading among various women in the Coventry community was the
gospel Luke 12.32, which advocated the giving of alms.[78] There was
less explicit reference to the local shrine of the Lady of the Tower than

---

[72] See below, p. 155.
[73] See below, p. 183; see also p. 153.
[74] See below, p. 102; see also pp. 142 and 156.
[75] See below, pp. 102, 116, 130, 141, 183, 195, 235.
[76] See below, p. 183.
[77] See below, pp. 103, 150, 157, 197, 198, 216, 235.
[78] See below, pp. 206, 227, 235.

there had been in the 1486 prosecution, although John Cropwell deposed that when he once went to make offerings to the image of Mary there, Robert Hachet told him, 'A, God help the, thow arte a foole'.[79]

The court book also shows, unsurprisingly, that the Coventry Lollards objected in various ways to the power held by ecclesiastical authorities. Balthasar Shugborow admitted, for instance, that he had held beliefs against the power of the Pope and other church officials. In some cases the objections the Lollards voiced were specifically related to their own encounters with the Church: Roger Landesdale, for instance, said that bishops and other ecclesiastical officials cannot render sentences of excommunication, and if they curse anyone their sentence is not to be feared.[80]

Our last encounters in the surviving historical record of the Coventry Lollards come from the investigations and prosecutions, again under-taken by Bishop Blyth, in 1515, 1520, and 1522. For these investigations, the evidence about Lollard beliefs is slender and somewhat unreliable. In his 1515 deposition, William Borodall told the bishop's commissaries that his parents had taught him not to believe in or receive the sacrament of the Eucharist, or at least not to confess before receiving it.[81] For the last prosecution between 1520 and 1522 of eight members of the Coventry community, at least seven of whom had been previously prosecuted in 1511–1512, we have only reports in John Foxe's *Acts and Monuments* and short accounts in various Coventry annals. Foxe tells his readers that the only cause of the arrest of the 'godly martyrs' in 1520 was that they taught their children and other family members the Lord's Prayer, the Creed, and the Ten Commandments in English, although he does note that they had all previously borne faggots several years before. He suggests that the bishop's men, who were ashamed of executing good people only for knowing English prayers, fomented false rumours about other unorthodox practices, such as breaking the Friday fasts. Foxe's named informant for the 1570 version of the burning of the Coventry Lollards, Mother Halle, also testifies that the accused were known for their piety and that they were particularly devoted to the Eucharist, although she suggests, perhaps with hindsight, that this was a pretence. She also noted that they would not use any oaths nor tolerate oath-making in others.[82] Given the evidence of the depositions offered in 1511–1512, it seems unlikely that those burned in 1520 and 1522 restricted themselves to the beliefs Foxe reports. The annalists, in

---

[79] See below, p. 212; see also p. 214.
[80] See below, pp. 118, 145.
[81] *Bishop Blythe's Visitations*, p. 101.
[82] See below, p. 311.

their brief entries on the Lollard prosecutions, also noted that the seven burned in 1520 were executed for having prayers in English, but they also report (as Foxe does not) that Robert Silkby was burned in 1522 for holding that Christ was not really present in the Eucharist.[83] Altogether, both Foxe and the annalists were probably working with very slender information in their accounts of the prosecutions in the early 1520s. We might assume that the Lollards who continued as active participants in their sect even after the prosecutions of 1511–1512 maintained the same kinds of beliefs with which they had been charged before.

The defendants and the practice of Lollardy

At the same time as we must acknowledge that being a member of a religious group entails matters of belief and conscience, we must also allow that people come to partake in particular religious activities because of social connections as well as intellectual or theological convictions.[84] Bishop Blyth recognized this and so, in his pursuit of heresy in his diocese, he focused mainly on uncovering the social networks of the Lollards. Association with heretics was itself an offence (one that the defendants abjured), but clearly Blyth was using the testimony about Lollards' interactions with one another as a means to discover new heretics and to force them to confess, if recalcitrant, when they in turn were questioned. While Blyth's approach to the heresy problem in his diocese does not allow us to make a sophisticated analysis of late Lollard thought, it does give us an unparalleled opportunity to see how Lollards in the early sixteenth century organized themselves and practised their beliefs.

Profile of the Coventry Lollards: sex, occupation, and social status

Coventry was a large and important city in late medieval England, but one whose fortunes had waned in the period for which evidence of significant Lollard activity survives. The foundation for Coventry's late medieval success lay in the textile industry, and its importance in this

[83] See below, pp. 315–317.
[84] Richard G. Davies' article, 'Lollardy and locality', *Transactions of the Royal Historical Society*, 6th series, 1 (1991), pp. 191–212, makes this point especially well. See also Bryan Wilson, *Religion in Sociological Perspective* (Oxford 1982), p. 118; Rodney Stark and William Sims Bainbridge, 'Networks of faith: interpersonal bonds and recruitment to cults and sects', *American Journal of Sociology*, 85 (1980), pp. 1376–1395.

sector allowed it to become the third or fourth city in the kingdom in size and economic importance by the mid-fifteenth century, with a population of perhaps 10,000 inhabitants. But when the country's cloth trade faltered, so also did Coventry's prosperity. The city entered a long-term economic and demographic decline in the 1440s that became even more serious in the early sixteenth century, culminating in a crisis between 1518 and 1525.[85]

Who were the Lollards of this city in decline, as revealed in the two bishops' registers and the court book? In the prosecutions of 1486–1490, 1511–1512, 1515, and 1520–1522, a total of seventy-nine people appeared as defendants before the bishops or their deputies, some more than once. In addition, the Lichfield Court Book and the depositions offered in 1515 implicated a substantial number of other people who apparently did not themselves appear before the authorities; if these are added, about 158 people altogether were implicated in heretical activities (108 of whom were from Coventry, the remainder inhabitants of other towns such as Birmingham, Leicester, and Bristol).[86] About two-thirds were men and one-third women, a proportion that is in line with the sex ratios found in the other Lollard communities for which we have good evidence.[87] They were also older rather than younger. For thirty-six of the defendants interrogated in 1511 and 1512, ages were recorded; these show that defendants ranged from age seventeen to age sixty-seven. But the average age was forty-one, and more than half (twenty-one of thirty-six) were forty or older, and six were age sixty or over. Three in the sixty-plus category were leaders in the community (Roger Landesdale, sixty-three; Robert Hachet, sixty; and Joan Warde, sixty); other leaders (Robert Silkby and Thomas Bown) were forty.[88] Of

---

[85] The classic study of the urban history of Coventry in the late Middle Ages is Phythian-Adams, *Desolation* (p. 35 for the population estimate). See also for maps of medieval Coventry, with medieval street names, Mary Lobel (general ed.), *The Atlas of Historic Towns*, II, *Coventry* (Baltimore MD, 1975).

[86] This total includes all who had some involvement in Lollard activities, even if they did not become fully involved in the sect. It includes Margery Goyte, Robert Clerke, and Richard Hyde; it excludes 'Symon' and John Olyver (apparently orthodox men offering information about Lollards in 1511–1512); it includes William Borodall, but not Ralph Lowe from 1515; it excludes Thomas Landesdale (who is named in the Bodleian annal as having been executed for Lollardy in 1520, but who is probably identical with Roger Landesdale). See Appendix 1, p. 321ff. below.

[87] Of the 79 who appeared as defendants, one was of indeterminable sex (a person named Pygstappe, first name illegible, who apparently abjured (see below, p. 275), although nothing more is known about him or her), 23 were women, and 55 were men (that is, 30 per cent women, 70 per cent men). Of the total number of 158 suspected of Lollard involvement, 50 were women, 107 were men, and one of unknown sex (that is, 32 per cent women and 68 per cent men). See Appendix 1, below, p. 321ff. On sex ratios in other communities, see McSheffrey, *Gender*, pp. 151–166.

[88] As with many other records in which ages were given in this period, there was a

the three leading women, Joan Smyth was fifty, Joan Warde sixty, and although Alice Rowley's age was not recorded she was probably at least in her mid-forties and likely older.[89] This suggests, unsurprisingly, that authority within the community was exercised by those of greater age. Many of those who took leading roles had also been long-standing members of the sect; the activities of Alice Rowley and Joan Warde, for example, stretched back to the 1480s.

Most of the men whose trades were named in the Lichfield Court Book were practising artisans, the majority of whom worked in cloth trades or leather trades, both in the processing of wool or animal skins (shermen, fullers, skinners, etc.) and in the creating of a finished product (tailors, shoemakers, pursers, glovers). Both cloth and leather production were strong elements of Coventry's manufacturing sector at this time,[90] so it is not surprising to find this pattern. A few other trades are also represented: cutlers, smiths, wiredrawers, coopers, butchers. Two men who were brought before the bishop were painters (part of the building trade), and a further three painters who lived in Leicester were also implicated by Coventry Lollards. As these men associated together, it seems clear that their trade was a key aspect of their recruitment to the Lollard community. A few men who appeared before the bishop were merchants – four mercers and a spicer. It is notable that all five of these men were fairly young, between the ages of twenty-five and thirty-four, and at least four of them (Bradeley, Lodge, Spenser, and Villers) associated together and apparently discussed heretical questions while on the job.[91]

Women's occupations are generally much less frequently recorded in medieval documents, and the records of the prosecution of Lollardy are no exception. Of the women, Katherine Revis was apparently a piemaker, four women were or had been servants, and Agnes Yong was a spinster. All these were lower-status occupations. On the other hand, evidence outside the court book suggests that Alice Rowley, widowed in 1506, was continuing her husband's business as a merchant in the period immediately after he died;[92] this was a common practice,

---

tendency to round off to the nearest decade or half-decade. Since we are interested in any case only in round figures, this should not pose a problem for our analysis.

[89] In 1506, when her husband died, Alice Rowley had an adult son, Thomas Rowley, named as heir in his father's will and about to enter political life (implying that he was about twenty-five or older in 1506, and thus that Alice was at least forty-five and likely to have been older in 1511). See below, n. 102; and PRO, PCC Prob. 11/15 (5 Adeane), fo. 34r, Will of William Rowley, 1506.

[90] Phythian-Adams, *Desolation*, pp. 40–41, 99–117.

[91] See below, p. 200.

[92] See the case in Chancery (PRO, C1/163/33), from soon after William Rowley's death in early 1506 (see above, n. 89), where the plaintiff complains that Alice Rowley has unjustly sued him for debt in the purchase of barley and malt, over which agreement had been made with William before his death.

although in most cases the widow's exercise of her husband's trade or craft was limited to a few years following his death.[93] Lollards of Coventry, as one might expect, did business with one another; some depositions imply that Lollards would give better terms to one another, and William Borodall testified that his father had ordered him at the age of thirteen or so to get his food from Landesdale and his shoes from Hachet.[94]

Then, perhaps even more than now, social status was tied to the occupation of the household's head; in a late medieval city like Coventry, merchants dominated the higher ranks of the city's socio-political hierarchy. Charles Phythian-Adams has defined four social levels among the inhabitants of Coventry in our period: at the top was the magisterial elite, comprising about 40 households; a second level of members of the ruling guilds, about 340 households; a third level of small masters and journeymen, about 1,000 households; and a fourth level of house-holds headed by labourers, widows, out-servants, and so on, perhaps 500 households.[95] The majority of those who appeared before the bishop probably fell into the third and fourth of these categories. As noted above, a few young men involved in the community were of merchant status (that is, probably in the second of Phythian-Adams's categories), but the leading men were two shoemakers (Silkby and Bown), a tailor (Landesdale), and a leatherdresser or shoemaker (Hachet), none of which were high-status trades. Within the community, a distinction should be drawn between those who were householders – and thus could hold gatherings in their homes – and those who were not. Although Hachet's trade of leatherdresser or shoemaker, for example, may not have given him high status in the city, he had a substantial enough household to employ servants (at least two of whom, Thomas Bown and Rose Furnour, were converted to Lollardy) and he hosted Lollard gatherings.[96]

Another of the leaders of the Lollard sect in Coventry is an enigma: Balthasar Shugborow was described as a gentleman (*generosus*), and since he was from Napton, he was probably related to the gentle family named Shugborow based in that area, although it is unclear what his exact relationship to the family was.[97] It is possible that he became

---

[93] Phythian-Adams, *Desolation*, pp. 91–92.

[94] See below, pp. 179, 203, 281.

[95] Phythian-Adams, *Desolation*, p. 131.

[96] See below, pp. 124–126, 147, 221–222. Robert's wife Katherine Hachet was not happy about the gatherings at their house – see below, pp. 125, 232.

[97] See below, p. 144 for Balthasar Shugborow, and *VCH Warws.*, IV, pp. 183, 216 for the family; a Thomas Shukborowe was Justice of the Peace for Warwickshire several times between 1502 and 1509, and commissioner of gaol delivery three times between 1503 and 1509 (*Calendar of Patent Rolls, 1494–1509*, London, 1916, pp. 359, 456, 663; *Letters & Papers of Henry VIII*, 21 vols, J.S. Brewer et al. (eds) (London, 1862–1932), nos

estranged from his family due to his Lollard activities. He apparently had financial problems – Thomas Warde said that he had lent Shugborow money[98] – and although he was evidently one of the leading members of the Lollard community, unlike other leaders there is no evidence that he hosted gatherings in his dwelling (in fact Thomas Flesshor said that Shugborow frequently stayed with him, so he may not even have had a residence in Coventry).[99] Gentry participation in Lollardy, once very substantial, had declined by the end of the fifteenth century, although in some communities the role of gentlefolk (such as the Durdants of Middlesex) was still important in the early sixteenth century.[100] There is, however, no evidence that Balthasar Shugborow's status as gentleman allowed him to act as patron or host in the way that the Durdants, for instance, were able.

But if the leading men of the Coventry Lollard community were mostly of relatively humble status, this was not true of two of its leading women: Alice Rowley and Joan Smyth were, by virtue of the status of their husbands, William Rowley and Richard Smyth (both former mayors of the city), of the highest category.[101] Alice Rowley was a widow in 1506, but her son Thomas soon after also became involved in Coventry civic government, acting at various times from 1510 to 1518 as warden, member of the common council, bailiff, and sheriff.[102]

282, 554). There is a will for a William Shukeborowe of Coventry, draper, probated 1514 (PRO, PCC Prob. 11/17, fos 245rv), but it makes no mention of Balthasar.

[98] See below, p. 203.

[99] See below, p. 106.

[100] See the essays in Margaret Aston and Colin Richmond (eds), *Lollardy and the Gentry in the Later Middle Ages* (Stroud and New York, 1997), especially Andrew Hope, 'The lady and the bailiff: Lollardy among the gentry in Yorkist and Early Tudor England', pp. 250–277; and McSheffrey, *Gender*, pp. 114–116, 125–128.

[101] Alice Rowley was married to William Rowley, who died in 1506 and had been sheriff and mayor of Coventry and Justice of the Peace in a long career as civic leader (see *Coventry Leet Book*, pp. 343–602 *passim*; PRO, PCC Prob. 11/15 (5 Adeane), fo. 34r, Will of William Rowley, 1506). Joan Smyth had been married three times: first to Richard Landesdale, a Lollard who was also active in civic politics at the junior level (*Coventry Leet Book*, pp. 482–601 *passim*) who died in or after 1502; he was probably Roger Landesdale's brother since Joan Smyth refers to Roger as her brother in 1515 (see below, p. 282). After Richard's death, according to her own deposition, she married John Padland (who presumably was not the man by the same name who appears in the *Coventry Leet Book* between 1474 and 1515, but may have been related to him), who died some time before 1511; and finally Richard Smyth, active in civic politics from 1474 until 1519, including the mayoralty in 1508 (*Coventry Leet Book*, pp. 390–665 *passim*). Richard Smyth must have died before Joan's condemnation and burning in early 1520, when she is described as a widow; it should be noted, however, that there is no indication that his political career was interrupted by his wife's public abjuration for heresy – he remained an elector and juror through 1511 and 1512 (*Coventry Leet Book*, pp. 631–636). See below, pp. 106, 116, 118, 124, 141.

[102] *Coventry Leet Book*, pp. 629–653 *passim*; see also his appointment to make inquisitions post-mortem for the Crown in 1517 and 1522 (*Letters & Papers of Henry VIII*, II, pt 2, no.

In neither Alice Rowley's nor Joan Smyth's case is there evidence that their high-status husbands were supportive of their heretical leanings (although Joan Smyth's first husband, Richard Landesdale, had converted her to Lollardy).[103] Indeed, in Alice Rowley's case, there is evidence that both her husband and her son were hostile: Joan Warde testified that she fled Coventry in the early 1490s out of fear of William Rowley, and in 1515 Thomas Rowley apparently sent his servants to spy on his mother's friend Joan Smyth.[104]

Neither Alice Rowley's nor Joan Smyth's status made them immune from prosecution, yet it is perhaps significant that Joan Smyth's execution in 1520 came after her third husband Richard Smyth died, and that Alice Rowley was apparently first accused of heresy in 1506, the

3014; and III, pt 2, no. 2214). We have not been able to find any record of him after 1522, nor have we located a will.

[103] Richard Landesdale (see below, p. 141), who died about 1503, is probably the man by the same name who participated in Coventry civic life at the junior level (see *Coventry Leet Book*, pp. 563, 579, 599–601, and Phythian-Adams, *Desolation*, pp. 118–121 on the structure of the civic elite); he was likely to have been Roger Landesdale's brother (see below, p. 000, where Joan refers to Roger as her brother[-in-law]). Joan Smyth also had another husband between Richard Landesdale and Richard Smyth, but his identity is less clear. He is referred to in the court book as John Padland, capper. A John Padland is very prominent in the *Coventry Leet Book*, but he did not die until 1516 at the earliest, so Joan could not have been his widow in 1511. The notary may have made an error in Master Padland's first name: Joan may instead have been the wife of Thomas Padland, John Padland's brother, who died about 1505. See McSheffrey, *Gender*, pp. 211–212, n. 64, for bibliographical references.

[104] See below, pp. 238, 282. It is not clear if Alice Rowley herself was still alive in 1515. A number of historians have assumed that William Rowley was sympathetic to, or even involved in, the Lollard community in Coventry along with his wife (see, for instance, Phythian-Adams, *Desolation*, p. 278, n. 9, and most recently P.J.P. Goldberg, 'Coventry's "Lollard" programme of 1492 and the making of Utopia', in Rosemary Horrox and Sarah Rees Jones (eds), *Pragmatic Utopias: Ideals and Communities 1200–1630* (Cambridge, 2001); our thanks to Dr Goldberg for allowing us to read this essay in advance of publication). This interpretation is apparently based on John Fines's statement that William Rowley read the epistles of St Paul to his wife (Fines, 'Heresy trials', p. 166), which itself derives from a misreading of a passage in the Lichfield Court Book. Fines refers to Roger Landesdale's deposition, which (in translation) reads, 'He [Roger Landesdale] also admits that within the last three months Alice Rowley came to this deponent's house carrying a book of St Paul's letters written in English and she heard the deponent reading from the book in the presence of his wife. Alice then took the book back to her own home' (see below, p. 116 for the Latin original). Neither this passage nor any other part of Landesdale's deposition says anything about William Rowley at all. The reading of Paul's epistles took place about August 1511, and as William Rowley died by 1506 he cannot have been present. The wife indicated in the deposition is clearly Margaret Landesdale, whom Roger is at pains (for some reason) to implicate, here and at other points in his deposition. Margaret corroborates that Alice Rowley visited her husband frequently (below, p. 219). William Rowley's will also indicates orthodoxy, including offerings to the religious houses of Coventry and one-third of his estate to be expended on his funeral and prayers for his soul (PRO, PCC Prob. 11/15 (5 Adeane), fo. 34r, Will of William Rowley, dated February 1505/6, proved March 1506).

same year in which she became a widow. Rowley's status may have protected her even then – she escaped punishment in 1506 when sixteen women were willing to swear to her good reputation. The three compurgators she later named – the wives of Duddesbury, Haddon, and Butler – were probably the wives of prominent men on the civic scene, commensurate with her own status as a widow of a former mayor.[105] Nonetheless, there is little evidence in the court book that Alice Rowley or Joan Smyth associated much with men and women of their own station, especially in relation to their Lollard beliefs. Alice Rowley had apparently confided her 'secrets' to 'Mistress Coke' – probably Joan Cook, wife of Richard Cook, also a former mayor[106] – who then counselled her to destroy her books, suggesting that she did not sympathize. For the sake of their religious beliefs Alice Rowley and Joan Smyth consorted mostly with men and, especially, women who were of significantly lower social station than they were. Alice Rowley, in particular, was probably able to use the prestige that her social station conferred to play roles within the Lollard community that were usually not available to women.

In addition to the well-documented participation of these two women of high station in the Lollard community in Coventry, there is also a possibility that a significant number of those men who constituted the magisterial elite in the late fifteenth and early sixteenth centuries were Lollards, even though they were never prosecuted for heresy. Various members of the urban oligarchy of Coventry were mentioned in the court book, indicating that there were rumours among the Coventry Lollards that Coventry civic leaders, and in some cases their wives, held ideas that were sympathetic to their own. Closely tied to the lay civic elite was James Preston, Doctor of Theology, vicar of St Michael's parish in Coventry from the 1480s until his death about 1507.[107] Alice Rowley reported that he had borrowed a book of the 'new law' from her and later returned it, and she thought that he favoured her and her sect.[108] Imogen Luxton has hypothesized that Preston and the members of the urban oligarchy were indeed heavily involved in the Lollard community of Coventry; apart from the evidence of the court book, she has used their wills (which she believes indicate Lollard

---

[105] See below, p. 155, n. 85.

[106] Joan or Jane Cooke, 'thridmaker', and widow of Richard Cooke, mercer, former mayor and MP for Coventry, who died in 1507. PRO, PCC 11/15, fos 229rv; *Coventry Leet Book*, pp. 431, 528, 601; Josiah Clement Wedgwood, *Biographies, History of Parliament, 1439–1509*, II (London, 1936), p. 216; *Calendar of Patent Rolls, 1494–1509*, pp. 230, 288, 474, 488.

[107] *BRUO to 1500*, pp. 1517–1518. Note that there appear to have been two Dr Prestons to whom deponents in the court book referred, one the vicar of St Michael's (below, p. 157) and the other a Franciscan friar (below, pp. 150, 222).

[108] See below, p. 157.

leanings) and evidence of ownership of English devotional works, including Bibles, to make this argument.[109] Further investigation, however, shows that neither wills nor the ownership of English scriptures and devotional works are good indicators of heretical leanings in this period. The wills of the men in question were, in any case, unexceptionably orthodox; the testators make bequests to religious houses, for example, and provision for masses for their souls (showing belief in purgatory), and for lights to be kept before the sacrament of the altar (showing reverence for the Eucharist). Book ownership is also tricky as evidence for heresy: for those of higher social status, including urban elites, possession of English devotional works was fairly common and by no means necessarily a sign of Lollardy.[110]

What remains, then, is the evidence of the court book, which shows that some of the Coventry Lollards believed that these men and women held ideas that were similar to theirs. It is striking that the deponents' allusions to these men and women of the civic elite are rather nebulous, most often involving rumours or reports that the people in question owned English books. This is the case even with Alice Rowley, who as widow of a past mayor might have been presumed to have greater familiarity with those of elite station. In a few cases, we hear reports that a Lollard had a conversation with a man or woman of high status that indicated that the person in question approved of English books, or disliked the clergy.[111] There is no evidence that members of the civic elite (always with the exception, of course, of Alice Rowley and Joan Smyth) participated in the community's gatherings in the way that Rowley, Smyth, and Shugborow clearly did.

Blyth was, however, apparently concerned about the rumours: he not only called back Hachet (presumably Robert Hachet) to question him specifically about the two most prominent families of Coventry, the Pysfords and the Wigstons, but he apparently also commissioned two 'trustworthy men within the city of Coventry' (unnamed, interestingly) to inquire diligently as to whether the rumours of heresy had any basis. In both cases, the answers were negative.[112]

There are two plausible interpretations of the reported rumours in the Lichfield Court Book that the civic elite of Coventry favoured Lollardy. In the first interpretation, a good proportion of the members of the civic oligarchy were indeed Lollards, but they apparently practised

---

[109] Luxton, 'Postscript'; see also Goldberg, 'Coventry's "Lollard" programme', and n. 104 above.

[110] This argument, with specific references to the wills in question, is made at length in McSheffrey, *Gender*, pp. 37–46 and 108–36, and so is given only summary treatment here.

[111] e.g. below, pp. 157, 185.

[112] See below, pp. 237, 251.

their faith separately from the lower-status Lollards who appeared before Bishop Blyth in 1511 and 1512. In this scenario, their social and political status protected them from prosecution, and Blyth's specific commission to the two 'trustworthy men' was nothing but a whitewash. This is an intriguing hypothesis, since it suggests that there may have been any number of high-status Lollards throughout England whose adherence to the sect remains obscure because their influential station left them immune from prosecution. It also suggests that the men in particular were master dissemblers, since so much of the political life of the late medieval English city – and Coventry was far from an exception here – involved the open and constant practice of the orthodox religion. In Coventry's case, the city's two major religious guilds was institutionally intertwined with the city's ruling councils (so that membership in the former was necessary for participation in the latter), and the mayor processed along with his aldermen to a daily Mass. Ultimately, however, this interpretation relies too much on the slender evidence of the rumours reported in the court book, since almost all other indications point towards orthodoxy.

The second interpretation – which is here held to be the more likely – is that the Coventry Lollards were simply mistaken in their belief that the men and women of the civic elite whom they named were Lollards. When a man named Derlyng (perhaps John Derlyng who held various civic positions) was several times reported to be hostile towards priests,[113] this might have been taken by the Lollards as support for their cause, although of course it was possible to be anti-clerical in late medieval England without being a Lollard. The Coventry Lollards may also have confused interest in English books with adherence to Lollardy. Authorities viewed possession of English writings – whether scriptures, orthodox devotional works, or Lollard tracts – by men and women of lower socio-economic station as constituting a heretical act. And indeed in intention, in the case of Lollards at least, it was an act of defiance against prevailing orthodoxy. But for men and women of the urban elites, or of gentle or noble status, possession of religious works in the vernacular, including the scriptures, was a common aspect of pious, orthodox devotion. A double standard – a supposition that those of higher station could be trusted to act appropriately if given direct access to the word of God, while the lower orders might misunderstand the message if it were not intepreted for them – can be seen in the thought of various figures of authority in the first half of the sixteenth century, for instance in the writings of Thomas More, or in legislation in the 1540s restricting access to Bible translations by

---

[113] See below, pp. 157, 185, 187; for his civic life, see *Coventry Leet Book*, pp. 516–629.

social status and gender.[114] Bishop Blyth himself evidently thought that it was dangerous for the lower orders to have direct access to the Bible, but the Lollards of Coventry themselves may not have drawn the same distinctions of social status as Blyth likely did. Thus we should not assume, when Thomas Wrixham testified that Thomas Bown had told him that Masters Wigston and Pysford had 'very beautiful books of heresy',[115] that the books in question were in fact technically heretical. Highly decorated books were in fact more likely to be psalters or primers, intended for use by urban or landed elites. They may even have been Wycliffite scriptural translations, but in fact many manuscripts of the Lollard biblical translation can be shown to have been in the hands of the unimpeachably orthodox, presumably unaware of the provenance of the translation.[116]

Recruitment

We know nothing about the genesis of heresy in Coventry, nor whether the heretics uncovered in 1486 by Bishop Hales had a long local pedigree. We do know that there was continuity between those Lollards prosecuted in 1486 and those prosecuted in 1511. A substantial number of those who were questioned in 1511 said that they had been led into heresy or instructed by Roger Brown, John Smyth, and Master John Phisicion (*alias* John Blumston).[117] Despite their abjurations in 1486, all three of these men apparently continued teaching heresy into the early years of the sixteenth century, although they were all dead by 1511.[118] John Jonson, for instance, said that when he moved to Coventry in the early years of the sixteenth century he stayed with Roger Brown, who instructed him in heretical opinions.[119] Roger Landesdale, a kingpin of the community in 1511, was also taught by Roger Brown.[120] There may have been other teachers in the late fifteenth or very early sixteenth centuries about whom we know next to nothing; although Thomas Bown acknowledged the influence of Landesdale, Hachet, and Silkby,

[114] Thomas More, *A Dialogue Concerning Heresies*, in Thomas M.C. Lawler, Germain Marc'hadour, and Richard C. Marius (eds), *The Complete Works of St Thomas More* (New Haven CT, 1981), VI, pt 1, p. 316; 'An Acte for thadvauncement of true Religion', 34 and 35 Henry VIII, ch. 1, *Statutes of the Realm*, III, p. 896.

[115] See below, p. 185, and p. 290, n. 112, and p. 295, n. 145 regarding Masters Wigston and Pysford.

[116] Hudson, *Premature Reformation*, pp. 233–234.

[117] e.g. below, pp. 106, 109, 114, 145, 152, 195, 200, 224.

[118] Smyth's and Brown's deaths are referred to below, p. 109; Brown's death, p. 114; Smyth's death, p. 145; and Blumston *alias* Phisicion's death, p. 200.

[119] See below, p. 109.

[120] See below, p. 114.

he said that he was first attracted to heresy by Richard Weston, once the servant of Bishop Hales, about whom we have no further information.[121]

An underground movement must make converts carefully, and most frequently recruits are sought through previously existing social networks. Social ties created through employment or trade were avenues through which people were drawn to the sect; as noted above, the spread of Lollardy through painters in Coventry and Leicester was almost certainly due to their common occupation, and in a number of cases servants were converted by their employers.[122] There are also many examples of relationships by blood or marriage,[123] suggesting that family ties were one of the primary ways in which interest in Lollardy was spread. Twenty-one-year-old William Borodall deposed that his mother and father, Margaret and Nicholas, induced him into heresies when he was a teenager, although he later became so angry with them that he screamed at them, calling them heretics.[124] In another case, the Villers family, a mother and three adult children, were implicated as heretics, although all might not have been equally committed. The mother of the family (whose first name we do not know) had apparently abjured heresy at Leicester at some time prior to Blyth's investigation in 1511–1512.[125] She was not summoned before the bishop, perhaps because she was dead by 1511. Her son, Thomas Villers, spicer, had been taught heretical views by his mother (as he admitted after several days of denial), and according to another deponent he also attempted to convert others to his creed.[126] Mother Villers's daughters, Thomasina Bradeley and the wife of Thomas Banbrooke (whose first name, again, we do not know), were married to Lollards, and both were accused by other deponents of partaking in Lollard activities.[127] The evidence against Thomasina was fairly strong, yet (as discussed above) she steadfastly denied her involvement in her appearances before the bishop and there is no evidence that she was forced to abjure. For Banbrooke's wife, the evidence is equivocal. She did not appear personally before the bishop; when her husband appeared on 28 November he denied any charges on her behalf, apparently successfully.[128] Although two

---

[121] See below, p. 130.

[122] See below, pp. 125, 127, 153, 157, 227.

[123] See McSheffrey, *Gender*, p. 34.

[124] See below, p. 281. For other examples of the reluctance of the children to respond to parental attempts to convert, see McSheffrey, *Gender*, p. 99.

[125] See below, pp. 146, 201, 207, 208.

[126] See below, pp. 111, 146, 147, 184, 191, 193, 194, 200, 201.

[127] Bradeley: see below, pp. 111, 118, 147, 156, 194, 200, 207, 243; Banbrooke, pp. 111, 156.

[128] See below, p. 195. Banbrooke at the same time denied his own involvement, but later admitted that he had partaken in heretical activities. In another case, that of

people bore witness against her, another deponent, Thomas Wrixham, suggested that she was opposed to the sect (or perhaps more precisely the dangers that it might bring) when he said that she urged her brother-in-law, Richard Bradeley, to hand all his books over to the bishop.[129] Family ties were of immense importance for the spread of Lollardy. In other Lollard communities, more men than women were recruited through familial ties, but the opposite pattern obtained in Coventry, probably both reflecting and explaining the relatively strong role that women played there.[130]

Precisely how those who did not have close family relationships with Lollards were drawn into the sect is not always clear, but recruitment seems for the most part to have proceeded through careful conversations. William Lodge testified that, in about 1508, when he and Thomas Villers, aged about twenty-two and twenty-four respectively, were rooming together (perhaps in Bristol, where Villers spent some of his apprenticeship as a spicer), Villers asked Lodge about his faith. Lodge responded, 'I believe whatever the Church teaches'. Villers then said, 'I tell you, a priest cannot make even the smallest fingernail, much less the Lord's body'. Lodge replied that he refused to accept this, and asked Villers why he continued to receive communion at Easter when he did not believe in it; Villers admitted that he did it only for show. Either before or, more likely, after his conversation with Villers, Lodge went on to hear Villers's brother-in-law, Richard Bradeley, reading in Bradeley's house, and on another occasion Thomasina Bradeley apparently expressed her hope about his conversion to her faith.[131] It appears, however, that Lodge was not convinced, and he was not named as a heretic by any deponent and there is no evidence that he abjured.[132]

Also proceeding at a slow pace – at least according to his own deposition – was the recruitment of John Spon into the community's activities. Spon admitted that he had heard Roger Landesdale reading from English books five or six times, but he claimed that when he first came to Landesdale's house he had no idea Landesdale was a heretic. Spon said that the readings he heard were from the lives of saints and

Richard Northopp and his wife (immediately following Banbrooke's in the manuscript), a husband also denied charges on his wife's behalf (see below, p. 196). While women usually answered for themselves in medieval ecclesiastical courts, there are other examples where husbands responded for their wives (e.g. diocese of London Commissary Court Act Book, London, Guildhall Library, MS 9064/3, fos 175r, 179v).

[129] See below, p. 185.
[130] See McSheffrey, *Gender*, pp. 34, 80–107.
[131] See below, p. 200.
[132] He was named in the examinations of Thomasina Bradeley and Thomas Villers (below, pp. 201, 207), but only as they responded to the accusations previously made against them in his deposition.

the epistles of Paul, rather than anything that attacked the doctrine of the Church, and he denied that he ever heard Landesdale or anyone else discussing opinions against the cult of saints, or the Eucharist, or any other orthodox teachings. Nonetheless, he admitted that after hearing Landesdale read it became obvious to him that he was a heretic. It is unclear from Spon's deposition if it was the fact of reading (unusual in itself for men of this station), or the contents of the readings and accompanying discussion that made Landesdale's heresy patent. Spon did admit that he had received a book of the Old Testament from Richard Gest and gave it to Robert Silkby, but said that he had already confessed this and performed penance. Spon's denials may, of course, be equivocation; the evidence against him given by other witnesses, however, is consistent with his being only on the margins of the sect.[133] His testimony, if valid, suggests that, in at least some cases, newcomers may have been courted through reading of scriptural material, or other texts of unexceptionable contents such as saints' lives, and would only gradually be initiated into discussions involving objections to the major doctrines of the Church.

Lollard practice in Coventry

Lollards practised their faith in various ways, but particularly through meeting together to listen to readings and to discuss Lollard ideas. They convened informally, perhaps only two people happening to meet one another while going about daily life, and they assembled in somewhat larger groups that the ecclesiastical authorities sometimes called conventicles. The evidence of the Lichfield Court Book indicates that gender, marital status, and pre-existing social relationships among members of the community shaped how Lollards participated in the sect.

In Coventry, such meetings did not consist of large gatherings (which would no doubt have attracted too much attention), but of groups of two to ten people who met, usually to hear one of the leading Lollards read from an English book, and to discuss various elements of belief, perhaps arising from the readings. Robert Silkby's depositions provide several examples of Lollard conventicles. Silkby said that he had been present with John Atkynson, John Davy, John Jonson, Balthasar Shugborow, and Thomas Flesshor in Flesshor's home, where they had

[133] Robert Silkby, Thomas Warde, Alice Rowley, and Rose Furnour said that they believed or had heard he was of the sect (although they do not seem entirely sure), but Balthasar Shugborow said that although he had seen Spon at gatherings he did not know whether or not Spon shared his opinions. See below, pp. 110, 116, 118, 125, 131, 145, 147, 156, 203, 222.

communication about the Gospels. He said that they had spoken these words, 'Whate can the preiste make of a morsel of brede, et cetera? Shuld he make God and ete hym todaie and do likewise tomorowe?' Silkby also said that he had been present at the home of Mother Margaret in Mill Lane, where Alice Rowley read from the Gospels before Silkby himself, Mother Margaret, and the wife of Roger Bromley. Similarly, Agnes Yong and her daughter Julian Yong also heard Rowley reading and Silkby communicating against the sacrament of the altar.[134] While the Coventry Lollards met in a number of private homes, it was to Roger Landesdale's house that they evidently resorted most often.[135] The Lollards of Coventry apparently had 'secret words', which Roger Landesdale reported to be, 'May we all drinke of a cuppe and at the departing, God kepe you and God blesse you'.[136] These words may have been passwords of a sort, or may point to a some kind of communion service; although there is no other evidence for this in Coventry, there are indications that other Lollard communities had such ceremonies.[137]

Lollards in Coventry also met out of doors, discussing heretical doctrines and reading while strolling in the Little Park to the southeast of the city. John Atkynson, for instance, testified that he had been in the park with John Holywod, Robert Silkby, and Thomas Flesshor, and that he had heard John Holywod reading there in a certain book against the sacrament of the altar.[138] John Cropwell had, according to one deponent, spoken of walking with Landesdale, and John Longhald admitted that he had frequently strolled with Landesdale both in the park and outside it.[139] It is possible, then, that the burning of the seven Lollards in 1520 took place in the Little Park precisely because it was the site of heretical activities (although the park may also simply have been the most convenient open space).[140]

[134] See below, pp. 102, 103, 146, 147.

[135] See below, pp. 102, 106, 116, 122, 125, 128, 208, 212.

[136] See below, p. 117; similar versions, less complete, were recorded on pp. 110, 125, 216.

[137] See Margaret Aston, *Lollards and Reformers*, pp. 49–51, 62–66; W.W. Shirley (ed.), *Fasciculi zizaniorum Magistri Johannis Wyclif cum tritico*, Rolls Series (London, 1858), pp. 423–424.

[138] See below, p. 115.

[139] See below, pp. 188, 198. Other references to discussions in the park: below, pp. 118, 131.

[140] For the 1520 burnings, see below, pp. 298, 310, 315. Foxe's relatively vague 1559 version of the story suggests that the executions took place at a ditch or hollow, which according to him henceforth was known as '"Heretics" Well or Hollow' (see below, p. 295). The site of Joan Warde's burning in 1512 is not clear – the register refers only to the '*summitatem dolii*' (below, p. 241), suggesting that the burning took place at a usual site of public punishment (Latham gives 'tun or cask' for *dolium*, but in London at least the word was used for the site of the pillory – at a prison called the Tun – and so the word

In a few cases, Lollards also testified about having discussions about Lollard doctrine in or near ecclesiastical sites. Perhaps there was a certain *frisson* in doing the forbidden in the very heart of Church territory – or perhaps, more prosaically, the Lollards simply treated such areas as public meeting places in the same way that their orthodox fellows did. Alice Rowley testified that she and Thomas Bown had talked about heretical opinions in the nave of the Benedictine priory church in Coventry, and reported that William Hawkyns had told her that he had heard Katherine Revis giving forth heretical opinions in the gardens of the Franciscan friary and the street nearby.[141] Two deponents also refer to a Lollard reading a book called *The Sykeman* in the cloister of a monastery; this might have been the cloister of the Benedictine priory in Coventry, or it might have been the cloister at the monastery of Maxstoke while the Lollards were being held there during their trials.[142]

As the meetings, wherever they were held, were fairly small, the Coventry community tended to congregate according to gender and marital status. Three loose groupings can be discerned from the court book evidence: groups of men, groups of married couples, and groups of women.[143] While these categories were by no means hard and fast, it is natural that the general tendencies of social interactions in medieval society would be duplicated within Lollard communities. Some men tended to be familiar, only or mostly, with other male members of the sect, such as Thomas Warde, who names Thomas Clerc, Thomas Bown, Robert Hachet, Balthasar Shugborow, Roger Brown, John Spon, Thomas Abell, and Thomas Banbrooke, but no women.[144] Conversely, some women appear to have had almost exclusively female contacts within the community, such as Agnes Jonson, *alias* 'litle moder Agnes', who was an active participant in the sect and who knew how to read, but whose connections were focused on women such as her daughter, Margaret Grey, and Alice Rowley, Agnes de Bakehouse, Joan Warde, and Rose Furnour.[145] When both husband and wife were Lollards, it

---

may have come more broadly to mean 'site of the pillory and stocks'.) Where such a site was in medieval Coventry is not clear, but it may well have been in the Little Park. The Bodleian annal also suggests that the burning took place in the Little Park (below, p. 315), but the annal does not seem altogether reliable concerning the execution(s) of 1512.

[141] See below, pp. 157, 158.

[142] See below, pp. 147, 202. It is also unclear who was doing the reading – Robert Silkby testified that Thomas Villers read the book, while Villers deposed that he had heard Silkby expounding from it.

[143] This question is more fully treated in McSheffrey, *Gender*, pp. 25–33.

[144] See below, p. 203.

[145] See below, pp. 158, 179, 180, 222, 239, 241. One man, Thomas Clerc, named her as a heretic (as 'moder Agnes'), and his connection with her may well have come through his wife, with whom Agnes Jonson had contact; see below, pp. 180, 188.

was natural that they would tend to participate in gatherings together: Thomasina and Richard Bradeley, for instance, held gatherings in their home and were frequently mentioned together by other Lollards.[146] Leading members of the group, especially Robert Silkby, Roger Landesdale, and Alice Rowley, were more likely to have contacts that spread over the whole community; Landesdale or Silkby, for instance, could sometimes be found reading to groups otherwise made up entirely of women, and for some men Rowley was the only woman Lollard they named.[147]

While, according to surviving records, other Lollard communities had conventicles made up of men, and in others there is evidence of mixed conventicles (with the women usually being the wives of men present), Coventry's Lollards are the only group for which there is evidence of all-female meetings.[148] This unusual situation may be traced to a number of factors. The urban situation facilitated women meeting together; Lollards who lived in rural areas often had to travel to meet with other Lollards, something that was much easier for men to do than for women. Coventry also had a critical mass of unattached women who participated in the sect; in most other Lollard communities, women Lollards were wives or daughters of male Lollards, and if they participated in gatherings, they did so in the company of their relatives. Single-women Lollards would have found that taking part in clandestine meetings, usually made up mostly of men, was very difficult or unwise in a culture that closely guarded women's sexual reputations; such an act might easily have been interpreted as unchaste. Indeed, a Lollard sermon praised the separation of the sexes in religious worship, since this kept men and women 'fro lecherye'.[149] Perhaps as a result of this, single women unrelated to male Lollards were very rare in other Lollard communities, but this problem was obviated by the all-female conventicles in Coventry. A last factor encouraging the participation of women in Coventry Lollard conventicles was the social prominence and probable charisma of several women leaders, especially Alice Rowley. Alice Rowley played a role as a teacher and leader that was not paralleled by any other woman Lollard, and Joan Smyth, Joan Warde, and Agnes Jonson (to name just three women) were very active in practising their faith. While committed women Lollards can certainly be found in other communities, their activities were often more constricted than those of the Coventry women.[150]

---

[146] See below, pp. 111, 147, 156, 200.

[147] e.g. below, pp. 106, 145, 148, 150, 156.

[148] See McSheffrey, *Gender*, pp. 29, 49–55.

[149] Anne Hudson and Pamela Gradon (eds), *English Wycliffite Sermons*, 5 vols (Oxford, 1983–1996), I, p. 355.

[150] McSheffrey, *Gender*, *passim*, esp. pp. 54–55.

Lollards in Coventry sometimes played host to visitors who came from elsewhere, evidently itinerant Lollards who travelled from one Lollard centre to another. Thomas Acton, for instance, testified about a certain notoriously defamed man, called 'a knowen man' in the vernacular,[151] who came to Acton's house and stayed there two nights, and was in Coventry for five or six nights altogether. During his stay at Acton's house, Alice Rowley came to him and they had communication on 'the deepest scriptures' (*profundis scripturis*). Silkby also came to visit him at Acton's house, gave him a pair of boots or leggings, and led him away, perhaps to the next house that would host him.[152] Joan Warde spoke of the same or perhaps another visitor when she reported that Silkby told her that Laurence Dawson, a good man, was then in the city.[153]

Such contacts with travelling Lollards exemplify the connections that Coventry Lollards had with heretics in other centres in England. Many other examples show the ties Coventry men and women had outside their city. Closely connected with the Coventry community were the Lollards in Birmingham and in Leicester, some of whom had previously been residents of Coventry. A number of Coventry Lollards were also closely familiar with the heretical community in Bristol – John Jonson deposed about them extensively in January 1512, and a number of Coventry witnesses testified about a man named Duke, who apparently visited Coventry and was later burned at Banbury, and who was possibly the same man as Henry Tuck, a wiredrawer of Bristol.[154]

The story of Joan Warde, *alias* Wasshingburn, shows how Lollards could use connections throughout the southern part of the kingdom when the need arose. In her testimony, she said that she had first fallen into heresy under the influence of Alice Rowley in the early 1490s. She was forced to flee Coventry, however, 'out of fear' of Alice's husband William Rowley, and she was escorted to Northampton by Robert Bastell. She stayed there at the home of a certain leatherdresser for about five months, after which she went to London. She stayed in the metropolis with a bedder named Blackburn whose wife was a Lollard, and within six months had married a Lollard shoemaker named Thomas Wasshingburn, whom ecclesiastical officials had investigated in the 1480s.[155] They lived in London for about three years, and then

---

[151] On this term, see Hudson, *Premature Reformation*, pp. 142–143.
[152] See below, p. 150.
[153] See below, p. 179.
[154] See below, pp. 103, 109, 126, 157, 180, 223.
[155] Wasshingburn was investigated in the Commissary Court of the Diocese of London for heresy in 1482; witnesses testified that he 'dixit quod Christus erat falsus patri suo dum vixit in terra, et beata Maria erat falsa qwen [queen – an epithet for prostitute]', and that he mocked a priest visiting the sick. He appeared before the judge and abjured.

moved to Maidstone, Kent. About 1495, Thomas and Joan were tried in Maidstone for heresy, renounced their opinions and were branded with the letter 'H' on their cheeks to signify their status as abjured heretics.[156] Some time after this, Joan returned to Coventry, apparently without Thomas (as he had previously abjured heresy, he may have been burned for relapse in Kent). There she began once again to consort with Alice Rowley and the other Lollards in that city and became an important figure, especially amongst the women. She was given the most severe of penalties in the 1511–1512 prosecution, being burned as a relapse in March 1512. Despite her sad end, Joan Warde had a long and varied career as a Lollard, and, notwithstanding the brand on her cheek, she had been able to continue in heretical activities for fifteen years after her first abjuration, apparently with little trouble from the authorities.

Lollards in Coventry also had contact with a number of clerics in nearby Leicestershire who were said to have heretical leanings. Robert Silkby mentioned the recently deceased William Kent, rector of Stoney Stanton (Leicestershire), as being sympathetic to heresy; as a result of Silkby's testimony, Bishop Blyth wrote to his counterpart in Lincoln to report that Kent 'by his lieff daies was maistr' of divers heretikes and had many books of heresy'. His nephew Ralph Kent, also a priest, was William Kent's executor and thus came into possession of his heretical books when William died about 1510; Ralph could read very well, Silkby reported, and had read to Silkby many times.[157] More shadowy

London, Guildhall Library, MS 9064/3, fo. 162v; William Hale, *A Series of Precedents and Proceedings in Criminal Causes, 1475–1640* (London, 1847), pp. 8–9.

[156] See below, p. 238; for other references to branding of Lollards, see Foxe, *A&M* (1570), pp. 917–919; *A&M* (1843), IV, pp. 123–124, 127 (on cheeks); Winchester, Hampshire Record Office, Reg. Fox, 2, fo. 87v (on hands); A.H. Thomas and I.D. Thornley (eds), *The Great Chronicle of London* (London, 1938), p. 290 (on cheeks); Charles Lethbridge Kingsford (ed.), *Chronicles of London* (Oxford, 1905), p. 226 (on cheeks). Although all these cases of Lollard branding date from the late fifteenth and early sixteenth centuries, branding had been used earlier in other instances of transgression. William of Newburgh reported that the twelfth-century heretical *Publicani* who visited England were branded on their foreheads as well as whipped (Richard Howlett (ed.), *Chronicles of the Reigns of Stephen, Henry II, and Richard I*, Rolls Series 82, 4 vols (London, 1884–1889), I, pp. 131–134; an English translation of the passage in question is available at <http://www.fordham.edu/halsall/basis/williamofnewburgh-two.html#13>). In the 1361 version of the Statute of Labourers, those who contravened the statute were to be branded with the letter 'F' on the forehead (for 'falsity') (*Statutes of the Realm*, 34 Edward III [1361], c. 10). John Bellamy notes that branding – on the hand – was used in the Elizabethan period for those who claimed benefit of clergy (so that they could not claim it more than once). J.G. Bellamy, *The Criminal Trial in Later Medieval England* (Stroud, 1998), pp. 137, 150. (Our thanks to Andrew Larsen and Kellie Robertson for these references.)

[157] See below, pp. 103, 108, 139 (quotation at p. 139); Fines, 'Heresy trials', p. 172. Stoney Stanton, as Thomson notices, lies on the road between Coventry and Leicester

is Sir Ralph Shor, whom Hachet believed had suspect books.[158] Hachet also reported that he had been told that Dr Alcock of Ibstock was of the sect, while Silkby testified that he had had possession of some of Alcock's books. John Alcock was rector of Ibstock, Leicestershire (north of Stoney Stanton), and in addition was a doctor of canon law and the holder of a number of benefices, including Ibstock, until he died around 1507. Alcock's possible involvement in Lollardy is curious, given that he was present among the group of clerics observing the proceedings during John Hales's prosecution of John Blumston and the others in 1486.[159] It is possible that this experience led him to become interested in the ideas of those who abjured. In any case, none of these men was centrally involved in the Coventry Lollard community; indeed the only person who evidently had direct contact with them was Robert Silkby.

Books and the importance of literacy

Coventry Lollards highly prized access to knowledge of vernacular prayers and devotional writings, particularly the scripture. Direct access to information, and in particular to the word of God as contained in the Christian scriptures, was central to the Lollard creed. As we have already seen, gatherings of Coventry Lollards consisted to a great extent of listening to a man or woman read aloud, and the members of the community expended a good deal of energy acquiring and trading English books. Bishop Blyth, who regarded such books as agents of the spread of heresy, saw this as especially dangerous. In his letter to the Bishop of Lincoln, he remarks that by imprisoning the suspects he has not only been able to get them to confess, but also 'by such meanes I have gete to my hands right many dampnable books, which shall noye no more by Godds grace'.[160]

Books are referred to throughout the Lichfield Court Book – receiving, possessing, or listening to 'books of heresy' was in itself a heretical act. One book, at least, was apparently heretical in content: John Atkynson said that he heard John Holywod reading in a book against the sacrament of the altar.[161] But while the records refer generically to the books in Lollard possession as 'books containing heresy', the great majority of the books that were specifically identified by the deponents were scriptural or otherwise orthodox. The Lollards of Coventry traded

and could conceivably have served as a resting-place between the two centres. Thomson, *Later Lollards*, p. 115.

[158] See below, p. 125.
[159] See below, pp. 74, 103, 125; *BRUC*, p. 6.
[160] See below, p. 139–140.
[161] See below, p. 115.

around and read to one another from all books of the Bible – copies of the Old and New Testaments are mentioned, along with a Psalter, the Book of Tobit, the Gospels, the Acts, the Epistles of Paul and James, and the Apocalypse (Book of Revelation).[162] They also made frequent mention of books '*de mandatis*' ('concerning the commandments'), which were probably commentaries on the decalogue rather than a simple translation.[163] In addition to the scriptural books, a few of the volumes mentioned by the Coventry Lollards appear to have been orthodox devotional works in English. The readings from the 'lives of the saints', the book 'of the passion of Christ and Adam', the primer (or book of hours) in English, and the book called *The Sykeman* (probably a book in the *ars moriendi* tradition) are all much more likely to be orthodox works than Lollard versions.[164]

These books were traded around among various members of the community. The leading members of the community – Robert Silkby, Roger Landesdale, and Alice Rowley – seem to have been most deeply involved in borrowing and lending. Silkby, for instance, gave Thomas Spenser a book of the epistles of Paul, gave Joan Warde a book on 'death and dying', brought a book of the Commandments to the home of Richard and Thomasina Bradeley and read to them from it, and bought from Richard Gest books of the Gospels, the Epistles and the Apocalypse.[165] Alice Rowley gave a book to Thomas Acton, lent an Old Testament 'in portable form' and a book of Paul's epistles to Roger Landesdale, and borrowed from Landesdale the Book of Tobit.[166] Sometimes books were given to Lollards outside Coventry. Thomas Banbrooke, for instance, lent Alice Rowley a book of the Gospels; she, in turn, lent it to 'a certain Dawson', apparently a Lollard traveller passing through Coventry, whereupon Banbrooke became angry with

---

[162] Old Testament: below, pp. 116, 118, 125, 132; New Testament: pp. 117, 157; Psalter: p. 155; Tobit: pp. 106, 116, 233, 241; Gospels: pp. 103, 106, 152, 156, 157, 173; Matthew: pp. 117, 146; John: pp. 118, 146; Gospels and Epistles: pp. 72, 146, 182; Acts: p. 117; Paul: pp. 116, 117, 130, 133, 147, 173, 197, 200; James: p. 155; Revelation: pp. 146, 150. Roger Landesdale mentioned a book 'of heretical depravity' that began, 'At the begynnyng whan God man' (p. 118); this may well have been Genesis (in the Wycliffite version, Genesis 1.1 is rendered 'In the bigynnyng God made of nou3t heuene and erthe'), but equally it may have been a Lollard or orthodox devotional text.

[163] See Appendix 2, below, p. 343.

[164] See Appendix 2. Primers and other books on the lives of saints, Christ's passion, and the art of dying were common in the late Middle Ages, and were among the more popular works coming off the early English presses. On these works, see Duffy, *Stripping of the Altars*, pp. 79, 209–286, 313–327. On the connection between orthodox vernacular devotion, including prayer, and Lollardy, see McSheffrey, 'Heresy, orthodoxy, and English vernacular religion'.

[165] See below, pp. 146, 147, 179, 194, 207.

[166] See below, pp. 116, 130, 150.

her as no doubt the book was now far from Coventry.[167] John Jonson
lent a book to Robert Silkby, who then took the book to Leicestershire;
when Jonson asked for the book back, Silkby gave him a 'tike of a
fedurbed' in recompense.[168]

There are indications in the Lichfield Court Book that the Coventry
Lollards sometimes copied, or had copied, the books that interested
them. Roger Landesdale twice mentioned borrowing books from Joan
Smyth, probably his former sister-in-law, and having them copied.[169]
Isabel Trussell admitted that she had a book copied or (less likely)
copied it herself (the passage is unclear).[170] Precisely how this copying
was accomplished is not at all clear. On the one hand, the skills of the
scrivener were highly specialized in the early sixteenth century and no
member of the Lollard community in Coventry is known to have
practised the trade. On the other hand, going outside the community
would have introduced a terrible risk, given the nature of the material
to be copied, and so it seems improbable that they would have simply
taken their books to a scrivener's shop. Two scenarios seem more likely
than others: that they took their books to London, or some other
centre, to be copied by scriveners sympathetic to their ideas, or that
some member of the community had acquired sufficient writing skills,
perhaps precisely for the purpose of making copies of Lollard books.[171]
Given the bishop's interest in preventing the spread of Lollard books,
it is surprising that Blyth did not pursue this question further.

In order for books to be read at Lollard gatherings, two things were
necessary: that books be available, and that there be someone present
who could read the books. There is considerable debate about general
literacy rates in the late medieval and early modern periods. Lollard
evidence indicates that the ability to read was not usual among
people of the social levels from which Lollard communities drew their
members.[172] Indeed, literacy could seem almost miraculous: Thomas

---

[167] See below, p. 157. On Dawson, see also p. 179.

[168] See below, p. 111. This might be the same book that, according to Silkby, was
subsequently in the hands of John Davy of Leicester (below, p. 146).

[169] See below, pp. 117, 118 (two different books are mentioned). In the first case, since
the verb is in the passive, it is not clear who is doing the copying. In the second example,
it is clearer that Roger had someone else copy it ('Fatetur [...] se quendam librum [...]
exemplandum habuisse.')

[170] See below, p. 248. The MS is damaged at this point and so the voice of the verb
is unclear; it is unlikely, however, that a woman would have had the skills to copy a
book.

[171] Possibly Balthasar Shugborow, who, as a gentleman, was likely to be better educated
than the others, served as the group's scribe.

[172] See Shannon McSheffrey, 'Literacy and the gender gap in the late Middle Ages:
women and reading in Lollard communities,' in Jane H.M. Taylor and Lesley Smith
(eds), *Women, the Book and the Godly* (Woodbridge, 1995), pp. 157–170.

Warde, for instance, heard Thomas Bown (a journeyman shoemaker) reading, and asked Bown's employer, Robert Hachet, how Bown could read when he did not know any letters. Hachet replied that Bown was inspired by the Holy Spirit.[173] As the Lichfield Court Book and other sources show, the ability to read was unusual enough that it could in itself be taken as evidence that an accused person was a heretic.[174] Relatively speaking, a fair number of Coventry Lollards were literate: deponents explicitly noted that ten men and six women could read.[175] Roger Landesdale was described reading far more frequently than any other Coventry Lollard, suggesting that his skills were the most highly developed.[176] The literacy of the women is particularly unusual: in other Lollard communities, evidence for women's literacy is rare, and this is probably both a reflection of, and reason for, the relatively high status of women in Coventry Lollardy.[177]

Leadership and influence in the Lollard sect were most likely to be exercised by the literate; John Foxe, for instance, sometimes described the most important members of the movement as 'principal readers'.[178] We must remember, though, that for late medieval and early modern people, reading was usually something that was done aloud and before a group, so that those unable to read still had access to the written word through the reading of others. Indeed sometimes illiterate people even had custody of books. Thomas Abell, for instance, had a book from Joan Warde, but since he did not know how to read he wanted to arrange for someone else to read it to him.[179] Roger Landesdale frequently read to many different groups of Lollards, and in his own

---

[173] See below, p. 203.

[174] See, e.g., Julian Yong's examination, below, p. 217. See also *Norwich Trials*, pp. 85, 169.

[175] Deponents testified that Thomas Bown (below, p. 203), Richard Bradeley (pp. 111, 200, 207), Thomas Clerc (pp. 126, 186, 188, 203, 247), Richard Dowcheman (p. 124), Robert Hachet (p. 125), John Holywod (p. 115), Roger Landesdale (see n. 176), Balthasar Shugborow (pp. 103, 106), Thomas Spenser (p. 171), Thomas Villers (p. 147), Thomasina Bradeley (p. 200), Agnes Jonson (pp. 179, 222), Alice Rowley (pp. 103, 106, 148, 157, 218), Joan Smyth (p. 197), Mother Villers (p. 205, 208), and Julian Yong (pp. 147, 148, 217) read or were literate. In addition, John Bull and Pygstappe appear to have signed their own names to their abjurations, and so were almost certainly literate (see below, pp. 271, 275), and the clergy on the fringes of the movement (such as Dr Alcock and the Kents) would have been able to read well (as Silkby indeed remarks regarding Ralph Kent, below, p. 108).

[176] See below, pp. 106, 110, 114, 116, 117, 122, 124, 125, 128, 130, 132, 139, 142, 156, 182, 187, 200, 210, 216.

[177] See McSheffrey, *Gender*, pp. 34, 58–59.

[178] Foxe, *A&M* (1570), p. 943; *A&M* (1843), IV, p. 214. See also Aston, *Lollards and Reformers*, p. 206; Hudson, *Premature Reformation*, pp. 185–187.

[179] See below, p. 179.

deposition he suggested that hearing him read was tantamount to heresy.[180]

Another means of access to religious texts was memorization, an activity that both literate and illiterate Lollards practised. According to various deponents, Matthew Markelond knew the Gospel of John (or perhaps its first chapter) by memory, Thomasina Bradeley could almost recite 'chapters of Paul', and Henry Tuke or Duke knew the Apocalypse by heart.[181] John Gest said that he had memorized the section of the epistle of Paul about charity, as well as the gospel in which the devil tempts God.[182] Memorization and recitation of scripture were both a means to convey the texts so important to the Lollards when books or readers were unavailable, and an act of piety and devotion.

The Lollard community, commitment, and the threat of prosecution

Although it was apparently possible to practise Lollardy virtually unmolested for years at a time, there was always the danger that eventually the bishop would come to hear of heresy in his diocese and prosecute – as Bishop Blyth indeed did. It was thus very important that proselytization be discreet, and that the secrets of the community be maintained. A number of defendants admitted that they had promised not to reveal the secrets of the community: twenty-year-old Julian Yong deposed that Alice Rowley instructed and warned her not to tell anyone about their activities, while Thomas Villers, who refused through several days of questioning to admit any involvement with heresy but finally broke down, told the prosecutors that he had tried to stay true to the oath he had sworn to Robert Silkby not to divulge any of their secrets and counsels.[183]

Yet it seems likely that some leakage from within the community was at least partly responsible for the prosecution of 1511–1512. A number of suspects said (in their own defence, of course) that they had previously confessed their heresies: John Spon said he had confessed to the vicar of Holy Trinity, Hugh Parrek said he had confessed to his curate, Rose Furnour confessed to a Franciscan friar, and Isabel Trussel surrendered her heretical book to her confessor.[184] These may all have been in response to a sentence of major excommunication fulminated by the bishop against those concealing heretics or books, probably just

---

[180] See above, n. 176.
[181] See below, pp. 124, 200, 224.
[182] See below, p. 154.
[183] See below, pp. 201, 218; see also pp. 108, 227, 231.
[184] See below, pp. 132, 210, 222, 248; see also p. 175.

before the proceedings recorded in the court book started.[185] Despite the theoretical confidentiality of confession, in one case at least, when a defendant confessed to one of the bishop's commissaries deputed in the heresy prosecutions, it was used against her. Agnes Brown denied any involvement with heresy in all her appearances before the court; after her last appearance in mid-February 1512, when she still refused to admit any heresy, a note was entered into the court book that she had 'secretly confessed her heresy' to Dr Wilcocks and that, nonetheless, she had not yet abjured.[186] It is possible, then, that as a result of other confessions information was passed to the episcopal authorities.[187] In any case, the relative success of Blyth's prosecutions in 1511–1512 was surely due to the detailed depositions given by the defendants, who garrulously offered a good deal of information about their fellows.

A wave of panic apparently went through the Coventry Lollards when the first arrests were made: one Lollard went to a man named Tuke or Duke when Silkby was first arrested to ask what Silkby had revealed, while the adolescent John Bull admitted in court that when he first heard about the arrest of Landesdale and the others that he had wanted to flee.[188] Alice Rowley, perhaps in a panic, gave some of her books to Joan Smyth before she went into custody, while Julian Yong tried to hide books under a mattress in Alice Rowley's house.[189] Some apparently did run away: Robert Hachet deposed on 31 October that his servant, Thomas Bown, was a heretic, but that he had fled (although he must have returned or been captured soon after since he appeared in court on 3 November), while Bown himself deposed that Robert Bastell, who had been active in Lollard activities from the early 1490s, had gone away somewhere unknown.[190]

Confessions and courtroom testimony about the sect indicate the strain that members of the Lollard communities felt, especially during times when prosecutions were imminent or underway. For some, involvement in the Lollard sect was perhaps somewhat experimental, and the danger that greater commitment would bring was more than they wanted to risk, especially in the face of prosecution and the threat of execution. It is characteristic of religious sects that some members remain adamant and lifelong adherents, while a good many others drift in and out, attracted at one point in their lives but later losing the

---

[185] See below, p. 132.

[186] See below, p. 252.

[187] It is possible that Joan Smyth caused detection of the group by giving over books to 'Master Longlond', who may have been an episcopal official, in mid-October 1511. See below, p. 142.

[188] See below, pp. 180, 215.

[189] See below, pp. 155, 217–218.

[190] See below, pp. 125, 131 (but cf. p. 110n.)

sense of commitment or, in the case of sects in which membership is dangerous or illegal, deciding that involvement is too hazardous.[191] This was almost certainly true of Lollardy: a number of Coventry defendants deposed that they had once held the beliefs of which they were accused, but that they had abandoned them, either when they realized that they were heretical, or when they felt that they were too risky. Thomas Warde, for instance, admitted that he had once listened to the reading of heretical books and favoured Lollard ideas, but that twelve years before, he had renounced these beliefs and done penance for them.[192] While obviously such statements may have been made by defendants as a way to deflect more serious charges (Warde abjured, for example, but was not given particularly difficult penance), it is also perfectly believable that men and women would repudiate heresy when the risks became manifest.

The Lollards of Coventry are a fascinating group: the unparelleled richness of the surviving records of their prosecution offer us tantalizing glimpses into the concerns, beliefs, hopes, and fears of the relatively ordinary people who made up this minority religious community. The documents also help us understand how authorities like Bishops Hales and Blyth tried to deal with this breach of their episcopal discipline, and how later polemicists like John Foxe used the example of their like-minded predecessors to inspire, validate, and justify. Altogether, the following sources present a unique opportunity to understand English society in the decades around 1500.

The documents

The bishops' registers and court books

In the pages that follow a number of different sorts of records kept by the bishops of Coventry and Lichfield and their administrators are presented. These include excerpts from the episcopal registers – the formal record of diocesan administration – of John Hales (bishop 1459–1490) and Geoffrey Blyth (bishop 1503–1531); the complete text of a notebook containing the relatively informal documentation of the trials of suspected heretics in 1511–1512, known as the Lichfield Court Book; and a short excerpt from a notebook kept by Bishop Blyth's vicar-

---

[191] See Frederick Bird and Bill Reimer, 'Participation rates in new religious and para-religious movements', *Journal for the Scientific Study of Religion*, 21 (1982), pp. 1–14.

[192] See below, p. 203; see also the case of Matthew Markelond, below, p. 152.

general as he made visitations in the diocese between 1515 and 1525. The registers, the Lichfield Court Book, and Bishop Blyth's visitation book together make up the surviving documentation of the bishops' proceedings against the heretics in their diocese.

The court book and the visitation book were the more informal, more complete, and almost certainly more immediate records: although we cannot be sure if the scribes drew up the entries from rough notes, the frequent deletions and insertions and untidy handwriting indicate that the material was recorded in some haste. The court book, devoted entirely to the special proceedings against the group of heretics the bishop uncovered in the autumn of 1511 and winter of 1512, is made up mostly of examinations or depositions of witnesses, but also includes a number of other types of records: formulaic questionnaires or inter-rogatories to which suspects presumably responded after they had been examined and indicated their willingness to abjure (literally 'to swear off') heresy; the original abjurations themselves, complete with crosses signed beneath the suspects' names (and sometimes original signatures); and the records of absolution and penance. In addition, there is a copy of a letter of warning, written in English, apparently sent from Bishop Blyth to William Smith, the Bishop of Lincoln, in early November 1511 regarding evidence Blyth had uncovered about Lollards in the city of Leicester. The book is one of only two such court or act books entirely devoted to the trials of Lollards known to survive from late medieval England, the other being the record of Bishop William Alnwick of Norwich's prosecutions in 1428–1431.[193] Others are known to have once existed, including those of Bishops Fitzjames and Tunstal of London and Longland of Lincoln.[194]

Two depositions from 1515 offer us further tantalizing clues about the subsequent history of the Lollard community in Coventry between the 1511–1512 prosecution and the burnings of 1520–1522. They are found now in Bishop Blyth's visitation book and were apparently taken in isolation, without any evidence of further action being taken by the bishop or his deputies at this time. They were recorded amongst a plethora of other proceedings, mostly the records of visitations of the diocese's religious houses conducted by Blyth's vicar-general, Thomas Fitzherbert, between 1515 and 1525.[195]

Unlike the court book and the visitation book, the bishops' registers did not include witness despositions, but were mainly an official record of abjurations, written in a neater and more formal hand. (It is interesting to note that, despite the presumably official status of the

[193] Published as *Norwich Trials*.
[194] For details see Fines, 'Heresy trials', p. 161, n. 2.
[195] For more information, see *Bishop Blythe's Visitations*, pp. xiv–xxviii, xxxii.

registers, it was to the more detailed court book that the bishop's representative apparently referred for evidence of previous conviction when a relapsed heretic, Robert Silkby, was captured and tried again in 1521 or 1522.)[196] Hales's register provided an individually tailored interrogatory for each person who abjured, dealing primarily with the heretical beliefs that were henceforth to be rejected. The abjurations recorded in Hales's register over four years, between 1486 and 1490, follow one another directly in the manuscript and apparently in the same handwriting – it is thus possible that the official record was entered all at the same time, at some date subsequent to Robert Clerke's abjuration in 1490. Unlike Hales's register, which provides some individualized information about the heretics' beliefs, in Blyth's register there were only two full confessions recorded – that of the first heretic to abjure formally, Thomas Flesshor, and that of Joan Warde *alias* Wasshingburn, who was the only suspect in 1511–1512 to be condemned to the stake as a relapsed heretic.[197] Other 1511–1512 suspects were said to abjure 'as Flesshor' or 'as above'.[198] There are some slight discrepancies between Blyth's register and his court book regarding dates of abjuration and other smaller details; in those cases, we have chosen to regard the court book, the immediate record, as more accurate.

The registers of Bishops Hales and Blyth, the Lichfield Court Book and Blythe's visitation book are all preserved in the Lichfield Record Office, along with the other archival records of the bishops of Coventry and Lichfield. The registers are described by David Smith, though without detailed references to the parts dealing with the trials in question.[199] The registers are in neat hands, fairly easy to read, and provide few problems to edit; usually the dates of the proceedings are indicated, although (as above) in some cases the dates are probably somewhat inaccurate.

The Lichfield Court Book, however, is very difficult to edit.[200] It appears to be, at least for the most part, the original record of the trials; the passages in Bishop Blyth's register, just mentioned, appear to be extracts from the court book written up in neat form. The court book is now a small paper folio volume of some twenty-six leaves with, in addition, three sheets of mounted fragments and a small portion of the vellum cover. It is devoted entirely to the proceedings for heresy in

---

[196] See the insertion of Silkby's condemnation in 1521 or 1522 into the Lichfield Court Book, below, p. 283.

[197] See below, pp. 135–136, 253, 263–264.

[198] For instance, below, pp. 163, 169, 290.

[199] D.M. Smith, *Guide to Bishops' Registers of England and Wales* (London, 1981), pp. 53 and 60–63.

[200] Fines, 'Heresy trials', pp. 160–161, describes the document and its history.

question and, with the exception of one document datable to 1521 or 1522, it refers exclusively to the prosecution of 1511–1512.

The Lichfield Court Book appears to have lain unnoticed until 1960: John Foxe shows no awareness of the prosecutions it records except for the proceedings against Robert Silkby in 1521–1522, knowledge of which he almost certainly obtained through other sources. When the book was rediscovered in the Lichfield Diocesan Registry in 1960 it was in a bad state, much damaged by damp in the centre and having the edges badly worn away. In addition to sizeable holes in various pages, some folios have been lost; the missing folios are probably few, however, shown in part by the fact that Bishop Blyth's register contains no names additional to those mentioned in the court book. Shortly after its rediscovery it was ably repaired and bound at Staffordshire Record Office; the original paper pages were mounted on pages of approximately the same size as the originals, measuring 35 cm (13.8 inches) by 26 cm (10.1 inches). At this time the manuscript was also given its present pagination/foliation (pages i–iv, folios 1–26). There is no evidence of an earlier numbering on the folios and it is not known how they were arranged before the rebinding. It is certain that the present order of folios at least postdates late 1521 or early 1522, as fo. 9, dealing with Robert Silkby's relaxation to the secular arm that year, is inserted following the earlier record of his examination and abjuration. It is likely, indeed, that at least some folios were originally ordered differently, as in some cases there is evidence that the scribe expected a folio other than in the current arrangment to follow.[201] In 1968, the book was moved, along with other records of the Diocesan Registry, to the Lichfield Joint Record Office (now the Lichfield Record Office), where it remains today, with the classification Lichfield Court Book, B/C/13.

Most of the handwriting in the book is of poor quality, frequently made worse, sometimes to the point of illegibility, by the damage done to the manuscript. Much of the material is undated or incompletely dated, though sometimes the dates given in Bishop Blyth's register come to the rescue. The contents of the book do not follow in a chronological sequence or in any other apparent order: this is the case at least as the folios are now bound together, but nothing suggests that a reordering of folios would produce a more coherent arrangement.

There is nothing unusual about the lack of order in the material. The records, for example, of the proceedings against Lollards of Bishop Alnwick of Norwich and Archbishop Warham of Canterbury similarly lack order, even though the latter are a neat copy written into Warham's

---

[201] For instance, below, p. 131, where the scribe's own cross-reference seems to indicate that fo. 4 once followed fo. 7.

register.[202] One can only assume that the scribes and their supervising authorities did not have the same obsession with chronology that would be presumed today: it was enough for them to have all the material, in whatever order, in a volume that was small enough to be perused with ease.

To print the material in the order in which it now stands in the court book would lead, at least for the modern reader, to large-scale incoherence and unintelligibility. It seems desirable, and with difficulty has been possible, to rearrange the material into a reasonably logical chronological order, though some uncertainty and conjecture remain. The reasoning behind the ordering of the documents is given in the appropriate places, in italics at the beginning of each entry.

John Foxe's Rerum in ecclesia gestarum *and* Acts and Monuments

In addition to the records of the episcopal authorities, valuable evidence for the fate of the Coventry Lollards is provided by two non-ecclesiastical sources: the writings of England's most famous Protestant martyrologist, John Foxe, and the civic annals of the city of Coventry. These sources are also presented below.

John Foxe (1517–1587),[203] author of *Acts and Monuments* (also known sometimes as *The Book of Martyrs*), was the leading English Protestant historian of the sixteenth century. Through his writings, Foxe hoped to provide both a historical justification for the Reformation and an alternative martyrology that traced a 'true' Christian church from the early centuries to his day. While in exile during Mary's reign, he published two Latin accounts of the persecution of Christians, *Commentarii rerum in ecclesia gestarum* (Strasbourg, 1554) and *Rerum in ecclesia gestarum [...] commentarii* (Basel, 1559). On his return to England with Elizabeth's accession, these were enlarged and translated into English as *Acts and Monuments of these latter and perillous dayes*, first published by John Daye in 1563. A second and substantially revised edition, entitled *The First (Second-) volume of the ecclesiasticall history [...]*, was published in 1570, and two subsequent editions appeared during Foxe's lifetime, in 1576 and 1583.[204]

---

[202] *Norwich Trials*, pp. 2–3; *Kent Heresy Proceedings*, pp. x and xxiv.

[203] This section on John Foxe and his writings was greatly improved by comments and suggestions made by Dr Thomas S. Freeman, and the editors gratefully acknowledge his help.

[204] On John Foxe and his martyrologies, see Thomas S. Freeman, 'Fate, faction, and fiction in Foxe's *Book of Martyrs*', *The Historical Journal*, 43 (2000), pp. 601–623; David

Foxe saw the Lollards as precursors of the Protestants of his own era, followers of the true light when most others were still in darkness. His accounts of the Lollard persecutions in *Acts and Monuments* (a title we will here use for all the different English versions of his history) have been used extensively by historians of the heretical movement. In his book, Foxe presented both translations of documents and oral histories he or his researchers gathered regarding the prosecution of heretics in the late medieval period. In some cases the documents he used still survive, but in others the records upon which he relied have since disappeared and in those cases the value of his account is substantial. The oral testimony he recorded is also of considerable interest. For the Coventry Lollards, Foxe's accounts provide us both with transcription of material that is still extant in the original and with information that we otherwise do not have, apparently gathered through interviews. While we must always keep Foxe's polemical purposes in mind when using the material he presents, his work cannot be ignored in the study of Lollardy.

Foxe presented different narratives of the Coventry Lollard pros-ecutions in his 1559 Latin work, *Rerum in ecclesia gestarum*, and in the 1563 and 1570 editions of *Acts and Monuments*, suggesting both that he and his researchers gathered more information about the prosecutions as he worked, and that he revised his account in response to critics.[205] The first account, which appeared in the 1559 Latin *Rerum*, written while Foxe was in exile during the reign of Mary I, is somewhat vague, recounting the story of the wife of a prominent man named Smyth

---

Loades (ed.), *John Foxe and the English Reformation* (Aldershot, 1997), esp. *idem*, 'Introduction: John Foxe and the editors', pp. 1–11, and David Newcombe, 'Appendix: A finding list of extant sixteenth- and seventeenth-century editions of John Foxe's *Acts and Monuments*', pp. 306–330.

[205] For the 1559, 1563 and 1570 versions, see below, pp. 296–314. The 1576 and 1583 editions reproduce the 1570 accounts of the Coventry Lollards with only minor changes in spelling and layout. See Freeman, 'Fate, faction,' regarding the successive revisions of Foxe's work. John King comments that modern scholars using Foxe have tended to rely on the nineteenth-century editions of Foxe, which are unsatisfactory in many ways (John King, 'Fiction and fact in Foxe's *Book of Martyrs*', in Loades, *John Foxe and the English Reformation*, pp. 12–13). This has been the case with scholarship on the Lollard movement (including work by the present editors). The nineteenth-century editions did not always accurately reproduce the 1583 edition of *Acts and Monuments* on which they were largely based; in addition, the comparison here shows that the 1563 edition has some material on Lollards that was subsequently omitted in the 1570 and later editions (although conversely the 1570 edition also includes some additions and clarifications). The sixteenth-century editions are to be preferred, but in addition reference will be made here to the nineteenth-century Townsend edition (*Acts and Monuments*, 8 vols, George Townsend (ed.) (London, 1843)), since it is more widely available.

who was burned with six others outside the town walls of Coventry. The woman, as the narrative tells it, was nearly spared the execution intended for the others, but as she was being escorted home, the man who led her by the arm discovered a paper in her sleeve on which was written the Lord's Prayer. Because of this, she was led back and consigned to the fire along with her companions. The episode is loosely dated as occurring around 1490 (about thirty years out of date). Foxe's source for this story may well have been his wife, Agnes Randall, or another member of her family; Agnes's father was a citizen of Coventry, and Foxe himself stayed briefly in the city in the 1540s.[206] Whoever Foxe's source was, that person remembered the harassment and execution of local Lollards and particularly the dramatic incident of Joan Smyth's near escape.

The subsequent revisions of Foxe's account of the Coventry martyrs indicate that he made further enquiries in order to flesh out the original story, probably on his return to England with the accession of Elizabeth. In the main part of the 1563 edition, Foxe included a revised and more complete version of seven martyrs, this time dating it to a more plausible April 1520. His naming of the mayor and sheriffs at the beginning of the account suggests that he used a mayoral list or civic annal for some of his information, but the story as a whole is far more extensive than anything found in such a source for this period. Foxe, or his agents, almost certainly gathered other parts of the story from local informants, one of whom was quite possibly the 'mother Halle' named in the 1570 version.[207]

In addition to the seven martyrs of 1520, Foxe also included in his 1563 version a translation of the abjurations recorded in Hales's register for those prosecuted in 1486 and 1488. This section was printed in an appendix near the end of the book (marked to be inserted before the account of the seven martyrs above), indicating that the material probably reached him just as the first edition was nearing completion in March 1563. It is likely that Foxe did not himself personally consult Hales's register but that someone else sent him a transcription or translation of the material. Foxe was in an excellent position to acquire

---

[206] J.F. Mozley, *John Foxe and His Book* (London, 1940), p. 27.

[207] As Thomas S. Freeman has pointed out to us, after Catholic attacks on the accuracy of the 1563 edition of *Acts and Monuments*, Foxe was particularly concerned in 1570 to name his sources. He was especially sensitive about the issue of execution for the reading of vernacular Bibles: Nicholas Harpsfield, in *Dialogi sex contra summi pontificatus, monasticae vitae, sanctorum Sacrarum imaginum oppugnatores et pseudomartyres* (Antwerp, 1566), pp. 827–828 and 833, had called him a liar for making this charge. Robert Parsons (in *A Treatise of Three Conuersions of England from Paganisme to Christian Religion* (St Omer, 1603–1604), II, pp. 409–415) would later continue the Catholic argument against Foxe on the issue of scripture with specific reference to the Coventry martyrs.

diocesan records from Coventry, since Thomas Bentham, Bishop of the diocese 1560–1579, and Thomas Lever, Archdeacon of Coventry, were close personal friends.[208] Either one of them could have sent him the original registers or copies thereof for his work. In neither the 1563 edition nor subsequent versions of *Acts and Monuments* did Foxe use the Lichfield Court Book, which he would surely have used had he known about it.

In the 1570 edition of *Acts and Monuments* Foxe inserted the 1486–1488 abjurations along with other material from the reign of Henry VII. The text remained almost identical to his 1563 appendix, with the addition of marginal notes highlighting particular doctrines and a shift in verb tense (the 1563 version translated verbs in their original present tense – 'that whoso beleueth as the church beleueth, beleueth ill' – while in 1570 Foxe emphasized the historical nature of the doctrines under discussion by shifting into the past tense – 'that who so beleued as the churche then did beleue, beleued ill'). Foxe more substantially revised his account of the 1520–1522 prosecutions. Some of the alterations were stylistic; the names of the prosecutors and the prosecuted are, for instance, presented in tabular form and some of the spellings of the names are changed. He retained one anecdote from the 1563 edition (the story told about Joan Smyth's scroll), but omitted another equally memorable but perhaps less credible story (the account of Robert Hachet's impassioned response to the bishop that the accused did no more than say English prayers). As above, he made the source of his information explicit in the 1570 edition, noting that one 'mother Halle', whom he identified as living in Bagington (now Baginton) near Coventry, remembered those who were executed as renowned for their piety. The rhetoric of the 1570 version of the story is muted in comparison to the 1563 edition: in both versions, the tone is one of righteous indignation that these 'men of good life, true dealing, and honest conuersation' were burned solely for having the Lord's Prayer in English, but the long passage about the 'vnmercifull Tyrantes and blodie papistes' who spread untrue rumours about other heretical acts is truncated in the later edition.

Historians have given various evaluations of Foxe's accuracy in his accounts of Lollard prosecutions.[209] A comparison between the material he presents regarding the 1486–1488 prosecutions and the documents

---

[208] Mozley, *John Foxe*, p. 50; London, British Library, MS 417, fos 99r, 103r, 121r (these references provided by Thomas S. Freeman).

[209] On the overall question of Foxe and accuracy, see Freeman, 'Fate, faction'; and Loades *John Foxe and the English Reformation*, esp. *idem*, 'Introduction', pp. 9–10; King, 'Fiction and fact', pp. 12–35. On Foxe as a source for Lollardy, see John A.F. Thomson, 'John Foxe and some sources for Lollard history: notes for a critical appraisal', *Studies in Church History*, 2 (1965), pp. 251–257; Fines, 'Heresy trials', pp. 173–174.

that survive confirms that he was substantially accurate in his translation of the register material, but that he (or those who provided the transcriptions for him) tended to omit what did not fit his polemical intentions. The articles in which Lollards were accused of beliefs that did not strictly conform with scripturalism are silently passed over, for instance.[210] In addition – and for this the present editors have a great deal of sympathy – he or his transcriber sometimes excluded articles if they were too difficult to read in the manuscript.[211] In his presentation of translated material, then, Foxe's sins are those of omission rather than commission, although on other occasions he was capable of more significant manipulation of the sources to serve his goal of portraying Lollards as proto-Protestant heroes and heroines.[212]

The Coventry civic annals

Further evidence for Lollard activities in the city of Coventry in the late fifteenth and early sixteenth century can be found in the Coventry civic annals.[213] Civic annals or town chronicles, sometimes called mayoral lists, are difficult sources to use.[214] They probably began as chronological listings of the civic leaders for each year, with short accounts about the noteworthy events that occurred during their year in office. Subsequent annalists copied earlier versions for their coverage of past events and gave contemporary accounts for their own day. In England most of these town chronicles survive only in versions dating from the late sixteenth century and after; the Coventry annals used here came into their present forms in the seventeenth and eighteenth centuries. The authorship and reliability of the annals' accounts of events from the fifteenth and early sixteenth century is thus impossible to assess.

A number of annals survive for Coventry, of which two are presented here, both clearly based on the same tradition judging by the similarity of wording, although differing in a few details.[215] The first, now in the Bodleian Library, dates from some time in the first half of the seventeenth century. The second, from the Birmingham City Archive, was compiled in the early eighteenth century. The information the annalists present about Lollards for the most part accords with surviving records

---

[210] See below, pp. 66, 68, and 88.

[211] For instance, the last article with which Thomas Butler was charged (below, pp. 70, 301).

[212] See McSheffrey, *Gender*, p. 13 and notes there.

[213] See below, pp. 315–318.

[214] On these sources, see Alan Dyer, 'English town chronicles,' *Local Historian*, 12 (1976–1977), pp. 285–292.

[215] For a discussion of Coventry annals, see *REED Coventry*, pp. xxxvii–xli.

and Foxe's account, with one exception: the two annals both suggest that seven heretics were burned in 1512. (Blyth's register records only one relaxation to the secular arm – Joan Warde's in 1512 – and the burning of seven heretics in 1520 is noted both by Foxe and the annalists.) Given the late date of compilation, and the uncertain provenance of the information provided in the annals, and barring other evidence for the burning of seven heretics rather than one in 1512, we have assumed here that the annalists were mistaken about the executions of 1512. It seems likely that the annalists confused the burning of Joan Warde in 1512 and the burning of the seven heretics in 1520.[216] Whether one or seven were burned in 1512, the annals do suggest that both the execution of Lollards and even the public penances of those who were not burned were notable events worthy of recording in the city annals.

[216] See below, pp. 255–258, 298, 304, 315, 317.

CHRONOLOGY OF EXAMINATIONS OF COVENTRY LOLLARD SUSPECTS, 1486–1522

Thursday, 9 March 1486	John Blumston, Richard Hegham, John Smyth, Robert Crowther, Thomas Butler, Richard Gilmyn, John Falks, and Roger Brown
Between Sunday, 12 March and Wednesday, 26 April 1486	John Blumston, Richard Hegham, Robert Crowther, John Smyth, Roger Brown, Thomas Butler, John Falks, and Richard Gylmyn
Tuesday, 8 April 1488	Margery Goyte
Saturday, 27 February 1490	Robert Clerke *alias* Teylour
Monday, 13 November 1503	John Sheperde
Before 28 October 1511	Robert Silkby John Jonson
Tuesday, 28 October 1511	Thomas Flesshor Robert Silkby John Jonson
Wednesday, 29 October 1511	John Atkynson Roger Landesdale
Thursday, 30 October 1511	John Atkynson
Friday, 31 October 1511	Roger Landesdale Symon Margery Locock Alice Rowley Robert Hachet
Sunday, 2 November 1511	John Atkynson
Monday, 3 November 1511	Thomas Bown John Spon Thomas Flesshor
Tuesday, 4 November 1511	Joan Smyth

	Richard Gest senior
	Balthasar Shugborow
Wednesday, 5 November 1511	Robert Silkby
	Thomas Acton
	Robert Peg
	Matthew Markelond
	Joan Gest
	John Gest
	Alice Rowley
	Joan Smyth
	Roger Landesdale, Robert Hachet, Thomas Bown, John Atkynson, Robert Peg, Thomas Acton, John Gest, and Joan Gest
	Richard Hyde
Thursday, 6 November 1511	Roger Landesdale, Robert Hachet, Thomas Bown, John Atkynson, Matthew Markelond, Thomas Acton, Robert Peg, John Gest, and Joan Gest
	Balthasar Shugborow
	Robert Peg
	Ralph Lye
	Balthasar Shugborow, Robert Peg, and Ralph Lye
	Ralph Lye and Robert Peg
Monday, 17 November 1511	Joan Warde *alias* Wasshingburn
Saturday, 22 November 1511	Thomas Abell
Tuesday, 25 November 1511	Thomas Wrixham
	Thomas Clerc
	Thomas Wrixham, Thomas Clerc, Thomas Abell, Thomas Villers, Robert Silkby, Richard Bradeley, Thomas Spenser, John Longhold, Thomas Banbrooke, William Hawkyns, and Thomas Warde
Thursday, 27 November 1511	Thomas Villers
Before 28 November 1511	Richard Bradeley
Friday, 28 November 1511	Thomas Villers
	Richard Bradeley
Saturday, 29 November 1511	Thomas Banbrooke
	Richard Northopp

Thomas Spenser
John Longhold
William Lodge
Thomas Villers
Thomas Warde
William Hawkyns
Robert Silkby, Thomas Wrixham,
Thomas Abell, Thomas Clerc, Richard
Bradeley, Thomas Spenser, John
Longhold, Thomas Banbrooke,
William Hawkyns, Thomas Warde, (and
Thomas Villers?)

Late November or early
December 1511

Thomasina Bradeley
Margaret Landesdale
Alice Lye
Thomas Kylyngworth
Hugh Parrek
William Revis
John Cropwell
Thomas Bown and Roger Landesdale
John Hebbis
David Clerc
John Bull
Thomas Lyeff
Elizabeth Gest
Julian Yong

Wednesday, 3 December
1511

Margaret Landesdale
William Revis
John Bull, Julian Yong, David Clerc,
Thomas Lyeff, and Thomas Villers
Hugh Parrek, Margaret Landesdale,
David Clerc, John Bull, Thomas Lyeff,
and Julian Yong

Friday, 16 January 1512

Rose Furnour
John Jonson
Rose Furnour
John Clerc
John Davy
Alice Rowley

Thursday, 22 January 1512

John Cropwell
Katherine Hachet
Agnes Jonson, Agnes Yong, and Agnes
de Bakehouse

	Agnes Corby
	Elizabeth Gest and Agnes Corby
	Agnes Jonson, Agnes de Bakehouse, Agnes Yong, Agnes Corby, Agnes Brown, and Elizabeth Gest
Saturday, 24 January 1512	[Robert?] Hachet
	Joan Wasshingburn *alias* Warde
	John Olyver
	Alice Rowley
Monday, 26 January 1512	Thomasina Bradley
Mid-January to mid-February 1512	Richard Rise
	Alice Acton
	Constance Clerc
	William Revis
	Katherine Baker
	Margaret Grey
	Thomas Kylyngworth
	Agnes Brown
	John Archer
	Isabel Trussell
Wednesday, 4 February 1512	John Cropwell
	John Holywod, John Cropwell, John Spon, John Archer, John Holbache, Roger Toft, Robert Haghmond, and Richard Rise
Friday, 13 February 1512	Agnes Brown
Thursday, 11 March 1512	Joan Warde *alias* Wasshingburn
Friday, 12 March 1512	Joan Warde *alias* Wasshingburn
Monday, 15 March 1512	Joan Warde *alias* Wasshingburn
Tuesday, 22 May 1515	William Borodall
	Ralph Lowe
Monday, 21 December 1521 or Monday, 13 January 1522	Robert Silkby

PROSECUTION OF THE COVENTRY LOLLARDS IN THE ECCLESIASTICAL RECORDS, 1486–1522

1486–1503

John Blumston, Richard Hegham, John Smyth, Robert Crowther, Thomas Butler, Richard Gilmyn, John Falks, and Roger Brown

[Reg. Hales, fo. 166r]

Acta in ecclesia sancti Michaelis Coventr',[1] ix° die mensis Marcii anno Domini millesimo cccclxxx quinto, coram reverendo in Christo patre ac domino domino Johanne Dei gracia Coventr' et Lich' episcopo.[a]

Negotium inquisicionis de et super crimine heretice pravitatis contra Johannem Blumston, Ricardum Hegham, Johannem Smyth, Robertum Crowther, Thomam Butler, Ricardum Gilmyn, Johannem Falks et Rogerum Browne, civitatis Coventr', dicti reverendi patris diocesis, super crimine heresis infamatos, accusatos atque detectos, ut patet in articulis subscriptis meram heresim continentibus seu saltem ad minus heresim[b] sapientibus.

[English translation]

Proceedings in St Michael's church in Coventry[1] on 9 March 1485/1486 before the Reverend Father and Lord in Christ, Lord John, by the grace of God Bishop of Coventry and Lichfield.

Enquiry concerning the the crime of heresy against John Blumston, Richard Hegham, John Smyth, Robert Crowther, Thomas Butler, Richard Gilmyn, John Falks, and Roger Browne, of the city of Coventry, of the diocese of the said reverend father, defamed, accused, and detected regarding the crime of heresy, as appears in the following articles involving pure heresy or at least savouring of heresy.

---

[a] Acta [...] episcopo *is the heading of the page.*
[b] sim *of* heresim *interlined.*

John Blumston

[Reg. Hales, fo. 166r]

In[a] primis videlicet Johannes Blumston de Coventria, Coventren' et Lich' diocesis, palam et publice infamatur, accusatur, nominatur et impetitur quod ipse Johannes fuit et sit verus hereticus pro eo et ex eo quod idem Johannes infra civitatem Coventr' predictam predicavit, docuit, tenuit, asseruit et dogmatizavit quod potestas attributa beato Petro in ecclesia Dei per salvatorem nostrum Iesum Christum immediate non fuit transitoria suis successoribus.

Item,[b] quod tanta virtus fuit in una herba sicut fuit in beata virgine Dei genitrice Maria.

Item,[c] quod oracio et elemosina non proficiunt defuncto quia incontinenti post mortem accedit vel ad celum vel ad infernum, sic ex consequenti nullum asserens esse purgatorium.

Item,[d] quod transire ad ecclesiam causa orandi vacuum esset quia quis possit ita bene fundere preces in domo propria sicut in ecclesia.

Item,[e] quod peregrinare ad ymagines beate Marie[f] de Dancastrie, Walsyngham vel de Turre civitatis Coventr'[2] fatuum esset, quia ita bene posset quis venerari beatam Virginem iuxta ignem in coquina sicut in locis predictis, et ita bene posset quis venerari beatam Virginem videndo matrem vel sororem sicut visitando ymagines, quia sunt tantomodo ligna mortua et lapides.

Item,[g] quod proterno vultu, ut apparuit, dixit in vulgari: 'A vengeance on all suche horeson prests for thay have gret envy that a pore man shulde gete hys levynge amonge hem'.

[English translation]

First, John Blumston of Coventry, of the diocese of Coventry and Lichfield, is openly and publicly defamed, accused, named, and charged that he has been, and is, a true heretic, inasmuch as within the said city of Coventry he preached, taught, held, asserted, and instructed that the power given to blessed Peter in the church of God by our

---

[a]   Contra Johannem Blumston i[us] articulus *in margin.*
[b]   2[us] articulus *in margin.*
[c]   3[us] articulus *in margin.*
[d]   4[us] articulus *in margin.*
[e]   5[tus] articulus *in margin.*
[f]   beate Marie *interlined.*
[g]   6[tus] articulus *in margin.*

saviour Jesus Christ did not directly pass to his successors.

Also, that there was as much virtue in one plant as in Mary the Blessed Virgin and mother of God.

Also, that prayer and alms do not benefit a dead person because he or she goes to heaven or to hell immediately after death, thereby asserting there is no purgatory.

Also, that to go to church to pray is pointless because people can pray equally well in their own house as in a church.

Also, that to make a pilgrimage to the images of Blessed Mary of Doncaster, of Walsingham or of the Tower of the city of Coventry[2] is foolish because people can equally well venerate the Blessed Virgin next to the fire in a kitchen as in the aforesaid places, and they can venerate the Blessed Virgin as well through seeing their mother or sister as through visiting images, for these are but dead wood and stones.

Also, that shamelessly, as it appeared, he said in the vernacular: 'A vengeance on all such whoreson priests for they have great envy that a poor man should get his living among them'.

Richard Hegham

[Reg. Hales, fo. 166r]

In[a] primis videlicet Ricardus Hegham de eadem civitate palam et publice infamatur, accusatur et impetitur ac nominatur quod ipse Ricardus fuit et sit verus hereticus pro eo et ex eo quod idem Ricardus infra civitatem Coventr' predictam palam et publice predicavit, docuit, tenuit, asseruit et dogmatizavit quod quilibet Christianus in articulo mortis constitutus renunciaret omnibus operibus suis bonis et malis et submiteret se misericordie divine.[b]

Item,[c] quod adorare[d] seu venerare ymagines beate Marie de Turre civitatis predicte seu aliorum sanctorum fatuum esse quia sunt nisi lingna et lapiedes.[e]

Item,[f] quod si ymago beate Marie de Turre civitatis predicte posita esset ad ignem, faceret bonum ignem.

Item,[g] quod melius esset erogare pecuniam pauperibus quam offerre

---

[a] Contra Ricardum Hegham *in margin.*
[b] divine *interlined.*
[c] 2[us] articulus *in margin.*
[d] ad *of* adorare *interlined.*
[e] lingna et lapiedes *[sic].*
[f] 3[us] articulus *in margin.*
[g] 4[tus] articulus *in margin.*

pecuniam ymaginibus[a] Christi et aliorum sanctorum, que sunt ligna mortua et lapides.

[English translation]

First, that Richard Hegham of the said city is openly and publicly defamed, accused, charged, and named that he has been, and is, a true heretic, inasmuch as within the said city of Coventry he openly and publicly preached, taught, held, asserted, and instructed that Christians at the hour of death should renounce all their works, both good and bad, and submit themselves to the divine mercy.

Also, that to adore or venerate images of Blessed Mary of the Tower of the said city, or of other saints, is foolish because they are but wood and stones.

Also, that if the image of Blessed Mary of the Tower of the said city were set alight, it would make a good fire.

Also, that it would be better to give money to the poor than to offer money to images of Christ and of other saints, which are dead wood and stones.

Robert Crowther

[Reg. Hales, fo. 166r]

In[b] primis videlicet Robertus Crowther de eadem civitate palam et publice infamatur, accusatur et impetitur ac nominatur quod ipse Robertus fuit et sit verus hereticus pro eo et ex eo quod idem Robertus infra civitatem Coventr' predicte palam et publice predicavit, docuit, tenuit, asseruit et dogmatizavit quod recipiens sacramentum altaris in mortali peccato vel extra caritatem nichil recipit nisi panem et vinum.

Item,[c] quod neque episcopi neque sacerdotes seu curati ecclesiarum habent potestatem in foro penitenciali ligandi atque solvendi.

Item,[d] quod vellet hec verba, 'qui conceptus est de Spiritu sancto, natus ex Maria virgine', extrahi a simbalo quia frustratorie ibidem sunt posita.

---

[a] ymaginibus *interlined*.
[b] Contra Robertum Crowther 1[us] articulus *in margin*.
[c] 2[us] articulus *in margin*.
[d] 3[us] articulus *in margin*.

Item,[a] quod peregrinare ad ymaginem beate Marie de Turre civitatis predicte fatuum esset, quia sunt nisi ligna et lepides.

[English translation]

First, that Robert Crowther of the same city is publicly defamed, accused, charged, and named that he has been, and is, a true heretic, inasmuch as within the said city of Coventry he openly and publicly preached, taught, held, asserted, and instructed that anyone who receives the sacrament of the altar in a state of mortal sin or outside charity receives only bread and wine.

Also, that neither bishops nor priests nor curates of churches have power in confession to bind and to loose.

Also, that he wished the words, 'who was conceived of the Holy Spirit, born of the Virgin Mary', were removed from the Creed because they were put there in vain.

Also, that to make a pilgrimage to the image of Blessed Mary of the Tower of the aforesaid city is foolish because it is only wood and stones.

John Smyth

[Reg. Hales, fo. 166v]

In[b] primis videlicet Johannes Smyth de eadem civitate palam et publice infamatur, accusatur, nominatur et impetitur quod ipse Johannes fuit et est verus hereticus pro eo et ex eo quod idem Johannes Smyth infra civitatem predictam predicavit, docuit, tenuit, asseruit et dogmatizavit videlicet quod quilibet tenetur scire dominicam orationem, salutacionem angelicam et simbolum in Anglic' si posset pro istis falcis presbiteris.

Item,[c] quod quilibet credens sicut sancta mater ecclesia credit, male credit; et quod necesse habet ad exercendum scolas per unum annum antequam cognoscat rectam fidem.

Item,[d] quod nullus presbiter habet potestatem absolvendi aliquem in foro penitenciali de peccatis suis.

---

[a] 4[us] articulus *in margin.*
[b] Contra Johannem Smyth articulus 1[us] *in margin.*
[c] 2[us] articulus *in margin.*
[d] 3[us] articulus *in margin.*

[English translation]

First, that John Smyth of the said city is openly and publicly defamed, accused, named, and charged that he has been, and is, a true heretic, inasmuch as within the said city he preached, taught, held, asserted, and instructed that all must know the Lord's Prayer, Hail Mary, and the Creed in English if they are to avail before these false priests.

Also, that anyone who believes as Holy Mother Church believes, believes falsely; and that it is necessary to attend school for a whole year before a person can know the correct faith.

Also, that no priest has power of absolving a person from sins in confession.

Roger Brown

[Reg. Hales, fo. 166v]

Rogerus[a] Browne de eadem palam et publice infamatur, accusatur, nominatur et impetitur quod ipse Rogerus fuit et est verus hereticus pro eo et ex eo quod idem Rogerus infra civitatem predictam predicavit, docuit, tenuit, asseruit et dogmatizavit quod quis non adoraret ymaginem beate Marie de Walsyngham nec sanguinem Christi apud Heylys,[3] sed adoraret dominum magnum et ipse dabit sibi quicquid petierit, asserens quod dominus nunquam effudit sanguinem in terra nec habuit matrem.

Item,[b] promisit cuidam quod sibi ostenderet certos libros heresim sapientes si iuraret quod non revelaret et si in eis crederet.

Item,[c] quod tempore levacionis eukaristie in manibus sacerdotis non elevat manus neque occulos ad sacramentum.

Item,[d] quod comedit carnes in xl[a, 4] et sic erat captus in comestione huiusmodi carnium.

Item,[e] si quis non erat confessus per totam vitam suam et in articulo mortis vellet confiteri et non possit, si haberet contricionem solum transiret ad gaudia sine purgatorio; et si esset confessus de aliquo peccato et solum iniunctum esset sibi ad dicendum unum Pater noster pro penitencia, si crederet quod aliquam penam haberet in purgatorio pro illo peccato nunquam iterum vellet confiteri pro aliquo peccato.

---

[a] Contra Rogerum Browne, 1[us] articulus *in margin.*
[b] 2[us] articulus *in margin.*
[c] 3[us] articulus *in margin.*
[d] 4[us] articulus *in margin.*
[e] 5[us] articulus *in margin.*

Item,[a] dicit quod omnia sunt perdita que data sunt presbiteris.

Item,[b] quod nullum esset purgatorium et quod Deus voluit remittere omnia peccata sine confessione et satisfaccione.

[English translation]

Roger Browne of the same city is openly and publicly defamed, accused, named, and charged that he has been, and is, a true heretic, inasmuch as within the said city he preached, taught, held, asserted, and instructed that people should not adore the image of Blessed Mary of Walsingham nor the blood of Christ at Hailes,[3] but they should adore the great Lord and he will give them whatever they ask, asserting that the Lord never shed his blood on earth and did not have a mother.

Also, he promised a certain man[c] that he would show him various books savouring of heresy, if he would swear that he would not reveal the matter, and if he would put his trust in the books.

Also, that at the moment the priest elevated the Eucharist in his hands, he would not raise his hands or eyes to the sacrament.

Also, he ate meat in Lent[4] and was caught while doing so.

Also, if anyone had not confessed throughout his life but at the hour of death wanted to confess but could not, if he had only contrition he would pass to bliss without purgatory; but if he had confessed some sin and had only been enjoined to say one Our Father as penance, if he believed that he would have some punishment in purgatory for that sin, he would never again want to confess a sin.

Also, he says that everything given to priests is lost.

Also, that there is no purgatory and God would remit all sins without confession and satisfaction.

Thomas Butler

[Reg. Hales, fo. 166v]

Thomas[d] Butler de eadem palam et publice infamatur, accusatur, nominatur et impetitur quod ipse Thomas fuit et est verus hereticus pro eo et ex eo quod idem Thomas infra civitatem predictam predicavit

---

[a] 6ᵘˢ articulus *in margin.*
[b] 7ᵘˢ articulus *in margin.*
[c] man: *the gender is unclear, could be woman.*
[d] Contra Thomam Butler, articulus primus

et palam ac publice docuit, tenuit, asseruit et dogmatizavit quod non erant nisi duo vie, ad celum videlicet et ad infernum, et quod nullus sustineret aliquam penam post mortem Christi pro aliquo peccato quia Christus moriebatur pro peccatis nostris.

Item,[a] quod nullum est purgatorium quia quilibet immediate post mortem transit ad celum vel ad infernum.

Item,[b] quod quilibet decedens in fide Christi et ecclesie, qualitercumque vixerit, salvabitur.

Item,[c] quod oraciones et peregrinaciones nullius sunt effectus et in nichilo prosunt ad obtinendum celum.

Item,[d] quod novit quando presbiter ascendit in pulpitum quid ipse vult dicere ita bene sicut ipse presbiter.

[English translation]

Thomas Butler of the same city is openly and publicly defamed, accused, named, and charged that he has been, and is, a true heretic, inasmuch as within the said city he preached and openly and publicly taught, held, asserted, and instructed that there are only two ways, namely to heaven and to hell, and that nobody undergoes any punishment for any sin after the death of Christ because Christ died for our sins.

Also, that there is no purgatory, because everyone passes immediately after death to heaven or to hell.

Also, that whoever dies in the faith of Christ and of the church, no matter how he has lived, will be saved.

Also, that prayers and pilgrimages are useless and of no worth for obtaining heaven.

Also, that when a priest goes up into the pulpit, he knows what the priest will say as well as the priest himself.

[a]   2[us] articulus *in margin.*
[b]   3[us] articulus *in margin.*
[c]   4[us] articulus *in margin.*
[d]   5[us] articulus *in margin.*

John Falks

[Reg. Hales, fo. 166v]

Johannes[a] Falkys de eadem palam et publice infamatur, accusatur, nominatur et impetitur quod ipse Johannes fuit et est verus hereticus pro eo et ex eo quod idem Johannes infra civitatem predictam publice predicavit, docuit, tenuit, asseruit[b] et dogmatizavit quod fatuum esset offerre ymagini beate Marie, dicendo in vulgari: 'Hyr hed shal be hoore or I offur to hur. What is hit but a blok? If hyt cothe speke to me, I wolde gyfe hit an halpeni worth of ale.'

Item,[c] quod quando presbiter differt languentibus seu infirmis corpus Christi, quare non differt eciam sanguinem Christi?

Item,[d] quod comedit lac vaccinium[5] in prima Dominica instantis xl.

Item,[e] quod quoad sacramentum penitencie et absolucionis, nullus presbiter habet potestatem absolvendi aliquem a peccatis suis, cum non possit creare unum capillum capitis sui.

Item, quod ymago beate Marie erat nisi lapis et truncus.

[English translation]

John Falkys of the same city is openly and publicly defamed, accused, named, and charged that he has been, and is, a true heretic, inasmuch as within the said city he publicly preached, taught, held, asserted, and instructed that it is foolish to offer to an image of the Blessed Mary, saying in the vernacular: 'Her head shall be old and grey[f] before I offer to her. What is it but a block? It if could speak to me, I would give it a halfpennyworth of ale.'

Also, that when a priest gives the body of Christ to the sick and infirm, why does he not also give Christ's blood?

Also, that he consumed cow's milk[5] on the first Sunday of this Lent.

Also, that regarding the sacrament of penance and absolution, no

---

[a] Contra Johannem Falkys *in margin.*
[b] primus articulus *in margin.*
[c] 2us articulus *in margin.*
[d] 3us articulus *in margin.*
[e] 4us articulus *in margin.*
[f] old and grey: *MS* hoore. *Cf. Geoffrey Chaucer, 'The Summoner's Tale', The Riverside Chaucer, 3rd edn, Larry D. Benson (ed.) (Boston, 1987), III: 2182 (p. 135): 'as that this olde cherl with lokkes hoore'; (our thanks to David Gormley for this reference). 'Hoore' could also mean, according to the OED, 'filth', 'hers', or 'whore'.*

priest has the power to absolve anyone of his sins, since he cannot make a single hair on his head.

Also, that the image of the Blessed Mary is only stone and a log.

Richard Gilmyn

[Reg. Hales, fo. 166v]

Ricardus[a] Gylmyn de eadem palam et publice infamatur, accusatur, nominatur et impetitur quod ipse Ricardus fuit et est verus hereticus pro eo et ex eo quod idem Ricardus infra civitatem predictam publice predicavit, docuit, tenuit, asseruit et dogmatizavit quod melius fuit erogare pecunias pauperibus quam decimas dare presbiteris vel offerre ymaginibus beate Marie et melius esset offerre ad ymaginem Dei creatam quam ad ymaginem Dei pyktam.

Item,[b] quod ipse habuit orationem dominicam et salvacionem angel-icam et simbolum in Anglic' et alium librum vidit et habuit continentem evangelia et epistolas in Anglic', et secundum illa voluit vivere, et per hoc credit se salvandum.

Item,[c] quod nullus presbiter melius loquitur in pulpito quam ille liber loquitur.

Item,[d] quod sacramentum altaris non est nisi panis et quod presbiteri hoc faciunt ad cecandum populum.

Item,[e] quod presbiter dum est in missa est presbiter, et post cele-brationem misse usque ad inchoacionem alterius misse est nisi laicus et nullam habet potestatem nisi ut merus laicus.

[English translation]

Richard Gylmyn of the same city is openly and publicly defamed, accused, named, and charged that he has been, and is, a true heretic, inasmuch as within the said city he publicly preached, taught, held, asserted, and instructed that it is better to give money to the poor than to pay tithes to priests or to offer to images of the Blessed Mary, and that it is better to offer to the created image of God than to a painted image of God.

[a] Contra Ricardum Gylmyn, articulus primus *in margin.*
[b] 2us articulus *in margin.*
[c] 3us articulus *in margin.*
[d] 4us articulus *in margin.*
[e] 5us articulus *in margin.*

Also, that he had the Lord's Prayer, Hail Mary, and the Creed in English, and he looked at and had another book containing the Gospels and Epistles in English, and he wished to live in accordance with them, and thereby he believed he would be saved.

Also, that no priest speaks better in the pulpit than that book speaks.

Also, that the sacrament of the altar is only bread, and priests make it in order to blind the people.

Also, that a priest is a priest while he is in the mass, and after the celebration of the mass until the beginning of another mass he is only a layman and has no power except as a mere layman.

John Blumston, Richard Hegham, Robert Crowther, John Smyth, Roger Brown, Thomas Butler, John Falks, and Richard Gilmyn

[Reg. Hales, fos 166v–167v]

Responsio predictorum Johannis Blumston, Ricardi Hygham, Roberti Crowther, Johannis Smyth, Rogeri Brown, Thome Boteler, Johannis Falkys et Ricardi Gylmyn separatim ad articulos supradictos:

[fo. 167r] Super quibus antea articulis omnibus et singulis supradictis, prefati Johannes, Ricardus, Robertus, Johannes, Rogerus, Thomas, Johannes et Ricardus coram dicto reverendo patre ad fideliter respondendum ad sacrosancta Dei evangelia coram ipso tunc aperta sponte iurati in forma iuris, eisdem articulis omnibus et singulis tam generaliter quam specialiter eisdem Johanni, Ricardo, Roberto, Johanni, Rogero, Thome, Johanni et Ricardo per prefatum reverendum patrem clare et distincte expositis separatim in vulgari responderunt publice in iudicio fatendo. Et confessi sunt et quilibet eorum confessus est omnes et singulos articulos hereticos et errores supradictos tunc ut premittitur tenuisse, predicasse, asseruisse, docuisse et dogmatizasse.

Demum tamen prefati Johannes, Ricardus, Robertus, Johannes, Rogerus, Thomas, Johannes et Ricardus per dictum reverendum patrem super veritate fidei et ortodoxe sanius instructi, submiserunt se correctioni dicti reverendi patris: et in iudicio sacrosancte ecclesie asserentes se fore paratos ad abiurandum omnes et singulos articulos hereticos et errores supradictos ac omnem et omnimodam heresim. Et tunc ibidem coram dicto reverendo patre et aliis notabilibus personis – videlicet Ricardo Coventry priore ecclesie cathedralis Coventr', Thoma Garstange, Johanne Preston, Ricardo Leylonde, Johanne Frysby, sacre theologie professoribus, Humfrido Hawardyn, legum doctore, Johanne

Alcok, decretorum doctore, Willelmo Gerarde, in theologia baccallario, Edmundo Hale et Johanne Sharpe in decretis bacallariis, Davide Clone in utrioque iure bacallario, magistris Hugone Lehe et Henrico Lewys, in artibus magistris, Roberto Pratt et Thoma Formewerke, notariis, et aliis quampluribus tunc presentibus – abiuraverunt et quilibet eorum abiuravit in forma subscripta tunc in vulgari.

In[a] the name of God, Amen. Before yowe the ryght reverent fadur in God John, by the grace of God bysshop of Coventre and Lichefeld, we, John Blumston, Ric' Hegham, Robert Crowther, John Smyth, Roger Browne, Thomas Butler, John Falks, and Ric' Gylmyn of the cety of Coventre of your diocese and jurisdiction, detectyd, difamyd, denouncyd and noysyd to your reverent fadurhed of heresy, errowrs and othur articlis evyl sownyng, beinge in dome and jugement before your sayde reverent fadurhed. And undurstondyng, knowynge and well persayvyge that afore thys houre we – the forsayd John, Ric', Robert, John, Roger, Thomas, John and Ric' – opynly sayde, affermyd, declaryd and expressyd dyverse articlis and opinions, errours and agaynns the fayth of hooly churche and contrari to the determination of the same and evyll sonynge in the eerys of wel disposyd cristyn men.

Wherfore we the forsayde John, Ric', Robert, John, Roger, Thomas, John and Ric' afore yowe the sayde reverent fadur, as hit is permittid, truly and faythfully enformyd, knolage and knowe well that ye sayde articlis above rehersyd bene eronyous and agayns the truwe beleve, fayth and determinatyon of hooly churche and ryght evyll sownyng to ye eerys of well disposyd cristyn peple.

Wyluynge with oure pure herts and fre wills to forsake the seyde errors and articlis and all othur errours, heresies and erronius opynions beynge ayaynns the truwe fayth and determination of hooly churche and the unite and determination of the sayde churche, and to beleve from hens forwarde aftur the techynge of all hooly churche and the determination of the same: forthermore the sayde errours, erronius opynyons and evyll sonynge articlis, as hyt is above sayde, and all maner of heresies, articlis, opynyons and doctrine that is ayaynns the truwe fayth and determination of hooly churche we forsake, renounce and abjure and sweyre apon this boke that aftur this houre we shall never opynly ne prively holde, declare ny teche herisy nor errors ny no maner doctrine agayns the fath and doctrine of hooly churche.

Ny we shal not receyve, favour ny concell ny defend, socour or supporte by oureselfe or any othur meane person prively or openly theyme that holdyth, techyth or meyntenyth eny suche fals doctrine, nothur to felishype with theyme wyttyngly ny confort theym, nethur

---

[a] Abiuracio Johannis Blumston, Ricardi Hegham, Roberti Crother, Johannis Smyth, Rogeri Browne, Thome Butler, Johannis Falk, Ricardi Gylmyn *in margin*.

receyve theym into oure howsus ny give thaym meyte ny drynke, clothynge ne money, nethur in any othur wise to socur hem.

Forthurmore we sware that if we mey knowe eny persons, men or wymen, suspecte of errors and heresyes or fautors, concelors, confortators, defensours, receptours or that make eny private conventiclis contrary to the comen doctrine of hooly churche, we shall denounce hem to your sayde reverent fadurhed or to your successours or ther offecers or to ther ordinarys as sone as we godely may.

So helpe us God and hali dome.

Facta huiusmodi abiuracione, prefati Johannes, Ricardus, Robertus, Johannes, Rogerus, Thomas, Johannes et Ricardus, saniori ducti consilio, bene inteligentes quod ipsi pro huiusmodi heresi maioris excommunicacionis sententiam a iure latam fuerunt involuti, a dicto reverendo patre ab ipsa excommunicacionis sententia se humiliter pecierunt absolvi.

Et tunc dictus reverendus pater predictos Johannem, Ricardum, Robertum, Johannem, Rogerum, Thomam, Johannem et Ricardum a dicta excommunicacionis sententia absolvit in forma iuris.

Ac contra eos et eorum quemlibet pronunciavit, declaravit atque processit sub modo et forma sequentibus.

In[a] Dei nomine, Amen. Nos Johannes, permissione divina Coventrensis et Lich' episcopus, contra vos, Johannem Blumston, Ricardum Hegham, Robertum Crowther, Johannem Smyth, Rogerum Browne, Thomam Butler, Johannem Falkys et Ricardum Gylmyn de Coventria nostre diocesis in negocio heretice pravitatis legitime procedentes.

Quia invemimus vos et quemlibet vestrum heretica dixisse, tenuise, asseruisse, predicasse et dogmatizasse articulos supradictos[b] separatim. Sed quia vultis, ut asseritis, et quilibet vestrum vult, corde puro et non ficto *[fo. 167v]* ad sanam doctrinam et ad unitatem ecclesie redire, ideo abiurata per vos et vestrum quemlibet penitus omni predicta heresi in speciali ac omni et omnimoda heretica pravitate, prestitaque caucione de parendo iuri ab excommunicacionis sentencia qua ea occasione perstetistis, vos et quemlibet vestrum absolvimus et sacramentis ecclesie restituimus.

Et[c] quia in Deum et sacrosanctam ecclesiam Romanam in ea parte deliquisti temere, vos et quemlibet vestrum in carceribus nostris mancipandos in partem penitencie vestre et salvo custodiendos usque ad

---

[a] Absolucio Johannis Blumston, Ricardi Hygham, Roberti Crother, Johannis Smyth, Rogeri Browne, Thome Butler, Johannis Falk, Ricardi Gylmyn *in margin*.

[b] heretica [...] articulos supradictos *[sic]*.

[c] Penitencia Johannis Blumston, Ricardi Hegham, Roberti Crother, Johannis Smyth, Rogeri Brown, Thome Butler, Johannis Falkys, Ricardi Gylmyn *in margin*.

diem Veneris[6] proximum post datum presentium decernimus in hiis scriptis.

Et pro malo exemplo quod Christi fidelibus in huiusmodi heresi vestra prebuistis, et ut pena vestra seu penitencia sit metus multorum, publicam penitenciam subscriptam vobis et cuilibet vestrum iniungimus, videlicet:

Quod die Veneris proximo post datum presentium vos et quilibet vestrum, nudus pedes et caput, solis liniis vestibus induti, ab ecclesia sancti Michaelis civitatis nostre Coventr' ad crucem in foro eiusdem civitatis unum fasciculum lignorum in humeris portet ante processionem solempnem circa horam undecimam ante meridiem coram curato vel vices eius gerenti. Totique populo circumstanti, abiuracionem heresis sue et omnimodam heresim ac quamcumque partem sue abiuracionis ac iuramenti supradicti sub modo et forma predictis, sicut profertur, ex eorum mera, libera, propria et spontanea voluntate sic fuisse et esse per ipsos factam palam et publice in vulgari fateantur et recognoscant, et eorum quilibet sic fateatur et recognoscat.

Deinde, post moram dimedietatis unius hore ibidem facte, pro eo quod ymaginem beate Marie de Turre infra precinctum domus Carmilitanorum civitatis nostre predicte situatam vilependerunt et blasfemaverunt, dictos fassiculos ut premittitur ad eandem ymaginem portantes, unam candelam precii unius denarii, cum denario in dicta candela affixo, una cum fasciculis antedictis, quilibet eorum devote peregrinando offerat tunc ibidem.

Deinde, die Dominica proximo tunc futuro,[7] prefati Johannes, Ricardus, Robertus, Johannes, Rogerus, Thomas, Johannes et Ricardus in ecclesia sancti Michaelis civitatis nostre predicte tempore processionis iuxta crucem in eadem processione differendi, solis vestibus liniis induti, nudi pedes et capita, singuli eorum unum fasciculum in humeris differens processionem procedat. Et sic, processione finita, ad superiorem gradum summi altaris usque ad offertorii completionem sic morentur et expectent. Et tunc, cum curato vel eius vicem gerenti preces et dicta consueta in pulpito dicturo, descendant. Et, ex opposito pulpito stando, permaneant quousque huiusmodi sua abiuratio in forma prescripta per curatum antedictum seu vices eius gerentes toti populo sic astanti palam, publice et expresse in vulgari plene exponatur. Deinde dictos fassiculos ad ymaginem beate Marie de Turre infra precinctum domus Carmilitanorum civitatis nostre predicte devote peregrinando offerant et quilibet eorum offerat.

[English translation]

Reply of the aforesaid John Blumston, Richard Hygham, Robert Crowther, John Smyth, Roger Brown, Thomas Boteler, John Falkys, and Richard Gylmyn, separately to the aforesaid articles:

[fo. 167r] Regarding all and each of the aforesaid articles, the said John, Richard, Robert, John, Roger, Thomas, John, and Richard swore of their own will in legal form before the said reverend father, on the Holy Gospels open in front of him, to reply in a trustworthy manner. After each and every one of the same articles, both generally and in particular, had been explained clearly and distinctly by the said reverend father to the same John, Richard, Robert, John, Roger, Thomas, John, and Richard, they replied individually in the vernacular language, publicly in the court, that they admitted the charges. Each and every one of them confessed that they had held, preached, asserted, and taught each and every one of the aforesaid heretical articles and errors as mentioned above.

Then the aforesaid John, Richard, Robert, John, Roger, Thomas, John, and Richard, having been soundly instructed by the said reverend father about the truth of the faith and of orthodoxy, submitted themselves to the correction of the said reverend father. They said, in the court of holy church, that they were ready to abjure each and every one of the aforesaid heretical articles and errors and each and every heresy. Then and there, before the said reverend father and other notable persons – namely, Richard Coventry, Prior of the Cathedral church of Coventry, Thomas Garstange, John Preston, Richard Leylonde, John Frysby, professors of sacred theology, Humphry Hawardyn, doctor of laws, John Alcok, doctor of decrees, William Gerarde, bachelor of theology, Edmund Hale and John Sharpe, bachelors of decrees, David Clone, bachelor in both laws, master Hugh Lehe and Henry Lewys, masters of arts, Robert Pratt and Thomas Formewerke, notaries, and many others then present – abjured and each of them then abjured in the vernacular language in the following form.

In the name of God, Amen. Before you the Right Reverend Father in God, John, by the grace of God Bishop of Coventry and Lichfield, we, John Blumston, Richard Hegham, Robert Crowther, John Smyth, Roger Browne, Thomas Butler, John Falks, and Richard Gilmyn of the city of Coventry of your diocese and jurisdiction, detected, defamed, denounced, and noised to your reverend fatherhood of heresy, errors, and other articles evil sounding, being in doom and judgement before your said reverend fatherhood. And understanding, knowing, and well perceiving that before this hour we – the aforesaid John, Richard,

Robert, John, Roger, Thomas, John, and Richard – openly said, affirmed, declared and expressed divers articles and opinions, errors and against the faith of Holy Church and contrary to the determination of the same and evil sounding in the ears of well disposed Christian men.

Wherefore we the aforesaid John, Richard, Robert, John, Roger, Thomas, John. and Richard before you the said reverend father, as it is permitted, truly and faithfully informed, acknowledge and know well that the said articles above rehearsed are erroneous and against the true belief, faith and determination of Holy Church and right evil sounding to the ears of well disposed Christian people.

Willing with our pure hearts and free wills to forsake the said errors and articles and all other errors, heresies, and erroneous opinions, being against the true faith and determination of Holy Church and the unity and determination of the said church, and to believe from henceforth after the teaching of all Holy Church and the determination of the same: furthermore, the said errors, erroneous opinions, and evil sounding articles, as it is above said, and all manner of heresies, articles, opinions, and doctrine that is against the true faith and determination of Holy Church we forsake, renounce, and abjure, and swear upon this book that after this hour we shall never openly nor privily hold, declare, nor teach heresy, nor errors, nor any manner of doctrine against the faith and doctrine of Holy Church.

Nor we shall not receive, favour, nor conceal, nor defend, succour, or support by ourself or any other mean person, privily or openly, those that hold, teach, or maintain any such false doctrine, neither to fellowship with them willingly, nor comfort them, neither receive them into our houses, nor give them meat nor drink, clothing, nor money, neither in any other wise to succour them.

Furthermore we swear that if we may know any persons, men or women, suspect of errors and heresies, favourers, concealers, comforters, defenders, receivers, or that make any private conventicles contrary to the common doctrine of Holy Church, we shall denounce them to your said reverend fatherhood, or to your successors, or their officers, or to their ordinaries as soon as we goodly may.

So help us God and holy doom.

After this abjuration, the said John, Richard, Robert, John, Roger, Thomas, John, and Richard, led by wiser counsel, knowing well that on account of the above heresy they had incurred by law the sentence of greater excommunication, humbly asked to be absolved by the said reverend father from the same sentence of excommunication.

Then the said reverend father absolved in legal form the aforesaid

John, Richard, Robert, John, Roger, Thomas, John, and Richard from the said sentence of excommunication.

And he pronounced, declared, and proceeded against them, and each one of them, in the following manner and form.

In the name of God, Amen. We John, by divine permission Bishop of Coventry and Lichfield, are legitimately proceeding in the matter of heresy against you, John Blumston, Richard Hegham, Robert Crowther, John Smyth, Roger Browne, Thomas Butler, John Falkys, and Richard Gylmyn of Coventry of our diocese.

We have found you, each and every one, to have stated, held, asserted, preached, and taught the above mentioned heretical articles individually. But because you wish, as you assert, and each one of you wishes, with a pure and unfeigned heart, to return to sound doctrine and to the unity of the Church, therefore since you have abjured all the aforesaid heresies in particular and every form of heretical deformity and have guaranteed to obey the law regarding the sentence of excommuniction that you have incurred, we absolve you, each and every one, and we restore you to the Church's sacraments

Because you have rashly deserted God and Holy Roman Church in this matter, we decree by this document that you, and each one of you, should be detained in our prisons as part of your penance, and should be kept secure until the Friday after the date of this document.[6]

On account of the bad example you have given to Christ's faithful by your heresy, and in order that your punishment or penance may instil fear into many people, we enjoin the following public penance upon each and every one of you:

On Friday after the date of this document, barefoot and with head uncovered, wearing only linen undergarments, you are to carry a faggot of wood on your shoulders at the head of the solemn procession at eleven o'clock in the morning, from the church of St Michael of our city of Coventry to the cross in the marketplace, before the curate or his substitute. While all the people are standing around, each and every one of you are to admit and recognize openly and publicly in the vernacular language that the abjuration of your heresy and every heresy, and every part of your abjuration and aforesaid oath, in the aforesaid manner and form, as is stated above, has been and is made by you with a pure, free, independent, and spontaneous will.

Then, after an interval of half an hour there, because you despised and blasphemed the image of Blessed Mary of the Tower within the precincts of the Carmelites' House in our said city, you are to carry your said faggot to this image and, devoutly making a pilgrimage to it, offer there a candle worth a penny, together with a penny stuck into the candle, and the said faggot.

Then, on the following Sunday,[7] in the church of St Michael of our said city, at the time of the procession, the said John, Richard, Robert, John, Roger, Thomas, John, and Richard, gathering near the cross in the same procession, wearing only linen undergarments, barefoot and with heads uncovered, shall go ahead of the procession, each one carrying a faggot on his shoulders. When the procession has ended, they shall wait on the top step of the high altar until the end of the offertory. Then, together with the curate or his substitute, who will say the prayers and customary words in the pulpit, they shall come down and remain standing opposite the pulpit until their abjuration in the above form has been explained openly, publicly, expressly, and fully in the vernacular language by the aforesaid curate or his substitutes to all the people standing around. Then all of them, devoutly making a pilgrimage, shall offer their faggots to the image of Blessed Mary of the Tower within the precincts of the Carmelites' House of our said city.

Between Sunday, 12 March and Wednesday, 26 April 1486

John Blumston, Richard Hegham, Robert Crowther, John Smyth, Roger Brown, Thomas Butler, John Falks, and Richard Gylmyn

[Reg. Hales, fos 167v–168r. The certificate was presumably drawn up sometime between the performance of the last penance, on Sunday 12 March 1486, and the last date allowed by the bishop for its submission, 26 April 1486.]

Certificatorium[a] vocationis Johannis Blumston, Ricardi Hegham, Roberti Crowther, Johannis Smyth, Rogeri Browne, Thome Butler, Johannis Falkys et Ricardi Gylmyn ad penitenciam.[b]

Reverendo in Christo ac patri ac domino domino Johanni Dei gratia Coventrensis et Lich' episcopo, vester humilis et devotus in Christo filius Ricardus Leylonde sacre theologie professor ac vicarii sancti Michaelis Coventr' vicem gerens, obediencias et reverencias cum honore et subiectione:

---

[a] Certificatorium *repeated in margin.*
[b] Certificatorium [...] penitenciam *is the heading.*

Litteras vestras reverendas nono die mensis Marcii ultimi iam preteriti[8] cum omni reverencia qua decuit noveritis me recepisse, tenorem
continens infrascriptam.

Johannes permissione divina Coventrensis et Lich' episcopus, dilecto in
Christo filio perpetuo vicario ecclesie parochialis sancti Michaelis Coventr' nostre diocesis eiusve vicem gerenti, salutem, gratiam et benedictionem.

Cum nuper Johannes Blumston, Ricardus Hegham, Robertus
Crowther, Johannes Smyth, Rogerus Browne, Thomas Butler, Ricardus Falkys et Johannis Gylmyn[a] de Coventria dicte nostre diocesis
de et super nonnullis articulis meram heresim sapientibus penes nos
infamati existunt et ea occasione auctoritate et mandato nostris capti,
adducti et aliquanto tempore pro huiusmodi crimine heresis legitime
incarcerati.

Deinde, coram nobis in ecclesia parochiali sancti Michaelis Coventr'
predicta pro trubunali iudicialiter sedentibus, huiusmodi heresim super
quam ut prefertur extiterant diffamati, prout in articulis precedentibus
separatim liculentius apparet, veraciter ut tunc expresse asseruerunt:
scientes articulos supradictos omnes et singulos fuisse et esse hereticos,
falsos et erroneos ac adversus doctrinam sancte matris ecclesie temere
procedentes. Volentesque, ut dixerunt, canonicam sequi doctrinam, ab
omni heretica pravitate recedere ac ad unitatem sacrosancte ecclesie
spontanea et propria voluntate redire, huiusmodi heresim et omnem et
omnimodam heresim libere et sponte coram nobis in iudicio palam et
publice se abiuraturos et abiurare fatebantur fore paratos.

Nosque, sacrorum canonum instituta immutari, ipsorumque Johannis, Ricardi, Roberti, Johannis, Rogeri, Thome, Ricardi et Johannis
tam corporum quam animarum vitam pariter et salutem salvari volentes
et intime affectantes prefatos Johannem, Ricardum, Robertum, Johannem, Rogerum, Thomam, Johannem et Ricardum, omnes et singulos
articulos supradictos, meram heresim ut liquide patet continentes,
necnon et omnem [fo. 168r] heresim sic in forma iuris abiurandam,
iudicialiter admisimus sub modo et forma infrascriptis.

In Dei nomine, Amen – ut supra in abiuratione et cetera. Nosque,
iuxta iuris peritorum consilium nobis in hac parte assidentium ulterius
legitime procedentes tam pro feliciori animarum ipsorum Johannis,
Ricardi, Roberti, Johannis, Rogeri, Thome, Johannis et Ricardi salute
et salubri correctione eorundemque omnium Christi fidelium per eorum
perversam doctrinam maxime infectorum seu inficiendorum, quod

---

[a] Ricardus Falkys et Johannis Gylmyn [sic]: presumably a scribal error for Johannes Falkys
et Ricardus Gylmyn.

absque reformatione prefatorum Johannis, Ricardi, Roberti, Johannis, Rogeri, Thome, Johannis et Ricardi abiuratione necnon partem salutaris penitencie eisdem ea occasione nostro arbitrio indicte in ecclesia vestra et in foro civitatis predicte publicandum fore decrevimus.[a] Que vero penitencia publica in ecclesia vestra et in foro civitatis predicte peragenda, per nos eisdem indicta, sequitur et est talis, videlicet.

Quod die Veneris proximo post datum presentium prefati Johannes, Ricardus, Robertus, Johannes, Rogerus, Thomas, Johannes et Ricardus et quilibet eorum, nudus pedes et caput, solis liniis vestibus indutus, ab ecclesia sancti Michaelis civitatis nostre predicte ad crucem in foro eiusdem civitatis unum fassiculum lignorum in humeris portet ante processionem solempnem circa horam undecimam ante meridiem coram curato vel vices eius gerenti. Totique populo circumstanti abiurationem heresis sue et omnimodam heresim ac quamcumque partem sue abiurationis ac iuramenti supradicti sub modo et forma predictis sic, ut prefertur, ex eorum mera, libera et spontanea voluntate sic fuisse et esse per ipsos factam palam et publice, eciam in vulgari, fateantur et recognoscant et eorum quilibet fateatur et recognoscat.

Deinde, post moram dimedietatis unius hore ibidem factam, pro eo quod ymaginem beate Marie de Turre infra precinctum domus Carmilitanorum civitatis nostre predicte situatam vilipenderunt et blasfemarunt, dictos fassiculos ut premittitur ad eandem ymaginem portantes, unam candelam precii unius denarii cum denario in dicta candela affixo una cum fassiculis antedictis quilibet eorum devote peregrinando offerat tunc ibidem.

Deinde die Dominica proximo tunc futuro prefati Johannes, Ricardus, Robertus, Johannes, Rogerus, Thomas, Johannes et Ricardus in ecclesia sancti Michaelis civitatis nostre predicte tempore processionis, iuxta crucem in eadem processione differendam, solis vestibus liniis induti, nudi pedes et capita, singuli eorum unum fassiculum in humeris differens processionem procedat. Et sic processione finita, ad superiorem gradum summi altaris usque ad offertorii completionem sic morentur et expectent. Et tunc cum curato vel[b] eius vicem gerente, preces et dicta consueta in pulpito dicturo, descendant et ex opposito pulpito stando permaneant quousque huiusmodi sua abiuratio in forma prescripta per curatum antedictum seu vices eius gerentes, toti populo sic astanti, palam, publice et expresse in vulgari plene exponatur. Deinde dictos fassiculos ad ymaginem beate Marie de Turre predictam devote peregrinando offerant et quilibet eorum offerat.

Quare vobis committimus et mandamus quatenus, dictis diebus ante huiusmodi processionis inceptionem, predictos Johannem Blumston,

---

[a] Nosque[...]decrevimus *[sic]: the grammar and syntax are often unclear.*
[b] et *deleted,* vel *interlined.*

Ricardum Hagham, Robertum Crowther, Johannem Smyth, Rogerum Browne, Thomam Butler, Johannem Falks et Ricardum Gylmyn ad huiusmodi penitenciam ut prefertur tunc peragendam palam et publice evocetis seu sic evocari faciatis. Nostramque huiusmodi penitencie iniunctionem ac ipsorum Johannis et ceterorum abiurationem ac iuramenti prestationem sic, ut prefertur, in vulgari exponatis seu sic exponi faciatis.

Et si prefati Johannes, Ricardus, Robertus, Johannes, Rogerus, Thomas, Johannes et Ricardus dictis die et loco coram vobis, ad vocacionem vestram, dictam penitenciam devote subituri comparuerint et fecerint et eorum quilibet comparuerit et fecerit, et quid in hac parte debite fecistis, nos citra xx^{um} sextum diem mensis Aprilis proximum futurum per litteras vestras patentes habentes seriem continentes, auctentice sigillatas, certificetis.

Datum Coventr' nostro sub sigillo ix° die mensis Marcii anno Domini millesimo cccclxxxv^{to} et nostre consecrationis anno xxvii°.

Quarum quidem litterarum reverendarum vigore et auctoritate, predictis diebus Veneris et Dominico in ecclesia parochiali sancti Michaelis predicta ante processionis huiusmodi inceptionem, prefatos Johannem Blumston et ceteros ad penitenciam huiusmodi, ut premittitur, peragendam palam et publice evocavi. Vestramque huiusmodi pariter penitencie iniunctionem ac ipsorum Johannis, Ricardi et ceterorum abiuracionem et iuramenti prestationem sic, ut prefertur, in vulgari exposui.

Qui quidem Johannes Blumston, Ricardus Hegham, Robertus Crowther, Johannes Smyth, Rogerus Browne, Thomas Butler, Johannes Falks et Ricardus Gylmyn dictis die et loco, ad dictam evocationem meam, penitenciam huiusmodi devote subituros personaliter statim comparuerunt et quilibet eorum comparuit. Penitenciamque huiusmodi humilime, ut apparuit, perfecerunt pariter et devote. Dictam abiuracionem heresis sue ac heresim quamcumque et quamcumque partem sue abiuracionis ac iuramenti prestacionis supradicte sub modo et forma predictis, sicut prefertur, ex eorum singulorum mera, libera, propria et spontanea voluntate fuisse et esse coram vobis per ipsos factas palam et publice eciam in vulgari recognoscendo et confitendo recognoverunt et confessi sunt tunc ibidem.

Et sic mandatum vestrum reverendum in omnibus humilime sum executus. In cuius rei.

[English translation]

Certificate of the summons to penance of John Blumston, Richard Hegham, Robert Crowther, John Smyth, Roger Browne, Thomas Butler, John Falkys, and Richard Gylmyn.

To the Reverend Father and Lord in Christ, Lord John, by the grace of God Bishop of Coventry and Lichfield, your humble and devoted son in Christ, Richard Leylonde, professor of sacred theology and taking the place of the vicar of St Michael of Coventry, obedience and reverence with honour and submission:

Know that I received your reverend letter on 9 March last[8] with all the reverence that is fitting, its contents being as follows.

John, by God's leave Bishop of Coventry and Lichfield, to our beloved son in Christ the perpetual vicar of the parish church of St Michael of Coventry of our diocese or his substitute: greetings, grace, and blessing.

John Blumston, Richard Hegham, Robert Crowther, John Smyth, Roger Browne, Thomas Butler, Richard Falkys, and John Gylmyn[a] of Coventry of our said diocese were recently denounced before us on account of various articles savouring of pure heresy. They were, therefore, arrested on our authority and command and were held and legitimately imprisoned for some time on account of this crime of heresy.

Then, before us sitting judicially in the said parish church of St Michael of Coventry, they truly and expressly admitted the heresy on account of which they had been denounced, as mentioned above, as clearly appears in particular in the preceding articles; acknowledging that each and every one of the aforesaid articles were and are heretical, false, and erroneous, and rashly contravening the teaching of Holy Mother Church. Wishing, as they said, to follow canonical teaching, to withdraw from all heretical perversity, and to return of their own will to the unity of Holy Church, they said they were ready to abjure freely and spontaneously, openly and publicly, before us in judgement, this heresy and all and every heresy.

Wishing to follow the rules of the sacred canons; also wanting and intimately desiring that the life and salvation, in both body and soul, of the said John, Richard, Robert, John, Roger, Thomas, Richard, and John be saved; we admitted judicially the said John, Richard, Robert, John, Roger, Thomas, John, and Richard, and each and every one of the aforesaid articles, which patently contain pure heresy, as well as

[a] Richard Falkys and John Gylmyn *[sic]: presumably a scribal error for* John Falkys and Richard Gylmyn.

every *[fo. 168r]* heresy that should thus be abjured in legal form, in the following manner and form.

In the name of God, Amen – as above in the abjuration etc. Legitimately proceeding further according to the advice of the legal experts assisting us in this matter, both for the salvation of the souls of the same John, Richard, Robert, John, Roger, Thomas, John, and Richard, and for the healthy correction of them and of all Christ's faithful who have been or would be greatly infected by their perverse teaching, we have decreed that, without the reform of the said John, Richard, Robert, John, Roger, Thomas, John, and Richard, the abjuration and the part of the saving penance enjoined upon them on this occasion by our judgement should be carried out in public in your church and in the marketplace of the aforesaid city.[a] This public penance, which we have enjoined upon them and which is to be performed in your church and in the marketplace of the said city, is as follows.

On Friday after the date of this document the aforesaid John, Richard, Robert, John, Roger, Thomas, John, and Richard, each one of them, barefoot and with head uncovered, wearing only linen undergarments, shall carry a faggot of wood on his shoulders at the head of the solemn procession around eleven o'clock in the morning, from the church of St Michael of our said city to the cross in the marketplace of the same city, in front of the curate or his substitute. While all the people are standing around, each and every one of them shall admit and recognize openly and publicly, and in the vernacular language, that the abjuration of their heresy and every heresy, and every part of their abjuration and aforesaid oath, in the aforesaid manner and form, as is stated above, has been and is made by them with a pure, free, and spontaneous will.

Then, after an interval of half an hour there, because they despised and blasphemed the image of Blessed Mary of the Tower within the precincts of the Carmelites' House in our said city, they shall carry the said faggot to this image and, devoutly making a pilgrimage to it, they shall offer there a candle worth a penny, together with a penny stuck into the candle, and the said faggot.

Then, on the following Sunday, in the church of St Michael of our said city, at the time of the procession, the said John, Richard, Robert, John, Roger, Thomas, John, and Richard, keeping close to the cross that is to be carried in the same procession, wearing only linen undergarments, barefoot and with heads uncovered, shall go ahead of the procession, each one carrying a faggot on his shoulders. When the procession has ended, they shall wait on the top step of the high altar

---

[a] *This sentence does not make grammatical or syntactical sense in the Latin.*

until the end of the offertory. Then, together with the curate, or his substitute who will say the prayers and customary words in the pulpit, they shall come down and remain standing opposite the pulpit until their abjuration in the above form has been explained openly, publicly, expressly, and fully in the vernacular language by the aforesaid curate or his substitutes to all the people standing around. Then all of them, devoutly making a pilgrimage, shall offer their faggots to the said image of Blessed Mary of the Tower.

We, therefore, commission and command you, on the said days before the start of the procession, to summon openly and publicly, or to have summoned, the aforesaid John Blumston, Richard Hagham, Robert Crowther, John Smyth, Roger Browne, Thomas Butler, John Falks, and Richard Gylmyn, to perform their penance as stated above. You shall explain or have explained, in the vernacular language, our injunction for the penance and the abjuration and oath-taking of the said John and others, as stated above.

If the said John, Richard, Robert, John, Roger, Thomas, John, and Richard appear before you, at your summons, on the said day and in the said place in order to undergo the said penance, you shall certify to us by the 26th day of next April, through your letters patent containing word to this effect and authentically sealed, regarding what you have duly done in this matter.

Given at Coventry under our seal on 9 March 1485/1486 in the 27th year of our consecration.

By virtue and authority of these reverend letters, I openly and publicly summoned the said John Blumston and others to perform the said penance on the said Friday and Sunday in the said parish church of St Michael, before the beginning of the procession, as stated above. I explained in the vernacular language your injunction for the penance and the abjuration and oath-taking of the said John, Richard and others, as stated above.

John Blumston, Richard Hegham, Robert Crowther, John Smyth, Roger Browne, Thomas Butler, John Falks, and Richard Gylmyn, each and every one of them, at once appeared on the said days and in the said places, according to my summons, in order devoutly to undergo the penance in person. They performed the penance, as it seemed, humbly and devoutly. They openly, publicly, and in the vernacular language acknowledged and confessed that the said abjuration of their heresy and of every heresy, and every part of their aforesaid abjuration and oath-taking in the manner and form stated above, had been and is made before you with a pure, free, independent, and spontaneous will in the case of each one of them.

I have, thus, humbly executed your respected order in all things. Wherefore.

Tuesday, 8 April 1488

Margery Goyte

[Reg. Hales, fos 168v–169v]

Acta in manerio de Beaudesert[9] octavo die mensis Aprilis anno Domini millesimo cccclxxxviii° coram reverendo in Christo patre et domino domino Johanne Dei gratia Coventrensis et Lich' episcopo.[a]

Negocium inquisicionis de et super crimine heretice pravitatis contra Margeriam Goyte, uxorem Jacobi Goyte, nuper de parochia de Assheburn[10] dicti reverendi patris diocesis, palam et publice super crimine heresis infamatam, accusatam atque detectam, ut patet in articulis subscriptis meram heresim continentibus seu saltem ad minus heresim sapientibus.

In[b] primis videlicet Margeria uxor Jacobi Goyte nuper de parochia de Assheburn Coventrensis et Lich' diocesis palam et publice infamatur, accusatur, nominatur et impetitur quod ipsa Margeria fuit et sit vera heretica pro eo et ex eo quod ipsa Margeria infra dictam parochiam de Assheburn et in[c] aliis locis circumvicinis predicavit, docuit, tenuit et asseruit quod illud quod presbiteri sublevant supra capita sua tempore misse non est verum corpus Christi, quia si sic esset presbiteri non frangerent illud in tres partes tam leviter et illud deglutirent sicut faciunt, quia corpus Domini habet carnem et ossa et sic non illud quod presbiteri tunc recipiunt.

Item,[d] dicta Margeria palam et publice ut supra infamatur, accusatur, nominatur et impetitur quod ipsa fuit et est vera heretica pro eo et ex eo quod ipsa palam et publice in locis predictis predicavit, docuit, asseruit, renuit et dogmatizavit quod sacerdotes ementes sexaginta panes pro obolo et monstrantes eos populo dicunt quod de singulis eorum conficitur corpus Christi, populum decipiendo et se ipsos ditando.

---

[a] Acta [...] episcopo *is the heading of the page.*
[b] Primus articulus *in margin.*
[c] in *interlined.*
[d] 2[us] articulus *in margin.*

Item,[a] dicta Margeria palam et publice ut supra infamatur, accusatur, nominatur et impetitur quod ipsa fuit et est vera heretica pro eo et ex eo quod in locis predictis predicavit, docuit, tenuit, asseruit et dogmatizavit quod cum Deus primo creasset hominem, quomodo potest homo creare Deum?

Item,[b] dicta Margeria palam et publice ut supra infamatur, accusatur, nominatur et impetitur quod ipsa fuit et est vera heretica pro eo et ex eo quod in locis predictis predicavit, docuit, tenuit, asseruit et dogmatizavit quod licet Christus natus fuit de beata Maria, tamen non de virgine, quia Joseph erat disponsatus Marie et pluries eam carnaliter cognovit, de cuius semine conceptus erat Christus sicut ipsa concepit filium de semine mariti sui.

Item,[c] dicta Margeria palam et publice ut supra infamatur, accusatur, nominatur et impetitur quod ipsa fuit et est vera heretica pro eo et ex eo quod in locis predictis predicavit, docuit, tenuit, asseruit et dogmatizavit quod puer conceptus inter parentes christianos non eget sacramento baptismatis.

Super[d] quibus autem articulis omnibus et singulis supradictis prefata Margeria, coram dicto reverendo patre ad fideliter respondendum ad sacrosancta Dei evangelia coram ipsa tunc aperta sponte iurata in forma iuris, eisdem articulis omnibus et singulis tam generaliter quam specialiter dicte Margerie per prefatum reverendum patrem clare et distincte expositis in vulgari respondit publice in iudicio fatendo. Et confessa est se omnes et singulos articulos hereticos et erroneos supradictos sic ut prefertur tenuisse, predicasse, docuisse et credidisse.

Demum tamen dicta Margeria Goyte, per dictum reverendum patrem super veritate fidei orthodoxe sanius instructa, submisit se correctioni dicti reverendi patris et in iudicio sacrosancte ecclesie, asserens se fore paratam ad abiurandum omnes et singulos articulos hereticos et errores supradictos ac omnem et omnimodam heresim.

Et tunc ibidem coram eodem reverendo patre et aliis notabilibus personis – videlicet magistris Georgio Strangeweys sacre theologie professore, Ricardo Salter decretorum doctore, Johanne Sharpe in decretis bacallario, magistro Hugone Lehe in artibus magistro, Roberto Pratt in utroque iure bacallario et Thoma Formewerke notario publico et aliis quampluribus tunc presentibus – abiuravit modo et forma subscriptis tunc ibidem in vulgari.

---

[a]   3[us] articulus *in margin.*
[b]   4[us] articulus *in margin.*
[c]   5[us] *in margin.*
[d]   Responsio predicte Margerie ad articulos supradictos *in margin.*

In[a] the name of God, Amen. Before yowe the ryght reverent fadur in God John by the grace of God bysshoppe of Coventre and Lich', I Margeri Goyte late of the parisshe of Assheburn of your *[fo. 169r]* diocese and jurisdiction, detectid, defamyd, denouncyd and noysyd to your reverend fadurhed of heresy, errorys and othur articlis evil sonynge, beynge in dome and jugement before your sayde reverend fadurhed and undurstondynge, knowynge and wel perceyvynge that afore this howre I have opynly sayde, affermyd, declaryd and expressyd diverse articlis and opinions erronious and agayns the fayth of hooly churche and contrari to the determination of the same and evill soynynge to the eeris of wel disposyd cristyn peple.

Wherfore I the forsayde Margeri afore yowe the sayde reverent fadur, as hit is permittyd truly and feythfully enformyd, knolage and kno well that the sayde articlis above rehersyd ben erronyous and agaynys the truwe beleve, fayth and determination of hooly churche and ryght evyll sownynge to the eers of wel disposyd cristin peple, willnynge with my pure herte and fre wille to forsake the sayde errours and articlis and all[b] othur errours, heresies and erronious opynyons beinge agaynns the truwe fayth and determination of hooly churche and the unite and determination of the sayde churche and to beleve from this tyme forwarde aftur the techynge of all hooly churche and the determination of the same.

Forthurmore the sayde errours, erronious opynyons and evyl sownynge articlis, as hit is above sayde, and all maner of heresyes, articlis, erronious opynyons and doctrine that is agaynns the truwe fayth and determination of hooly churche I forsake, renounce and abjure and swayre apon this boke that aftur this houre I shall never opynly ny privily holde, declare ny teche heresi nor errours ny no maner doctrine agayns the fayth or doctrine of hooly churche. Ne I shall receyve, favour ny concell, defende, succour ny supporte by myselfe or any othur meane person privili or opynly theyme that holds, techys or mayntenis any suche fals doctrine, nethur to felishyp with theyme, nethur receyve theyme into my hows ny yiffe theyme mete ny drynke, clothynge ny monay, nethur eny othur wise to socour hem.

Forthermore I swayre that if Y may knowe any persons, men or women, suspecte of errours and heresies or fautors, concelours, confortatours, defensours, receptours or that make eny private conventiclis contrari to the comen doctrine of hooly churche, I shall denounce hem to your seyde reverent fadurhed or to your successours or ther offecers or to ther ordinaris as sone as I godeli mey.

So helpe me God and holi dome.

---

[a] Abiuracio eiusdem Margerie *in margin.*
[b] all *interlined.*

Facta huiusmodi abiuracione, prefata Margeria, saniori ducta consilio, bene inteligens quod ipsa pro huiusmodi heresi maioris excommunicacionis sentencia a iure lata fuit involuta, a dicto reverendo patre ab ipsa excommunicacionis sentencia se humiliter peciit absolvi. Et tunc dictus reverendus pater predictam Margeriam Goyte a dicta excommunicacionis sentencia absolvit in forma iuris.

Ac contra eam pronunciavit, declaravit atque processit sub modo et forma sequentibus.

In[a] Dei nomine, Amen. Nos Johannes, permissione divina Coventrensis et Lich' episcopus, contra te, Margeriam Goyte nuper de parochia de Assheburn nostre diocesis, in negocio heretice pravitatis legitime procedentes.

Quia invenimus te heretica dixisse, tenuisse et asseruisse articulos supradictos sed vis, ut asseris, corde puro et non ficto ad sanam doctrinam et ad unitatem ecclesie redire. Ideo, abiurata per te penitus omni predicta heresi in speciali ac omni et omnimoda heretica pravitate, prestitaque cautione de parendo iuri, ab excommunicacionis sententia, in qua ea occasione perstetisti, te absolvimus et sacramentis ecclesie restituimus.

Et quia in Deum et sacrosanctam ecclesiam Romanam in ea parte temere deliquisti, pro malo exemplo quod Christi fidelibus in huiusmodi heresi tua prestitisti, ut pena tua seu penitencia publica per te peragenda sit metus aliorum, penitenciam publicam subscriptam tibi iniungimus.

Videlicet quod die *[fo. 169v]* Sabbati ante Dominicam in Albis,[II] nuda pedes, aliis vestimentibus induta, ab ecclesia de Assheburn usque ad crucem in foro ville predicte unum fassiculum lignorum in humeris portes, processionem procedas circa horam undecimam ante meridiem. Et ibidem, coram vobis seu vices vestras gerente, totique populo circumstanti, abiuracionem heresis tue et omnimodam heresim ac quamcumque partem tue abiuracionis ac iuramenti supradictorum sub modo et forma predictis sic, ut premittitur, ex tua mera, libera[b] et spontanea voluntate sic fuisse et esse per te factam palam et publice eciam fatearis et recognoscas.

Deinde, dictis articulis et abiuracione publice perlectis, dictum fassiculum ad predictam ecclesiam coram processione deportes, et illud unacum candela ardente ad ymaginem crucifixi in ecclesia predicta devote peregrinando offeras.

Et consimilem penitenciam peragas per tres dies mercati ibidem. Et si dictam penitenciam per unum diem mercati ibidem devote peragas, ceteri respectuantur sub spe bone gesture.

---

[a] Absolucio dicte Margerie *in margin.*
[b] *illegible word deleted:* libera *interlined.*

[English translation]

Proceedings in the manor at Beaudesert[9] on 8 April 1488 before the Reverend Father and Lord in Christ, Lord John, by the grace of God Bishop of Coventry and Lichfield.

Enquiry concerning the crime of heresy against Margery Goyte, wife of James Goyte, recently of Ashbourne parish[10] of the diocese of the said reverend father, openly and publicly defamed, accused, and detected of the crime of heresy, as appears from the following articles containing pure heresy or at least savouring of heresy.

First, that Margery, the wife of James Goyte, recently of Ashbourne parish of Coventry and Lichfield diocese is openly and publicly defamed, accused, named, and charged that she was, and is, a true heretic, inasmuch as within the said Ashbourne parish and other neighbouring places she preached, taught, held, and asserted that what priests hold up above their heads at the time of mass is not the true body of Christ; because if it was, priests would not break it so readily into three parts and swallow it as they do, since the body of the Lord has flesh and bones, and therefore it is not what priests receive at that time.

Also, the said Margery is openly and publicly defamed, accused, named, and charged that she was, and is, a true heretic, inasmuch as in the aforesaid places she openly and publicly preached, taught, asserted, denied, and instructed that priests buy sixty pieces of bread for a halfpenny and show them to the people, and then say that the body of Christ is made from each one of them, thereby deceiving the people and enriching themselves.

Also, the said Margery is openly and publicly defamed, accused, named, and charged that she was, and is, a true heretic, inasmuch as in the aforesaid places she preached, taught, held, asserted, and instructed that since God first created humans, how can a human create God?

Also, the said Margery is openly and publicly defamed, accused, named, and charged that she was, and is, a true heretic, inasmuch as in the aforesaid places she preached, taught, held, asserted, and instructed that although Christ was born of Blessed Mary, he was not, however, born of a virgin, because Joseph was betrothed to Mary and he had sexual intercourse with her many times, so Christ was conceived of Joseph's seed, just as Margery conceived her son from the seed of her husband.

Also, the said Margery, as above, is openly and publicly defamed, accused, named, and charged that she was, and is, a true heretic, inasmuch as in the aforesaid places she preached, taught, held, asserted, and instructed that a child conceived of Christian parents does not need the sacrament of baptism.

Regarding each and every one of the said articles, the said Margery, having sworn of her own accord in legal form, on God's Holy Gospels open before her, in front of the said reverend father, to reply faithfully to each and every one of the said articles, replied publicly to each and every one of the same articles, which were clearly and distinctly explained in the vernacular language to the said Margery, both generally and in particular, by the said reverend father, and she acknowledged them in the court. She confessed that she had held, preached, taught, and believed each and every one of the aforesaid heretical and erroneous articles as stated above.

Then the said Margery Goyte, having been soundly instructed by the said reverend father about the truth of the orthodox faith, submitted herself to the correction of the said reverend father and to the judgement of Holy Church, saying that she was ready to abjure each and every one of the aforesaid heretical articles and errors and each and every heresy.

Then and there, before the same reverend father and other notable persons – namely, Masters George Strangeweys, professor of sacred theology, Richard Salter, doctor of decrees, John Sharpe, bachelor in decrees, Master Hugh Lehe, master of arts, Robert Pratt, bachelor in both laws, and Thomas Formewerke, notary public, and many others then present – she abjured in the vernacular language in the following manner and form.

In the name of God, Amen. Before you, the Right Reverend father in God, John, by the grace of God Bishop of Coventry and Lichfield, I, Margery Goyte, late of the parish of Ashbourne of your *[fo. 169r]* diocese and jurisdiction, detected, defamed, denounced, and noised to your reverend fatherhood of heresy, errors and other articles evil sounding, being in doom and judgement before your said reverend fatherhood and understanding, knowing, and well perceiving that before this hour I have openly said, affirmed, declared, and expressed divers articles and opinions erroneous and against the faith of Holy Church and contrary to the determination of the same and evil sounding to the ears of well disposed Christian people.

Wherefore I, the aforesaid Margery, before you, the said reverend father, as it is permitted truly and faithfully informed, acknowledge and know well that the said articles above rehearsed were erroneous and against the true belief, faith, and determination of Holy Church and right evil sounding to the ears of well disposed Christian people, willing with my pure heart and free will to forsake the said errors and articles, and all other errors, heresies, and erroneous opinions being against the true faith and determination of Holy Church and the unity and determination of the said church, and to believe from this time forward after the teaching of all Holy Church and the determination of the same.

Furthermore, the said errors, erroneous opinions, and evil sounding articles, as it is abovesaid, and all manner of heresies, articles, erroneous opinions, and doctrine that is against the true faith and determination of Holy Church I forsake, renounce, and abjure, and swear upon this book that after this hour I shall never openly nor privily hold, declare, nor teach heresy, nor errors, nor any manner of doctrine against the faith or doctrine of Holy Church. Nor shall I receive, favour, nor conceal, defend, succour, nor support by myself or any other inter-mediate person, privily or openly, those who hold, teach, or maintain any such false doctrine, neither to fellowship with them, nor receive them into my house, nor give them meat or drink, clothing or money, nor in any other wise to succour them.

Furthermore, I swear that if I may know any persons, men or women, suspect of errors and heresies, or favourers, concealers, com-forters, defenders, receivers or those that make any private conventicles contrary to the common doctrine of Holy Church, I shall denounce them to your said reverend fatherhood, or to your successors, or their officers, or to their ordinaries as soon as I goodly may.

So help me God and holy doom.

After making this abjuration, the said Margery, led by wiser counsel, well aware that she had incurred by law the sentence of greater excommunication on account of this heresy, humbly asked that she might be absolved from this sentence of excommunication by the said reverend father. Then the said reverend father absolved in legal form the aforesaid Margery Goyte from the said sentence of excommunication.

And he pronounced, declared and proceeded against her in the following manner and form.

In the name of God, Amen. We, John, by divine permission Bishop of Coventry and Lichfield, are legitimately proceeding against you, Margery Goyte, recently of Ashbourne parish of our diocese, in the matter of heresy.

We have found that you have stated, held, and asserted the aforesaid heretical articles. But you wish, as you assert, to return with a pure and unfeigned heart to sound doctrine and to the unity of the church. Therefore, now that you have wholly abjured every aforesaid heresy in particular and each and every heretical deformity, and have guaranteed to obey the law, we absolve you from the sentence of excommunication that you incurred and we restore you to the church's sacraments.

Because you rashly departed from God and Holy Roman Church in this matter, for the bad example that you gave to Christ's faithful in your heresy, and in order that the public punishment or penance that you will perform might instil fear in others, we enjoin the following public penance upon you.

Namely, that on the Saturday before Whit Sunday,[11] barefoot but otherwise clothed, you shall carry a faggot of wood on your shoulders from Ashbourne church to the cross in the marketplace of the town, going ahead of the procession around eleven o'clock in the morning. There, before the vicar or his substitute, with all the people standing around, you shall openly admit and acknowledge that the abjuration of your heresy, and every heresy, and every part of your abjuration and oath in the aforesaid manner and form, as stated above, was and is made by your own pure, free, and spontaneous will.

Then, after the said articles and abjuration have been read out in public, you shall carry the said faggot in front of the procession to the said church and, devoutly making a pilgrimage, you will offer it together with a burning candle to the image of the crucifix in the said church.

You will do similar penance there for three market days. But if you devoutly perform the said penance for one market day, the other days may be remitted in the hope of good conduct.

Saturday, 27 February 1490

Robert Clerke *alias* Teylour

[Reg. Hales, fo. 169v]

Acta in palacio reverendi in Christo patris et domini domini Johannis Dei gratia Coventrensis et Lich' episcopi infra civitatem predictam[12] coram eodem xxvii die mensis Februarii anno Domini millesimo cccclxxxix.[a]

Negotium[b] inquisicionis super crimine heretice pravitatis contra Robertum Clerke alias Teylour de parochia sancti Michaelis Coventr' dicti reverendi patris diocesis, palam et publice super crimine heresis accusatus, infamatus et detectus ut patet in articulis subscriptis meram heresim continentibus seu saltim sapientibus.

---

[a] Acta [...] cccclxxxix *is the heading.*
[b] Clerke *in margin.*

In^a primis dictus Robertus Clerke alias Teylour palam et publice infamatur, accusatur, nominatur et impetitur quod ipse fuit et est verus hereticus pro eo et ex eo quod idem Robertus infra civitatem predictam predicavit, docuit, tenuit, asseruit et dogmatizavit quod oracio Dominica et salutacio angelica non sunt alicuius effectus et quod dampnabile esset dicere Pater noster et Ave Maria, sed quod totus effectus orationis est in symbolo. Ad quem articulum dictus Robertus respondebat sub hac moderamine, quod oracio Dominica non esset dicenda ab aliquo existente extra caritatem quia tunc esse pocius ad dampnacionem dicentis quam ad edificacionem.

Item,^b quod presbiteri habent omnes divicias mundi et tenent aurum et argentum ultra capita sua tempore misse, que melius essent distribuenda inter pauperes. Negat articulum, tamen dicit quod plura bona sunt collata ad ecclesiam que melius essent distribuenda inter pauperes.

Item,^c quod ipse scivit facere homines loqui cum Deo, ore ad os.

Item,^d dictus Robertus requisitus respondere dictis articulis in vim iuramenti sui, dixit quod noluit iurare coram sacerdote licet mortem sustineret. Demum tamen idem Robertus, per dictum reverendum patrem super veritate fidei orthodoxe sanius instructus, submisit se correctioni dicti reverendi patris et in iudicio sancte matris ecclesie, asserens se fore paratum ad abiurandum omnes et singulos errores et hereticas pravitates et omnem et omnimodam heresim. Et tunc ibidem, coram dicto reverendo patre et aliis notabilibus personis, omnem et omnimodam heresim penitus abiuravit et crucem propria manu in signum abiuracionis sue huiusmodi fecit.

Factaque huiusmodi abiuracione, predictus Robertus, saniori ductus consilio, bene inteligens quod ipse pro huiusmodi heresi maioris excommunicacionis sentenciam a iure latam fuit involutus, a dicto reverendo patre ab ipsa excommunicacionis sentencia se humiliter peciit absolvi. Et tunc dictus reverendus pater dictum Robertum a dicta excommunicacionis sentencia absolvit in forma iuris et penitenciam subscriptam iniunxit.

Videlicet quod die Dominica ex tunc proximo sequente dictus Robertus, nudus pedes et caput, ante processionem unum fasciculum lignorum in humeris portet. Et sic stando coram pulpito, dictos articulos sibi per executorem officii publice perlectos fateatur et recognoscat se penitus abiurasse, et tunc ibidem publice abiuret cum effectu.

---

^a i^{us} articulus *in margin.*
^b 2us articulus *in margin.*
^c 3us articulus *in margin.*
^d 4us articulus *in margin.*

Et curatus certificaverit viva voce quod dicta penitencia fuit humiliter peracta.

[English translation]

Proceedings in the palace of the Reverend Father and Lord in Christ, Lord John, by the grace of God Bishop of Coventry and Lichfield, within the said city,[12] conducted before him on 27 February 1489/1490.

Enquiry about the crime of heresy against Robert Clerke, *alias* Teylour, of the parish of St Michael of Coventry of the diocese of the said reverend father, who is openly and publicly accused, defamed, and detected of the crime of heresy as appears in the following articles containing, or at least savouring, of pure heresy.

First, the said Robert Clerke, *alias* Teylour, is openly and publicly defamed, accused, named, and charged that he was, and is, a true heretic, inasmuch as within the said city he preached, taught, held, asserted, and instructed that it is damnable to say the Our Father and Hail Mary, because the whole efficacy of prayer is in the Creed. Robert replied to this article with this qualification, that the Lord's Prayer should not be said by anyone outside charity because this would then be to his damnation rather than for his edification.

Also, that priests have all the riches of the world, and they hold gold and silver above their heads at the time of mass, which would better be distributed among the poor. He denies the article but says that many goods have been given to the church that would have better been distributed to the poor.

Also, that he knew how to make people speak with God face to face.

Also, the said Robert, when required to respond to the said articles by virtue of his oath, said that he was unwilling to swear before a priest even if he had to suffer death. Then, however, being soundly instructed by the said reverend father regarding the truth of the orthodox faith, he submitted himself to the correction of the said reverend father and to the judgement of Holy Mother Church, stating that he was ready to abjure each and every error and heretical deformity, and each and every heresy. Then and there, before the said reverend father and other notable persons, he wholly abjured each and every heresy, and he made a cross with his own hand as a sign of his abjuration.

After making this abjuration, the said Robert, led by wiser counsel, and well aware that he had incurred by law the sentence of greater excommunication on account of his heresy, humbly asked to be absolved from the sentence of excommunication by the said reverend father.

And then the said reverend father absolved the said Robert in legal form from the sentence of excommunication and he enjoined the following penance.

That is to say, on the next Sunday, the said Robert, barefoot and with head uncovered, shall carry a faggot of wood on his shoulders in front of the procession. And while standing before the pulpit, he shall admit and acknowledge that he has wholly abjured the said articles publicly read to him by an executor of the office, and then and there he shall abjure them with effect.

The curate certified orally that the said penance had been humbly performed.

Monday, 13 November 1503

John Sheperde

[Reg. Blyth, fo. 72r]

Acta habita in ecclesia cathedrali Lich' xiii die mensis Novembris anno Domini millesimo quingentesimo tercio coram venerabilibus viris magistris Johanne Yotton, decano, et Georgio Strangwais, eiusdem ecclesie canonico residente, sacre theologie professoribus, reverendi in Christo patris et domini domini Galfridi permissione divina Coventr' et Lich' episcopi in negocio inquisicionis de et super crimine heretice pravitatis contra Johannem Sheperde parochie de Bolton super Moores[13] dicto reverendi patre super crimine heresis infamatum, accusatum atque detectum, ut patet in articulis meram heresim continentibus, seu saltem heresim ad minus sapientibus, commissariis specialiter deputatis sufficienterque constitutis.

In the name of Gode, before you[a] right worshipfull maisters M. John Yotton and George Strangwais, doctors of divinite and yn thys behalfe commissaries to the reverend fader in God Geffrey by the grace of God busshopp of Coventr' and Lich' sufficiently deputed, I John Scheperde of the paresh of Bolton on the Mooris of the diocese and jurisdiction of the seyd reverend fadre detected, diffamed, accused, denownced and noysed to the fore reheresed reverende fadre of errowris, heresy and other articles evyll sownyng; being in dome and jugement of the seyd reverend fadre and you his commissaries, and

---

[a] you *interlined.*

undrestondyng, knowyng and well perceving that afore thys howr I the foreseyd John opynly seyde, affermed, declared and expresly held diverse articles and opynyons erroneows and agenst the fayth of the holy church and contrary to the determination of the same and evyll sowyndyng in the eris of well disposid cristen men.

Wherefore I the foreseyd John, afore you worshypfull maisters John and George, commissaries to the reverend fadre above named sufficientlie deputed, as it is permitted, trulie and feythfully enformed, knowledge and know well that the seyd articles rehersed bene erroneows and agenst the true beleve, fayth and determinacion of hooly church and right evyll sowndyng to the eris of well disposed cristin people; willing with my pure hart and free will to forsake the seyd erroures and articles and all other erroures, heresies and erronyows opinions being agenst the true faith and determinacion of holy church and unitee of the same and to beleve from hensforward aftur the techyng of all holye churche and the determinacion of the same.

Furthermore the seyd erroures, erronyous opinions and evil sowndyng articles, as it is above seyd, and all other maner of heresies, articles, opinions and doctrine that be agenst the true feyth and determinacion of hoolie church I forsake, renownce and abjure and swer apon thys booke that aftur thys howre I shall never opynlye ne privelie holde, declare ne teche heresie, errowres ne eny othyr maner of doctrine agenst the faith and doctrine of hoolie church; ne yet shall nott receive, favour ne councell ne defend, socour or maynteyneth ony such false doctrine nether to felishipp with them wetinglie ne comforte them nether receve them into my howse, gete them mete as drincke, clothing ne money, nether in ony other wise to socour them.

Furthermore I swere that yef Y may know ony persons, men or women, suspecte of erroures and heresies or faverers, concelers, conforters, defenders, receptors or that make ony private conventicles contrary to the common doctrine of hoolie churche, I shall denownce them to the seid reverende fadre or to his successors, ther officers or ther ordinaries as soone as I goodlie may. Soo help me god and hoolie doome.

Facta huiusmodi abiuracione, prefatus Johannes Sheperde, saniori ductus consilio, bene intelligens quod ipse pro huiusmodi heresi maioris excommunicacionis sentenciam a iure lata fuerat involutus, a dictis venerabilibus commissariis humiliter peciit se ab ipsa excommunicacionis sentencia absolvi. Et tunc alter commissarius predictus, videlicet magister [...],[a] predictum Johannem a dicta excommunicacionis.[b]

[a] *blank space in MS.*
[b] *paragraph ends sic.*

In Dei nomine, Amen. Nos, Johannes Yotton, sacre theologie professor, decanus ecclesie cathedralis Lich', reverendi in Christo patris et domini domini Galfridi permissione divina Coventr' et Lich' episcopi in hac parte commissarius, cum ea clausula 'coniunctim et divisim' sufficienter et legitime deputatus, contra te Johannem Sheperde, dicti reverendi patris diocesis in negocio heretice pravitatis legitime procedentes. Quia invenimus te heretica dixisse, tenuisse, asseruisse, predicasse et dogmatizasse articulos tibi obiectos separatim, sed quia vis, ut asseris, corde puro et non ficto ad sanam doctrinam et ad unitatem ecclesie redire. Ideo, abiurata per te penitus omnimoda predicta heresi in speciali, ac omni et omnimoda heretica pravitate in generali, prestitaque cautione de parendo iuri ab excommunicacionis maioris sentencia qua ea occasione perstetisti, te absolvimus et sacramentis ecclesie restituimus. In nomine Patris etc.

[English translation]

Proceedings in the Cathedral church of Lichfield on 13 November 1503 before the venerable men, Masters John Yotton, Dean, and George Strangwais, canon resident of the same church, professors of sacred theology, commissaries of the reverend father and Lord in Christ, Lord Geoffrey, by divine permission Bishop of Coventry and Lichfield, specially deputed and sufficiently constituted, in the enquiry concerning the crime of heresy against John Shepherde of the parish of Bolton on the Moors,[13] defamed, accused, and detected regarding the crime of heresy, as appears in articles containing pure heresy, or at least savouring of heresy.

In the name of God, before you right worshipful masters, Masters John Yotton and George Strangwais, doctors of divinity and in this behalf commissaries to the Reverend Father in God, Geoffrey, by the grace of God Bishop of Coventry and Lichfield, sufficiently deputed, I, John Sheperde of the parish of Bolton on the Moors of the diocese and jurisdiction of the said reverend father, detected, defamed, accused, denounced, and noised to the afore rehearsed reverend father, of errors, heresy, and other articles evil sounding; being in doom and judgement of the said reverend father and you his commissaries, and understanding, knowing, and well perceiving that before this hour, I, the aforesaid John, openly said, affirmed, declared, and expressly held divers articles and opinions erroneous and against the faith of the Holy Church and contrary to the determination of the same, and evil sounding in the ears of well disposed Christian men.

Wherefore, I, the aforesaid John, before you, the worshipful masters John and George, commissaries to the reverend father above named sufficiently deputed, as it is permitted, truly and faithfully informed, acknowledge, and know well that the said articles rehearsed were erroneous and against the true belief, faith and determination of Holy Church and right evil sounding to the ears of well disposed Christian people; willing with my pure heart and free will to forsake the said errors and articles, and all other errors, heresies, and erroneous opinions being against the true faith and determination of Holy Church and unity of the same, and to believe from henceforward after the teaching of all Holy Church and the determination of the same.

Furthermore the said errors, erroneous opinions, and evil sounding articles, as it is abovesaid, and all other manner of heresies, articles, opinions, and doctrine that be against the true faith and determination of Holy Church I forsake, renounce, and abjure, and swear upon this book that after this hour I shall never openly nor privily hold, declare, nor teach heresy, errors, nor any other manner of doctrine against the faith and doctrine of Holy Church; nor yet shall not receive, favour, nor counsel, nor defend, succour, or maintain any such false doctrine, neither to fellowship with them wittingly, nor comfort them, nor receive them into my house, get them meat or drink, clothing or money, nor in any other wise to succour them.

Furthermore I swear that if I may know any persons, men or women, suspect of errors and heresies, or favourers, concealers, comforters, defenders, receivers, or that make any private conventicles contrary to the common doctrine of Holy Church, I shall denounce them to the said reverend father or to his successors, their officers, or their ordinaries as soon as I goodly may. So help me God and holy doom.

After making this abjuration, the said John Sheperde, led by wiser counsel, and well aware that he had incurred by law the sentence of greater excommunication for his heresy, humbly asked to be absolved from the sentence of excommunication by the said venerable commissaries. Then one of the said commissaries, namely Master [...],[a] [absolved] the said John from the said excommunication.

In the name of God, Amen. We, John Yotton, professor of sacred theology, Dean of the Cathedral church of Lichfield, commissary of the Reverend Father and Lord in Christ, Lord Geoffrey, by divine permission Bishop of Coventry and Lichfield, sufficiently and legitimately deputed in this matter with the clause 'collectively and individually', are legitimately proceeding in the matter of heresy against

[a] *blank space in MS.*

you, John Sheperde, of the diocese of the said reverend father. We have found you to have stated, held, asserted, preached, and taught the heretical articles individually objected against you. But you wish, as you assert, to return with a pure and unfeigned heart to sound doctrine and to the unity of the Church. Therefore, now that you have wholly abjured every aforesaid heresy in particular and each and every heretical deformity in general, and have guaranteed to obey the law, we absolve you from the sentence of major excommunication which you have incurred and we restore you to the Church's sacraments. In the name of the Father etc.

Before 28 October 1511

Robert Silkby

[LCB, fo. 2r. Dated 'said day'; as Silkby's biographical information is recorded here, it is conjectured that this is his first examination and so must predate his examination 'denuo' dated 28 October 1511 (below, p. 108). There are large holes in the middle of fo. 2, leaving gaps of several words at a time.]

Robertus Silkby civitatis Coventr', sutor, dictis die et loco, etatis xl annorum.

Iuratus et examinatus, et primo ubi moram traxit, dicit quod in Leicestria et xviii annis Coventr'.

Preterea interrogatus an unquam conversatus fuit cum Johanne Holywode et aliis communicantibus contra sacramentum altaris, dicit quod interfuit cum Johanne Peyntour alias Atkynson[a] juniore et Johanne Peyntour alias Davy[b] seniore necnon Johanne Cutler alias Jonson, Balthasar Shugborowgh et Thoma Flesshour in domo eiusdem Thome, ubi communicacionem habuerunt de evangeliis. Et fatetur se habuisse hec verba: 'Whate can the preiste make of a morsell of brede et cetera? Shuld he make God[c] and ete hym todaie and do likewise tomorowe?' Et similiter de his verbis, 'hoc est corpus meum', ut supra in deposicione Johannis Holywod.[14]

Et fatetur Aliciam Rowley huiusmodi communicacioni sepius interfuisse in domo sua. Que, ut asserit, heretica est.

Et Rogerus Londesdale eiusdem secte est. Qui in domo sua propria, presente tunc Johanne Davy una cum isto deponente, disputavit contra sacramentum altaris et cetera, ut supra.

Dicit[d] insuper Rogerum, Hachet,[15] Thomam Bond et uxorem[e] cuiusdam[f] Gaest senioris[g] de [...] Jonson, cutler, de eadem eiusdem secte esse.

---

[a] alias Atkynson *interlined.*
[b] Davy *interlined.*
[c] hym *deleted.*
[d] Johannes *in margin.*
[e] Johannis *deleted.*
[f] cuiusdam *interlined.*
[g] an *deleted.*

[...] Shugbrowgh erat executor testamenti magistri Johannis [...] Coventr'.

Preterea fatetur se dixisse quod magis conferret ad salutem anime erogare pecuniam in elemosinam quam in oblaciones ymaginum, quas truncos mortuos appellavit.

Dicit etiam quod interfuit in domo Thome Flesshour sepenumero [...] Balthaser Shugborowgh publice legentem librum continentem heresim [...] Balthaser satis bene novit istum fuisse [...] deponentem publice verba habuisse contra [...] atque ritum suum approbavit [...].

[...] preterea quod Johannes Bouway de Bristol'[16] [...] opiniones suas tam contra sacramentum altaris [...] et cetera. Et secum disputacionem habuit in [...] Johannis Holywod.

Fatetur insuper se interfuisse [...] manent' in Mylne[a] lane[17] unacum Alicia [...], ubi audivit dictam Aliciam publice legentem evangelia [...] scripta. Et preterea audivit eam dicentem de [...] ymaginibus fiendas,[b] asserendo quod melius applic' [...] pauperum. Et non vult aspicere sacramentum elevacionem [...] istum deponentem ut non intueretur illud et [...] passionis Christi, ita quod acciperet eum [...] passionis Christi et non pro vero corpore.

Interrogatus an unquam habuit haec verba vel eis similia in effectu, 'It is a prety falshod of [...] preistes to buy a C caks for a peny and sell them ageyn for [...] obol', dixit quod credit se talia verba habuisse.

Interrogatus an aliquos libros habuit aut habet continentes heresim, habuit ut asserit sed non habet. [...] dicit quod erant doctoris de Ybstock,[18] cui eosdem remisit [...] magistri Kent rectoris de Staunton,[19] quos eidem remisit.

———

[English translation]

Robert Silkby of the city of Coventry, shoemaker, on the said day and place, forty years old.

Sworn and examined, and first where he lived, he said in Leicester and for eighteen years in Coventry.

Asked whether he ever conversed with John Holywode and others speaking against the sacrament of the altar, he says he was with John Peyntour *alias* Atkynson junior, and John Peyntour *alias* Davy senior,

[a] Margaret' in Myln' lane *in margin*.
[b] necnon *deleted*.

and also John Cutler *alias* Jonson, Balthasar Shugborowgh, and Thomas Flesshour in the house of the same Thomas, where they talked about the Gospels. He admits these words: 'What can the priest make of a morsel of bread etc. Should he make God and eat him today and do likewise tomorrow?' And likewise these words, 'This is my body', as above in John Holywod's deposition.[14]

He admits that Alice Rowley was often present at communication of this kind in his house. She is, he says, a heretic.

And Roger Londesdale belongs to the same sect. He, in his own house, in the presence of John Davy and this deponent, disputed against the sacrament of the altar etc., as above.

He says that Roger, Hachet,[15] Thomas Bond, and the wife of a certain Gaest senior of [...] Jonson, cutler, of the same city, belong to the same sect.

[...] Shugbrowgh was an executor of the testament of Master John [...] Coventry.

He admits he said that it benefits more the soul's salvation to give money in alms than in offerings to images, which he called dead logs.

He says also he was very often in the house of Thomas Flesshour, [...] Balthasar Shugborowgh publicly reading a book containing heresy [...]. Balthasar knew sufficiently well that he was [...] publicly deposing to have spoken words against [...] and he favoured his rite [...].

[...] moreover that John Bouway of Bristol[16] [...] his opinions both against the sacrament of the altar [...] etc. And he had a disputation with him in [...] of John Holywod.

He admits, furthermore, that he had been present [...] living in Mylne[a] lane[17] together with Alice [...], where he heard the said Alice publicly reading the Gospels [...] written. And, furthermore, he heard her saying of [...] to be made to images, asserting that they would be better applied [...] of the poor. And he is not willing to look at the sacrament at the elevation [...] this deponent and he would not look at it and [...] of the passion of Christ, so that he would accept [...] of the passion of Christ and not for his true body.

Asked whether he ever spoke these or similar words, 'It is a pretty falsehood of [...] priests to buy a hundred cakes for a penny and sell them again for [...] halfpennies', he said he believed he had spoken such words.

Asked whether he had or has any books containing heresy, he said he had but no longer. [...] he says that they belonged to the doctor of Ybstock,[18] to whom he returned them [...] of Master Kent, rector of Staunton,[19] which he returned to him.

---

[a]   Margaret in Myln lane *in margin*.

John Jonson

[LCB, fo. 2v. Date illegible. The examination continued on 'the 28ᵗʰ day' (below, p. 109); October is the most likely month, both because it follows in the MS Robert Silkby's deposition (see previous entry), and because John Spon and Richard Gest, examined on 3 or 4 November (below, pp. 132 and 143), apparently responded to questions derived from his deposition on the 28ᵗʰ.]

[...] die mensis anno Domini et loco supradictis.[a]

Johannes Jonson de Byrmyngham, cutler, etatis circa xl annorum.[b]

Comparens coram domino et interrogatus de articulis omnibus quibus Robertus Sylkby et alii respondebant, nichil effectualiter voluit fateri.

[English translation]

[...] the day of the month, year of the Lord and place as above.

John Jonson of Birmingham, cutler, about forty years of age.

Appearing before the lord and asked about all the articles to which Robert Sylkby and others were replying, he wished effectively to admit nothing.

Tuesday, 28 October 1511

Thomas Flesshor

[LCB, fo. 8r. Dated '28ᵗʰ day'; the examination resumes 3 November 1511 (below, p. 134).]

Prefatis die mensis, anno et loco et die xxviii.[c]

Thomas Flesshour etatis lxvii annorum civitatis Coventr', ubi moram traxit per spacium xl annorum, natus fuit in parochia de Preston in Amundrernes,[20] ut asserit.

Iuratus et diligenter examinatus ut supra, et primo an novit aliquos

---

[a]   [...] die mensis anno Domini et loco supradictis *is the heading of the page.*
[b]   etatis circa xl annorum *interlined.*
[c]   Prefatis [...] et die xxviii *is the heading of the page.*

suspectos de heresi, dicit quod Balthaser Shugborowe, Robertus Sylkby, Johannes Peyntour junior[21] et Johannes Peyntour senior[22] necnon Rogerus Landesdale atque Rogerus Bromley sporier, qui iam mortuus est, sepenumero communicacionem habuerunt de evangeliis et sacramento altaris; et presertim Alicia Rowley, Rogerus Landesdale, Johannes Peyntour junior in domo dicti Rogeri, ubi etiam alius extraneus cum uxore sua interfuit, communicacionem contra presbiteros habuerunt.

Fatetur se recepisse in domo sua dictum Balthaser et alios atque audivit prenominatum Balthaser legentem evangelia atque mandata Anglice scripta, prout continentur in quibusdam libris remanentibus iam apud dominum, tunc autem in sua custodia existentibus.

Interrogatus a quo habuit huiusmodi libros, dicit quod circiter annos xviii elapsos habuit eosdem libros a quodam Rogero Brown,[a] ea lege ut ipsos supranominato Balthaser traderet: quod infra novem dies immediate sequentes fecit. Et Balthaser huiusmodi libros recepit et penes se per spacium trimestre servavit. Deinde quosdam illorum [...] sit dictus Balthaser ad[b] istum deponentem, quosdam vero penes se retinuit. Et idem Balthaser multotiens hospitatus apud istum deponentem, huiusmodi libros legit, presentibus Roberto Silkby et aliis.

Interrogatus an cremavit huiusmodi libros aut eosdem ordinario denunciavit, dicit quod non.

Audivit Aliciam Rowley circiter festum sancti Michaelis ad annum emensum in domo Rogeri Landesdale librum de mandatis legisse, et Landesdale alium librum post lecturam dicte Alicie.

Dicit preterea dictam Aliciam fuisse et esse suspectam de et super heretica pravitate multis annis.

Fatetur etiam se audivisse dictos Balthaser, Aliciam, Rogerum Landesdale, Sylkby et alios verba habuisse contra venerationes et oblationes ymaginibus fiendas atque contra peregrinaciones et cetera.

Dicit etiam quod Rogerus, Hachet[23] et Thomas Bonde cum aliis supranominatis [...] interfuerunt et communicaverunt de et super premissis,[c] et presertim de quodam libro intitulato super vita Thobie[24] et cetera.

Dicit[d] quod Matheus Maklyn, fullor, habuit libros varios de et super heresi et quod idem Matheus est hereticus et cetera.

Fatetur quod [...] Johanna, nuper relicta Padland nunc autem uxor magistri Smythe, fuit et est [...].

---

[a] qua *deleted*.
[b] ad *interlined*.
[c] qu' *deleted*.
[d] Matheus Maklyn habuit libros *in margin*.

[English translation]

The day of the month, year and place and 28th day as above.

Thomas Flesshour, sixty-seven years old, of Coventry city, where he has lived for forty years, born in the parish of Preston in Amounderness,[20] as he says.

Sworn and carefully examined as above, and first whether he knows any persons suspected of heresy, he says that Balthasar Shugborowe, Robert Sylkby, John Peyntour junior,[21] and John Peyntour senior,[22] as well as Roger Landesdale and Roger Bromley spurrier, who is now dead, often conversed about the Gospels and the sacrament of the altar; and especially Alice Rowley, Roger Landesdale, and John Peyntour junior talked against priests, in the house of the said Roger, where another stranger was present with his wife. He admits he received in his home the said Balthasar and others, and he heard the said Balthasar reading the Gospels and the Commandments written in English, as is contained in certain books that are now with the bishop but were then in his custody.

Asked from whom he received the books, he says that about eighteen years ago he had them from a certain Roger Brown, on condition that he hand them over to the said Balthasar: which he did within the following nine days. Balthasar took the books and kept them with him for three months. Then the said Balthasar [...] some of them to this deponent and kept some of them himself. Balthasar frequently stayed with this deponent, and read the books in the presence of Robert Silkby and others.

Asked whether he burned the books or denounced them to the ordinary, he says no.

He heard Alice Rowley reading a book about the Commandments in the house of Roger Landesdale a year ago around the feast of St Michael, and Landesdale reading another book after Alice had finished.

He says the said Alice has been for many years and is suspected of heresy.

He admits he has heard the said Balthasar, Alice, Roger Landesdale, Sylkby, and others speaking against the veneration of images and offerings to them and against pilgrimages etc.

He also says that Roger, Hachet,[23] and Thomas Bonde and others named above were present and conversed about the aforesaid matters and especially about a certain book entitled 'On the Life of Tobit'[24] etc.

He says that Matthew Maklyn, fuller, had various heretical books and that this same Matthew is a heretic etc.

He admits that [...] Joan, recently the widow of Padland and now the wife of master Smythe, was and is [...].

Robert Silkby

[LCB, fo. 8v. Dated '28ᵗʰ day'; the examination resumes 5 November (below, p. 146).]

xxviii die mensis anno domini et loco supradictis.[a]

Robertus[b] Silkby, examinatus denuo de et super conversacione sua cum aliis, utputa Margeria Lacock quondam relicta Hugonis Stubbe, dicit quod Balthaser Shugborowe et iste deponens interfuerunt insimul cum ipsa Margeria et communicacionem habuerunt de et super articulis contra sacramentum altaris et cetera.

Dicit etiam quod dicta Margeria est eiusdem secte et opinionis cum Balthaser et aliis supranominatis.

Interrogatus utrum ab aliis complicibus suis ei consultum fuit et sub iuramento confirmatus ut secreta sua non celaret, dicit quod non.

Et dicit quod dominus Radulphus Kent, nepos magistri Willelmi Kent nuper rectoris de Staunton,[25] post obitum dicti M. Kent venit ad istum deponentem et nunciavit ei de obitu dicti magistri Kent.

Et fatetur se dixisse antea Johanni Holywod quod dictus dominus Radulphus optime scivit legere et quod multociens ei in libris continentibus heresim legit.

Dicit preterea dictum dominum Radulphum executorem fuisse in testamento dicti magistri Kent, de qua re presumendum est. Et ita credit iste quod idem dominus Radulphus huiusmodi libros penes se servat, satisque bene novit istum deponentem et avunculum suum predictum eiusdem secte et opinionis fuisse.

———

[English translation]

On the 28ᵗʰ day of the month in the year of the Lord and the place mentioned above.

Robert Silkby, examined again about his conversations with other people, including Margery Lacock, formerly the widow of Hugh Stubbe, says that Balthasar Shugborowe and this deponent were present, together with the said Margery, and they conversed about articles against the sacrament of the altar etc.

He also says that the said Margery is of the same sect and opinion as Balthasar and the others named above.

Asked whether he had been told by the other accomplices and confirmed under oath not to reveal their secrets, he says no.

[a] xxviii [...] supradictis *is the heading of the page.*
[b] Lacok *in margin.*

He says that Sir Ralph Kent, nephew of Master William Kent, recently rector of Staunton,[25] came to this deponent after the death of the said Master Kent and told him about the death of the said Master Kent.

He admits that he said before John Holywod that the said Sir Ralph knew very well how to read, and that he often read to him books containing heresy.

He says the said Sir Ralph was an executor of the will of the said Master Kent, which must be presumed to be so. Thus he believes the same Sir Ralph keeps the books with him and knows well enough that this deponent and his aforesaid uncle are of the same sect and opinion.

John Jonson

[LCB, fos 2v–3r. Continued from before 28 October 1511 (above, p. 105; see entry there regarding dating to October).]

Demum, xxviii° die mensis et anno atque loco suprascriptis, idem Johannes, oneratus iuramento corporali ad dicendum veritatem super interrogatis, et examinatus primum de etate, dicit quod agit xxxvii^{mum} annum sue etatis et natus erat in Skelton prope civitatem Ebor'.[26] Et erat apprentitius cum quodam Ricardo Wilcocks, bladesmythe in Seecole lane prope carcerem de Flete.[27] Cum quo Ricardo, ut asseruit, moram traxit per spacium xiiii annorum. A Londinio venit ad May-destone,[28] ubi cum quodam Dunham, cutler, operatus est per spacium semestris.[a]

Et postea mansit cum Rogero Brown[b] in civitate Coventr', antea abiurato. Qui eum in opinionibus hereticis primo instruxit una cum confiliis magistri Johannis Physici et Johannis Smyth, scissoris, qui iam mortui sunt. Et a civitate Coventr' recessit Gloucestriam,[29] ubi cum quodam Roberto Gilbert, cutler, per annum et dimidium moratus est. Ab eo autem oppido contulit se demum civitati Coventr'. Ibique, cum quodam Lodge, quasi per spacium semestris mansit. Inde venit ad prioratum de Maxstock,[30] ubi duos [...] moram [...].

Post hoc adiit Bristolliam atque ibi in parochia sancti [...][c] cum quodam W[...] est ferme per spacium trium annorum, ubi conversatus est [...] Ratcliff strete,[d, 31] [...] Bouway,[e] textore, et patre suo,[f, 32] et Henrico

[a] A Londinio [...] semestris *inserted in margin.*
[b] ab *deleted.*
[c] in parochia sancti [...] *interlined.*
[d] [...] Ratcliff strete *interlined.*
[e] Duke *probably in margin.*
[f] et patre suo *interlined.*

Padwell, cutler, qui iam [...]. Et cum ipsis habuit communicacionem contra sacramentum [...], oblaciones, ymagines et peregrinaciones. Et ipsi similiter communicaverunt cum isto deponente. Et dicit prefatum Bouway et alios super suspicionem heretice pravitatis deprehensos fuisse et[a] penitenciam egisse, ut postea [...].

[...] Bristollia accessit ad Taunton,[33] ubi morabatur ad ix[em] septimanas [...] in Britoniam.[34] Et a Britonia ad Burdewos,[35] ubi [...] Sanctorum usque initum xl[me]. A Burdewos [...] prope Holbourn cross,[36] bladsmyth, per [...]. A Londinio iterum rediit Coventriam, ubi cum [...] Brown mansit per spacium dimidium anni et [...] Rogero Landesdale, qui eum instruxit contra [...] est, quemadmodum omnibus notum est [...] affirmat eque malus et perversus in opinionibus [...]. Idem,[b] dicit de Roberto Hachet et Boune,[c] qui heretic' [...] preterea quendam Robertum Bastell[d] una cum [...]own et Alicia Rowley. Que Alicia dedit ei [...] sepenumero et communicavit contra peregrinaciones, ecclesiam et presbiter' [...],[e] isto deponente presente.

Et interrogatus de conversacione [...] dicit quod[f] in consciencia sua erat eo tempore dicta Alicia [...] secreto vocabulo inter eos, ubi convenerunt simul dicit [...] '[...] and God blesse you'. Et dicit quod opinio est inter eos quod non faci[...] sculptele.

Dicit etiam uxorem Rogeri Landesdale sepe audivisse sponsum [...] legentem et heretica est sua opinione.

A[g] Coventria contulit se ad Byrmyngham, ubi nunc moram trahit et traxit ad spacium iiij[or] annorum. Et conversatus erat ibidem cum Ricardo Gest et Johanne Gest atque uxore sua. Idem Ricardus et Johannes habuerunt cum isto sepe communicacionem contra peregrinaciones, ymagines sanctorum et oblaciones necnon contra sacramentum altaris.

Et dicit quod Ricardus Gest, ut recolit, tribus annis elapsis, misit *[fo. 31]* istum deponentem ad quendam Spon, lanium civitatis Coventr', pro quodam libro remanente in custodia eiusdem Spon. Et idem Spon respondit se velle tradere sibi librum pro eo quod nummos pro huiusmodi libro ab eis, quorum nomina iste nescit, colligere non potuit. Non tamen eo tempore deliberavit isti deponenti librum. Tercia tamen vice iste deponens comitatus est eum ad domum Rogeri Londesdale et ibi dictus Spon tradidit ei librum. Quem vero librum continuo iste deponens commisit custodie Roberti Silkby. Et postea, quando iste

---

[a] ut credit *deleted*.
[b] Robert Lech alias Bestel obiit *in margin*.
[c] Boune *interlined*; Bonde *deleted*.
[d] Bastell *in margin*.
[e] [...] *deleted*.
[f] pr *deleted*.
[g] Gest *in margin*.

deponens rediit ad dictum Silkby pro huiusmodi libro, responsum erat eidem a prenominato Silkby quod eundem librum attulit[a] in comitatu Leicestr' et, petenti isti nummos pro eodem libro, dedit ei a tike of a fedurbed.

Interrogatus an novit effectum huiusmodi libri, dicit quod erat de huiusmodi perversis opinionibus quas Ricardus Gest et Johannes predicant et favent. Fatetur verba contra sacramentum altaris fuisse prolata ab omnibus per eum superius accusatis, sub eo tenore qui continetur in deposicione Roberti et Johannis Holywod. Dicit quod audivit Bradeley legentem ad [...] annos elapsos [...] domo sua.

Et dicit quod Villers fuit sue opinionis et mutuatus est isti nummos variis temporibus et conversatus est secum. Novitque istum fuisse hereticum et Bradeley idem novit. Et Villers habuit communicacionem cum isto contra peregrinaciones et ymaginum veneraciones. Et Bradeley idem fecit. Non tamen habent verba contra sacramentum altaris.

Idem dicit de Bambrooke, a quo sepius audivit huiusmodi verba que ab aliis prenominatis. Credit quod uxores Bradeley et Bambrooke sunt eiusdem secte, que erant audientes communicacionem maritorum suorum.

[English translation]

Finally, on the 28th day of the month in the year and the place aforesaid, the same John, placed under corporal oath to tell the truth when questioned, and examined first about his age, says he is in his thirty-seventh year of age and was born in Skelton near York.[26] He was apprenticed with a certain Richard Wilcocks, bladesmith in Seacoal Lane, near the Fleet prison.[27] He spent fourteen years with the said Richard, he says. From London he came to Maidstone,[28] where he worked for six months with a certain Dunham, cutler.

Afterwards, he lived in the city of Coventry with Roger Brown, who abjured earlier. Roger Brown first instructed him in heretical beliefs, together with the godchildren of Master John Physician and John Smyth, tailor, who are now dead. From Coventry he withdrew to Gloucester,[29] where he stayed for a year and a half with a certain Robert Gilbert, cutler. From that town he returned to Coventry, and remained there with a certain Lodge for almost six months. From there he came to Maxstock Priory,[30] where for two [...] he lived [...].

Afterwards, he went to Bristol and in the parish of saint [...] with a certain W[...] almost for three years, where he conversed [...] Ratcliff

---

[a] attulit *interlined*; misit *deleted*.

street[31] [...] Bouway, weaver, and his father[32] and Henry Padwell, cutler, who now [...]. He talked with them against the sacrament [...], offerings, images, and pilgrimages. They likewise talked with this deponent. He says the said Bouway and others were arrested on suspicion of heresy and did penance, as afterwards [...].

[...] Bristol he went to Taunton[33] where he stayed for nine weeks [...] to Britanny.[34] From Brittany to Bordeaux,[35] where [...] of saints until the beginning of Lent. From Bordeaux [...] near Holborn Cross,[36] bladesmith, for [...]. From London he returned again to Coventry, where he remained for half a year with [...] Brown and [...] Roger Landesdale, who instructed him against [...], inasmuch as it is known to all [...] he affirms he is equally bad and perverse in the opinions [...]. He says the same of Robert Hachet and Boune, who heretic' [...] besides[a] a certain Robert Bastell together with [...]own and Alice Rowley. The said Alice gave him [...] very often and talked against pilgrimages, the church, and priest' [...], in the presence of this deponent.

Asked about the conversation, [...] he says that to his knowledge the said Alice was at that time [...] secret saying among them, when they came together [...] '[...] and God bless you'. He says the opinion among them that not [...] carved.

He says the wife of Roger Landesdale often heard her husband [...] reading and she is a heretic, in his opinion.

From Coventry he came to Birmingham where he now lives, having lived there for the past four years. He conversed there with Richard Gest, and John Gest and his wife. The same Richard and John have often talked with him against pilgrimages, the images of saints, and offerings as well as against the sacrament of the altar.

He says that Richard Gest, as he remembers, three years ago, sent [fo. 3r] this deponent to a certain Spon, butcher of Coventry city, for a book in Spon's keeping. Spon replied that he was willing to hand over the book to him because he was not able to collect the money for the book from certain persons, whose names the deponent does not know. But he did not then hand over the book to this deponent. On a third occasion, however, this deponent accompanied him to the house of Roger Londesdale, and there the said Spon handed the book over to him. This deponent immediately gave the book to Robert Silkby. Afterwards, when this deponent returned to the said Silkby for the book, Silkby told him that he had taken it to Leicestershire, and when he asked him for money for the book, he gave him a tick of a featherbed.

Asked whether he knows the effect of the book, he says that it contained those perverse beliefs that Richard Gest and John preach and favour. He admits that all the persons whom he accused above

[a] Robert Lech *alias* Bestel died *in margin*.

spoke against the sacrament of the altar, in accordance with the deposition of Robert and John Holywod. He says he heard Bradely reading to [...] years ago [...] in his home.

He says Villers was of his opinion and lent money to this deponent on various occasions and conversed with him. He knows he was a heretic and Bradely knows the same. Villers conversed with this deponent against pilgrimages and the veneration of images and Bradeley did the same. They do not speak, however, against the sacrament of the altar.

He says the same of Bambrooke. He heard similar words spoken by him as by the others named above. He believes the wives of Bradeley and Bambrooke belong to the same sect and they listened to what their husbands said.

Wednesday, 29 October 1511

John Atkynson

[LCB, fo. 5r. Dated '29th day'; examination resumes 'penultimate day' (30 October, below, p. 115) and again on 2 November (below, p. 127, explicitly dated).]

xxix[no] die mensis anno et loco supradictis.[a]

[Johan]nes Atkynson civitatis Coventr' peyntour etatis circiter xxii annorum.

Iuratus atque examinatus et cetera ut supra, et primo ubi natus fuit, dicit quod in parochia de Garstange prope monasterium de Cokersand.[37]

Interrogatus ulterius de conversacione sua cum Balthaser, Silkby et aliis supranominatis, negat omnino conversationem cum eisdem aut noticiam opinionis eorundem.

Et sic remisit eum dominus carceribus.

[English translation]

On the 29th day of the month in the year and the place given above.

John Atkynson of Coventry city, painter, aged about twenty-two.

Sworn and examined etc. as above, and first where he was born, he says in the parish of Garstang, near Cokersand Monastery.[37]

---

[a] xxix[no] [...] supradictis *is the heading of the page.*

Asked about his dealings with Balthasar, Silkby, and others named above, he entirely denies contact with them, or knowledge of their beliefs. Therefore the bishop sent him back to prison.

Roger Landesdale

[LCB, fo. 5v. Dated 'as given above'; follows John Atkynson's examination of 29 October 1511. Examination resumes last day of month, i.e. 31 October 1511 (below, p. 116).]

Die, mense, anno Domini et loco suprascriptis.[a]

Rogerus Landesdale civitatis Coventr', scissor, etatis lxiii annorum.

Iuratus atque examinatus,[b] confessus est prima fronte se annum[c] ante diem obitus Rogeri Brown[d] opiniones hereticas favisse et libros de et super heresi confectos legisse.

[English translation]

The day, month, year of the Lord and place as given above.

Roger Landesdale of Coventry city, tailor, aged sixty-three.

Sworn and examined, he confessed immediately that the year before the death of Roger Brown he favoured heretical opinions and read heretical books.

---

[a] Die [...] suprascriptis *is the heading of the page*
[b] et primo Ac *deleted.*
[c] per annos *deleted.*
[d] ante [...] Brown *interlined.*

Thursday, 30 October 1511

John Atkynson

[LCB, fo. 5r. Continued from 29 October 1511 (above, p. 113). Dated 'penultimate day'; resumption of this examination dated 2 November (below, p. 127).]

Postea, videlicet penultimo die mensis anno Domini et loco supradictis, interrogatus prefatus Johannes Atkynson an habuit conversationem cum Silkby et aliis, ratificando opiniones eorundem, fatetur se interfuisse in parco unacum Johanne Holywod, Silkby et Flesshour[a] et quod audivit prenominatum Johannem Holywod legentem ibidem in quodam libro contra sacramentum altaris et cetera. Negat tamen se favisse opinioni eorundem.

Et ubi Silkby repetit ei in facie coram domino quod eiusdem opinionis et secte erat cum ipso[b] Silkby, omnino negavit.

[English translation]

Later, namely on the penultimate day of the month in the year of the Lord and the place given above, the aforesaid John Atkynson, asked whether he had contact with Silkby and others, supporting their beliefs, admits he was in a park together with John Holywod, Silkby, and Flesshour, and that he heard John Holywod reading there a book against the sacrament of the altar etc. He denies, however, that he supported their opinion.

When Silkby repeated to his face, before the bishop, that he was of the same belief and sect as Silkby, he utterly denied it.

[a] negat tamen *deleted.*
[b] ipso *interlined.*

Friday, 31 October 1511

Roger Landesdale

[LCB, fos 5v–6r. Continued from 29 October 1511 (above, p. 114). Dated 'last day of the month'.]

Et idem Rogerus, die ultimo mensis anno Domini et loco[a] supranominatis, comparens coram domino, fatebatur quod uxor sua audivit eum legentem sepenumero in huiusmodi libris et quod opinionibus hereticis favet.

Et quod Johannes Davy peyntour, nunc Leicestriam commorans, unacum fratre eiusdem Johannis, etiam pictore, ut credit, presente Silkby, audivit istum deponentem multotiens in[b] et super huiusmodi libris legisse. Et in hac parte accusat Johannem Atkynson pictorem.

Dicit insuper quod Thomas Acton, purser, et Robertus Peg, pictor, civitatis Coventr',[c] audiverunt eum legentem. Unius et eiusdem secte cum eo sunt.

Fatetur insuper quod Johannes Spon, dicte[d] civitatis lanius, eum legentem in huiusmodi libris sepius audivit et quod opinionibus suis hereticis favebat.

Idem[e] dicit de uxore Roberti Hachet.

Fatetur etiam quod infra trimestre emensum, Alicia Rowley accessit ad domum istius deponentis, afferens secum librum super epistolis Pauli Anglice scriptum. Et audivit istum deponentem legere super eodem libro in presentia uxoris sue. Et librum ipsum denuo ad domum suam propriam dicta Alicia reportavit.[38] Dicit preterea se mutuo alium librum de tota vetere lege Anglice confectum, ad modum portiforii, per manus Thome Bown, servientis Roberti Hachet, ad annum et ultra de predicta Alicia Rowley habuisse.[f] Et deponit ulterius quod prenominata Alicia habuit eo tempore ab isto deponente librum intitulatum De vita Thobie. Et quod infra duos annos superiores, eadem Alicia Rowley istum deponentem audivit sepe legentem et insimul communicacionem habuerunt contra sacramentum altaris sub hiis verbis: 'Cum videris sacrosancti dominici corporis levationem in altari, cogita de vero corpore Christi in celis et non de hostia et cetera.' Et fatetur quod non credidit

---

[a] uxor Londesdale *in margin.*
[b] de *deleted;* in *interlined.*
[c] eum *deleted.*
[d] Spon *in margin.*
[e] uxor Hachet *in margin.*
[f] Rowley *in margin.*

verum dominicum corpus ibi fuisse sed in celis. Interrogatus ubi et a
quibus libros habuit,[a] quos in domo sua tenuit,[b] dicit etiam[c] quod a
Johanna, nunc uxore Ricardi Smythe, quendam librum [...] habuit.[d]
Quem, postquam eundem exemplatus est, tradidit predicte Johanne.
Que Johanna [...] librum habuit intitulatum Actus apostolorum in[e]
Anglicis translatum.

Dicit [...] librum alium[f] super epistolis Pauli in amplo volumine a
quodam Johann' [...] nunc mortuo habuisse.

De quo autem librum de mandatis habuit, nescit deponere.

Reliquos vero libros ad numerum quinque confessus se habuisse de
dicta Johanna Smyth. Quam asserit esse eiusdem secte et opinionis
cum eo. Et fatetur quod infra sex septimanas audivit istum deponentem
dicta Johanna legentem.

Est alius etiam, ut asserit, Ranulphus [...],[g] textor[h] apud Allesley[39] ex
opposito ecclesie in vico ducente versus parcum manens, huiusmodi
secte et opinionis favens.[i] Cum quo, ad duos annos elapsos, communicaciones in quadam clausura [...] suam de et super opinionibus
hereticis habuit.

Interrogatus de secreto vocabulo inter eos dicit,[j] 'May we all drinke
of a cuppe and at the departing, God kepe you and God blesse you'.

Interrogatus[k] de Thoma Bayly,[40] dicit[l] quod semel ad spatium sex
annorum, ut recolit, iste deponens in domo eiusdem Thome Bayly cum
eodem Thoma communicacionem habuit super evangeliis Mathei. Ex
eo tempore nullam conversacionem cum dicto Thoma habuit, ut asserit.
[fo. 6r] Dicit insuper dictum Thomam Bayly habuisse varios libros quos
non novit[m] nisi ex relatu. Deponit etiam quod Robertus Hachet sepe
conversatus fuit cum prenominato Thoma Bayly.

Interrogatus de Gest seniore et juniore, dicit quod cum Gest juniore
et Johanne Jonson, cutler, communicaciones habuit contra sacramenta
ecclesie, non tamen cum eisdem simul et coniunctim sed divisim. Et
dicit quod Gest senior habuit librum valde pulcrum de et super nova

---

[a] habuit *interlined.*
[b] habuit *deleted.*
[c] etiam *interlined.*
[d] habuit *interlined.*
[e] Johanna Smythe *in margin.*
[f] a quodam *deleted.*
[g] *blank space in MS.*
[h] qui *deleted.*
[i] favens *interlined; two illegible words deleted.*
[j] quod *deleted.*
[k] Bayly *in margin.*
[l] dicit *interlined.*
[m] sed *deleted.*

lege in Anglic' traductum, quem Spon postea habuit et Silkby ab eodem Spon.

Interrogatus de conversacione domini Thome Gest capellani, nescit, ut asserit, deponere.

Interrogatus de Balthaser, dicit quod sepe communicaverunt insimul de et super opinionibus huiusmodi hereticis, ut supra in deposicionibus tam sua quam aliorum.

Dicit etiam quod Matheus Markelond in parvo Parke strete,[a, 41] eiusdem secte et opinionis est cum eo et aliis supranominatis. Qui secum de huiusmodi opinionibus hereticis multotiens communicavit. Et idem Matheus librum habet, ut asserit, de evangeliis sancti Johannis.

Idem[b] dicit de quodam Ricardo, alienigeno,[c] pictore, nunc commorante apud Leicestriam cum Johanne Davy, pictore. Dicit preterea quod opinionem tenuerunt episcopos et alios iudices ecclesiasticos non posse excommunicacionis sentenciam fulminare, sed quod si alicui maledixerint, non est[d] timenda eorum sentencia.

Dicit preterea quod [...][e] Wrixam, glover, ex opposito[f] signi Corone[42] moram trahens in Coventria, interfuit secum multotiens et communicationem habuit secum de opinionibus hereticis ut supra.

Idem Rogerus interrogatus preterea quare credit Johannem Spon fuisse hereticum,[g] dicit quod ob eam causam quod idem Johannes attulit sibi quendam librum de et super vetere iure in Anglic' traductum.

Fatetur insuper dictus deponens se quendam librum de et super heretica pravitate, continentem in primo folio, 'At the begynnyng whan God man', [...] Johanna nuper relicta magistri Padland, nunc autem uxore magistri Ricardi Smyth, exemplandum habuisse. Quem librum iste idem prenominate Johanne postea remisit, ut asserit.

Dicit[h] quod Bradeley unacum uxore sua[i] et Bambrooke presentes fuerunt sepius in domo Bambrooke. Et audierunt istum communicantem, ut supra.

Hawkyns est eiusdem opinionis, ut iste et Bown asserunt.[j, 43]

Holbache[k] et uxor sua fuerunt eiusdem secte et iste habuit communicacionem secum in parco.

---

[a]   in parvo Parke strete *interlined.*
[b]   Ricardo Ducheman *in margin.*
[c]   *possibly* alieninge.
[d]   te *deleted.*
[e]   *blank in MS.*
[f]   Wrixam *in margin.*
[g]   Spon *in margin.*
[h]   Bradeley et uxor et Banbrooke *in margin.*
[i]   unacum uxore sua *interlined.*
[j]   Bown et Londesdale J' *in margin.*
[k]   Holbache *in margin.*

Derlyng[a] sepe habet communicationem de 4[or] ordinibus ecclesie.
Fatetur[b] de Davy Clerc coryer.[c]
Dicit[d] etiam quod Revys fuit eiusdem secte et opinionis.

Dicit[e] quod Thomas Kylyngworth, cooper in Flete strete Coventr',[44] interfuit cum isto et audivit istum communicantem contra sacramentum altaris et cetera. Et idem dicit de Johanne Cropwell,[f] wyer drawer. Et isti duo, ut asserit, favebant opinionibus suis, et hoc ad x[cem] vel xii[cem] annos.

Idem[g] dicit de Hugone Parret, qui interfuit cum isto infra quaternum anni et audivit atque favebat ut supra.[h]

[English translation]

The same Roger, appearing before the bishop on the last day of the month in the year of the Lord and the place given above, admitted that his wife often heard him reading books of this kind and that she favours heretical beliefs.

And that John Davy, painter, now living in Leicester, together with John's brother, also a painter, as he believes, and in the presence of Silkby, often heard this deponent reading books of this kind. In this matter he accuses John Atkynson, painter.

He also says that Thomas Acton, purser, and Robert Peg, painter, of Coventry city, heard him reading. They are of one and the same sect with him.

He admits that John Spon, butcher of the said city, often heard him reading these books and that he favoured his heretical opinions.

He says the same about Robert Hachet's wife.

He also admits that, within the last three months, Alice Rowley came to this deponent's house carrying a book of St Paul's Letters written in English and she heard the deponent reading from the book in the presence of his wife. Alice then took the book back to her own home.[38] He says, too, that he had on loan for a whole year and more, from the said Alice Rowley through the hands of Thomas Bown, servant of Robert Hachet, another book of the whole Old Testament,

---

[a] Derlyng *in margin.*
[b] Davy Clerc *in margin.*
[c] dicat *deleted.*
[d] Revys *in margin.*
[e] Kylyngworth *in margin.*
[f] Cropwell *in margin.*
[g] Hugo Parret *in margin.*
[h] fatetur quod uxor Lye nuper relicta Lodge est heretica *deleted*; Lodge *also deleted from margin.*

written in English and in a form that could be carried around. He says
that Alice at that time had from the deponent a book entitled 'On the
Life of Tobit'. During the above two years, Alice often heard him
reading and together they spoke against the sacrament of the altar in
these words: 'When you see the elevation of the sacred body of the
Lord at the altar, think of Christ's true body in heaven and not of the
host etc.' He admits that he did not believe the Lord's true body was
there but in heaven. Asked when and from whom he received the
books that he kept in his house, he says he had one book [...] from
Joan, now the wife of Richard Smyth. He returned the book to Joan
after it had been copied. The same Joan [...] had a book entitled Acts
of the Apostles translated into English.

He says [...] had another book of St Paul's Letters in a large volume
from a certain John [...] now dead.

From whom, however, he had the book on the Commandments, he
does not know.

He confessed he had the other five books from the said Joan Smyth.
He asserts that she is of the same sect and opinion as he. He admits
that Joan heard him reading within the last six weeks.

Another person favouring this sect and its beliefs is, he asserts, Ralph
[...],[a] weaver, who lives in Allesley[39] opposite the church in the lane
leading to the park. For the last two years the deponent conversed with
him in a private place [...] about heretical beliefs.

Asked about their secret saying, he says, 'May we all drink of a cup
and at the departing, God keep you and God bless you'.

Asked about Thomas Bayly,[40] he says that once about six years ago,
as he remembers, he talked with the said Thomas in Thomas's house
about Matthew's Gospel. Thereafter, he had no contact with the said
Thomas, he says. [fo. 6r] He also says that Thomas Bayly had various
books, of which he has no knowledge except by report. He says that
Robert Hachet often talked with Thomas Bayly.

Asked about Gest senior and junior, he says he spoke against the
church's sacraments with Gest junior and John Johnson, cutler, but
with them individually not together. He says Gest senior had a very
beautiful book of the New Testament translated into English, which
Spon had later, and then Silkby had it from Spon.

Asked about the behaviour of Sir Thomas Gest, chaplain, he does
not know anything, he says.

Asked about Balthasar, he says they often conversed together about
these heretical beliefs, as above in his and others' depositions.

He says that Matthew Markelond in Little Park Street[41] is of the
same sect and opinion as he and the others named above. Matthew

---

[a] *blank space in MS.*

often spoke with him about heretical beliefs. Matthew has, he says, a book of St John's Gospels.

He[a] says the same about a certain Richard, foreigner, painter, now living in Leicester with John Davy, painter. He says, moreover, that they believed that bishops and other ecclesiastical judges could not fulminate sentences of excommunication, but if they cursed anyone their sentence should not be feared.

He says that [...][b] Wrixam, glover, living opposite the sign of the Crown[42] in Coventry, was often with him and spoke with him about heretical beliefs as above.

The same Roger, asked why he believed John Spon was a heretic, says because John brought him a book of the Old Testament in English.

The said deponent, moreover, admits he had a copy made of a heretical book containing on the first folio the words, 'At the beginning when God man', [...] Joan recently the widow of Master Padland and now the wife of Master Richard Smyth. He later returned the book to the said Joan, he says.

He says that Bradeley, together with his wife and Bambrooke, were often present in Bambrooke's house. They heard him speaking, as above.

Hawkyns is of the same opinion, he and Bown say.[43]

Holbache and his wife belonged to the same sect and he conversed with them in the park.

Derlyng frequently spoke about the four orders of the church.

He admits concerning Davy Clerc, currier.

He says Revys was of the same sect and opinion.

He says that Thomas Kylyngworth, cooper in Fleet Street in Coventry,[44] was with him and heard him speaking against the sacrament of the altar etc. He says the same about John Cropwell, wiredrawer. The two of them, he says, favoured his beliefs and this for ten or twelve years.

He says the same about Hugh Parret, who was with him within the last three months and listened to and agreed with him as above.[c]

[a] Richard Ducheman *in margin.*
[b] *blank space in MS.*
[c] He admits that Lye's wife, recently the widow of Lodge, is a heretic *deleted;* Lodge *also deleted from the margin.*

Symon

[LCB, fo. 6r. Undated. Follows Roger Landesdale's examination of 31 October 1511 (see previous entry), but it is at the foot of the page, separate from the preceding text.]

Symon deposuit coram domino quod Hugo Parret, Landesdale et uxor sua rettulerunt sibi quod Jo Clerc fuit hereticus.

[English translation]

Symon deposed before the bishop that Hugh Parret, Landesdale, and his wife told him that Jo Clerc was a heretic.

Margery Locock

[LCB, fo. 6v. Dated 'last day of the month'. Follows Roger Landesdale's examination of 31 October 1511 (above, p. 116).]

Ultimo die mensis anno Domini et loco supradictis.[a]

Margeria Locock, uxor Henrici Locock, civitatis Coventr', girdeler, nuper uxor Hugonis Stubbe.

Iurata et examinata, dicit quod non modo temporibus primi mariti sui, videlicet Hugonis antedicti, verum etiam in diebus istius Henrici, conversabatur cum Landesdale, Silkby et aliis. Et presertim infra annum in domo prefati[b] Rogeri Landesdale, unacum uxore eiusdem Rogeri, lecturam a sepenominato Rogero in libris heresim continentibus audivit et opiniones hereticas favebat.

Eisdem opinionibus tunc publice coram domino prorsus renunciavit.[c]

Sed dominus, propterea quod timetur de repudiacione a viro suo facienda, distulit abiurationem solempnem[d] eidem iniungere faciendam. Et eam, ad perimplendum penitenciam sibi iniungendam iuramento corporali[e] oneratam ad cautelam, absolvit et cetera.

---

[a] Ultimo [...] supradictis *is the heading of the page.*
[b] prefati *interlined;* eiusdem *deleted.*
[c] et abiuravit *deleted.*
[d] solempnem *interlined.*
[e] *two illegible words deleted.*

[English translation]

The last day of the month in the year of the Lord and the place given above.

Margery Locock, wife of Henry Locock, of Coventry city, girdler, recently the wife of Hugh Stubbe.

Sworn and examined, she says that not only in the time of her first husband, Hugh Stubbe, but also in the time of the said Henry, she conversed with Landesdale, Silkby, and others. Especially within the last year, in the house of the said Roger Landesdale, together with Roger's wife, she heard the oft-mentioned Roger reading heretical books and she favoured heretical opinions.

Then she wholly renounced these beliefs publicly before the bishop.

The bishop, however, fearing she might be repudiated by her husband, deferred ordering her to make a solemn abjuration. While, by way of precaution, binding her under oath to perform the penance that would be imposed, he absolved her etc.

Alice Rowley

[LCB, fo. 6v. Dated 'the same day'. Examination follows Margery Locock's, dated last day of month (see previous entry), and resumes 5 November 1511 (below, p. 155).]

Eisdem die et loco comparuit coram domino Alicia Rowley civitatis Coventr', relicta Willelmi Rowley eiusdem civitatis Coventr' nuper mercatoris, de et super certis opinionibus hereticis accusata.

Iurata et examinata et[a] primo utrum antea propter suspitionem heresis fuerat conventa in iudicio, fatebatur quod sic, presertim coram domino apud Coventriam.

Interrogata an ab anno Domini millesimo quingentesimo sexto conversata fuit cum Rogero Landesdale et aliis supranominatis, aut eorundem aliquem in libris heresim continentibus legentem audivit, vel opinionibus eorundem favebat, negat.

[English translation]

The same day and place, Alice Rowley of Coventry, widow of William

---

[a] de *deleted*.

Rowley, recently a merchant of the same city, appeared before the bishop accused of certain heretical opinions.

Sworn and examined, first regarding whether she had been summoned in judgement on suspicion of heresy before, she admitted she had been, and especially before the bishop in Coventry.

Asked whether since 1506 she had conversed with Roger Landesdale and others named above, or had heard any of them reading heretical books, or had supported their beliefs, she says no.

Robert Hachet

[LCB, fo. 7r. Dated 'the aforesaid day', following others dated 31 October 1511 (see previous two entries). Hachet abjures 5 November 1511 (below, p. 165).]

Prefatis die et loco comparuit coram domino Robertus Hachet civitatis Coventr', alutarius, etatis lx annorum,[a] de et super heretica pravitate detectus et cetera.

Iuratus atque examinatus et primo de conversacione sua cum Landesdale, Silkby et aliis, fatetur se interfuisse cum eisdem sepenumero et audivisse eosdem contra sacramentum altaris verba habuisse, ut supra.

Dicit etiam quod Matheus Maclyn,[45] fullo in parvo Parke strete proxime domo magistri [...],[b] scit memoriter evangelium, 'In principio erat verbum'.[46] Et dictus Matheus sepenumero conversabatur cum Landesdale, Silkby et aliis.

Fatetur etiam quod Alicia Rowley audivit Landesdale legentem in presentia istius.

Est preterea alienigena pictor apud Leicestriam, qui in huiusmodi libris continentibus heresim[c] adeo[d] instructus est et expertus, ac ipse idem in oracione Dominica est, cuius nomen Londesdale scit et adduxit[e] eum ad istum deponentem.

Dicit insuper quod Robertus Peg, pictor in Gosforde strete,[47] fuit eiusdem secte per vii annos elapsos cum isto et ceter'.

Balthaser Shugborowe etiam hereticus[f] est, de quo deponit cum aliis.

Dicit insuper quod Johanna relicta Padland, nunc autem uxor Ricardi Smyth, suspecta est de heresi. Nam, ut asserit, quemadmodum publica vox se habet, eadem Johanna libros continentes heresim habuit.

[a] etatis lx annorum *interlined*.
[b] Fullo [...] [...] *interlined*.
[c] continentibus heresim *interlined*.
[d] perf' *deleted*.
[e] ist' est deponen *deleted*.
[f] xl *deleted*.

Dicit[a] etiam quod Johannes Spon, lanius, interfuit bis vel ter in domo Landesdale ad duos annos elapsos, audiendo eundem Landesdale unacum isto deponente legentes libros heresim et cetera.

Deponit quod Thomas[b] Bownd,[c] famulus suus, hereticus est. Qui iam aufugit.[48]

Uxor[d] Thome Trussell, hosier, librum habet de veteri testamento. Mulier est gravida et prope partum. Liber erat Thome Forde.

Thomas Acton purser de Coventr', prope Jordan Well[e, 49] erat unus de primis qui istum ad huiusmodi hereses provocavit et allexit. Et sepenumero conversabatur cum Alicia Rowley.

Relatum etiam erat, ut asserit, quod doctor Alcock de Ybstock[50] erat huiusmodi secte.

Credit[f] quod dominus Radulphus Shor libros habet erroneos.

Dicit etiam quod Gest senior et junior sunt suspecti. Et Gest senior librum habuit de heresi. Et eundem librum dominus Thomas Gest habuit secum per annum in domo patris sui.

Interrogatus de vocabulo secreto inter eos,[g] 'May we[h] drinke of the same cupp'.

Dicit[i] insuper uxorem suam novisse secreta et opiniones suas. Non tamen eisdem, ut asserit, favisse.

Dicit[j] preterea quod uxor Thome Acton predicti est heretica cum viro suo.

Interrogatus quare dicit Gest seniorem esse huiusmodi secte, respondit propterea quod audivit eundem Gest, postquam maritavit uxorem Johannis Smyth, nuper de Coventr' scissoris abiurati,[k] dicentem sibi quod uxor sua allexit eum ad opiniones suas hereticas, quibus, ipse affirmavit, favebat.

Et dicit quod uxor Gest junioris pessima est in opinionibus hereticis et quod erat famula uxoris dicti Johannis Smythe [...] erat in huiusmodi opinionibus et cetera.

Est alius Ranulphus [...][l] textor [...] eiusdem secte et opinionis.

---

[a] Spon *in margin.*
[b] Baud' *deleted.*
[c] Bownd *interlined.*
[d] Trussell' *in margin.*
[e] [...] *interlined.*
[f] Shore *in margin.*
[g] dc' *deleted.*
[h] we *interlined;* ye *deleted.*
[i] uxor Hachet *in margin.*
[j] uxor Acton *in margin.*
[k] abiurati *interlined.*
[l] *blank space in MS.*

Thomas[a] Clerc, hosier, serviens [...],[b] fuit eiusdem secte et legebat super quodam libro heresim continente – qui liber ut iam credit transmissus ad Bristolliam et ibidem crematus erat – isti deponenti ad vii annos elapsos.

[English translation]

The same day and place Robert Hachet of Coventry, tawyer, aged sixty, appeared before the bishop detected of heresy etc.

Sworn and examined and first about his contacts with Landesdale, Silkby, and others, he admits he was often with them and heard them speaking against the sacrament of the altar, as above.

He says that Matthew Maclyn,[45] fuller in Little Park Street, next to the house of Master [...],[c] knows by heart the Gospel, 'In the beginning was the Word'.[46] The said Matthew frequently talked with Landesdale, Silkby, and others.

He also admits that Alice Rowley heard Landesdale reading in his presence.

There is also a foreign painter in Leicester who is well instructed and expert in these heretical books, and likewise in the Lord's Prayer. Londesdale knows his name and led him to this deponent.

He says that Robert Peg, painter in Gosford Street,[47] belonged to the same sect with him for the last seven years.

Balthasar Shugborowe is also a heretic; he deposes about him with the others.

He says that Joan, the widow of Padland and now Richard Smyth's wife, is suspect of heresy. For, as he says is rumoured, she had heretical books.

He says that John Spon, butcher, was in Landesdale's house two or three times during the last two years, hearing Landesdale and this deponent reading heretical books etc.

He deposes that Thomas Bownd, his servant, is a heretic. Thomas has now fled.[48]

The wife of Thomas Trussell, hosier, has a book of the Old Testament. She is pregnant and close to giving birth. The book belonged to Thomas Forde.

Thomas Acton, purser of Coventry, near Jordan Well,[49] was one of the first who provoked and drew this deponent to these heresies. He frequently conversed with Alice Rowley.

---

[a] Clerc *in margin.*
[b] serviens [...] *interlined.*
[c] *illegible.*

It was reported, he says, that Doctor Alcock of Ibstock[50] belonged to the sect.

He thinks that Sir Ralph Shor has erroneous books.

He says that Gest senior and junior are suspect. Gest senior had a heretical book. Sir Thomas Gest had the same book with him for a year in his father's house.

He was asked about the secret saying among them, 'May we drink of the same cup'.

He says his wife knew his secrets and beliefs, but she did not, he says, agree with them.

He says the wife of the said Thomas Acton is a heretic, together with her husband.

Asked why he says that Gest senior belongs to the sect, he replies that he heard the said Gest saying – after he married the wife of John Smyth, recently a tailor of Coventry, who abjured – that his wife drew him to his heretical beliefs, which, he affirmed, she supported.

He says that the wife of Gest junior is wicked in heretical beliefs, and that she was the servant of the said John Smyth's wife [...] was in these beliefs etc.

There is another Ralph [...]ᵃ weaver [...] of the same sect and belief.

Thomas Clerc, hosier, servant [...], belonged to the same sect and read a heretical book to this deponent seven years ago: the book, as he now believes, was taken to Bristol and there burnt.

Sunday, 2 November 1511

John Atkynson

[LCB, fo. 5r. Examination continues from 30 October 1511 (above, p. 115).]

Tandem tamen, videlicet ii^do die mensis Novembris anno Domini et loco supradictis, idem Johannes Atkynson, comparens coram domino, fatebatur quod conversatus fuit cum Roberto Silkby et Johanne Davy, peyntour. Qui eum primo, ut asserit, allexerunt ad hereses.

Interrogatusᵇ cuius etatis erat quando primo a patria sua venit, dicit quod circiter etatem octo annorum. Et tunc venit ad quendam dominum

---

ᵃ *blank space in MS.*
ᵇ quo *deleted.*

Willelmum Coor,[a, 51] avunculum suum,[b] cum quo moram traxit per spacium trium annorum. Et postea erat apprenticius Coventr' cum quodam Jacobo Reynesford. Et ibi moratus est ultra tres annos. Deinde rediit ad dictum avunculum suum et mansit secum per dimidium anni. Ab avunculo suo contulit se ad Warwicum,[52] ubi morabatur per annum et dimidium. Et a Warwico migravit ad dominum Latemer, doctorem,[53] cum quo moram traxit per annum. Deinde rediit Warwic', ubi mansit per annum. Ab[c] eo loco venit ad Stichall,[54] ibique moratus est per annum. Et a Stichall venit Coventr', ubi operatus est in Signo Angeli[55] per annum et ultra. Et ab eo tempore continuo moram traxit apud Coventriam quasi per spacium duorum annorum.

Et dicit se primum audivisse dictos Robertos[d] Sylkby et Johannem Davy et eorum dictis credidisse eo tempore quo operatus est in Signo Angeli, videlicet ad tres annos preteritos. Et fatetur dictos Robertum et Johannem Davy dogmatisasse[e] contra sacramentum altaris, peregrinaciones et cetera, ut supra continetur in deposicionibus aliorum, quorum dogmatisacionibus fidem habuit.

Dicit[f] insuper quod Abel et, ut recolit, Silkby retulerunt ei quendam Willelmum Grevis,[56] skynner, Coventr',[g] esse opinionis et secte eorundem. Sed [...] hac parte dixerunt necne nescit deponere quandoquidem non [...] cum dicto Willelmo, ut asserit.

Audivit preterea Thomam Bown [...] sonant' heresim, que non recolit sed credit ipsum Thomam esse unius secte et opinionis cum ipso et aliis.

Fatetur etiam se multotiens interfuisse in domo Rogeri Landesdale et eum in libris continentibus heresim legentem audivisse.

Et fatetur articulum de Johanne Davy et Ricardo Dowcheman, qui ambo sunt heretici, ut asserit. Et idem Ricardus habet librum in vernacula sua.[57]

Et[h] dicit se audivisse a Thoma Bown quod magister Pisford[58] est huiusmodi secte et opinionis.

Dicit[i] ad tres annos elapsos[j] se fuisse in domo Thome Acton, ubi vidit librum de mandatis ablatum extra quendam cistam in tabula per dictum Thomam et cetera.

---

[a] yn *deleted*.
[b] vicarius de Corby *in margin*.
[c] h' *deleted*.
[d] Robertos *[sic]*.
[e] de *deleted*.
[f] Int' Abell' *in margin*.
[g] Revys *in margin*.
[h] Int' Bown *in margin*.
[i] Acton *in margin*.
[j] elapsos *interlined*.

[English translation]

Finally, however, on 2 November in the year of the Lord and the place given above, John Atkynson, appearing before the bishop, admitted that he had conversed with Robert Silkby and John Davy, painter. They first, he says, drew him towards heresies.

Asked about his age when he first came from his country, he says about eight years old. He then came to Sir William Coor, his uncle,[a, 51] and stayed with him for three years. Afterwards he was apprenticed in Coventry with James Reynesford, and he stayed there more than three years. He then returned to his said uncle and remained with him for half a year. From his uncle he went to Warwick,[52] and lived there for a year and a half. From Warwick he moved to Sir Latemer, doctor,[53] and stayed with him for a year. Then he returned to Warwick and remained there a year. From there he came to Stivichall[54] and stayed there for a year. From Stivichall he came to Coventry, where he worked at the sign of the Angel[55] for more than a year. Since then he has lived continuously in Coventry for almost two years.

He says he first heard Robert Sylkby and John Davy and believed their teaching when he was working at the sign of the Angel, that is to say, for the past three years. He admits that the said Robert and John Davy taught against the sacrament of the altar, pilgrimages etc., as is contained above in the depositions of others, and he believed in their teachings.

He[b] says, moreover, that Abel and, as he remembers, Silkby, told him that William Grevis,[56] skinner of Coventry, was of their beliefs and sect. But [...] in this matter they said, and he is unable to state, since not [...] with the said William, as he says.

He heard Thomas Bown [...] savouring of heresy; he does not remember but believes the said Thomas is of the same sect and beliefs as he and others.

He admits he was often in Roger Landesdale's house and heard him reading heretical books.

He admits the article concerning John Davy and Richard Dowcheman, both of whom are heretics, he asserts. The same Richard has a book in his vernacular language.[57]

He[c] says he heard from Thomas Bown that Master Pisford is of the same sect and beliefs.[58]

He says that, three years ago, he was in Thomas Acton's house and

---

[a] vicar of Corby *in margin.*
[b] Ask Abell *in margin.*
[c] Ask Bown *in margin.*

he saw there a book of the commandments, which had been brought
out of a chest onto a table by the said Thomas etc.

Monday, 3 November 1511

Thomas Bown

[LCB, fos 7v, 4v.]

iii Novembris anno Domini et loco suprascriptis.[a]
    Thomas Bowne civitatis Coventr', sutor, etatis xl annorum.
    Iuratus et examinatus et primo ubi natus fuit, dicit quod apud
Chorlebury prope Banbury.[59] Et a decimo sue etatis anno traxit
moram continuam apud Coventriam, ut asserit, ubi audivit Rogerum
Londesdale legentem in libris continentibus heresim et conversabatur
cum Roberto Hachet, Roberto Silkeby et aliis.
    Et dicit quod quidam Ricardus Weston, quondam famulus domini
Johannis Halse, nuper Coventr' et Lich' episcopi,[60] eum primo allexit
et provocavit ad huiusmodi hereses.
    Fatetur insuper quod audivit dictum Rogerum et alios commun-
icantes contra sacramentum altaris, prout continetur in deposicionibus
aliorum.
    Dicit etiam quod opinionibus contra peregrinationes, ymaginum
oblationes et sanctorum venerationes favebat.
    De Roberto Peg, concordat cum Hachet et Londesdale.
    Et fatetur quod quendam librum de epistolis Pauli, ut recolit, infra
tres annos elapsos ab Alicia Rowley habuit mutuo nomine Rogeri
Londesdale. Quem librum ad eundem Rogerum continuo attulit.
    Et eadem Alicia infra idem tempus dogmatisavit isti deponenti quod
tempore elevationis eucaristie crederet hostiam ibidem esse oblatam
spiritualiter in memoriam passionis Christi, et sic reciperet hostiam
spiritualiter recolendo passionem Christi. Dogmatisavit etiam dicta
Alicia isti deponenti, 'Quomodo potest creatura Deum, creatorem
suum, formare?' et cetera, ut in depositionibus aliorum; et hoc infra
tres annos.
    Et quidam Robertus Bastell, unacum isto deponente, infra iiii[or] annos

---

[a] iii Novembris [...] suprascriptis *is the heading of the page.*

audivit ipsam Aliciam sic dogmatisantem: qui nunc recessit, quo tamen nescit.[a]

[fo. 4v] Fatetur insuper Thomas Bown quod Thomas Acton civitatis Coventr' purser, Robertus Peg, [...][b] Wrixam glover, Thomas Clerc, Matheus Marklond et Ranulphus textor de Allesley atque Gest senior de Birmyngham sunt heretici et opinionis sue.

Et dicit quod Gest prenominatus habuit communicacionem cum Roberto Hachet et isto deponente quasi ad viii annos preteritos[c] inter eundem ad parcum de et super opinionibus hereticis, et quod dixit eisdem uxorem suam eum allexisse ad huiusmodi opiniones.

Interrogatus de Spon, dicit quod non novit eum pro heretico. Audivit tamen Silkby dicentem dictum Spon esse huiusmodi opinionis et secte et cetera.

Thomas Abell est huiusmodi secte, ut asserit.

[English translation]

3 November in the year of the Lord and the place given above.

Thomas Bowne of Coventry, shoemaker, aged forty.

Sworn and examined and first where he was born, he says in Charlbury near Banbury.[59] And from his tenth year he lived continuously in Coventry, as he says, and there he heard Roger Londesdale reading heretical books and conversed with Robert Hachet, Robert Silkeby, and others.

He says that Richard Weston, once a servant of Sir John Halse, recently Bishop of Coventry and Lichfield,[60] first attracted and drew him to these heresies.

He admits that he heard the said Roger and others speaking against the sacrament of the altar, as is contained in the depositions of others.

He says also that he agrees with opinions against pilgrimages, offerings to images, and the veneration of saints.

Concerning Robert Peg, he agrees with Hachet and Londesdale.

He admits that within the last three years he had, as he recalls, a book of St Paul's Letters on loan from Alice Rowley, in Roger Londesdale's name. He immediately brought the book to the said Roger.

Within the same time, the same Alice taught him that at the time of

[a] Respice folio proximo ad the signum Z *follows. The deposition continues on fo. 4v, indicated in the margin by another letter* Z.

[b] *blank in MS.*

[c] de *deleted.*

the elevation of the eucharist he should believe the host was offered spiritually in memory of Christ's passion, and thus he should receive the host spiritually by recalling Christ's passion. Alice also taught him, 'How can a creature fashion God, his creator?' etc., as in other depositions; this within the three years.

A certain Robert Bastell and the deponent heard her teaching in this way within the last four years: he has now gone away, the deponent knows not where.[a]

[fo. 4v] Thomas Bown also admits that Thomas Acton of Coventry, purser, Robert Peg, [...][b] Wrixam glover, Thomas Clerc, Matthew Marklond, and Ralph the weaver of Allesley, and Gest senior of Birmingham are heretics and share his beliefs.

He says that the aforesaid Gest spoke with Robert Hachet and the deponent almost eight years ago in a park about heretical beliefs, and that Gest told them that his wife drew him to these beliefs.

Asked about Spon, he says he does not know him for a heretic. However, he heard Silkby saying that Spon held these beliefs and belonged to the sect etc.

Thomas Abell belongs to the sect, he says.

John Spon

[LCB, fo. 7v. Dated 'same day'. Follows Thomas Bown's examination, dated 3 November]

Johannes Spon civitatis Coventr', lanius, dictis die et loco comparuit coram domino, etatis xl annorum et ultra, natus ut asserit in Allesley, ubi moram traxit et in civitate Coventr' toto vite sue tempore.

Iuratus et examinatus et primo an novit Londesdale fuisse suspectum de et super heresi, dicit quod non nisi postquam audiverat eum legentem.

Et interrogatus de quodam libro quem a Ricardo Gest seniore habuit, fatetur receptionem eiusdem libri et quod erat liber[c] de veteri iure[d] in anglicis traductus,[e] in quo libro audivit Londesdale legentem. Et post-quam audivit lecturam sentencie maioris in ecclesia solemniter factam, aggressus est magistro Bowde, tunc vicario perpetuo ecclesie parochialis

---

[a] Look on the next folio at the letter Z *follows. The deposition continues on fo. 4v, indicated in the margin by another letter* Z.

[b] *blank space in MS.*

[c] super epistolis Pauli *deleted.*

[d] de veteri iure *interlined.*

[e] de *deleted.*

sancte Trinitatis Coventr',[61] et peccata sua, presertim de custodia huiusmodi libri, eidem magistro Bowde confitebatur.

Interrogatus ulterius an unquam audivit dictum Rogerum Londesdale, seu alium quempiam, verba habuisse private aut publice contra sacramentum altaris, sanctorum venerationes aut peregrinationes et cetera, dicit quod non.

Interrogatus preterea an opinione sua credidit dictum Rogerum aut alios fuisse suspectos de et super heretica pravitate, dicit quod sic.

Interrogatus insuper an ipse sit suspectus aut pro tali reputatus in Coventr', dicit quod non quantum conjicere possit.

Interrogatus an conversationem habuit cum dicto Landesdale aut aliis huiusmodi secte postquam credidit eos fuisse suspectos, negat prorsus.

Interrogatus quotiens audivit Landesdale legentem, dicit quod quinquies aut sexies.

Interrogatus qui erat effectus huiusmodi lecture, dicit quantum recolit erat de vitis sanctorum et epistolis Pauli. Nichil tamen contra ymaginum venerationes,[a] sacramentum altaris aut aliquod aliud contra sanam doctrinam ecclesie audivit, ut asserit, in huiusmodi lectura.

[English translation]

John Spon of Coventry, butcher, appeared before the bishop on the same day and in the same place, aged forty and more, born as he says in Allesley, where and in Coventry he has lived all his life.

Sworn and examined and first whether he knew Londesdale was suspected of heresy, he says not until after he had heard him reading.

Asked about a book that he had from Richard Gest senior, he admits receiving the book and that it was a book of the Old Testament translated into English and that he heard Londesdale reading it. After the solemn reading of the greater sentence in the church, he approached Master Bowde, then perpetual vicar of Holy Trinity parish church in Coventry,[61] and confessed his sins to him, especially his keeping of the book.

Asked whether he ever heard Roger Londesdale or anyone else speaking privately or publicly against the sacrament of the altar, the veneration of saints, or pilgrimages etc., he says no.

Asked whether, in his opinion, he thought the said Roger or the others were suspected of heresy, he says yes.

[a] aut *deleted.*

Asked whether he himself was suspected or reputed to be a heretic in Coventry, he says no, insofar as he knows.

Asked whether he conversed with the said Landesdale or any others of the sect after he believed they were suspected, he entirely denies it.

Asked how often he heard Landesdale reading, he says on five or six occasions.

Asked about what was read, he says that, insofar as he remembers it, was saints' lives and Paul's Letters. He heard nothing in the reading against the veneration of images, the sacrament of the altar, or anything else against the Church's sound teaching, he says.

Thomas Flesshor

[LCB, fos 8r, 24v; Reg. Blyth, fo. 98r. Examination (first section) continued from 28 October 1511 (above, p. 105). Note that the questionnaire ministered to Flesshor, in the second and third sections below, probably formed the model that subsequent questionnaires were to follow (see below, pp. 162, 165 and 175). For Flesshor's abjuration, see below, pp. 260–265.]

[fo. 8r] Tandem idem Flesshour, iii° [...] die Novembris, recognoscens errores [...] et omnimode heretice pravitati sponte renunciavit et abiuracionem legit [...] seque submisit iudicio ecclesie. Et dominus, prestita per dictum Thomam Flesshour [...] de parendo iuri et mandatis ecclesie, eundem ab excommunicationis sentencia absolvit.

Ac iniunxit eidem quod die Veneris proximo sequente eat coram processione generali apud Coventr', portando in humeris suis fasciculum lignorum donec processio finiatur. Et die Dominica extunc sequente eat similiter ante processionem in ecclesia parochiali sancti Michaelis, deferendo fasciculum lignorum ut supra, et intersit sermoni ibidem aᵃ principio in finem. Atque ad preceptum predicantis, tempore declarationis articulorum, levet huiusmodi fasciculum humeris suis donec finiatur articulorum declaratio. Reliqua pars penitencie sue differtur in visitacionemᵇ quousque dominus decreverit eum vocare. Quoᶜ tempore habet in mandatis ad comparendum coram domino, ulteriorem penitenciam subiturum, si et quatenus domino videbitur expedire.

[fo. 24v] Acta coram dicto reverendo patre apud Maxstock, iii° die Novembris anno Domini supradicto. Quo die Thomas Flesshour civitatis Coventr', faber, comparuit coram dicto reverendo patre. Contra

---

ᵃ s' *deleted.*
ᵇ proximam et eo *deleted.*
ᶜ quousque [...] quo *interlined.*

quem articuli subscripti ministrati erant. Et ad fideliter respondendum eisdem iuramentum prestitit corporale.[a]

In primis objicimus et articulamur tibi Thome Flesshour civitatis Coventr', fabrum,[b] quod tu es nostre Coventr' et Lich' diocesis. Fatetur.

Item, quod tu scienter cum hereticis et heretice pravitatis fautoribus conversationem habuisti et lecturis[c] eorundem sepius interfuisti. Fatetur.

Item, quod opinionibus eorundem – et presertim Rogeri Londesdale, Roberti Silkby, Balthaser Shugborow et aliorum – erroneis favisti easdemque tenuisti. Fatetur.

Item, quod tu eosdem contra sacramentum altaris, venerationes ymaginum et peregrinaciones sanctorum dogmatisare et verba sepius habere audivisti. Fatetur.

Item, quod tu libros reprobate lectionis in domo tua tenuisti eosque et alios in custodia aliorum existentes celavisti et ordinario non denunciasti. Fatetur.

Item, quod tu suspectos de et super heretica pravitate in domum tuam recepisti: et cum eisdem tam in domo quam aliis in locis communicacionem contra sanam ecclesie doctrinam habuisti. Fatetur.

Item, quod tu in civitate Coventr', et aliis locis convicinis eidem, de et super huiusmodi heretica pravitate suspectus et[d] diffamatus[e] publice et notorie existis. Fatetur.

Deinde legit dictus Thomas Flesshour abiurationem subsequentem coram dicto reverendo patre. Presentibus tunc ibidem dompno Willelmo Dykons, priore domus sive prioratus de Maxstock, magistris Radulpho Cantrell, decretorum doctore, Willelmo Skelton et Willelmo Wilton, artium magistris, necnon Johanne Blyth, in decretis bacallario, fratre Henrico Eliot, suppriore dicti prioratus, Henrico Big et aliis. Et ipsis presentibus, signum crucis propria sua manu[f] subscripsit.

[*Reg. Blyth, fo. 98r*] Acta habita in prioratu de Maxstock [...] permissione divina Coventr' et Lich' episcopo tercio die mensis Novembris anno Domini millesimo quingentesimo xi, in negocio inquisicionis heretice pravitatis contra et adversus Thomam Flesshor civitatis Coventr' de et super crimine heretice pravitatis publice diffamatum, detectum, denunciatum et accusatum. In primis ministrati erant sibi articuli subscripti;[g] quibus idem Thomas, iuramento corporali oneratus, respondebat ut patet.

---

[a] Acta [...] corporale *is the heading of the page.*
[b] fabrum *[sic], presumably* fabro *is meant.*
[c] eiusdem sep *deleted.*
[d] et *interlined.*
[e] et *deleted.*
[f] s *deleted.*
[g] subscripti *interlined.*

In primis objicimus et articulamur tibi Thome Flesshor civitatis Coventr', fabro, quod tu es nostre Coventr' et Lich' diocesis. Fatetur.

Item, quod tu scienter cum hereticis et heretice pravitatis fautoribus conversacionem habuisti et lecturis eorundem sepius interfuisti. Fatetur.

Item, quod opinionibus eorundem – et presertim Rogeri Londesdale, Roberti Sylkby, Balthaser Shugborough et aliorum – erroneis favisti easdemque tenuisti. Fatetur.

Item, quod tu eosdem contra sacramentum altaris, veneraciones imaginum et peregrinaciones sanctorum dogmatizare et verba sepius habere audivisti. Fatetur.

Item, quod tu libros reprobate lectionis in domo tua tenuisti eosque et alios in custodia aliorum existentes celavisti et ordinario non denunciasti. Fatetur.

Item, quod tu suspectos de et super heretica pravitate in domum tuam recepisti et cum eisdem tam in domo quam aliis in locis communicationem contra sanam ecclesie doctrinam habuisti. Fatetur.

Item, quod tu in civitate Coventr' et aliis locis convicinis eidem de et super huiusmodi heretica pravitate suspectus et diffamatus publice et notorie existis. Fatetur.

Tandem die mensis, anno Domini et loco quibus supra, idem Thomas Fleshor, recognoscens errores suos, eisdem atque omni et omnimode heretice pravitati sponte renunciavit et abiuracionem legit prout sequitur postea, seque submisit iudicio ecclesie. Et prefatus reverendus pater, prestita per dictum Thomam Fleshor caucione de parendo iuri et mandatis ecclesie, eundem ab excommunicationis sententia absolvit.

Ac iniunxit eidem quod die Veneris proximo sequente eat coram processione generali apud Coventrim, portando in humeris suis fasciculum lignorum donec processio finiatur. Et die Dominica extunc sequente eat similiter ante processionem in ecclesia parochiali sancti Michaelis Coventr', deferendo[a] fasciculum lignorum ut supra, et intersit sermoni ibidem a principio in finem; atque ad preceptum predicantis tempore declaracionis articulorum, levet huiusmodi fasciculum in humeris suis donec finiatur articulorum declaratio. Reliqua pars penitencie sue differtur in visitacionem quousque dominus decreverit eum vocare. Quo tempore habet in mandatis ad comparendum coram domino, ulteriorem penitenciam subiturum, si et quatenus domino videbitur expedire.

---

[a] fascili *deleted.*

[English translation]

[fo. 8r] Finally the same Flesshour, on the third [...] day of November, recognizing the errors [...] and spontaneously renounced every heresy and read the abjuration [...] and submitted himself to the Church's judgement. The bishop, after [...] taken by the said Thomas Flesshour [...] about obeying the Church's law and commandments, absolved him from the sentence of excommunication.

The bishop enjoined upon him that next Friday he shall go before the general procession in Coventry, carrying a faggot of wood on his shoulders until the procession finishes. And on the following Sunday he shall go likewise before the procession in St Michael's parish church, carrying a faggot of wood as above, and shall be present at the sermon there from beginning to end. And when the preacher orders it, at the time that the articles are declared, he shall raise the faggot to his shoulders until the declaration of the articles is finished. The rest of his penance is deferred until the bishop's visitation when he may decide to summon him. He is bound to appear before the bishop at that time, to undergo further penance, if and insofar as the bishop may decide.

[fo. 24v] Proceedings before the said reverend father in Maxstoke on 3 November in the aforesaid year of the Lord. On this day Thomas Flesshour of Coventry, smith, appeared before the said reverend father. The following articles were proposed against him and he swore corporally to reply faithfully to them.

First, we accuse and charge you, Thomas Flesshour of Coventry, smith, that you belong to our diocese of Coventry and Lichfield. He admits this.

Also, that you knowingly conversed with heretics and supporters of heresy and were often present at their readings. He admits this.

Also, that you supported their beliefs and held them, especially those of Roger Londesdale, Robert Silkby, Balthasar Shugborow, and others. He admits this.

Also that you often heard them teaching and speaking against the sacrament of the altar, the veneration of images, and pilgrimages to saints. He admits this.

Also, that you kept in your house books of forbidden readings and kept secret these and other books kept by others and did not reveal them to the ordinary. He admits this.

Also, that you received into your house persons suspected of heresy and spoke with them against the Church's sound doctrine both in your home and in other places. He admits this.

Also, that you were publicly and notoriously suspected and defamed of heresy in Coventry and other neighbouring places. He admits this.

Then, the said Thomas Flesshour read the following abjuration before the said reverend father. Present then and there were Sir William Dykons, Prior of the house or Priory of Maxstoke, Masters Ralph Cantrell, doctor of decrees, William Skelton and William Wilton, masters of arts, and John Blyth, bachelor of decrees, Brother Henry Eliot, subprior of the said priory, Henry Big, and others. In their presence he made underneath a sign of the cross in his own hand.

[*Reg. Blyth, fo. 98r*] Proceedings in the Priory of Maxstoke [...] by divine permission, Bishop of Coventry and Lichfield, on 3 November 1511 in the enquiry concerning heresy against Thomas Flesshor of Coventry, publicly defamed, detected, denounced, and accused of heresy. The following articles were proposed to him and he replied under corporal oath as follows.

First, we accuse and charge you, Thomas Flesshor of Coventry, smith, that you belong to our diocese of Coventry and Lichfield. He admits this.

Also, that you knowingly conversed with heretics and supporters of heresy and were often present at their readings. He admits this.

Also, that you supported their beliefs and held them, especially those of Roger Londesdale, Robert Sylkby, Balthasar Shugborough and others. He admits this.

Also, that you heard them often teaching and speaking against the sacrament of the altar, the veneration of images and pilgrimages to saints. He admits this.

Also, that you kept in your house books of forbidden readings and kept secret these and other books kept by others and did not reveal them to the ordinary. He admits this.

Also, that you received into your house persons suspected of heresy and spoke with them against the Church's sound doctrine both in your home and in other places. He admits this.

Also, that you were publicly and notoriously suspected and defamed of heresy in Coventry and other neighbouring places. He admits this.

Then, on the same day in the year of the Lord and in the place given above, the same Thomas Fleshor, recognizing his errors, spontaneously renounced them, and each and every heresy, and he read his abjuration as follows afterwards and submitted himself to the Church's judgement. The said reverend father, after Thomas Fleshor had guaranteed to obey the Church's law and commandments, absolved him from the sentence of excommunication.

And the bishop enjoined upon him that next Friday he shall go before the general procession in Coventry carrying a faggot of wood on his shoulders until the procession finishes. And on the following Sunday he shall go likewise before the procession in St Michael's parish church in Coventry, carrying a faggot of wood as above, and shall be present at the sermon there from beginning to end; and when the preacher orders it, at the time that the articles are declared, he shall raise the faggot to his shoulders until the declaration is finished. The rest of his penance is deferred until the bishop's visitation when he may decide to summon him. He is bound to appear before the bishop at that time, to undergo further penance, if and insofar as the bishop may decide.

Letter of Geoffrey Blyth, Bishop of Coventry and Lichfield, to William Smith, Bishop of Lincoln

[LCB, fo. 24r]

In my most hertie maner I recommend me unto your good lordshipp.

Please it the same to undrestond that by the confession of the most noted heretikes now found within my diocese I have knowleage that one John Davy payntour, late of Coventr' now dwelling in Leicestr', and another Richard Dowcheman of his occupation abiding with the seid John, as they reporte, hath been and yet be of ther dampnable opynyons as well ageinst the sacrament of the alter as pilgremages, wurshipping of ymages and other which your lordshipp at more leasure shall[a] playnely undrestond and have sufficient recorde to convicte them if they will denye.[62]

The broder of the forseid John is also detected by the confession of one man onely called Roger Landesdale, which affermeth that the seid John[b] and his brother hard hym at sundry tymes rede lectures of heresy.

There is also, as it is supposed, within your diocese one Sir Rafe Kent preiste, executour to one M. William Kent, late person of Staunton in Leicestre shyre,[63] which by his lief daies was maistr' of divers heretikes and had many books of heresy, which of liklyhod shuld cum to the hands of the seid Sir Rafe, stonding that he is executour to his seid uncle. He knewe well, as it is deposid by Robert Silkeby one of the chief heretikes here, that the same M. William Kent his uncle was an heretike with such other as com to hym and hard hym. And also the seid sir Rafe, aftre the deceas of the forseid M. William Kent, com to the seid Robert Sylkeby and showed hym that his uncle was departed, for whate entent your Lordship may enquyre farther. I praie God ye may cum to the seid books, for by such there be many corrupted.

They will not confesse but by payne of prisonment. And by such

---

[a] more *deleted*.
[b] is also detected *deleted*.

meanes I have gete to my hands right many dampnable books, which shall noye no more by Goddes grace, who kepe your good Lordship in good and long lief.

From Maxstock the iii^d daie of Novembre.

Prescriptas litteras dominus misit ad episcopum Lincoln'[64] anno Domini supradicto.

[English translation]

In my most hearty manner I recommend me unto your good Lordship.

Please it the same to understand that by the confession of the most noted heretics now found within my diocese I have knowledge that one John Davy, painter, late of Coventry, now dwelling in Leicester, and another Richard Dowcheman, of his occupation, abiding with the said John, as they report, have been, and yet be, of their damnable opinions as well against the sacrament of the altar as pilgrimages, worshipping of images, and other which your Lordship at more leisure shall[a] plainly understand and have sufficient record to convict them if they will deny.[62]

The brother of the foresaid John is also detected by the confession of one man only called Roger Landesdale, which affirms that the said John[b] and his brother heard him at sundry times read lectures of heresy.[b]

There is also, as it is supposed, within your diocese, one Sir Ralph Kent, priest, executor to one Master William Kent, late parson of Staunton in Leicestershire,[63] which by his life days was master of divers heretics and had many books of heresy, which of likelihood should come to the hands of the said Sir Ralph, standing that he is executor to his said uncle. He knew well, as it is deposed by Robert Silkeby, one of the chief heretics here, that the same Master William Kent, his uncle, was a heretic with such others as came to him and heard him. And also the said Sir Ralph, after the decease of the foresaid Master William Kent, came to the said Robert Sylkeby and showed him that his uncle was departed, for what intent your Lordship may enquire farther. I pray God ye may come to the said books, for by such there be many corrupted.

They will not confess but by pain of imprisonment. And by such means I have gotten to my hands right many damnable books, which shall annoy no more by God's grace, who keep your good Lordship in good and long life.

From Maxstock the third day of November.

---

^a more *deleted.*
^b is also detected *deleted.*

The bishop sent the above letter to the Bishop of Lincoln[64] in the aforesaid year of the Lord.

Tuesday, 4 November 1511

Joan Smyth

[LCB, fo. 4r]

iiii^{to} die mensis Novembris anno Domini supradicto.[a]

Johanna, annorum l^{ta} et ultra,[b] uxor Ricardi Smyth civitatis Coventr' mercer, nuper relicta Johannis Padland dicte civitatis capper, detecta super heresia, comparuit coram domino.

Et eadem iurata et examinata et cetera, primo fatebatur se opiniones hereticas tenuisse per spacium xi^{cem} annorum et quod Ricardus Landesdale, maritus suus primus, eam induxit ad huiusmodi hereses ad tres annos ante obitum eiusdem Ricardi.

Et dicit quod tempore elevacionis eucaristie non credidit ibi verum fuisse corpus dominicum sed panem substancialem.

Et fatetur se opiniones tenuisse contra peregrinaciones.

Eadem interrogata de libris de et super heretica pravitate, dicit quod diversos libros heresim continentes habuit et quosdam illorum tradidit custodie Rogeri Londesdale. Interrogata quare ita fecit, dicit ob illum finem quod non deprehenderentur in custodia sua.

Interrogata an novit vel credit se fuisse suspectam de et super heresi et diffamatam, fatetur articulum in toto.

Et recognovit coram domino varios libros qui in domo Rogeri[c] Londesdale inventi fuerant, quos dominus eidem Johanne ostendit, fuisse quondam libros[d] Ricardi[e] Londesdale, viri sui, et quod ipsa eosdem libros secum servavit a tempore obitus eiusdem Johannis[f] usque trimestre emensum.

Interrogata preterea an unquam[g] audivit alios ita dicentes, 'May a

---

[a] iiii^{to} die [...] supradicto *is the heading of the page.*
[b] annorum l^{ta} et ultra *interlined.*
[c] Rogeri *interlined.*
[d] Johannis *deleted.*
[e] Ricardi *interlined.*
[f] Johannis *[sic]; possibly a scribal error for* Ricardi.
[g] habuit verba vel *deleted.*

preiste make God todaie and ete hym and doo likewise tomorowe etc.',
fatetur et cetera.

Dicit preterea se quendam librum de passione Christi et Ada, ut
recolit,[a] magistro Longlond[65] ad tres septimanas preteritas deliberasse.

Et dicit quod quando Rogerus Londesdale legit eidem, ipsa in aulam,[b]
clauso ostio eiusdem, cum dicto Rogero intravit.

Et iacente ista deponente in cubili suo infirma, Alicia Rowley accessit
ad eam et, ostenso eidem Alicie per istam deponentem quod ipsa
tradidit quendam librum ut supra magistro Longlond, respondit eadem
Alicia, quantum recolit,[c] si ipse liber[d] nondum fuisset traditus, non esset
opus ut deliberaretur.

Fatetur etiam se opiniones[e] tenuisse contra ymagines.

[English translation]

4 November in the aforesaid year of the Lord.

Joan, aged fifty and more, wife of Richard Smyth, mercer of
Coventry, recently the widow of John Padland, capper of Coventry,
detected of heresy, appeared before the bishop.

Sworn and examined etc., first she admitted she had held heretical
beliefs for eleven years and that Richard Landesdale, her first husband,
drew her into these heresies three years before his death.

She says that, at the moment of the elevation of the Eucharist, she
did not believe the Lord's true body was there, but rather the substance
of bread.

She admits she held opinions against pilgrimages.

Asked about heretical books, she says she had various heretical books
and she handed some of them over to Roger Londesdale. Asked why
she did this, she says so that they would not be found in her keeping.

Asked whether she knows or believes she was suspected and defamed
of heresy, she admits all of this.

She acknowledged before the bishop that various books, which had
been found in Roger Londesdale's home and which the bishop showed
to her, had once belonged to Richard Londesdale, her husband, and
that she had kept these books with her from the time of John's[f] death
until three months ago.

---

[a] ut recolit *interlined.*
[b] aulam *interlined*; secretum cubiculum *deleted.*
[c] quantum recolit *interlined.*
[d] *illegible word deleted.*
[e] opiniones *interlined.*
[f] *possibly a scribal error for* Richard's.

Asked whether she heard others saying, 'May a priest make God today and eat him and do likewise tomorrow etc.', she admits this etc.

She says she delivered a book on Christ's passion and Adam, as she recalls, to Master Longlond[65] three weeks ago.

She says that when Roger Londesdale read to her, she entered into a hall with the doors closed.

When she lay ill in bed, Alice Rowley visited her, and when she told Alice that she had given a certain book as above to Master Longlond, Alice told her, as far as she remembers, that if the book had not yet been passed on, it would not be necessary to hand it over.

She also admits she held opinions against images.

Richard Gest senior

[LCB, fo. 4v. Undated. The examination likely took place 3 or 4 November 1511, since the entry follows the continuation of Thomas Bown's examination 3 November (above, p. 130), and Joan Smyth's examination, dated 4 November, is on the recto of the same folio (above, p. 141).]

Ricardus Gest senior de Byrmyngham etatis lx annorum et ultra, natus in Northfeld,[66] ubi et infra Brymyngham predict' moram [traxit] toto tempore vite sue.

Iuratus et examinatus, et primum an habuit conversacionem[a] seu communicacionem cum Thoma Bown et Roberto Hachet, fatetur se[b] communicacionem habuisse cum eisdem; et quod Hachet dogmatisavit eidem Ricardo de[c] eucaristia quod Christus tempore ascensionis sue ministravit corpus suum discipulis suis.

Interrogatus an unquam audivit eos dogmatisantes contra peregrinaciones et cetera ut supra, dicit quod sic; et quod[d] voluisset detegere huiusmodi communicationem[e] cum ipsi dixerunt, 'Ve illi per quem scandalum venit',[67] et cetera.

Interrogatus de libro continente heresim, dicit cum Jonson cutler. Interrogatus quare non denunciavit huiusmodi librum ordinario, dicit quod ratio sua in hac parte non sufficiebat sibi. Et fatetur quod novit librum fuisse de et super heretica pravitate confectum, relatu domini Thome Gest, filii sui, ut asserit. Interrogatus preterea quanto tempore

---

[a] cum *deleted.*
[b] habuisse *deleted.*
[c] corpore *deleted.*
[d] v' *deleted.*
[e] q' *deleted.*

remansit liber huiusmodi penes eum, dicit quod per spacium ferme trimestris.

Interrogatus ulterius an novit Johannem Jonson et Johannem Gest, filium suum, fuisse huiusmodi opinionis, dicit quod suspicatus est male de eis per annum, non tamen novit eos veraciter fuisse huiusmodi opinionis. Et dicit quod nunquam habuit fidem dogmatisationibus Hachet et Bown neque alicuius alterius et cetera.

[English translation]

Richard Gest senior of Birmingham, aged sixty and more, born in Northfield,[66] where and in Birmingham he has lived all his life.

Sworn and examined, and first whether he had conversation or communication with Thomas Bown and Robert Hachet, he admits he had communication with them; and that Hachet taught him, concerning the Eucharist, that Christ at the time of his ascension gave his body to his disciples.

Asked whether he ever heard them teaching against pilgrimages etc. as above, he says yes; and that he had wanted to reveal this communication when they said, 'Woe to that man by whom the scandal cometh',[67] etc.

Asked about a heretical book, he agrees with Jonson, cutler. Asked why he did not denounce the book to the ordinary, he says the matter was not sufficiently important to him, but he admits he knew the book was heretical on the report of Sir Thomas Gest, his son, as he says. Asked how long the book remained with him, he says for almost three months.

Asked whether he knew that John Jonson and John Gest, his son, were of this opinion, he says he suspected ill of them for a year but he did not know for certain that they were of this opinion. He says he never trusted the teachings of Hachet and Bown, nor of anyone else etc.

Balthasar Shugborow

[LCB, fo. 19v. The examination continues on 6 November 1511 (below, p. 171).]

iiii^to die Novembris anno Domini et loco supradictis.[a]

---

[a] iiii^to die [...] supradictis *is the heading of the page.*

Balthaser Shugborogh, generosus, parochie de Napton,[68] etatis quinquaginta annorum.

Iuratus et diligenter examinatus et primo de conversacione sua et presertim a tempore quo primum lapsus erat in heresim, dicit quod a xiiii^cim annis preteritis, solicitacionibus^a cuiusdam Johannis Smyth de Coventr' nunc mortui, ipse^b in huiusmodi heresim, videlicet contra sacramentum altaris, potestatem pape, episcoporum et aliorum, necnon contra ymaginum venerationes.

Et dicit quod Alicia Rowley habuit librum ad quinque vel sex annos preteritos de primario in Anglic', rubro velamine coopertum.

Dicit insuper Matheum Markland fuisse sue opinionis.

Idem dicit de Thoma Clerc hosier.

Dicit etiam quod Spon erat sepe in consortio suo. Non tamen novit an favebat aut tenuit opiniones huiusmodi.

Dicit etiam Johannem Clerc, hosier, in Erle strete[69] variisque in locis audivisse istum communicantem contra veram ecclesie doctrinam et favet opinionibus suis.

[English translation]

4 November in the year of the Lord and the place given above.

Balthasar Shugborogh, gentleman, of Napton parish,[68] aged fifty.

Sworn and carefully examined, and first about his conduct, especially from the time he first lapsed into heresy, he says from fourteen years ago, at the urgings of a certain John Smyth of Coventry, now dead, he fell into this heresy: namely, against the sacrament of the altar, the power of the Pope, bishops, and others, and against the veneration of images.

He says that for the last five or six years Alice Rowley had a primer in English in a red cover.

He says Matthew Markland was of his opinion.

He says the same about Thomas Clerc, hosier.

He says Spon was often in his company. However, he does not know whether Spon favoured or held these opinions.

He says he often heard John Clerc, hosier, in Earl Street[69] and various other places speaking against the Church's true teaching and he favours his opinions.

---

^a s *deleted.*
^b cum *deleted.*

Wednesday, 5 November 1511

Robert Silkby

[LCB, fos 8v, 3v. The examination on fo. 8v is continued from 28 October 1511 (above, p. 108). The material on fo. 3v is undated; it may have been a continuation of the record of his examination on 5 November or of his earlier examination (above, p. 102).]

Deinde iste examinatus denuo quinto die mensis Novembris anno Domini et loco supradictis, dicit quod quidam Wrixham de Coventr' habuit parvum librum de mandatis in Anglic' et parvum quaternum de evangeliis[a] sancti Johannis.

Et[b] dicit quod Johannes Davy, pictour apud Leicestriam, habuit librum illum quem iste a Gest habuit pro decem[c] [...] solidis.[d] Et liber ille erat super evangeliis et epistolis in Anglic'. Et habuit alium librum de evangeliis Mathei et aliud volumen de Apocalipsi de isto eodem.

Interrogatus de Roberto Peg,[e] Wrixham, Thomas Clerc hosier et Matheus Markelond, sunt eiusdem secte et opinionis.

Et credit Thomam Acton huiusmodi opinionis et secte esse, propterea quod plurimum conversabatur cum Alicia Rowley.

Dicit insuper quod Ranulphus textor de Allesley[70] habuit communicacionem cum isto sepius de et super opinionibus hereticis et cetera.

Thomas[f] Villers, ut credit, est de huiusmodi secta et opinionibus, propterea quod mater eius erat abiurata apud Leicestreiam[71] [...] in hac re, ut asserit.

Quedam[g] Agnes Yong, vidua [...] scissoris, que in filo faciendo iam agit dies suos [...] et spectant' ad Aliciam Rowley. Et circiter festum purificacionis [...] beate Marie [...][h] ultimum preteritum legit super quodam libro Mathei in domo [...] est Agne' [...], presente tunc ibidem isto Silkeby.

De[i] Johanne Clerc, hosier, dicit [...] credit est ipsius opinionis et

---

[a] evangeliis *sic.*
[b] Interrogat' de [...] et cetera *in margin.*
[c] libris *deleted.*
[d] [...] solidis *interlined.*
[e] Wxixh' *deleted.*
[f] Interrogat' Wrixham, Villers *in margin.*
[g] Agnes Yong *in margin.*
[h] *some illegible words interlined.*
[i] Johannes Clerc *in margin.*

secte cum aliis et cetera. Thomas[a] Clerc, ut asserit et putat, scit amplius deponere in hac re.

Et[b] dicit quod Spon, ut credit, est huius opinionis. Johannes[c] Jonson cutler, ut asserit, scit verum in hac parte dicere.

Dicit[d] quod Thomas Villers legit the Sykeman in clau[...] monasterii, sed tempus[e] ignorat.

Fatetur[f] de Thoma Warde, quod Ricardus Brown dixit sibi ipsum esse opinionis illorum et quod omnia novit. Hachet affirmat idem.[72]

Lyeff[g] est unus illius[h] illorum, ut Landesdale asseruit isti deponenti. Et Hachet idem asserit.

Dicit[i] insuper Ricardum Bradeley, Thomasinam uxorem eius, Thomam Villers et seipsum semell[j] interfuisse legendo in domo Ricardi Bradeley.[k]

David[l] Clerc, coryar, favebat eis et celabat opinione illorum, unusque illorum est. Robertus Hachet idem dicit.

Idem[m] ipse et Hachet dicunt de Longhold.

Thomas[n] Spenser habuit libros de Silkeby de epistolis Pauli ad ix annos preteritos. Prima familiaritas inter eos fuit in domo Hachet, ubi interfuit pater[o] ipsius Spenser, unacum isto deponente, qui egit penitenciam publicam post abiuracionem in Bristollia.

Dicit[p] quod filia Agnetis Yong, que scit bene legere, est eiusdem opinionis et, ut dicitur, copulabitur [...] Ricardo Dowcheman pictori apud Leicestr'.

Dicit[q] quod Katerina, uxor cuiusdam pistoris in Gosford strete[73] est eiusdem secte et instructa per magistram suam Aliciam Flaxrell.

Et bene novit Hawkyns per [...] esse illius opinionis.

---

[a] Interrogat' Thom' Clerc *in margin*.
[b] Spon *in margin*.
[c] Interrogat' Johann' cutler *in margin*.
[d] Villers *in margin*.
[e] g *deleted*.
[f] Warde *in margin*.
[g] Lyeff *in margin*.
[h] illius *sic*.
[i] Bradeley et Villers *in margin*.
[j] semell *interlined*.
[k] Thomas *deleted*.
[l] David *in margin*.
[m] Longhold *in margin*.
[n] Spenser *in margin*.
[o] ist *deleted*
[p] filia Agnetis Yong et Ricardus Dowcheman *in margin*.
[q] Katerina pistoris *in margin*.

[fo. 3v] Sylkeby[a]

Uxorem Bluet suspectam opinatur propterea quod famula erat uxoris Bentham et nulla alia de causa.

Dicit etiam quod male suspicatur de Rogero Bromley the bedder solummodo quia idem Bromley erat apprenticius cum magistro Forde.[74]

Et de uxore dicti Bromley, dicit quod Alicia Rowley rettulit[b] sibi eam esse sue opinionis.

Et preterea dicit quod interfuit uxor Bromley supranominati cum eo et dicta Alicia in domo matris Margarete in Mylne, audiendo communicacionem de et super heretica pravitate. Alicia[c] Rowley scit deponere.

De Agnete Yong et filia sua, dicit quod sepenumero audiverunt istum communicantem contra sacramentum et cetera. Et legente Alicia Rowley, filia dicte Agnetis eam correxit et legit continuo.

[English translation]

Then, examined again on 5 November in the year of the Lord and the place given above, he says that a certain Wrixham of Coventry had a small book of the Commandments in English and a small quire of St John's Gospels.

He says John Davy, painter in Leicester, had the book that he had from Gest for ten [...] shillings. The book was about the Gospels and Epistles in English. He had another book of Matthew's Gospels and another volume of the Apocalypse from the same person.

Asked about Robert Peg, Wrixham, Thomas Clerc, hosier, and Matthew Markelond, they are of the same sect and opinion.

He believes Thomas Acton is of this sect and opinion because he talked much with Alice Rowley.

He says Ralph, the weaver, of Allesley[70] often communicated with him about heretical beliefs etc.

Thomas Villers,[d] he believes, is of the same sect and opinions, because his mother abjured at Leicester[71] [...] in this regard, he says.

Agnes Yong, widow [...] of the tailor, who now passes her days in making thread [...] and looking at Alice Rowley. Around the last feast of the purification [...] of blessed Mary, [...] [she][e] read a book of

---

[a] Sylkeby *is the heading of the page. There is a hole in the MS before* Sylkeby, *so it is impossible to know whether a first name was once there.*

[b] isti *deleted.*

[c] Interrogat' Rowley *in margin.*

[d] Ask Wrixham, Villers *in margin.*

[e] She: *possibly* he; *the subject of the verb is not clear.*

Matthew in the house [...] is Agnes [...], in the presence there of Silkby.

About John Clerc, hosier, he says [...] he believes he is of the same opinion and sect with the others etc. Thomas Clerc,[a] as he says and thinks, knows well what to say in this matter.

He says that Spon, he believes, is of the same opinion. John Jonson, cutler,[b] he says, knows the truth in this matter.

He says that Thomas Villers read *The Sick Man* in the cloister [...] of a monastery but he does not know when.

He says of Thomas Warde, that Richard Brown told him that Thomas is of their opinion and he says that Thomas knows all. Hachet affirms the same.[72]

Lyeff is one of them, as Landesdale told this deponent. And Hachet says the same.

He says that Richard Bradeley, Thomasina his wife, Thomas Villers, and he were once together reading in Richard Bradeley's home.

David Clerc, currier, supported them and concealed their beliefs and he is one of them. Robert Hachet says the same.

He and Hachet say the same about Longhold.

Thomas Spenser had from Silkeby books of St Paul's Letters nine years ago. They first became friends in Hachet's house, when this deponent was also present, along with Spenser's father, who did public penance after abjuring in Bristol.

He says that Agnes Yong's daughter, who can read well, is of the same opinion and, as it is said, will marry [...] Richard Dowcheman, painter at Leicester.

He says that Katherine, the wife of a miller in Gosford Street,[73] belongs to the same sect and was taught by her mistress Alice Flaxrell.

He knows well that Hawkyns [...] is of the same opinion.

[fo. 3v] Sylkeby

He thinks that Bluet's wife is suspect because she was the servant of Bentham's wife and for no other reason.

He thinks ill of Roger Bromley, the bedder, only because the same Bromley was an apprentice with Master Forde.[74]

Of the wife of the said Bromley, he says that Alice Rowley told him that she is of her opinion.

He says that the wife of the said Bromley was present with him and the said Alice in the house of Mother Margaret in Mylne, hearing them talk about heresy. Alice[c] Rowley can testify.

Concerning Agnes Yong and her daughter, he says that they often

---

[a] Ask Thomas Clerc *in margin.*
[b] Ask John cutler *in margin.*
[c] Ask Rowley *in margin.*

listened to him speaking against the sacrament etc. And while Alice
Rowley was reading, Agnes's daughter corrected her and immediately
read herself.

Thomas Acton

[*LCB, fo. 20r*]

Quinto die mensis Novembris anno Domini et loco.[a]

Thomas Acton civitatis Coventr' purser etatis quinquaginta annorum
et ultra, natus in Cestr',[75] ubi et in Coventria per totum vite sue tempus
continuam moram traxit.

Iuratus et examinatus et cetera, dicit quod sepe audivit Aliciam
Rowley sepius communicaciones habuisse in domo istius deponentis
infra iiii[or] annos preteritos de epistolis et evangeliis; et inter cetera
dogmatisasse quod non esset offerendum ymaginibus, ymmo potius
distribuendum pauperibus.

Dicit preterea quod ad tres annos elapsos quidam notorie diffamatus,
ut ipse in vernacula profert a knowen man, ad destinationem Alicie
Rowley[b] venit ad domum istius deponentis, ubi hospitatus erat duabus
noctibus, et moram traxit in Coventria per quinque vel sex dies. Ad
quem[c] accessit dicta Alicia et communicacionem habuit cum eodem in
profundis scripturis. Et Silkby itidem aggressus est eum et traduxit eum
secum, donando sibi par sotularium seu ocrearum.

Nec potest iste deponens ire inficiari quin audivit dictam Aliciam et
Bown communicantes de libro vocato Apocalipsi infra duos annos, ut
recolit.

Et dicit dictam Aliciam eum primo ad huiusmodi sectam allexisse et
provocasse.[d] Cui quidem secte, ut asserit, duobus annos non favebat sed
prorsus renunciavit eidem. Nec unquam male sentiebat de sacramento
altaris, ut affirmat.

Dicit preterea se semper solitum fuisse confiteri doctori Preston, fratri
minori.[76] Et fatetur se habuisse librum a dicta Alicia, quem tradidit
eidem infra triennium.

---

[a] Quinto [...] loco *is the heading of the page.*
[b] per *deleted.*
[c] venit *deleted.*
[d] Aj *deleted.*

[English translation]

5 November in the year of the Lord and the place.

Thomas Acton of Coventry, purser, aged fifty and more, born in Chester,[75] where and in Coventry he has lived continuously all his life.

Sworn and examined etc., he says he often heard Alice Rowley speaking in his house during the last four years about the Epistles and Gospels; and she taught, among other things, that money should not be offered to images but rather should be given to the poor.

He says that three years ago a notoriously defamed person – a known man, as he said in the vernacular – came, on his way to Alice Rowley, to this deponent's house, where he was given hospitality for two nights, and then he stayed for five or six days in Coventry. Alice Rowley came to him and conversed with him about the deepest scriptures. Silkby also met him and took him with him, giving him a pair of shoes or leggings.

The deponent cannot deny he heard the said Alice and Bown talking about the book called Apocalypse within the last two years, as he remembers.

He says that the said Alice first attracted and drew him to the sect. For two years he has not favoured the sect, he says, but rather has wholly rejected it. Nor did he ever think ill of the sacrament of the altar, he says.

He says he was always accustomed to confess to Doctor Preston, friar Minor.[76] He admits he had a book from the said Alice, which he handed back to her within three years.

Robert Peg

[LCB, fo. 20r. Undated. Follows Thomas Acton's examination dated 5 November (above, p. 150) and is resumed on 6 November 1511 (below, p. 173).]

Robertus Pegge civitatis Coventr' pictor etatis xxx annorum, natus in Coventria ubi moram traxit omni tempore vite sue.

Iuratus et examinatus et cetera, dicit quod sepe interfuit communicationibus Londesdale, Hachet et Bown. Et audivit eos proferentes verba contra sacramentum altaris, peregrinationes et sanctorum veneraciones. Negavit tamen se fuisse opinionis eorundem. Et continuo Robertus Hachet affirmabat in facie sua quod ipse didicit heresim apud Vies,[77] quod non potuit negare idem Robertus Pegge.

Et tunc fatebatur ipse Pegge quod xii^{cem} annis preteritis venit a Vies ad Coventriam.

[English translation]

Robert Peg of Coventry, painter, aged thirty, born in Coventry where he lived all his life.

Sworn and examined etc., he says he was often present at the conversations of Londesdale, Hachet, and Bown. He heard them speaking against the sacrament of the altar, pilgrimages, and the veneration of saints. But he denied he shared their opinions. Robert Hachet, however, immediately said to his face that he learnt heresy in Devizes,[77] which the same Robert Pegge could not deny.

Pegge then admitted that twelve years ago he came from Devizes to Coventry.

Matthew Markelond

[LCB, fo. 20v]

Quinto Novembris.[a]

Matheus Markland civitatis Coventr' fullo etatis lviii° annorum, natus in Hawton,[78] ubi et in civitate Coventr' toto vite sue tempore moram traxit.

Iuratus et examinatus, dicit quod fuit huiusmodi secte cum Landesdale et aliis. Sed renunciavit eidem secte, ut asserit,[b] diebus domini Halse[79] eo tempore quo Smyth et alii erant abiurati;[80] et quod tunc cremavit librum quem[c] in Anglic' de evangeliis habuit. Et dicit se favisse omnibus ipsis opinionibus quas Londesdale tenuit, sed eisdem omnibus et singulis tunc expresse renunciavit et abiuravit.

[English translation]

5 November.

Matthew Markland of Coventry, fuller, aged fifty-eight, born in Hawton,[78] where and in Coventry he lived all his life.

Sworn and examined, he says he belonged to the same sect with Landesdale and others. But he renounced the sect, he says in the time

---

[a] Quinto Novembris *is the heading of the page.*
[b] dict' *deleted.*
[c] habuit *deleted.*

of Bishop Halse,[79] when Smyth and others abjured;[80] and he then burnt the book of the Gospels in English which he had. He says he had favoured all the beliefs that Londesdale held but he then expressly renounced and abjured all of them.

Joan Gest

[LCB, fo. 20v]

Quinto Novembris.[a]

Johanna, uxor Johannis Gest junioris, de Byrmyngham, etatis xl annorum, nata in Abbots Bromley.[81]

Iurata et examinata et cetera, dicit quod erat famula cuidam Johanni Smyth scissoris civitatis Coventr'. Qui quidem Johannes eam primo ad hereticam pravitatem allexit et provocavit.

Et fatetur quod opinionem de peregrinationibus non fiendis tenuit. Et dubitabat de sacramento altaris, propterea quod audivit dictum Johannem dicentem, 'Faber lignarius domum, non domus fabrum, fabricat', et sic de creatore et presbitero.

Interrogata quis primo instruxit maritum suum in huiusmodi opinionibus erroneis, videlicet contra sacramentum altaris et cetera, dicit quod ipsa eum primo informavit in ea parte.

Et dicit quod parata est iam ad renunciandum huiusmodi hereses et submittendum se iudicio ecclesie.

Interrogetur Gest junior de conversacione Willelmi [...] manentis in Napton[82] in [...].[83]

[English translation]

5 November.

Joan, wife of John Gest junior, of Birmingham, aged forty, born in Abbots Bromley.[81]

Sworn and examined etc., she says she was the servant of a certain John Smyth, tailor, of Coventry, who first attracted and drew her into heresy.

She admits she held the opinion that pilgrimages should not be made, and she doubted the sacrament of the altar because she heard the said John saying, 'The carpenter makes the house, the house does

---

[a] Quinto Novembris *is a heading.*

not make the carpenter', and likewise regarding the Creator and a priest.

Asked who first instructed her husband in these erroneous opinions, namely against the sacrament of the altar etc., she says that she first informed him in this matter.

She says she is now ready to renounce these heresies and to submit herself to the Church's judgement.

Gest junior is asked about the conduct of William [...] living in Napton[82] in [...].[83]

John Gest

[LCB, fo. 25v. Undated. Conjectured that he was examined the same day as his wife, Joan (above, p. 153) and the same day as he abjured (below, p. 165).]

Johannes Gest junior de Byrmyngham, sutor, etatis xxx annorum et ultra, natus in Brymyngham predicta, ubi moram traxit toto vite sue tempore.

Interrogatus de conversacione sua, dicit et fatetur quod circiter xi annos elapsos, solicitacionibus Johanne uxoris sue, incidit in heresim – videlicet contra sacramentum altaris, peregrinaciones et venerationes ymaginum – et recitavit epistolam Pauli in Anglic' de caritate et evangelium in quo diabolus tentat Deum et cetera.[84]

Et dicit uxorem suam opinionem tenere contra decimas, dicendo huiusmodi decimas non debere prestari presbiteris.

Interrogatus de conversacione sua cum Johanne Jonson cutler, dicit quod multotiens communicacionem habuit secum in epistolis et evangeliis.

Nec potest negare quin favebat opinionibus eorum ut supra.

[English translation]

John Gest junior of Birmingham, shoemaker, aged thirty and more, born in Birmingham, where he has lived all his life.

Asked about his conduct, he says and admits that, about eleven years ago, at the promptings of his wife Joan, he fell into heresy – namely against the sacrament of the altar, pilgrimages, and the veneration of images – and he recited Paul's Letter on charity in English, and the Gospel in which the devil tempts God etc.[84]

He says his wife held a belief against tithes, saying that these tithes should not be paid to priests.

Asked about his relations with John Jonson, cutler, he says he often spoke with him about the Epistles and Gospels.

Nor can he deny that he supported their opinions as above.

Alice Rowley

[LCB, fos 6v, 7r, 5r. Continued from 31 October 1511 (above, p. 123). As the scribe ran out of room on fo. 6v, he apparently first moved to fo. 7r (keyed for insertion by a letter 'T') and then onto the bottom of fo. 5r. The assignment of this last section on fo. 5r to Alice Rowley's deposition is somewhat insecure (the witness is not identified), but on balance it seems probable. The style and marginal notes are similar to what has followed before in Rowley's testimony on 5 November, and evidence is offered about Rowley's conversations with her servant, the wife of Roger Bromley, in Mother Margaret's house, a matter concerning which Silkby had, earlier the same day, suggested that Rowley could depose (see above, p. 148).]

[fo. 6v] Sed postea, quinto die mensis Novembris anno Domini et loco supradictis, eadem Alicia, comparens coram domino, fatebatur se purgacionem fecisse de et super heretica pravitate. Et dicit quod[a] uxores Duddesbury, Haddon, Butler et cetere ad numerum xvi erant compurgatrices sue.[85]

Interrogata quinam erant libri quos dedit Johanne Smyth[b] ante adventum suum ad dominum, dicit quod unus erat psalterium in Anglic' et alius de mandatis. Et[c] dicit se misisse ad dominum post recessum eiusdem Alicie a Beaudesert[86] per Willelmum Alen[87] duos libros, unum de mandatis, alium de epistolis Jacobi.

Interrogata de illo [...] quem Acton vocat a knowen man, noluit veritatem fateri.

Fatetur[d] [...] de Agnete Yong, prout continetur in deposicione Silkby.

Dicit[e] preterea [...] mansisse apud New Yate[88] huius opinionis cuius nomen scit Flesshour [...].

Et fatetur se tenuisse quod decem peccata venialia faciunt mortale peccatum.

Interrogata preterea an verba habuit cum aliquo contra sacramentum altaris vel audivit aliquem alium contra huiusmodi sacramentum dogmatisasse, negat.

---

[a] quod *interlined.*
[b] de *deleted.*
[c] Notatur pro Willelmo Alen *in margin.*
[d] Agnes Yong *in margin.*
[e] Interrogat' Flesshour *in margin.*

Interrogata an habuit huiusmodi verba, 'How can the preiste make God?', fatetur.

Et fatetur articulum de libris traditis magistro Longland, prout continetur in deposicione Johanne uxoris Ricardi Smyth.

Fatetur insuper se in domo Londesdale unacum Hachet audivisse Londesdale[a] legentem et cetera a tempore quo idem Londesdale migravit ad domum in quo iam inhabitat.

Dicit preterea se dogmatisasse contra oblaciones ymaginibus fiendas et cetera et contra peregrinaciones.

Dicit[b] quod Spon infra quaternium anni cum ipsa emeret carnes ab eo, allocutus est eam de lege. Et Hachet novit optime de eo et quod est illius opinionis.

Hawkyns,[c] skynner, est illius opinionis et erat cum Landesdale, Silkby, Hachet et Bown familiaris.

Uxor[d] Acton est etiam eiusdem secte et bene novit de communicacione inter istam deponentem et virum suum.

Magister[e] Bayly[89] ostendebat isti librum de 4^{or} evangeliis. Et dicit eum esse eiusdem opinionis et Katherinam Garton.[f]

Idem[g] dicit de Agnete Corby.

Dicit quod, ut credit, due filie Johanne Smyth sunt illius secte. Nam uni illarum librum tradidit matri sue deliberandum ad septimanas ad adventum suum ad me.

Dicit[h] etiam quod Bradley et Bambrooke cum uxoribus suis, filiabus Villers, sunt eiusdem opinionis.

Dicit[i] idem de Spenser [...] Northopp cum uxore, filia uxoris Smyth, pro certo idem affirmat.

Et ulterius dicit quod habuit communicaciones cum Bradley et[j] uxore, que fuit filia Villers.[k]

[fo. 7r][l] Dicit[m] quod Bradeley, veniens ad eam pro filo ad preculas et cetera,[n] sepe intravit in secretum locum cum ea et communicacionem

---

[a]   Londesdale *interlined;* Hachet *deleted.*
[b]   Spon *in margin.*
[c]   Hawkyns interrogat' *in margin.*
[d]   uxor Acton *in margin.*
[e]   Bayly *in margin.*
[f]   Katerina Garton *in margin.*
[g]   Corby *in margin.*
[h]   Bradley, Banbrooke cum uxoribus suis *in margin.*
[i]   Spenser, Northopp, [...] filie Smyth *in margin.*
[j]   Villers *in margin.*
[k]   *The letter* T *follows in the margin. The deposition continues at the bottom of fo. 7r, indicated in the margin by another letter* T.
[l]   *A* T *in the margin marks the insertion of this text.*
[m]   Bradeley *in margin.*
[n]   et cetera *interlined.*

habuit. Et dixit deberemus oblaciones facere ymagini Dei, qui est homo, non autem ad ymagines manu hominis factas. Et ultimo huiusmodi communicacionem habuit in autumpno.

Dicit[a] quod Banbrooke,[b] tempore quo heretici erant abiurati apud Leicestriam,[90] mutuo tradidit isti librum de evangeliis. Quem librum, ut recolit, ipsa mutuatus[c] est cuidam Dawson; ob quod idem Banbrooke obiurgavit eam.

Et Rogerus Cutler,[91] Johanna Smyth et ipsa simul intraverunt in domum[d] Banbrooke, ubi[e] ista legebat, Banbrooke presente, in libro evangeliorum. Robertus Bastell ibidem interfuit.

Dicit[f] quod Spenser et Bradeley sunt in magna[g] familiaritate.

De[h] uxore Acton, dicit quod audivit istam communicantem in domo ipsius Acton sepius in causis hereticis, presente Acton.

Audivit quod Northopp est eiusdem secte. Qui erat[i] serviens Johanne Smyth, cuius filiam duxit.

Interrogata de eo qui erat incarceratus cum Silkby pro receptione cuiusdam Duke, qui erat crematus apud Banbury.[92]

Dicit quod vicarius iam mortuus, videlicet doctor Preston,[93] habuit librum ab ea de nova lege, quem restituit eidem denuo. Et favebat eidem et ceteris, ut asserit.

Uxor[j] Willelmi Revis,[k] skynner, que est pye maker, ut ista[l] audivit ab Hawkyns, est eiusdem secte. Et Hawkyns audivit eam sepe[m] verba habentem sonantia heresim in ortis et vico prope fratres minores.[94]

Magistra Cooke[95] novit secreta sua, quia consiluit eidem ut omnes libros suos deleret.

Hawkyns magnus est cum Bown.

Sepe[n] communicavit cum Abell.

Derlyng,[o, 96] infestus est presbiteris et multum loquitur contra ecclesiam, dicendo quod presbiteri omnia possident et omnino elati sunt.[p]

---

[a] Banbrooke *in margin.*
[b] ad *deleted.*
[c] mutuatus: *sic, error for* mutuata.
[d] Londesdale *deleted.*
[e] ip *deleted.*
[f] Spenser *in margin.*
[g] s *deleted*
[h] Northopp, uxor Acton *in margin.*
[i] *MS.* erant.
[j] Revis, Hawkyns *in margin.*
[k] ser' *deleted.*
[l] ut ista *interlined.*
[m] e' *deleted.*
[n] Abell *in margin.*
[o] Ee(?) Clerc, Derlyng *in margin.*
[p] *illegible letter/word deleted.*

Dicit quod suspicio laborat contra filiam Agnetis Brown, nuptam Dawney, et Thomam Brown.

De Davy Clerc coryer, Hawkyns scit deponere.

Fatetur[a] de Elizabeth Gest quod est eiusdem opinionis et ista habuit communicacionem cum matre sua contra peregrinationes et cetera.

Dicit[b] quod Rise shomaker ad xx[ti] annos elapsos [...] isti librum de mandatis.

De[c] uxore Lye, quondam relicta Lodge, dicit quod audivit male de ea.

[fo. 5r][d] Agnes[e] de Bakehouse interfuit vigesies cum Rowley, Silkby et moder Margaret.

Credit[f] quod Revis est eiusdem opinionis et secte. Cum quo communicationem habuit in domo cuiusdam chaundeler in grere freres lane[97] de et super opinionibus suis hereticis post sermonem factam.

Dicit[g] uxorem Bluet, quondam servientem Bentham,[h] esse suspectam.

Balthaser[i] scit et Johanna Warde dicit quod moder Agnes dixit sibi ipsam esse unam.

Famula[j] Rowley,[k] uxor Rogeri Bromley the bedder, est eiusdem secte et vir suus reputatur unius illorum; propterea sed quod servus magistri Forde erat. Et eadem uxor sepe fuit in communicacione cum ea in domo matris Margarete.

Et credit quod Johannes Harris, frater uxoris Bluet, esse eiusdem opinionis; propterea quod servus erat Johannis Tailiour heretici.

Dicit[l] quod Hebbis is such a man and M. John the phisicion showed him soo.

Dicit[m] quod Cropwell semel audivit istam et Bown communicantes in navi ecclesie prioratus Coventr' de huiusmodi opinionibus.

---

[a] Inquirat' Gest *in margin.*
[b] Rise *in margin.*
[c] uxor Lye *in margin.*
[d] *see the beginning of this section regarding the insertion of this text here.*
[e] Agnes de Bakehous' *in margin.*
[f] Revys *in margin.*
[g] uxor Bluet *in margin.*
[h] quondam servientem Bentham *interlined.*
[i] Interrogat' Baltheser *in margin.*
[j] uxor Bromley *in margin.*
[k] Famula Rowley *interlined.*
[l] Hebbys *in margin.*
[m] Cropwell *in margin.*

[English translation]

[fo. 6v] Afterwards, on 5 November in the year of the Lord and the place given above, the same Alice, appearing before the bishop, admitted she had purged herself of heresy. She says that the wives of Duddesbury, Haddon, Butler, and others to the number of sixteen were her compurgators.[85]

Asked which were the books she gave to Joan Smyth before her appearance before the bishop, she says one was a psalter in English and another was of the Commandments. She[a] says that, after she had left Beaudesert,[86] she sent to the bishop, through William Alen,[87] two books, one of the Commandments, the other of James's Epistles.

Asked about the man [...] whom Acton calls a knowen man, she was unwilling to tell the truth.

She admits [...] of Agnes Yong, as is contained in Silkby's deposition.

She[b] also says [...] to have stayed at New Gate,[88] of this opinion, whose name Flesshour knows [...].

She admits she held that ten venial sins make a mortal sin.

Asked whether she spoke against the sacrament of the altar or heard anyone else teaching against the sacrament, she denies this.

Asked whether she spoke the words, 'How can the priest make God?', she admits this.

She also admits the article about the books brought to master Longland, as is contained in the deposition of Joan, the wife of Richard Smyth.

She admits she heard Londesdale reading etc. in his house together with Hachet from the time Londesdale moved to the house in which he now lives.

She says she taught against making offerings to images etc. and against pilgrimages.

She says that within the last three months when she would buy meat from Spon, he spoke to her about the law. Hachet knows best about him and that he is of that opinion.

Hawkyns,[c] skinner, is of that opinion and was familiar with Landesdale, Silkby, Hachet, and Bown.

Acton's wife belongs to the same sect and knows well the communication between the deponent and her husband.

Master Bayly[89] showed her a book of the four Gospels. She says he is of the same opinion, and so is Katherine Garton.

She says the same about Agnes Corby.

---

[a] Noted for William Alen *in margin.*
[b] Ask Flesshour *in margin.*
[c] Ask Hawkyns *in margin.*

She says that, as she believes, the two daughters of Joan Smyth belong to the sect. For she brought a book to one of them to be given to her mother for the weeks until she came to me.

She says that Bradley and Bambrooke and their wives, Villers's daughters, are of the same opinion.

She says the same about Spenser [...] Northopp and his wife, the daughter of Smyth's wife, she affirms the same for certain.

She says she communicated with Bradley and his wife, who was Villers's daughter.[a]

[fo. 7r] She says that Bradeley, when he came to her for thread for beads etc., often entered into a secret place with her and talked. He said we ought to make offerings to the image of God, which is the human person, and not to images made by humans. They last communicated in this way in the autumn.

She says that Banbrooke, at the time when the heretics abjured in Leicester,[90] gave her on loan a book of the Gospels. She lent the book, as she remembers, to a certain Dawson, and for this the same Banbrooke rebuked her.

Roger Cutler,[91] Joan Smyth, and she went together to Banbrooke's house and there she read, in Banbrooke's presence, a book of the Gospels. Robert Bastell was present there.

She says that Spenser and Bradley are very familiar.

Of Acton's wife, she says she often heard her talking in Acton's house about heretical things, in Acton's presence.

She heard that Northopp belongs to the sect. He was the servant of Joan Smyth, whose daughter he married.

She was asked about the man who was imprisoned with Silkby for receiving a certain Duke, who was burned in Banbury.[92]

She says that the vicar who is now dead, namely Doctor Preston,[93] had a book of the New Testament from her, which he eventually returned to her. He favoured her[b] and the others, she says.

The wife of William Revis, skinner, who is a piemaker, as she heard from Hawkyns, belongs to the same sect. Hawkyns ofter heard her speaking words savouring of heresy in gardens and in the lane near the friars Minor.[94]

Mistress Cooke[95] knows her secrets since she advised her to destroy all her books.

Hawkyns is intimate with Bown.

She often communicated with Abell.

---

[a] *The letter* T *follows in the margin. The deposition continues at the bottom of fo. 7r, indicated in the margin by another letter* T.

[b] her: *MS* eidem; *possibly means* it (the book).

Derlyng[96] is hostile to priests and speaks much against the church, saying that priests own everything and are extremely proud.

She says there is suspicion against Agnes Brown's daughter, the wife of Dawney, and against Thomas Brown.

About Davy Clerc, currier, Hawkyns can testify.

About[a] Elizabeth Gest, she admits she is of the same opinion and she talked with her mother against pilgrimages etc.

She says that Rise, shoemaker, twenty years ago [...] a book of the Commandments to her.

About Lye's wife, formerly the widow of Lodge, she says she heard ill of her.

[fo. 5r] Agnes de Bakehouse was twenty times with Rowley, Silkby, and Mother Margaret.

She believes that Revis is of the same opinion and sect. She communicated with him about her heretical opinions, after a sermon, in the house of a chandler in Grey Friars Lane.[97]

She says Bluet's wife, who was once Bentham's servant, is suspect.

Balthasar[b] knows, and Joan Warde says, that Mother Agnes told her that she is one.

Rowley's servant, the wife of Roger Bromley, the bedder, belongs to the same sect. Her husband is reckoned one of them, for he was Master Forde's servant. The same wife often communicated with her in Mother Margaret's house.

She believes that John Harris, the brother of Bluet's wife, is of the same opinion, for he was the servant of John Tailiour, heretic.

She says that Hebbis is such a man, and Master John the physician showed him so.

She says that Cropwell once heard her and Bown talking about these opinions in the nave of the church of the Priory in Coventry.

Joan Smyth

[LCB, fo. 22v; Reg. Blyth, fo. 98v. The following interrogatory is virtually identical in form to other formulae of enquiry, all probably based on that ministered to Thomas Flesshor (see pp. 135, 165 and 175). The formulaic nature of this questionnaire, despite its attribution in the heading to Joan Smyth, is indicated by the blank space where the name was to be inserted and by the grammatically masculine gendering of the abjurer. Note also that the last two paragraphs below refer to 'each and every one' of those whose names were recorded on the abjuration on fo. 23r (including Joan Smyth herself, below, p. 271), and so it is likely that

---

[a] Inquire [about?] Gest *in the margin.*
[b] Ask Balthasar *in margin.*

the questionnaire was used for each of these suspects, whose abjurations took place between 5 November 1511 and 24 January 1512.]

[fo. 22v] Johanne uxori Ricardi Smyth Coventr', quinto Novembris.[a]

In primis objicimus et articulamur tibi [...][b] quod tu es nostre Coventr' et Lich' diocesis.

Item, quod tu scienter cum variis personis, quos hereticos seu[c] de heretica pravitate[d] suspectos fuisse aut esse novisti, conversacionem sepius habuisti et lecturis eorundem multotiens interfuisti. Fatetur.

Item, quod tu eosdem contra sacramentum altaris, peregrinaciones atque ymaginum veneraciones dogmatisare et verba sepius habere audivisti. Fatetur.

Item, quod tu opinionibus eorundem erroneis scienter favisti easque tenuisti. Fatetur.

Item, quod tu scienter libros reprobate lecture in domo tua tenuisti; eosque, vel saltem tales penes alios existentes, celavisti et ordinario non denunciasti. Fatetur.

Item, quod tu scienter suspectos de heresi in domo tua recepisti; et cum eisdem communicasti atque conversatus[e] fuisti contra sanam ecclesie doctrinam. Fatetur.

Item, quod tu in civitate Coventr' et aliis locis eidem convicinis de et super huiusmodi heretica pravitate palam, publice et notorie suspectus et diffamatus[f] extas. Fatetur.

Eadem Johanna, recognoscens se hereticam fuisse et contra sanam ecclesie doctrinam sensisse, saniori ducta consilio, volens iam ad unitatem ecclesie redire, huiusmodi heresi et opinionibus hereticis ac aliis omnibus male sonantibus prorsus renunciavit et abiuravit et signum crucis manu sua propria [...].

Lecta fuit huiusmodi abiuracio die mensis, anno Domini et loco[g] in folio sequente specificatis,[98] presentibus tunc ibidem omnibus et singulis quorum nomina in eodem folio continetur.

Et sciendum est[h] quod omnibus abiuratis solemniter iniunctum fuit [...] ut non conversentur neque familiaritatem [...] illorum[i] haberent, sub pena relapsus.

[fo. 98v] Acta habita in prioratu de Maxstocke coram domino episcopo

---

[a] Johanne [...] Novembris *is the heading of the page.*
[b] *blank space in MS.*
[c] hereticos seu *interlined.*
[d] hereticos seu saltem *deleted.*
[e] conversatus *[sic] in MS.*
[f] suspectus et diffamatus *sic in MS.*
[g] sup *deleted.*
[h] est *interlined.*
[i] illorum *interlined.*

antedicto, quinto die mensis Novembris anno Domini millesimo quingentesimo undecimo, in negocio inquisitionis heretice pravitatis contra
Johannam, uxorem Ricardi Smyth civitatis Coventr'.[a]

In primis objicimus et articulamur tibi Johanne, uxori Ricardi Smyth
civitatis Coventr', quod tu es nostre Coventr' ac Lich' diocesis. Fatetur.

Item, quod tu scienter cum variis personis, quos hereticos seu de
heretica pravitate suspectos fuisse et esse novisti, conversacionem sepius
habuisti et lecturis eorundem multociens interfuisti. Fatetur.

Item, quod tu eosdem contra sacramentum altaris, peregrinaciones
atque ymaginum veneraciones dogmatizare et verba sepius habere
audivisti. Fatetur.

Item, quod tu opinionibus eorundem erroneis scienter favisti easque
tenuisti. Fatetur.

Item, quod tu scienter libros reprobate lectionis et lecture in domo
tua tenuisti; eosque, vel saltem tales penes alios existentes, celavisti et
ordinario non denunciasti. Fatetur.

Item, quod tu scienter suspectos de heresi in domum tuam recepisti;
et cum eisdem communicasti atque conversata fuisti contra sanam
ecclesie doctrinam. Fatetur.

Item, quod tu in civitate Coventr' et aliis locis eidem convicinis de
et super huiusmodi heretica pravitate palam, publice et notorie suspecta
et diffamata extas. Fatetur.

Quibus articulis eidem declaratis, obiectis et confessis, eadem
Johanna, recognoscens se hereticam fuisse et contra sanam ecclesie
doctrinam sensisse, saniori ducta consilio, volens iam ad unitatem
ecclesie redire, huiusmodi heresi et opinionibus hereticis ac aliis omnibus
male sonantibus prorsus renunciavit et abiuravit. Et signum crucis manu
sua propria signavit ceteraque fecit prout continetur in abiuracione
Flesshour. Et habet consimilem penitenciam cum Flesshour peragendam
et cetera, quam fecit.

[English translation]

[fo. 22v] To Joan, the wife of Richard Smyth of Coventry, 5 November.

First, we accuse and charge you [...][b] that you belong to our diocese
of Coventry and Lichfield.

Also, that you knowingly and often conversed with various persons
whom you knew to be heretics or to have been suspected of heresy
and you frequently attended their readings. She admits this.

Also, that you often heard the same persons teaching and speaking

[a] Acta [...] Coventr' *is the heading.*
[b] *blank space in MS.*

against the sacrament of the altar, pilgrimages, and the veneration of images. She admits this.

Also, that you knowingly favoured and held their erroneous opinions. She admits this.

Also, that you knowingly kept books of forbidden readings in your house: and these, or at least some kept by others, you kept secret and did not denounce to the ordinary. She admits this.

Also, that you knowingly received into your house persons suspected of heresy: and you communicated and conversed with them against the Church's sound teaching. She admits this.

Also, that you are openly, publicly, and notoriously suspected and defamed of heresy in Coventry and other neighbouring places. She admits this.

The same Joan, acknowledging that she had been a heretic and had thought contrary to the Church's sound teaching, led by sounder counsel and wishing now to return to the Church's unity, wholly renounced and abjured this heresy, and heretical and all other ill sounding opinions: and [...] the sign of the cross in her own hand.

The abjuration was read on the day of the month and in the year of the Lord and the place specified on the next folio;[98] present then and there were each and every one of those whose names are mentioned on the same folio.

Let it be known that all those who abjured were solemnly enjoined [...] that they should not converse nor be familiar [...] of them, under pain of relapse.

[fo. 98v] Proceedings in the Priory of Maxstoke before the said Lord Bishop on 5 November 1511 in the enquiry concerning heresy against Joan, the wife of Richard Smyth of Coventry.

First, we accuse and charge you Joan, the wife of Richard Smyth of Coventry, that you belong to our diocese of Coventry and Lichfield. She admits this.

Also, that you often conversed with various persons whom you knew to be heretics or to have been suspected of heresy and you often attended their readings. She admits this.

Also, that you often heard the same persons teaching and speaking against the sacrament of the altar, pilgrimages, and the veneration of images. She admits this.

Also that you knowingly favoured and held their opinions. She admits this.

Also, that you knowingly kept in your house books of forbidden readings and these, or at least some kept by others, you kept secret and did not denounce to the ordinary. She admits this.

Also, that you knowingly received into your house persons suspected of heresy and you communicated and conversed with them against the Church's sound teaching. She admits this.

Also, that you were openly, publicly and notoriously suspected and defamed of this heresy in Coventry and other neighbouring places.

After these articles had been declared and charged to her and confessed, the same Joan, acknowledging that she had been a heretic and had thought contrary to the Church's sound teaching, led by wiser counsel, and wishing now to return to the Church's unity, wholly renounced and abjured this heresy, and heretical, and all other ill sounding opinions. She drew a sign of the cross with her own hand and did the other things that are mentioned in Flesshour's abjuration. She has to undergo the same penance with Flesshor etc., which she did.

Roger Landesdale, Robert Hachet, Thomas Bown, John Atkynson, Robert Peg, Thomas Acton, John Gest, and Joan Gest

[LCB, fo. 23v. Although this formula and record of abjuration are dated 5 November, it may have been administered to some or all of the abjurers on 6 November – Robert Peg's examination, for instance, continued on 6 November, and another abjuration recorded for him on that day (below, pp. 173, 175–176), and the records of abjuration in Blyth's register are dated 6 November (below, pp. 169 and 177). See below, p. 266, for the abjuration these suspects signed.]

Quinto die Novembris et cetera.[a]

In primis objicimus et articulamur tibi [...][b] quod tu es nostre Coventr' et Lich' diocesis.

Item, quod tu scienter cum variis personis, quas de heresi suspectas fuisse seu saltem hereticos[c] esse novisti, communicationem sepius hab-uisti et lecturis eorundem multotiens interfuisti.

Item, quod tu eosdem contra sacramentum altaris, peregrinaciones atque ymaginum veneraciones dogmatisare et verba sepius habere audivisti.

Item, quod tu contra sacramentum altaris, peregrinaciones atque ymaginum venerationes sepe[d] et scienter dogmatisasti atque opinionem in hac parte perversam et erroneam[e] tenuisti.

---

[a] Quinto [...] cetera *is the heading of the page.*
[b] *blank space in MS.*
[c] fuisse *deleted.*
[d] dog *deleted.*
[e] et erroneam *interlined.*

Item, quod tu scienter libros reprobate lecture in domo tua tenuisti; eosque, vel saltem tales in custodia aliorum existentes, celavisti et ordinario non denunciasti.

Item, quod tu scienter suspectos de heresi in domum tuam recepisti; et cum eisdem communicavisti et conversatus fuisti contra sanam ecclesie doctrinam.

Item, quod tu in comitatu Warwic' et presertim in Coventria ac aliis locis eidem convicinis de et super huiusmodi heresi palam, publice et notorie suspectus et diffamatus extas.

Isti articuli suprascripti erant ministrati Rogero Landesdale, Roberto Hachet, Thome Bown, Johanni Atkynson, Roberto Pegge, Thome Acton, Johanni Gest parochie de Brymyngham^a et Johanne uxore sue, singillatim. Et Landesdale, Hachet, Bown, Atkynson, Gest et Johanna uxor eius fatebantur ipsos omnes et singulos. Peg et Acton ita fatebantur omnes^b preter iii^{um} et quartum.

Et submiserunt se omnes et singulos iudicio sancte matris ecclesie et opinionibus suis hereticis renunciaverunt atque abiuraverunt ut sequitur, quilibet in persona sua.

Et ipsis per dominum absolutis, iniuncta erat eadem^c penitencia publica que^d continetur in penitencia Thome Flesshour.

Et iniuncta erat^e consimilis penitencia Johanni Gest et Johanne uxori sue, peragenda in ecclesia de Byrmyngham^f per unum diem Dominicum proximum sequentem. Et reliqua pars penitencie ex parte mulieris differtur sub spe se bene gerende erga [...] ecclesiam et^g maritum suum.

Lecta fuit huiusmodi abiuratio et signa crucis subscripta quinto die mensis anno Domini et loco supradictis, coram dicto reverendo patre, presentibus tunc ibidem venerabilibus et discretis viris dompno Willelmo Dikons, priore de Maxstock, magistris Radulpho Cantrell, decretorum doctore, Willelmo Skelton et Willelmo Wilton, artium magistris, Thoma Barker et Johanne Blyth, in decretis bacallariis, fratribus Thoma Danyell et David Jacob de ordine Observant', cum nonnullis aliis, et cetera.

---

^{a} parochie de Brymyngham *interlined.*
^{b} omnes *interlined.*
^{c} eadem *interlined.*
^{d} que *interlined*; prout *deleted.*
^{e} iniungit *deleted;* iniuncta erat *interlined.*
^{f} in ecclesia de Byrmyngham *interlined.*
^{g} uxorem *deleted;* [...] ecclesiam et *interlined.*

[English translation]

5 November etc.

First, we accuse and charge you [...]^a that you belong to our diocese of Coventry and Lichfield.

Also, that you often knowingly communicated with various persons whom you knew to have been suspected of heresy, or at least to be heretics, and you often attended their readings.

Also, that you often heard the same persons teaching or speaking against the sacrament of the altar, pilgrimages, and the veneration of images.

Also, that you often and knowingly taught against the sacrament of the altar, pilgrimages, and the veneration of images, and you held a perverse and erroneous opinion in this matter.

Also, that you knowingly kept books of forbidden readings in your house, and these, or at least some kept by others, you concealed and did not denounce to the ordinary.

Also, that you knowingly received into your house persons suspected of heresy, and you communicated and conversed with them against the Church's sound teaching.

Also, that you are openly, publicly, and notoriously suspected and defamed of this heresy in the county of Warwick, and especially in Coventry and other neighbouring places.

The above articles were presented individually to Roger Landesdale, Robert Hachet, Thomas Bown, John Atkynson, Robert Pegge, Thomas Acton, John Gest of Birmingham parish, and Joan his wife. Landesdale, Hachet, Bown, Atkynson, Gest, and Joan his wife admitted each and every one of them. Peg and Acton admitted all of them except the third and fourth.

Each and every one of them submitted himself or herself to the judgement of Holy Mother Church, and they renounced and abjured their heretical opinions as follows, each one in person.

And after they had been absolved by the bishop, the same public penance as is contained in the penance of Thomas Flesshour was enjoined.

And the same penance was enjoined on John Gest and Joan his wife, to be performed in Birmingham Church on the following Sunday. The rest of the woman's penance was deferred in the hope of her good conduct towards [...] the Church and her husband.

The abjuration was read and the signs of the cross were subscribed on the fifth day of the month in the year of the Lord and the place

^a *blank space in MS.*

given above, before the said reverend father, in the presence then and there of the venerable and prudent men, Sir William Dikons, Prior of Maxstoke, Masters Ralph Cantrell, doctor of decrees, William Skelton, and William Wilton, masters of arts, Thomas Barker and John Blyth, bachelors in decrees, brothers Thomas Danyell and David Jacob of the Observant order, and others, etc.

Richard Hyde

[LCB, fo. 23v. This undated passage appears at the bottom of fo. 23v, following other material dated 5 November 1511. There is no evidence that Hyde was a Lollard; it seems rather that he was simply negligent in his observances of orthodoxy.]

That is to sey, bicause I have moste parte of this xxii yeres not cum to the chirche, hering divyne service as a true cristen man oght to doo, ne being confessed nother receiving the blessed sacrement of the aulter,[a] and ouer this seyeng not my Pater noster, Ave and Credo, ne yet takyng holy brede ne holy water as I oght to doo.

+

Ricardus Hyde

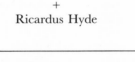

[English translation]

That is to say, because I have most part of these twenty-two years not come to the church, hearing divine service as a true Christian man ought to do, nor being confessed neither receiving the blessed sacrament of the altar, and over this not saying my Our Father, Hail Mary and Creed, nor yet taking holy bread nor holy water as I ought to do.

+

Richard Hyde

---

[a]   *illegible word deleted.*

Thursday, 6 November 1511

Roger Landesdale, Robert Hachet, Thomas Bown, John Atkynson, Matthew Markelond, Thomas Acton, Robert Peg, John Gest, and Joan Gest

[Reg. Blyth, fo. 99r. Dated 'the 6th day of the month' following the entry for Joan Smyth, dated 5 November 1511 (see above, p. 161). See also above, p. 165 for a record of abjuration attributed to the same accused – with the exception of Matthew Markelond – on November 5. See also below, pp. 173–174, 175–177 for Robert Peg. See below, p. 266, for the abjuration these suspects signed.]

Item, vi^{to} die mensis et anni Domini suprascriptorum apud Maxstock predicta, Rogerus Landesdale, Robertus [Hachet], Thomas Bown, Johannes Atkynson,[a] Matheus Markeland et Thomas Acton civitatis Coventr', [...] detecti super crimine heretice pravitatis, comparuerunt coram dicto reverendo patre. Et tandem ministratis articulis suprascriptis, fatebantur omnes et singulos preter iii^{um} et quartum, quos Markeland, Pegge[b] et Acton penitus negaverunt.

Similiter Johannes Gest parochie de Brymyngham et Johanna uxor eius dictis die et loco comparentes, ipsos articulos omnes et singulos confessi publice in iudicio.

Quare prenominatus reverendus pater, post humiles submissiones omnium et singulorum supranominatorum, renunciatis primitus per eos omnibus et omnimodis opinionibus hereticis, factaque per eos singillatim abiuracione quemdadmodum continetur in abiuracione Flesshor – preterque a Markeland et Acton, qui tercium et iiii^{tium} articulos prorsus negaverunt – et signo crucis per quemlibet ipsorum sub nomine suo subscripto, iniunxit eis consimilem penitenciam cum Flesshor peragendam.

Johannes tamen Gest et uxor eius habent penitenciam suam in ecclesia parochiali de Brymyngham peragendam. Et uxor eius unicum tamen diem habet in casu quo bene se gerat erga maritum suum et ecclesiam imposterum; alioquin equam penitenciam cum Flesshor, ut prefertur, habet et cetera.

Quam penitenciam omnes et singuli suprascripti postea humiliter peregerunt et cetera.

Lecta erat abiuracio illorum die et loco suprascriptis, presentibus tunc ibidem venerabilibus et discretis viris dompno Willelmo Pollesworthe

---

[a] C *deleted.*
[b] Pegge *interlined.*

ecclesie cathedralis Coventr' et Willelmo Dykons[a] de Maxstocke, prioribus, necnon magistris Radulpho Cantrell, decretorum doctore, Willelmo Skelton, Willelmo Wylton, artium magistris, Thoma Barker et
Johanne Blyth, in decretis bacallariis, necnon Thoma Danyell et David
Jacobi, fratribus de ordine Observant', cum nonnullis aliis.

[English translation]

On the 6th day of the aforesaid month and year of the Lord at the
said Maxstoke, Roger Landesdale, Robert [Hachet], Thomas Bown,
John Atkynson, Matthew Markeland, and Thomas Acton of Coventry,
[...] detected regarding the crime of heresy, appeared before the said
reverend father. After the articles mentioned above had been presented,
they admitted each and every one of them except the third and fourth
which Markeland, Pegge, and Acton wholly denied.

Likewise John Gest of Birmingham parish and Joan his wife, appearing on the aforesaid day and in the aforesaid place, publicly confessed
in the court each and every one of the articles.

Following, therefore, the humble submissions of each and every one
of the above named, after they had renounced each and every one of
the heretical opinions, after they had individually made an abjuration
as is contained in Flesshor's abjuration – except Markeland and Acton
who wholly denied the third and fourth articles – and after each of
them had made a sign of the cross underneath his or her name, the
said reverend father enjoined upon them the same penance as Flesshor.

John Gest and his wife, however, are to do their penance in
Birmingham parish church. His wife, moreover, has only one day if
afterwards she conducts herself well towards her husband and the
Church; if not, she has the same penance as Flesshor, as stated above,
etc.

Each and every one of the above named subsequently humbly
performed the penance etc.

Their abjuration was read on the day and in the place given above,
in the presence of the venerable and prudent men, the Lords William
Pollesworthe of Coventry Cathedral church and William Dykons of
Maxstoke, priors, and Masters Ralph Cantrell, doctor of decrees,
William Skelton, William Wylton, masters of arts, Thomas Barker and
John Blyth, bachelors in decrees, and Thomas Danyell and David
Jacob, friars of the Observant order, and several others.

---

[a] P *deleted.*

Balthasar Shugborow

[LCB, fo. 19v; Reg. Blyth, fo. 99r. Examination in LCB continued from 4 November 1511 (above, p. 144). The record in Blyth's register is dated 'the same day', following an entry dated 6 November (see previous entry). For Shugborow's abjuration, see below, p. 273.]

[fo. 19v] Tandem vi^{to} die mensis antedicti, idem Balthaser Shugborow huiusmodi heresi atque opinionibus hereticis omnibus et singulis per eum iudicialiter confessis prorsus coram domino renunciavit. Atque eisdem omnibus et singulis ac aliis quibuscumque contra veram ecclesie doctrinam sanam^a palam et publice tunc ibidem abiuravit, submittens se iudicio sancte matris ecclesie. Lecta per eum^b abiuracione ut supra, dominus, prestita per dictum Balthaser caucione de parendo iuri et perimplendo penitenciam iniungendam, eundem Balthaser ab excommunicacionis [sentencia] absolvit.

Et iniunxit eidem quod die Dominica proxima sequente in ecclesia cathedrali sua Coventr' coram^c processione ibidem eat, portando fasciculum in humeris suis. Et finita processione, conferat se ad ecclesiam parochialem sancti Michaelis, et ibidem intersit toto tempore sermonis, et ad mandatum predicantis ibidem levet fasciculum suum cum aliis.^d Reliqua pars penitencie sue differtur in adventum domini tempore visitacionis sue proxime. Et iniungitur eidem ut eo tempore aggrediatur dominum ad ulterius audiendum voluntatem domini et cetera.

Et^e continuo idem Balthaser fatebatur quod Thomas Spenser civitatis Coventr', mercer, est huiusmodi secte et opinionis. Et audivit istum legentem heresim circa xii^{cem} annos preteritos. Et favebat opinionibus suis, ut supra.

Et dicit se audivisse quod Warde erat eiusdem secte et quod Silkby ita retulit sibi.

[Reg. Blyth, fo. 99r] Eisdem die et loco Balthasar Shugborowe parochie de Napton, detectus ut supra, comparuit coram pretexato reverendo patre.

Qui ministratos articulos supraspecificatos omnes et singulos, iuramento oneratus ad fideliter respondendum eisdem, publice fatebatur tunc in iudicio, humiliter se submittens iudicio sancte matris ecclesie. Lectaque per eum abiuracione ut supra ac prestita caucione de parendo

---

^a renu' *deleted.*
^b eum *interlined.*
^c ibidem *deleted.*
^d Reliq *deleted.*
^e Spenser *in margin.*

iuri et perimplendo penitenciam eidem iniungendam, dominus eum a sentencia excommunicacionis absolvit.

Et iniunxit eidem penitenciam subscriptam. Videlicet, quod die Dominica proxima sequente in ecclesia sua cathedrali Coventr' procedat processionem ibidem, fasciculum ligneum humeris suis deportando. Finitaque processione, conferat se ad ecclesiam parochialem sancti Michaelis Coventr' predictam et intersit ibidem unacum aliis supranominatis toto sermonis tempore, atque ad mandatum predicantis levet fasciculum suum cum aliis.

Reliquam partem penitencie sue dominus distulit in tempus proxime visitacionis sue. Quo tempore iniungitur eidem quatenus accedat personaliter ad dictum reverendum patrem, decretum suum in hac parte ulterius ponendum – si et quatenus dicto reverendo patri videbitur expediens – auditurus et cetera.

[English translation]

[fo. 19v] Finally, on the 6th day of the aforesaid month, Balthasar Shugborow wholly renounced before the bishop this heresy and each and every heretical opinion that he had confessed in the trial. Then and there, he openly and publicly abjured all of them and any others against the Church's true and sound teaching, submitting himself to the judgement of Holy Mother Church. After he had read the abjuration as above, and after the said Balthasar had guaranteed to obey the law and to perform the penance that would be enjoined, the bishop absolved the same Balthasar from [the sentence] of excommunication.

The bishop enjoined upon him that on the next Sunday he should go in front of the procession in his Cathedral church of Coventry, carrying a faggot on his shoulders. At the end of the procession he shall go to St Michael's parish church and stay there throughout the sermon, and, when the preacher orders him, he shall raise his faggot with the others. The rest of his penance is deferred until the bishop's next visitation. He is enjoined to come to the bishop at that time in order to hear further the bishop's will etc.

Straightaway, the same Balthasar admitted that Thomas Spenser of Coventry, mercer, is of the same sect and opinion. He heard him reading heresy about twelve years ago; and he favours his opinions, as above.

He says he heard that Warde belonged to the same sect and Silkby told him so.

[Reg. Blyth, fo. 99r] On the same day and in the same place Balthasar

Shugborowe of Napton parish, detected as above, appeared before the said reverend father.

Under oath to reply truthfully, he publicly confessed in the court to each and every one of the above articles as they were proposed to him, humbly submitting himself to the judgement of Holy Mother Church. After he had read the abjuration, as above, and guaranteed to obey the law and to perform the penance that would be enjoined upon him, the bishop absolved him from the sentence of excommunication.

The bishop enjoined upon him the following penance. On the next Sunday he shall go in front of the procession in his Cathedral church of Coventry, carrying a faggot of wood on his shoulders. At the end of the procession, he shall go to St Michael's parish church in Coventry and stay there throughout the sermon with the others named above, and, when the preacher gives the order, he shall raise his faggot with the others.

The bishop deferred the rest of his penance until his next visitation. He is enjoined to come in person to the bishop at that time to hear etc. his further decision in the matter if and insofar as it seems expedient to the bishop.

Robert Peg

[LCB, fo. 20r. Continued from examination of 5 November 1511 (above, p. 000); dated 'the 6th day of the aforesaid month', following in the MS Thomas Acton's examination dated 5 November (above, p. 150). See below, p. 273, for Peg's abjuration.]

Deinde vi^{to} die mensis antedicti prenominatus Robertus Pegge, denuo coram domino comparens, dixit quod quidam Christoferus, sutor, tunc manens apud Vies, dogmatisavit sibi quod non crederet dictis presbiterorum qui, incontinenter viventes, falsum predicant. Et audivit dictum Christoferum legentem sibi in epistolis Pauli et evangeliis in vernacula.ᵃ Qui vero Christoferus, ut asserit, erat postea ignibus traditus.⁹⁹

Et idem Robertus Pegge preterea dixit quod postquam accessit iterum ad Coventriam, mediis et solicitacionibus Thome Bown et Sylkby inductus erat in heresim et opiniones suprascriptas.

Quos errores, hereses et opiniones fatebatur se tenuisse et eisdem credidisse. Eisdem tunc omnibus et singulis atque aliis quibuscunque contra sanam ecclesie doctrinam sonantibus coram domino renunciavit et abiuravit, ut [...], seque iudicio ecclesie humiliter submisit. Absolutus

ᵃ P *deleted.*

itaque et iuratus de perimplendo penitenciam, iniungitur eidem penitencia publica prout continetur in penitencia Thome Flesshour.

[English translation]

Then, on the 6th day of the aforesaid month, the said Robert Pegge,
appearing again before the bishop, said that a certain Christopher,
shoemaker, then living at Devizes, taught him that he should not
believe the sayings of priests, who, living incontinently, preach falsely.
And he heard Christopher reading to him Paul's Letters and the
Gospels in English. Christopher, he says, was later burnt.[99]

Robert Pegge also said that after he had come again to Coventry,
he was led into heresy and the above mentioned heretical opinions by
means of and through the solicitations of Thomas Bown and Sylkby.

He admitted that he had held and believed in these errors, heresies
and opinions. Then he renounced and abjured before the bishop each
and every one of them and any others contrary to the Church's sound
teaching, [...], and he submitted himself to the Church's judgement.
He was, therefore, absolved. And after he had sworn to perform the
penance, the public penance was enjoined on him as is contained in
Thomas Flesshour's penance.

Ralph Lye

[LCB, fo. 21r. See below, p. 273, for the abjuration Lye signed.]

vi^{to} Novembris.[a]

Ranulphus Lye, textor apud Allesley, etatis circiter quinquaginta
annorum, natus, ut asserit, in civitate Cestr' et nutritus apud Coventriam, ubi et in Allesley moram pro maiori parte vite sue moram^{b}
traxit.

Iuratus et examinatus et cetera, dixit quod audivit quendam Ste-
phanum^{c} Frayne, Silkby, Hachetts et Bown sepenumero dogmatisantes
et verba habentes tam contra sacramentum altaris, ymaginum venerationes et peregrinationes, ut supra in depositionibus aliorum latius
continetur. Et fatebatur se huiusmodi opinionibus atque heresi credidisse.

---

[a] vi^{to} Novembris *is the heading of the page.*
[b] moram *repeated in MS.*
[c] *illegible letter deleted.*

Quibus omnibus et singulis atque aliis huiuslibet contra catholicam fidem male sonantibus tunc ibidem coram domino palam et aperte prorsus renunciavit et abiuravit, submittendo se iudicio sancte matris ecclesie.

[English translation]

6 November

Ralph Lye, weaver in Allesley, aged about fifty, born, he says, in Chester and brought up in Coventry, where and in Allesley he has lived for most of his life.

Sworn and examined etc., he said he heard a certain Stephen Frayne, Silkby, Hachetts and Bown often teaching and speaking against the sacrament of the altar, the veneration of images and pilgrimages, as is contained more fully above in the depositions of others. He admitted he believed in opinions and heresy of this kind.

Then and there he wholly renounced and abjured, openly and publicly before the bishop, each and every one of them and any others contrary to the Catholic faith, submitting himself to the judgement of Holy Mother Church.

Balthasar Shugborow, Robert Peg, and Ralph Lye

[LCB, fo. 25v. As with the other examples of interrogatories, this formula of enquiry may or may not have applied specifically to the suspects named in the final paragraph, but note that the third and fourth articles (which Robert Peg is said to have denied, above, pp. 166 and 169) are marked out by the letters 'B' and 'a' in the margin, perhaps indicating that they were to be omitted in Peg's case. The 'subsequent abjuration' referred to in the final paragraph is probably that appearing on fo. 22r (below, p. 273), signed by these three men.]

In primis objicimus et articulamur tibi [...]ᵃ quod tu es nostre Coventr' et Lich' diocesis. Fatetur.

Item, quod scienter cum variis personis, quos de heresi novisti suspectos atque hereticos esse, conversacionem sepius habuisti et lecturis eorundem multotiens interfuisti. Fatetur quamlibet partem articuli.

Item,ᵇ quod opinionibus eorundem erroneis favisti easque tenuisti. Fatetur quamlibet articuli partem.

ᵃ *blank space in MS.*
ᵇ B *in margin.*

Item,[a] quod tu eosdem contra sacramentum altaris, ymaginum venerationes atque peregrinaciones dogmatisare et verba sepius habere audivisti. Fatetur.

Item, quod tu scienter[b] libros reprobate lectionis in domo tua tenuisti eosque, vel saltem tales in custodia aliorum existentes, celavisti et ordinario non denunciasti. Fatetur.

Item, quod tu scienter[c] suspectos de et super heretica pravitate in domum tuam recepisti, et cum eisdem conversatus fuisti et communicasti contra sanam ecclesie doctrinam. Fatetur.

Item, quod tu in civitate Coventr' et aliis locis eidem convicinis de et super huiusmodi heretica pravitate palam, publice et notorie diffamatus [...] suspectus [...]. Fatetur.

Lecta fuit subsequens abiuratio per Balthaser Shukburgh, Robertum Peg et Ranulphum Lye et cetera coram domino apud Maxstock vi[to] die mensis Novembris anno Domini supradicto. Presentibus tunc ibidem venerabilibus et discretis viris dompnis Willelmo Pollesworthe ecclesie cathedralis Coventr',[d] et Willelmo Dykons prioratus de Maxstock, prioribus, necnon magistris Radulpho Cantrell, decretorum doctore, Willelmo Skelton et Willelmo[e] Wilton, artium magistris, Thoma Barker [...][f] et Johanne Blyth in decretis bacallariis, fratribus Thoma Danyell et David Jacobi fratribus Observantibus, cum nonnullis aliis et cetera.

[English translation]

First we propose that you [...][g] that you belong to our diocese of Coventry and Lichfield. He admits this.

Also, that you knowingly and often conversed with various persons whom you knew to have been suspected of heresy and to be heretics, and you often attended their readings. He admits each part of the article.

Also,[h] that you supported their erroneous opinions and held them. He admits each part of the article.

---

[a] a *in margin.*
[b] scienter *interlined.*
[c] scienter *interlined.*
[d] priore *deleted.*
[e] Willelmo *repeated in MS.*
[f] *blank space in MS.*
[g] *blank space in MS.*
[h] B *in margin.*

Also,[a] that you heard them teaching and often speaking against the sacrament of the altar, the veneration of images and pilgrimages. He admits this.

Also, that you knowingly kept in your house books of forbidden readings, or at least you concealed some kept by others, and did not denounce them to the ordinary. He admits this.

Also, that you knowingly received into your house persons suspected of heresy and you conversed and communicated with them against the church's sound teaching. He admits this.

Also, that you are openly, publicly and notoriously defamed [...] suspected [...] of this heresy in Coventry and its neighbourhood. He admits this.

The following abjuration was read by Balthasar Shukburgh, Robert Peg, and Ralph Lye etc. before the bishop at Maxstoke on 6 November in the aforesaid year of the Lord. Present then and there were the venerable and prudent men, the Lords William Pollewsorthe of Coventry Cathedral church and William Dykons of Maxstoke Priory, priors, and Masters Ralph Cantrell, doctor of decrees, William Skelton and William Wilton, masters of arts, Thomas Barker [...][b] and John Blyth, bachelors in decrees, brothers Thomas Danyell and David Jacob, Observant friars, and several others etc.

Ralph Lye and Robert Peg

[Reg. Blyth, fo. 99r. This entry is undated. Although it follows material dated 3 December 1511 (after a gap), it has been dated here to 6 November 1511 due to the date of abjuration recorded in LCB (preceding entry). See p. 273 for their abjuration.]

Ranulphus Lye parochie de Allesley cum Roberto Pegge supranominato consimilem confessionem publice in iudicio emisit.

Abiuravit et renunciavit opinionibus suis et cetera.

Habetque penitenciam cum Silkeby, unica tamen die, et cetera.[c]

---

[a] a *in margin.*
[b] *blank space in MS.*
[c] Ranulphus Lye parochie [...] *deleted at the foot of the page.*

[English translation]

Ralph Lye of Allesley parish with the above named Robert Peg made the same confession publicly in the court.

He abjured and renounced his opinions etc.

And he has the penance with Silkeby, but one day only, etc.

Monday, 17 November 1511

Joan Warde *alias* Wasshingburn

[LCB, fos 21r, 20v]

xvii° die Novembris anno Domini supradicto.[a]

Johanna Warde alias Wasshingburn civitatis Coventr' etatis circiter lx annorum, detecta, impetita et accusata super crimine heretice pravitatis.

Comparens et iurata atque examinata ut supra, dicit quod apud Maydeston' erat accusata de et super huiusmodi heresi xvi annis elapsis et abiurata erat[b, 100]

Fatebatur se habuisse communicationem cum Alicia Rowley, Rogero Landesdale, Roberto Sylkby, Hachette et Bown contra sacramentum altaris.

Interrogata quantum tempus effluxit a tempore huiusmodi conversationis, dicit quod annus preteriit.

Et fatetur quod infra triennium emensum habuit[c] pessimam communicationem contra sacramentum altaris, peregrinationes et ymaginum venerationes. Et domino interrogante nomina aliorum cum quibus conversabatur, subiunxit: 'Quia certum est quod moriar culpis exigentibus, nolite spiritum meum inquietare.'

Deinde interrogata an unquam penituit, respondit quod sic.

Ulterius[d] interrogata de[e] causa residivationis sue,[f] dixit quod carentia[g] gracie erat potissima causa residivationis sue huiusmodi.

---

[a] xvii° [...] supradicto *is the heading.*
[b] *a gap of two or three lines follows in the MS.*
[c] h *deleted.*
[d] rogata *deleted.*
[e] interrogata de *interlined.*
[f] *illegible word deleted.*
[g] g' *deleted.*

Et[a] dicit preterea quod Silkby tradidit ei unum librum parvum de mortuo aut egrotante, ut recolit, dicendo quod esset optimus liber, ad duos annos elapsos. Quem librum ista deponens tradidit Abell et cetera, et Abell asserens nescire legere dixit quod voluit efficere ut per alium legeretur.

Dicit[b] etiam quod Agnes Jonson de Spon Cawsey[101] infra triennium legit in libro de mandatis isti deponenti.

Idem[c] dicit de Agnete Corby, non ad lecturam sed ad conversacionem. Quidam[d] Yate, scissor, intimavit isti deponenti quod dominus maximo favore prosecutus est Agnetem Corby.

Erat[e] quedam Rosa, famula Hachetts, eiusdem secte. Quam Agnes Jonson instruxit, ut credit. Et manet dicta Rosa apud Atherston.[102]

Et[f] deponit quod Silkby dixit ad eam, biennio elapso,[g] quod Laurentius Dawson est nunc in civitate et est bonus socius.

Et[h] audivit Bown dicentem quod Warde erat huiusmodi secte. Tunc illa, 'Vade ergo ad illum et mutua corium ab eodem in auxilium tuum si talis fuerit.'

De[i] Lieff, dicit se credere quod duxit in uxorem filiam uxoris Landesdale. Quod si sic, dicit quod est eiusdem opinionis et cetera. Et Hachet fatetur idem de dicto Lieff.[103]

Audivit[j] Longhold esse suspectum et est de [...] Landesdale

Fatetur[k] insuper quod Agnes de Bakehouse est eiusdem secte.

Et[l] Agnes Margareta[m] White, serviens Rowley is of the same breking in tantum quod dicit, 'I wuld have my husband of thi mynde'.

De[n] uxore Londesdale plane fatetur.[o]

[fo. 20v] Dicit[p] quod Agnes Brown in Weston Hard,[104] quondam uxor Thome Brown,[q] cuius frater erat pessimus, rettulit sibi quod erat in

[a] Abell *in margin.*
[b] Agnes Jonson, litle moder Agnes *in margin.*
[c] Corby *in margin.*
[d] Yate *in margin.*
[e] Rosa/Banbrooke serviens est *in margin.*
[f] Laurentius Dawson *in margin.*
[g] biennio elapso *interlined.*
[h] Warde *in margin.*
[i] Lyeff *in margin.*
[j] Longhold *in margin.*
[k] Agnes de Bakehouse *in margin.*
[l] Agnes White *in margin.*
[m] Margareta *interlined above* Agnes.
[n] uxor Landesdale *in margin.*
[o] *The letter 2 follows. The deposition continues at the bottom of fo. 20v, indicated in the margin by another letter 2, and then returns to fo. 21r again.*
[p] Agnes Brown *in margin.*
[q] pessim' *deleted.*

societate cum magistro Bayly. Et ista deponens hospitabatur cum eadem Agnete ad tres septimanas, cum quibus Johannes Jonson cutler[a] conversabatur.

Dicit[b] se audivisse moder Agnetem dicentem quod uxor Thome Clerc est illius opinionis. Et dixit isti deponenti: 'Quare non venis domum? Sponsus meus habet optimum librum'.

Dicit[c] quod audivit Hachet et Flesshour dicentes quod Katerina Revis et sponsus sunt eiusdem secte.

Elizabeth[d] Gest, filia Agnetis Corby, fuit sepius in communicacione cum ipsa.

Uxor[e] Willelmi Grey, filia litle modre Agnes, est [...]. Et credit quod prima uxor dicti Willelmi superstes est.

[fo. 21r] Hawkyns,[f] ut audivit ab aliis, est fautor hereticorum et est in magna familiaritate cum Alicia Rowley.

Katerina,[g] uxor cuiusdam pistoris in Gosford strete,[105] dixit isti deponenti se esse confessam magistro Flemmyng[106] quod non bene credebat de sacramento altaris. Et venit ad quendam Tuke cum Sylkby primum deprehensus erat et rogabat eundem quatenus declareret Silkby [...] coram vicario.

[English translation]

17 November in the aforesaid year of the Lord.

Joan Warde *alias* Wasshingburn of Coventry, aged about sixty, detected, charged, and accused concerning the crime of heresy.

Appearing and sworn and examined as above, she says that she had been accused of this heresy in Maidstone sixteen years ago and she had abjured.[h, 100]

She admitted she communicated with Alice Rowley, Roger Landesdale, Robert Sylkby, Hachette, and Bown against the sacrament of the altar.

Asked how long ago this conversation was, she says a year ago.

She admits that within the last three years she took part in a wicked conversation against the sacrament of the altar, pilgrimages, and the

---

a cutler *interlined.*
b uxor Thome Clerc *in margin.*
c Revis et uxor *in margin.*
d Elizabeth Gest *in margin.*
e filia litle modre Agnes *in margin.*
f Hawkyns *in margin.*
g Katerina *in margin.*
h *a gap of two or three lines follows in the MS.*

veneration of images. When the bishop asked about the names of the other persons with whom she conversed, she replied: 'Since it is certain that I will die for my faults, do not disturb my spirit.'

Asked then whether she ever repented, she said yes.

Asked further about the cause of her relapse, she said that lack of grace was the chief cause of her relapse.

She says that two years ago Silkby gave her a small book concerning a dead or sick man,[a] as she recalls, saying it was an excellent book. The deponent gave the book to Abell etc. and Abell, saying he could not read, said he would like it to be read by someone else.

She says that, within the last three years, Agnes Jonson of Spon Cawsey[101] read from a book of the Commandments to the deponent.

She says the same about Agnes Corby, not about reading but about conversation. A certain Yate, tailor, intimated to the deponent that the bishop prosecuted Agnes Corby with the greatest partiality.

A certain Rose, servant of Hachett's, belonged to the same sect. Agnes Jonson instructed her, she believes. Rose lives in Atherstone.[102]

She says that Silkby told her, two years ago, that Laurence Dawson is now in the city and is a good companion.

She heard Bown saying that Warde belonged to the sect. Then she said, 'So go to him and borrow leather from him to help you, if he is such a one'.

About Lieff, she says she believes he married the daughter of Landesdale's wife. If this is so, she says he is of the same opinion etc. Hachet admits the same about Lieff.[103]

She heard that Longhold is suspected and he is [...] Landesdale.

She admits further that Agnes de Bakehouse belongs to the same sect.

Agnes Margaret White, servant of Rowley, is of the same breaking,[b] inasmuch as she says, 'I would have my husband of thy mind'.

She admits fully concerning Londesdale's wife.[c]

[fo. 20v] She says that Agnes Brown in Weston Hard,[104] formerly the wife of Thomas Brown, whose brother was wicked, told her that she associated with Master Bayly. The deponent stayed with the same Agnes for three weeks and John Jonson, cutler, conversed with them.

She says she heard Mother Agnes saying that Thomas Clerc's wife is of that opinion. And she told the deponent: 'Why not come home? My husband has an excellent book'.

She says she heard Hachet and Flesshour saying that Katherine Revis and her husband belong to the sect.

---

[a] *or* from a dead or sick man.

[b] *MS* breking: *meaning unclear.*

[c] *The letter 2 follows. The deposition continues at the bottom of fo. 20v, indicated in the margin by another letter 2, and then returns to fo. 21r again.*

Elizabeth Gest, daughter of Agnes Corby, often communicated with her.

William Grey's wife, the daughter of Little Mother Agnes, is [...]. She believes that the said William's first wife is still alive.

[fo. 21r] Hawkyns, as she heard from others, is a supporter of heretics and is very familiar with Alice Rowley.

Katherine, the wife of a miller in Gosford Street,[105] told the deponent that she confessed to Master Flemmyng[106] that she did not believe properly in the sacrament of the altar. And she came to a certain Tuke, when Sylkby was first arrested, and asked him how much Silkby would declare [...] before the vicar.

Saturday, 22 November 1511

Thomas Abell

[LCB, fo. 21v. For Abell's abjuration, see below, p. 260.]

xxii^{do} die mensis Novembris anno Domini 1511°.ᵃ

Thomas Abell civitatis Coventr' sutor, natus in parochia sancte Werburge Cestrie[107] [...], etatis xlii annorum.

Iuratus et cetera, dicit quod circa xii^{mum} sue etatis annum erat apprenticius cum quodam Henrico Flemyng sutor apud Canarvan',[108] cum quo moratus est vi annis.ᵇ Deinde^c rediit Cestriam, ubi mansit ad tres annos. Et post hoc apud Staff'[109] fecit moram et in Coventria. In qua civitate Coventr' per^d Robertum Hachet^e ad duos annos elapsos primum inductus erat in heresim et non ante, ut asserit.

Et dicit quod mediis illius Roberti Hachet aggressus est Rogerum Londesdale.^f Quem audivit legentem in libris Anglic' scriptis de evangeliis et epistolis, presentibus secum dicto Hachet et Bown.

Et negat se novisse prenominatos Londesdale, Hachet et Bown fuisse opinionis heretice.

ᵃ xxii^{do} [...] 1511° *is the heading of the page.*
ᵇ annis *[sic].*
ᶜ venit *deleted.*
ᵈ contra Hachet *in margin.*
ᵉ per *deleted.*
ᶠ ubi *deleted.*

Fatetur[a] tamen se audivisse eosdem contra sacramentum altaris dogmatisasse, videlicet: 'That God made man and not man God, as the carpenter doith make the howse and not the howse the carpenter. And that he shuld take it as a token or a remembraunce of Crists passion and not as the very body of Cryste', et cetera.

Et fatetur se [...] Wyclyffe, ad instructiones aliorum superius nominatorum, credidisse dictis illorum et quod non erat peregrinandum. Nec peregrinaciones observavit ab eo tempore, a quo etiam tempore ymaginum venerationes detestabatur, ut affirmavit.

Fatetur libri receptionem a Johanna Warde et dicit quod tradidit eundem librum dicte Johanne [...].

Volens tamen redire ad unitatem ecclesie et cetera, abiuracionem legit ut supra.

[English translation]

22 November 1511.

Thomas Abell of Coventry, shoemaker, born in St Werburgh's parish in Chester[107] [...], aged forty-two.

Sworn etc., he says that when aged about twelve he was apprenticed with Henry Flemyng shoemaker in Caernarvon,[108] and remained with him for six years. Then he returned to Chester, where he remained for three years. After this, he lived in Stafford[109] and in Coventry. It was in Coventry two years ago, and not before, that he was first drawn into heresy by Robert Hachet,[b] he says.

He says that through Robert Hachet he met Roger Londesdale. He heard the latter reading books of the Gospels and Epistles written in English while the said Hachet and Bown were present with him.

He denies he knew that the said Londesdale, Hachet, and Bown were of an heretical opinion.

He admits, however, that he heard them teaching against the sacrament of the altar, namely: 'That God made man and not man God, as the carpenter makes the house and not the house the carpenter. And that he should take it as a token or a remembrance of Christ's passion and not as the very body of Christ', etc.

He admits that he [...] Wycliffe, on the instructions of others named above, to have believed their sayings, and that pilgrimages should not be made. And from that time he did not make pilgrimages and he detested the veneration of images, he said.

---

[a] se *deleted.*
[b] Against Hachet *in the margin.*

He admits receiving a book from Joan Warde and he says he returned
it to her [...].
Wishing, however, to return to the unity of the Church etc., he read
the abjuration as above.

Tuesday, 25 November 1511

Thomas Wrixham

[LCB, fo. 18v. For Wrixham's abjuration, see below, p. 260.]

xxv^{to} die Novembris anno Domini supradicto.^a

Thomas Wrixham civitatis Coventr' cyrothecarius etatis^b xl annorum
et ultra, ut asserit, natus apud Castrum de Holt^{110} et apprenticius
London' cum magistro Birell aramatario circa xii^{mum} sue etatis annum,
cum quo ad vi annos moram traxit. Et a London' rediit ad Wrixham,^{111}
ubi cum patre suo mansit. Et in ipsa villa addidicit artificium suum,
manendo ibidem ad vii^{tem} annos. Deinde venit Coventriam ubi pro
maiori parte mansit et cetera.

Iuratus et examinatus an unquam habuit in custodia sua^c libros super
heretica pravitate, dicit quod sic. Sed eundem librum^d tradidit domino,
ut asserit.

Et quantum ad conversacionem cum Landesdale et Abell, fatetur.
Dicit tamen quod nunquam credidit secte illorum.

Et^e dicit preterea quod Villers, Banbrooke et Bradeley, ut credit, sunt
heretici.

Et tandem fatebatur se eam fidem tenuisse quam Landesdale et
ceteri tenuerunt.

Dicit^f insuper quod Willelmus Revys et Katherina, uxor eius, sunt
heretici. Nam cum primum Landesdale deprehensus erat, dixerunt
quod idem Landesdale erat vir bonus et dolendum erat de vexatione
sua. Et audivit eundem Revis communicantem contra sacramentum
altaris et cetera.

---

^a xxv^{to} die [...] supradicto *as heading of the page.*
^b l *deleted.*
^c b *deleted.*
^d libros [...] librum *sic.*
^e Et *interlined;* Villers, Bambroke et Bradeley *in margin.*
^f Revys et uxor *in margin.*

Idem[a] dicit de Hawykins skynner, addendo quod Warde reputatus[b] est eiusdem secte et optimus communicator.[c]

Et[d] audivit Bown dicentem quod magistrum[e] Wiggeston et Pysford[112] habent pulcherrimos libros de heresi et cetera.

Addit[f] preterea quod Thomas Spenser mercer est, ut credit, eiusdem secte.

Ricardus Northopp cum uxore sua sunt etiam heretici et cetera.

Audivit[g] communicationem factam de magistro Bayly et Roberto filio eiusdem[113] quod fuerunt eiusdem opinionis.

Dicit[h] insuper quod Johannes Davy, pictor a Leicestr',[i] multotiens accessum habuit ad Abell, Silkeby et Bown, nova a quodam vocato Annesty[j] pseudo propheta afferendo. Et prophetias huiusmodi Bown interpretatus est.[k]

Et[l] Derling omnino adversatur presbiteris, ut asserit.

Thomas[m] Lyeff, sherman, et Johannes Longhald, sherman, semper cum Landesdale spaciabantur.[n]

Holbache[o] fuit sepe cum Silkby et cetera.

Et[p] dicit se audivisse Banbrooke dicentem quod[q] Willelmus Banwell, mercer,[114] erat cognitus inter eos et eiusdem secte.

De[r] uxore Trussell, dicit cum ceteris.

Dicit quod uxor Banbrooke dixit ad Bradeley: 'Tu habes librum de heresi, quare non tradis eum domino episcopo? Faxit Deus ut comburentur huiusmodi libri'.

Volens tamen ad unitatem ecclesie et cetera redire et cetera, abiuracionem legit et cetera. Quem dominus absolvit penitenciamque iniunxit.

---

[a] Hawkyns, Warde *in margin.*
[b] reputatus *interlined.*
[c] est *deleted.*
[d] Pysford et Wiggeston *deleted in margin.*
[e] Pysford *deleted.*
[f] Thomas Spenser et Ricardus Northopp *in margin.*
[g] Bayly *in margin.*
[h] Johannes Davy, Anesty *in margin.*
[i] a Leicestr' *interlined.*
[j] pſp *deleted.*
[k] Dicit insuper [...] interpretatus est *underscored.*
[l] Derling *in margin.*
[m] Lyeff, Longhald *in margin.*
[n] uxor Lye, nuper relicta Lodge cutler, est eiusdem opinionis et cetera *deleted;* uxor Lye *in margin.*
[o] Holbache *in margin;* de Maxstock *deleted.*
[p] Interrogat' Banbroke *in margin.*
[q] Banwell *in margin.*
[r] Trussell *in margin.*

Dicit[a] quod ex relatu Thome Clerc, inter eundem domum, audivit quod Willelmus Revis et Thomas Archer audiverunt eundem Thomam legentem in libro suo pessimo.

[English translation]

25 November in the aforesaid year of the Lord.

Thomas Wrixham of Coventry, glover, aged forty and more, as he says, born at Holt Castle.[110] He was apprenticed in London with Master Birell, spicer, when aged about twelve, and he spent six years with him. From London he returned to Wrexham,[111] where he lived with his father. In that town he learnt his trade, remaining there for seven years. Then he came to Coventry, where for the most part he has remained etc.

Sworn and examined whether he ever had heretical books in his custody, he says yes, but he handed over the same book to the bishop, he says.

Regarding conversation with Landesdale and Abell, he admits this. But he says he never believed in their sect.

He says that Villers, Banbrooke, and Bradeley, as he believes, are heretics.

Finally, he admitted that he held the faith that Landesdale and the others held.

He says that William Revys and Katherine, his wife, are heretics. For when Landesdale was first arrested, they said that Landesdale was a good man and they were sorry about his ill treament. He heard the same Revis speaking against the sacrament of altar etc.

He says the same about Hawkyns, skinner, adding that Warde is reputed to belong to the same sect and to be an excellent speaker.

He[b] heard Bown saying that Master Wiggeston and Pysford[112] have very beautiful books of heresy etc.

He adds that Thomas Spenser, mercer, belongs, he believes, to the sect.

Richard Northopp with his wife are also heretics, etc.

He heard it said of Master Bayly and his son Robert[113] that they were of the same opinion.

He says also that John Davy, painter from Leicester, often visited Abell, Silkeby, and Bown, bringing news from a pseudo-prophet called Annesty. Bown interpreted these prophecies.

Derling is completely opposed to priests, he says.

[a] Revis et Archer *in margin.*
[b] Pysford and Wiggeston *deleted in margin.*

Thomas Lyeff, sherman, and John Longhald, sherman, were always walking with Landesdale.[a]

Holbache was often with Silkby etc.

He says he heard[b] Banbrooke saying that William Banwell, mercer,[114] was known among them and belonged to the sect.

About Trussell's wife, he agrees with the others.

He says that Banbrooke's wife said to Bradeley: 'You have a heretical book, why do you not hand it over to the lord bishop? God would cause these books to be burnt.'

Wishing, however, to return etc. to the Church's unity etc., he read the abjuration etc. The bishop absolved him and enjoined a penance.

He says that, according to Thomas Clerc, within the same house, he heard that William Revis and Thomas Archer heard the same Thomas reading his wicked book.

Thomas Clerc

[LCB, fo. 19r. Dated 'aforesaid day'; follows in MS Thomas Wrixham's examination, dated 25 November 1511 (see previous entry). For Clerc's abjuration, see below, p. 260.]

Prefatis die et loco.[c]

Thomas Clerc hosier civitatis Coventr', natus in Harding prope Northampton,[115] etatis l annorum et ultra, ubi moram traxit et Coventr' tota vita sua.

Iuratus et cetera, dicit quod mediis Landesdale et cuiusdam Willelmi Heywod, qui iam mortuus est, ad xii^{cem} annos elapsos incidit in hereticas opiniones, tenendo perversas hereses, quas prenominatus Landesdale et alii tenuerunt ut supra.

Et[d] dicit quod in principio, videlicet ad x^{cem} annos preteritos,[e] Thomas Warde conversabatur cum Landesdale. Et audivit eundem legentem unacum isto deponente et Roberto Hachetts. Silkby et Landesdale sciunt, ut asserit, plura deponere in hac re.

Et[f] Johannes Clerc erat,[g] voce quorundam, huiusmodi opinionis.

De[h] Derling, concordat cum Wrixham.

---

[a] Lye's wife, recently the widow of Lodge, cutler, is of the same opinion etc. *deleted.*
[b] Ask Banbrooke *in margin.*
[c] Prefatis die et loco *as a heading*
[d] Warde *in margin.*
[e] videlicet [...] preteritos *interlined.*
[f] Johannes Clerc *in margin.*
[g] quemadmodum fa *deleted.*
[h] Rise, Derling *in margin.*

De Rise shomaker, dicit quod Abell scit deponere.

De[a] Banwell, dicit se audivisse quod erat eiusdem secte.

Interrogatus de libro pessimo atque erroribus pleno, dicit quod habuit a Willelmo Heywod.

De[b] Lyeff, dicit quod[c] imitatus est vestigia parentis et cetera. Et de eodem atque Langhald, dicit quod magni erant cum Landesdale.

Uxor[d] Thome Acton magna est cum magistra Cooke. Et ipsa magistra Cooke habuit sponsum iam mortuum eiusdem secte.[116] Credit[e] Thomam Acton et Londesdale plura scire in hac re.

Dicit[f] quod Hawykyns fuit familiaris cum Londesdale.

De[g] moder Agnes, dicit quod heretica est.

In recessu, fatebatur se tenuisse contra benedictionem episcopi.

Volens tamen ad unitatem ecclesie redire et cetera, abiuracionem legit et cetera. Iuratusque ad perimplendum penitenciam et cetera, absolutus est a domino.[h]

Dicit[i] quod Johannes Cropwell, wyer drawer, rettulit isti quod fuit conversatus cum Landesdale et spaciatus est cum eodem.

Et[j] dicit quod Cristiana, uxor sua, audivit eum legentem variis vicibus et nouit de libro pessimo quem iste habuit. Dicit tamen quod non legebat ei opiniones hereticas. Verumtamen fatetur quod uxor sua voluit eum cremare librum suum huiusmodi.

[English translation]

The day and place as given above.

Thomas Clerc, hosier of Coventry, born in Harding near Northampton,[115] aged fifty and more, where and in Coventry he has lived all his life.

Sworn etc., he says that through Landesdale and a certain William Heywood, who is now dead, he fell into heretical opinions twelve years ago, holding perverse heresies which Landesdale and others held as above.

[a] Banwell *in margin.*
[b] Lyeff, Langhald *in margin.*
[c] *illegible word deleted.*
[d] uxor Acton', uxor Cooke *in margin.*
[e] Interrogat' Acton et Londesdale *in margin.*
[f] Hawkyns *in margin.*
[g] moder Agnes *in margin.*
[h] *A short gap follows. The subsequent marginal note,* uxor Thome Clerc, *identifying* uxor sua, *indicates that the remainder belongs to Thomas Clerc's deposition.*
[i] Interrogat' Londesdale *in margin.*
[j] uxor Thome Clerc *in margin.*

He says that in the beginning, namely ten years ago, Thomas Warde conversed with Landesdale. He heard Landesdale reading together with this deponent and Robert Hachetts. Silkby and Landesdale, he says, can say more about this.

John Clerc was, according to some, of the same opinion.

About Derling, he agrees with Wrixham.

About Rise, shoemaker, he says that Abell can testify.

About Banwell, he says he heard that he belonged to the same sect.

Asked about a wicked book full of errors, he says that he had it from William Heywod.

About Lyeff, he says he followed in the footsteps of his parent etc. About Lyeff and Langhald, he says they were close with Landesdale.

Thomas Acton's wife is intimate with Mistress Cooke. Mistress Cooke had a husband, now dead, who belonged to the same sect.[116] He believes Thomas Acton and Londesdale know more about this.

He says that Hawkyns was familiar with Londesdale.

About Mother Agnes, he says she is a heretic.

On leaving, he admitted he opposed the blessing of a bishop.

Wishing, however, to return to the Church's unity etc., he read the abjuration etc. And having sworn to perform the penance etc., he was absolved by the bishop.

He says[a] that John Cropwell, wiredrawer, told him that he talked with Landesdale and walked with him.

He says that Christian,[b] his wife, heard him reading on various occasions and knew the wicked book which he had. But he says he did not read heretical opinions to her. He admits, however, that his wife wanted him to burn the book.

Thomas Wrixham, Thomas Clerc, Thomas Abell, Thomas Villers, Robert Silkby, Richard Bradeley, Thomas Spenser, John Longhold, Thomas Banbrooke, William Hawkyns, and Thomas Warde

[Reg. Blyth, fo. 99r. Dated 'the 25th day of the month'; the entry follows others in Blyth's register dated November (see above, pp. 161 and 169). Although the first two men named, Thomas Wrixham and Thomas Clerc, are recorded as having abjured 25 November (see previous two entries), the abjurations of some, or all of the others in the list may be more correctly dated to 29 November. Thomas Villers, for instance, was still denying heresy on 27 November (below, p. 192); Richard Bradeley and others were still being questioned on the 28 and 29 November, and

[a] Ask Landesdale *in margin.*
[b] Wife of Thomas Clerc *in margin.*

the entry in LCB recording the abjurations of most of the same men is dated 29 November (below, p. 205). See also the text of the abjurations with names subscribed (below, pp. 260 and 266).]

Vicesimo quinto die mensis et anni suprascriptorum apud Maxstock predict' coram prenominato reverendo patre, Thomas Wrixham, Thomas[a] Clerc hosyer, Thomas Abell, Thomas Villers, Robertus Silkeby, Ricardus Bradeley, Thomas Spenser, Johannes Longhold, Thomas Banbrooke, Willelmus Hawkyns et Thomas Warde, detecti et cetera ut supra.

Post eorum confessionem in iudicio factam, articulis prescriptis ministratis, atque submissiones suas humiliter in hac parte, facta abiuracione per ipsorum quemlibet prima ut supra in abiuracione Flesshor, dominus eos omnes et singulos a sentencia excommunicationis – prestita primitus per eos et eorum quemlibet caucione de perimplendo penitenciam et cetera in forma ecclesie consueta – absolvit.

Et Wrixham, Silkeby, Clerc et Abell consimilem penitenciam iniunxit cum Landesdale, Flesshor et aliis. Reliquam partem penitencie sue dominus distulit in visitacionem suam ut supra.

Bradeley, Spenser, Longhald et Hawkyns habent penitenciam peragendam die Veneris extunc proxime sequente circa civitatem in processione.

Bambrooke vero habet interesse apud crucem in foro cum fasciculo, quem adveniente processione levet humeris suis et cum supranominatis processionaliter, more penitentis, eat in ecclesiam sancti Michaelis et cetera.

Et omnes supranominati habent in monitione quod interim nichil operis in opellis suis exerceant aut aliis locis operentur. Nec ingrediantur ecclesiam usque in diem Dominicam extunc proximam sequentem. Quo die habent ad interessendum sermoni in ecclesia parochiali predicta cum Sylkeby et aliis, sed sine fasciculis.

[English translation]

On the twenty-fifth day of the aforesaid month and year, at Maxstoke, before the said reverend father, Thomas Wrixham, Thomas Clerc, hosier, Thomas Abell, Thomas Villers, Robert Silkeby, Richard Bradeley, Thomas Spenser, John Longhold, Thomas Banbrooke, William Hawkyns, and Thomas Warde, detected etc. as above.

After their confession had been made in the court, after the aforesaid

---

[a] hosyer *deleted.*

articles had been proposed to them, after their humble submissions in the matter; after each one of them had made an abjuration as above in Flesshor's abjuration, and after each and every one of them had first guaranteed to perform the penance etc. in the Church's customary form, the bishop absolved each and every one of them from the sentence of excommunication.

He enjoined upon Wrixham, Silkeby, Clerc, and Abell the same penance as Landesdale, Flesshor and others. He deferred the rest of the penance until his visitation as above.

Bradeley, Spenser, Longhald, and Hawkyns must perform their penance around the city in the procession on the following Friday.

Bambrooke must be present with a faggot at the cross in the marketplace. When the procession approaches, he shall lift the faggot onto his shoulders and he shall go in procession with the others named above, in the manner of a penitent, to St Michael's church etc.

All the above named are warned that in the meantime they shall not practise their trades in their shops or elsewhere. Nor shall they enter a church until the following Sunday, and on that day they must be present at the sermon in the aforesaid parish church with Sylkeby and others, but without faggots.

Thursday, 27 November 1511

Thomas Villers

[LCB, fo. 21v. Dated 27ᵗʰ day of month following an entry on the same folio dated 22 November 1511. This indicates that the date of the abjuration recorded in Blyth's register, 25 November (above, p. 190), is inaccurate by several days, at least for Villers and possibly for others, as Villers cannot have abjured while he still denied his heresies. The LCB records his abjuration as taking place 29 November (below, p. 205). This examination resumes on the 28ᵗʰ (below, p. 193).]

xxvii° die mensis et anni supradictorum.[a]

Thomas Villers civitatis Coventr' aromaticarius xxvii annorum, ut asserit, ubi natus erat.

Iuratus et examinatus et cetera, dicit quod artificium suum in Bristollia et partibus[b] extraneis didicit.

[a] xxvii° [...] supradictorum *is the heading.*
[b] Bristollie *deleted.*

Et tandem duxit uxorem filiam[a] Thome Redhell de Byrmyngham, a quo tempore continue moram traxit apud Coventriam.

Interrogatus an unquam conversatus erat cum supranominatorum abiuratorum aliquo aut legit, vel audivit eos legentes,[b] in libris continentibus heresim, negat prorsus.

Interrogatus an unquam audivit quod uxores Bradeley et Banbrooke fuerunt suspecte de et super heretica pravitate, negat.

[English translation]

27th day of the aforesaid month and year.

Thomas Villers of Coventry, spicer, aged twenty-seven, as he says, where he was born.

Sworn and examined etc., he says he learnt his craft in Bristol and in foreign parts.

Afterwards, he married the daughter of Thomas Redhell of Birmingham and from that time he lived continuously in Coventry.

Asked whether he had ever conversed with any of the above named who abjured, or read, or heard them reading heretical books, he wholly denies this.

Asked whether he ever heard that the wives of Bradeley and Banbrooke were suspected of heresy, he denies this.

Before 28 November 1511

Richard Bradeley

[LCB, fo. 10r. Undated. His examination resumed the 28th day of the month (below, p. 194); November is the most likely month due to his dated abjuration 29 November (below, p. 205), although October remains possible. Note also that Blyth's register dates his abjuration to 25 November, but as this is clearly not an accurate date in the case of Thomas Villers (see previous entry), it is probably not in Bradeley's case either.]

Ricardus Bradeley civitatis Coventr' mercer etatis xxxiiii annorum,

---

[a] filiam *interlined.*
[b] vel audivit eos legentes *interlined.*

natus in comitatu Staff' in parochia de Kinges Swyneford,[117] ubi et in civitate predicta moram omnino traxit, ut asserit.

Iuratus et examinatus et cetera an nunquam conversatus fuit cum eis vel illorum aliquo qui huiusmodi secte erant et cetera ut supra, negat conversacionem, noticiam secte aut lecture illorum presentiam et cetera. Quare dominus mancipavit eum carceribus.

[English translation]

Richard Bradeley of Coventry, mercer, aged thirty-three, born in the county of Stafford in the parish of Kingswinford,[117] where and in Coventry he has always lived, he says.

Sworn and examined etc. whether he ever conversed with those, or any of them, who belonged to the sect etc. as above, he denies such conversation, knowledge of the sect, or attending their readings. The bishop therefore committed him to prison.

Friday, 28 November 1511

Thomas Villers

[LCB, fo. 21v. Continued from 27 November (above, p. 191). The examination resumed again on 29 November (below, p. 201).]

Deinde xxviii° die mensis et anni supradictorum, comparens coram domino et cetera et examinatus ut supra, negat omnino. Quare mancipatus est carceribus.

[English translation]

Then on the 28th day of the aforesaid year and month, appearing before the bishop etc. and examined as above, he denies all. Therefore he was committed to prison.

Richard Bradeley

[LCB, fo. 10r. Continued from before 28 November 1511 (above, p. 192; see entry there regarding dating to November). See below, pp. 205 and 260, for his abjuration.]

Deinde xxviii° die mensis et anni supradicto, interrogatus et cetera ut supra, negat conversacionem secte, noticiam aut lecture[a] audite. Nec voluit omnino confiteri. Negat etiam conversacionem aut communicacionem cum Alicia Rowley ut[b] emptionem cum eadem. Negat insuper conversacionem aut communicacionem cum Landesdale et ceteris in hac parte.

Tandem tunc fatetur quod opiniones tenuit contra peregrinaciones et ymaginum veneraciones, et quod Jonson cutler exposuit eis scripturas, presente Silkeby.

Fatetur de Banbrooke.

Dicit etiam quod Spenser rettulit ei se esse opinionis sue.

Dicit[c] insuper quod Villers habuit sepe verba secreta contra peregrinaciones et cetera.

Et dicit quod Silkby attulit in domo istius librum de mandatis, quem [...].[d]

Dicit uxorem suam Thomasinam esse eiusdem secte et opinionis.

Volens tunc, ut asseruit, ad unitatem fidei redire et huiusmodi opinionibus et aliis quibuscumque, ut supra, hereticis prorsus renunciare, abiuracionem et cetera legit, signum crucis sub nomine suo subscribens. Et tunc dominus eundem, ad perimplendum penitenciam subscriptam iuratum, absolvit.

[English translation]

Then on the aforesaid 28th day of the month and year, examined etc. as above, he denies contact with the sect, knowledge, or hearing readings. He was entirely unwilling to confess. He also denies conversation or communication with Alice Rowley, or buying with her. He also denies conversation or communication with Landesdale and others in this matter.

Finally, then, he admits that he held opinions against pilgrimages and the veneration of images, and that Jonson, cutler, explained the scriptures to them in Silkeby's presence.

[a] presentiam *deleted.*
[b] ut *sic, possibly* aut *is meant.*
[c] Villers *in margin.*
[d] *blank space in MS.*

He admits regarding Banbrooke.

He says that Spenser told him that he was of his opinion.

He says that Villers often spoke secretly against pilgrimages etc.

He says that Silkby brought into his house a book of the Commandments, which [...].[a]

He says his wife, Thomasina, is of the same sect and opinion.

Wishing then, as he said, to return to the unity of the faith and to renounce wholly these and any other heretical opinions, as above, he read the abjuration etc. and wrote a sign of the cross under his name. Then the bishop absolved him after he had sworn to perform the following penance.

Saturday, 29 November 1511

Thomas Banbrooke

[LCB, fo. 10r. Undated; follows in MS Richard Bradeley's examination begun before 28 November 1511 (above, pp. 192 and 194). This entry is assigned the date of 29 November because of the reference to Banbrooke's abjuration; the records variously date this both 25 November and 29 November, although the latter date is to be preferred (see pp. 189 and 205). See below, p. 260, for the abjuration Banbrooke signed.]

Thomas Banbrook civitatis Coventr' pandaxator etatis lii annorum et ultra, natus in Coventr' ubi et in civitate Coventr'[b] moram traxit.

Iuratus et examinatus et cetera ut supra, negat ut supra tam de se quam uxore sua.

Tandem tunc fatetur cum ceteris.

Et dicit quod conversatus erat magistro Johanne Phisico et audivit eundem communicantem contra ymaginum venerationes et per-egrinationes.

Et dicit quod magister Johannes rettulit ei 'that the hoste consecrate was not the very body of our Lorde but a figur'. Et ita credidit isti. Quem, ut asserit, magister Johannes primo instruxit in huiusmodi opinionibus hereticis.

Volens tunc, ut asseruit, ad fidei unitatem redire et opinionibus huiusmodi atque aliis quibuscunque hereticis prorsus renunciare, abi-

---

[a] *blank space in MS.*

[b] Coventr' *[sic].*

uracionem legit ut supra, signum crucis sub nomine suo subscribendo. Quem dominus, [...] ad perimplendum penitenciam et cetera iuratum, absolvit.

[English translation]

Thomas Banbrook of Coventry, brewer, aged fifty-two and more, born in Coventry, where and in Coventry he has lived.

Sworn and examined etc. as above, he denies as above, for both himself and his wife.

Finally, then, he admits with the others.

And he says that he had conversed with Master John Phisicion and heard him speaking against the veneration of images and pilgrimages.

He says that Master John told him 'that the consecrated host was not the very body of our Lord but a figure'. And he believed him. Master John first instructed him in these heretical opinions, he says.

Wishing then, as he said, to return to the unity of the faith and to renounce wholly these and any other heretical opinions, he read the abjuration as above and wrote a sign of the cross under his name. The bishop absolved him [...] after he had sworn to perform the penance etc.

Richard Northopp

[LCB, fo. 10v. Undated; follows in MS Thomas Banbrooke's examination (see previous entry).]

Ricardus Northopp civitatis Coventr' mercer etatis circiter xxxi annorum, natus in Myrfeld prope Wakefeild.[118]

Iuratus et cetera atque examinatus ut supra folio precedente, negat cum ceteris non modo pro se verum etiam pro uxore sua.

[English translation]

Richard Northopp of Coventry, mercer, aged about thirty-one, born in Mirfield near Wakefield.[118]

Sworn etc. and examined as in the preceding folio above, he denies with the others not only for himself, but also for his wife.

Thomas Spenser

[LCB, fo. 10v. Undated; follows in MS Richard Northopp's examination (see previous entry). This entry is assigned the date of 29 November, because of the reference to Spenser's abjuration; the records variously date this both 25 November and 29 November, although the latter date is to be preferred (see pp. 189 and 205). See below, p. 260, for the abjuration he signed.]

Thomas Spenser civitatis Coventr' merser etatis xxxi annorum et ultra, natus in Wynchecombe.[119]

Iuratus et examinatus, negat conversacionem ut supra.

Fatetur tamen se habuisse librum a Silkeby de epistolis Pauli, ut Silkeby asseruit.

Et pater suus misit ipsum ad Bown pro quodam libro. Quem librum, ut affirmat, postquam erat ei traditus, dimisit in mensa vocata le war' borde. Et magister suus Ricardus Londesdale[a] eundem librum habuit, ut credit.

Negat conversacionem cum Balthaser aut lecture eiusdem audite.

Dicit quod audivit Silkeby dicentem quod ymagines in memoriam sanctorum fabricate sunt[b] nihil aliud quam trunci mortui.

Idem dicit de Bradeley.

Dicit quod Johanna Smyth[c] multotiens accersuit ad eam filias suas et, clauso ostio, legat ad eas.

Et Silkeby primum introduxit eum ad huiusmodi hereses.

Volens tunc ad unitatem ecclesie redire et cetera, abiurationem legit et cetera. Iuratusque ad perimplendum penitenciam et cetera, absolutus est, ut continetur.

[English translation]

Thomas Spenser of Coventry, mercer, aged thirty-one and more, born in Winchcombe.[119]

Sworn and examined, he denies conversation as above.

He admits, however, that he had a book of St Paul's Letters from Silkeby, as Silkeby asserted.

His father sent him to Bown for a book. The book, he says, after it

---

[a] Ricardus Landesdale *interlined.*
[b] *illegible word deleted.*
[c] [...] Smyth *interlined.*

had been given to him, he left on a table called the ware board.ᵃ And his master, Richard Londesdale, had the book, he thinks.

He denies conversing with Balthasar or hearing him read.

He says he heard Silkeby saying that images made in memory of saints are nothing but dead logs.

He says the same about Bradeley.

He says that Joan Smyth often summoned her daughters and read to them behind closed doors.

Silkeby first introduced him to these heresies.

Wishing then to return to the unity of the Church etc., he read the abjuration etc. And having sworn to perform the penance etc., he was absolved, as is contained [...].ᵇ

John Longhold

[LCB, fo. 11r. Undated; follows in MS Thomas Spenser's examination (see previous entry). This entry is assigned the date of 29 November because of the reference to Longhold's abjuration; the records variously date this both 25 November and 29 November, although the latter date is to be preferred (see pp. 189 and 205). See below, p. 260, for the abjuration he signed.]

Johannes Longhald civitatis Coventr' sherman etatis circiter xxxiiiiᵒʳ annorum, natus in parochia sancti Johannis de la murᶜ prope Laghton' in Mornyng.¹²⁰

Iuratus et examinatus et cetera ut supra, dicit quod audivit Landesdale verba habentem contraᵈ ymaginum veneracionesᵉ dicendo quod idolatria erat.

Et fatetur quod sepenumero spaciatus est cum Landesdale tam in parco quam extra.

Interrogatus quotiens audivit Londesdale communicantem contra ymaginum venerationes, dicit quod longe pluries quam par est. Interrogatus an favebat opinioni Londesdale in ea parte, fatetur; et quod audivit eum dicentem, 'iste ymagines sunt nisi trunci mortui et nihil possunt tibi conducere', cui assertioni iste tunc credidit.

Et sepius audivit eum communicantem de Thobia.

ᵃ ware board: *MS* le war' borde: *war' may mean 'ware', as in goods for sale; board means 'table'. See OED, s.v. 'board' and 'ware' n.3.(5). This probably means the table on which goods were displayed for sale in a shop.*

ᵇ *Breaks off here, presumably* above *implied.*

ᶜ *possibly* mor.

ᵈ peregrinationes *deleted.*

ᵉ ymaginum veneraciones *interlined.*

Ita dicit de peregrinacione, quod melius est pecunia distribuenda in elemosinis quam in huiusmodi peregrinacione.

Volens tunc, ut asseruit, eisdem opinionibus hereticis et aliis quibuscumque contra sanam ecclesie doctrinam sonantibus penitus renunciare atque ad unitatem ecclesie redire, opinionibus huiusmodi hereticis omnibus et omnimodis aliis prorsus tunc expresse renunciavit et abiuracionem legit et cetera ut supra, signumque crucis sub nomine suo subscripsit. Deinde iuratum ipsum ad perimplendum penitenciam et cetera, dominus absolvit.

[English translation]

John Longhald of Coventry, sherman, aged about thirty-four, born in the parish of St John on the Moor, near Laughton en le Morthen.[120]

Sworn and examined etc. as above, he says he heard Landesdale speaking against the veneration of images, saying it was idolatry.

He says he often walked with Landesdale, both in the park and outside.

Asked how often he heard Londesdale speaking against the veneration of images, he says very often indeed. Asked whether he favoured Londesdale's opinion in this matter, he admits this; and that he heard him saying, 'these images are only dead logs and cannot benefit you at all', a statement that he then believed.

He often heard him speaking about Tobit.

He says about pilgrimages, that it is better for the money to be given in alms than spent on such a pilgrimage.

Wishing then, as he said, to renounce wholly these heretical opinions and any others against the Church's sound teaching and to return to the Church's unity, he wholly and expressly renounced all these heretical opinions and any others. He read the abjuration etc. as above and he wrote a sign of the cross under his name. Then after he had sworn to perform the penance etc., the bishop absolved him.

William Lodge

[LCB, fo.11r. Undated; dated tentatively to 29 November, because it follows in MS entries dated to 29 November (see previous entries), and because Lodge's deposition is referred to in Thomas Villers's examination on 29 November (see next entry). Lodge apparently did not abjure with the others who appeared that day, perhaps because his deposition does not indicate clear involvement in heretical activities and because his testimony helped secure Villers's confession.]

Willelmus Lodge civitatis Coventr' mercer etatis xxv annorum, natus in Coventr'.

Iuratus et examinatus, fatetur quod semel interfuit in domo cum Bradeley et uxore sua audiens Bradeley legentem in libro de epistolis Pauli.

Et dicit quod uxor eiusdem Bradeley scit bene legere et pene memoriter novit recitare capitula Pauli.

Dicit insuper quod semel intravit in domum Banbrooke ubi Landesdale quandam lecturam Bradeley et uxori sua[a] exposuit et continue Landesdale tacuit. Cui uxor Bradeley dixit, 'Noli timere, spero istum esse filium gracie'.

Dicit[b] preterea quod ad tres annos elapsos, ut recolit, iste in[c] eodem lecto iacuit cum Thoma Villers et Villers interrogavit istum de fide sua, cui iste respondit,[d] 'credo quemadmodum docet ecclesia'. Cui Villers, 'dico tibi presbiterum non posse minimum unguem facere, ergo nec a fortiori nequit[e] corpus dominicum efficere'. Cui iste, 'relinque hanc opinionem. Et que est causa quod illud corpus dominicum recipis in Paschale cum non credis firmiter?' et cetera. At Villers, 'hoc facio in[f] vanam gloriam [...] quemadmodum ceteri faciunt'.

Et credit iste deponens quod quidam puer[121] iam manens cum Villers nuper autem cum magistro Johanne Phisico – qui commisit ipsum eundem puerum prenominato Villers et legavit post mortem Balthaser Shugborow eodem puero varios libros heretice pravitatis – est eiusdem secte; presertim quod varios viros prestantes in magistros habere potuit, immo[g] longe prestantiores quam Villers.[h]

Et dicit quod Robertus Lye, qui duxit matrem suam, minatus est ei, asserendo quod detexit matrem suam propriam.

[English translation]

William Lodge of Coventry, mercer, aged twenty-five, born in Coventry.

Sworn and examined, he admits he was once at home with Bradeley and his wife, hearing Bradeley reading a book of St Paul's Letters.

[a]   leg *deleted.*
[b]   insu *deleted.*
[c]   v *deleted.*
[d]   Ego *deleted.*
[e]   *illegible word deleted.*
[f]   glosa' *deleted.*
[g]   Villers *deleted.*
[h]   quam Villers *interlined.*

He says that Bradeley's wife can read well and can almost recite from memory the chapters of Paul.

He says he once entered Banbrooke's house, where Landesdale was explaining a reading to Bradeley and his wife, and immediately Landesdale became silent. Bradeley's wife said to Landesdale, 'Do not fear, I trust he is a son of grace'.

He says that three years ago, as he recalls, he was sharing a bed with Thomas Villers, and when Villers questioned him about his faith, he replied, 'I believe whatever the church teaches'. Villers answered him, 'I tell you, a priest cannot make even the smallest fingernail, much less the Lord's body'. The deponent replied, 'Give up this opinion. Why do you receive the Lord's body at Easter when you do not believe firmly?' etc. But Villers said, 'I do this for vainglory [...] just as others do'.

The deponent believes that a boy,[121] who is now staying with Villers but was recently with Master John Phisicion – who entrusted the boy to Villers and left the boy various heretical books to come to him when Balthasar Shugborow dies – belongs to the same sect; especially because he could have had various eminent men as masters, far more eminent than Villers.

He says that Robert Lye, who married his mother, threatened him, saying that he had betrayed his own mother.

Thomas Villers

[LCB, fo. 21v. Continued from 28 November 1511 (above, p. 193). The men named as being present were all in the court on 29 November, testifying or abjuring their heresies (see previous entry and p. 205).]

Tandem, penultimo die mensis et anni supradictorum, prenominatus Thomas Villers comparens atque – presentibus Roberto Silkby, Ricardo Bradeley, Thoma Banbrooke, Willelmo Lodge, Rogero Landesdale et Johanne Jonson – [...] examinatus, fatetur se dixisse et tenuisse quemadmodum continetur in depositione Lodge, Bradeley et aliorum. Sed penitenciam egit in ea parte.

Interrogatus quare noluit hoc fateri antea, dicit quod propter juramentum per eum [...] de consiliis et secretis illorum non detegendis [...] presertim Robert' Silkeby. Et fatetur se dixisse Willelmo Lodge[a] quod mater sua docuit eum ipsam opinionem[b] que continetur in depositione eiusdem Willelmi Lodge.

---

[a] p'nt *deleted.*
[b] quod *deleted.*

Et dicit quod non credidit perfecte sed he wavered and stode in doubt.

Et dicit quod non bene credidit eo tempore quo Silkby eum communicantem audivit, sed iam plene et perfecte credit ut asserit.

Fatetur quod audivit Silkby exponentem librum de Sikeman[122] in claustro.

[English translation]

At last, on the penultimate day of the aforesaid month and year, the said Thomas Villers, appearing and – in the presence of Robert Silkby, Richard Bradeley, Thomas Banbrooke, William Lodge, Roger Landesdale, and John Jonson – [...] examined, admits that he said and held what is contained in the deposition of Lodge, Bradeley, and others. But he did penance in the matter.

Asked why he refused to confess this earlier, he says on account of an oath by him [...] about not revealing their counsels and secrets [...], especially Robert Silkeby. And he admits he told William Lodge that his mother taught him the opinion that is contained in the same William Lodge's deposition.

He says he did not believe perfectly, but he wavered and stood in doubt.

He says he did not believe well at the time when Silkby heard him speaking, but now he believes fully and perfectly, he says.

He admits he heard Silkby explaining the book about *The Sick Man*[122] in a cloister.[a]

Thomas Warde

[LCB, fo. 1v. Date in the heading is partially illegible – between 20–29 November 1511 – but the final paragraph is marginally dated the penultimate day of November. The abjuration to which the entry refers is recorded on the same folio and is also dated 29 November (below, p. 205). Cf. also the abjuration in the register recorded 25 November (above, p. 189). See below, p. 273, for the abjuration he signed.]

xx[...] Novembris [...].[b]

Thomas Warde civitatis Coventr', barker, etatis lxiii annorum, natus in Rutlond[123] et a presencia moram trahens Coventr'.

---

[a]   cloister: *MS* claustro; *could be translated as* closed room, *but cf. above pp. 147 and 149.*
[b]   xx [...] Novembris [...] *is the heading of the page.*

Iuratus et examinatus et cetera, interrogatus an unquam audivit Thomam Clerc legentem hereses, fatetur.

Et fatetur se audivisse Bown legentem et cetera. Et incontinenter interrogavit Hachett quomodo legit iste cum litteras non noverit. Cui respondit Hachetts, 'Spiritus sanctus eum inspiravit'.

Interrogatus preterea an favebat opinionibus illorum, fatetur sed non per spacium xii^{cem} annorum. Et ipsas hereses prorsus renunciavit, se submittendo iudicio sancte matris ecclesie.

Dicit etiam se mutuo dedisse Balthasar Shugborow aureum et mutuatum esse Bown corium variis temporibus.

Et cum Hachetts, Bown, Clerc et Brown sepe conversatus erat.

Audivit[a] quod Spon erat eiusdem secte.

Idem dicit de Abell, cum quo communicacionem habuit quemadmodum cum Hachetts.

Dicit quod Banbrooke reputabatur vivente Brown pro uno opinionis illorum.

Ipsis[b] tunc hereticis opinionibus et aliis quibuscumque contra sanam ecclesie doctrinam sonantibus penitus renunciavit et abiuravit, ut supra continetur. Signumque crucis sub nomine suo subscripsit. Et eundem iuratum, ad perimplendum penitenciam iniungendam iuratum, dominus absolvit. Et penitenciam distulit in adventum suum ad Coventriam.

[English translation]

Twenty-[...] of November [...].

Thomas Warde of Coventry, barker, aged sixty-three, born in Rutland[123] and now living in Coventry.

Sworn and examined etc., asked whether he heard Thomas Clerc reading heresies, he admits this.

He admits he heard Bown reading etc. Immediately he asked Hachett how Bown read since he was unlettered. Hachetts answered him, 'The holy Spirit inspired him'.

Asked whether he agreed with their opinions, he says yes but not for twelve years. And he wholly renounced these heresies, submitting himself to the judgement of Holy Mother Church.

He says he lent gold to Balthasar Shugborow and lent leather to Bown at various times.

He had often conversed with Hachetts, Bown, Clerc, and Brown.

He heard that Spon belonged to the same sect.

[a] Spon *in margin.*
[b] penultimo Novembris *in margin.*

He says the same about Abell, with whom he communicated as with Hachetts.

He says that Banbrooke was reputed as one of their opinion when Brown was alive.

Then,[a] he wholly renounced and abjured these heretical opinions, and any others contrary to the Church's sound teaching, as is contained above, and he wrote a sign of the cross under his name. After he had sworn to perform the penance to be enjoined, the bishop absolved him. The bishop deferred the penance until his coming to Coventry.

William Hawkyns

[LCB, fo. 1v. Dated penultimate day of November in margin. The abjuration to which the entry refers is recorded on the same folio and is similarly dated 29 November (see next entry). Cf. also the abjuration in the register recorded 25 November (above, p. 189). See below, p. 260, for the abjuration he signed.]

Willelmus[b] Hawkyns civitatis Coventr', skynner, natus in parochia de Penkrich[124] etatis circiter xlviii annorum.

Iuratus et cetera, dicit quod solicitacionibus Hachet, Sylkby et Londesdale, inductus erat in opiniones hereticas. Et eisdem favebat atque opinionibus eorum. Volens tunc, ut asseruit, ad fidei unitatem redire et cetera, abiuracionem legit et cetera. Fecit ut continetur infra.

[English translation]

William[c] Hawkyns of Coventry, skinner, born in Penkridge parish,[124] aged about forty-eight.

Sworn etc., he says he was led into heretical opinions through the promptings of Hachet, Sylkby, and Londesdale. He favoured them and their opinions. Wishing then, as he said, to return to the unity of the faith etc., he read the abjuration etc. He did as is contained below.

---

[a] Penultimate day of November *in the margin.*
[b] penultimo Novembris *in margin.*
[c] Penultimate day of November *in the margin.*

Robert Silkby, Thomas Wrixham, Thomas Abell, Thomas Clerc, Richard Bradeley, Thomas Spenser, John Longhold, Thomas Banbrooke, William Hawkyns, Thomas Warde, (and Thomas Villers?)

[LCB, fo. 1v. Note that most of the men listed here are recorded in Blyth's register as having abjured 25 November (above, p. 189). The date of this entry is here considered more accurate, both because various examinations of men named here apparently took place between 25 and 29 November (see pp. 191–204), and because the LCB was likely a more immediate record than Blyth's register. For Thomas Villers's possible presence, see the final paragraph of this entry and note there. For the abjurations these men signed, see below, pp. 260, 270 and 273.]

Penultimo die Novembris anno Domini[a] et loco supradictis, Robertus Sylkby, Thomas Wryxham, Thomas Abell, Thomas Clerc, Ricardus Bradeley, Thomas Spenser, Johannes Longhold, Thomas Banbrooke et Willelmus Hawkyns et Thomas Warde[b] legerunt abiuraciones. Et abiurati erant solemniter prout continetur in abiuracione Flesshor.

Et ipsis iuratis ad perimplendum penitenciam eis et eorum cuilibet iniungendam, dominus absolvit [...].

Et iniungitur Silkeby, Clerc, Wryxham et Abell consimilis penitencia cum Flesshour [...], videlicet quinto die mensis Decembris et die Dominica ex tunc sequentibus agenda[c] [...]. Reliqua pars penitencie sue differtur in adventum domini ad Coventriam.

Reliqui quinque[d] eorum – videlicet Bradeley, Spenser, Longhold,[e] et Hawkyns – habent penitenciam cum fasciculis peragendam in die Veneris[f] proximo sequenti. Et habet Banbrooke interesse apud crucem in foro cum fasciculo et adveniente processione transeatur cum ceteris in ecclesiam parochialem sancti Michaelis.

Et interim habent omnes supranominati in mandatis quod nihil operentur in opellis suis aut aliis locis aperte et quod nec ingrediantur ecclesiam usque post ipsum diem Dominicam nec insimiliter conversentur unus eorum cum aliis.

Et die Dominica habent interesse sermoni in ecclesia parochiali predicta cum Sylkeby et ceteris, sed sine fasciculis.

Et[g] audivit matrem suam legere in vernacula lingua evangelium illud,

---

[a] et *deleted.*
[b] et Thomas Warde *interlined.*
[c] Res *deleted.*
[d] quinque *[sic]: note that Banbrook's name has been deleted* (see following note).
[e] Banbrooke *deleted.*
[f] ex tunc *deleted.*
[g] *This passage follows immediately after* sine fasciculis, *on the same line. It is unclear to whom it refers, but it is possible that Thomas Villers is the subject. His mother was involved in the Lollard*

'Noli timere pusillus grex'.[125] Submisit se tandem iudicio ecclesie. Et abiuracionem legit et cetera ut supra. Et penitenciam habet ut continetur.[a]

[English translation]

On the penultimate day of November in the year of the Lord and the place given above, Robert Sylkby, Thomas Wryxham, Thomas Abell, Thomas Clerc, Richard Bradeley, Thomas Spenser, John Longhold, Thomas Banbrooke, and William Hawkyns and Thomas Warde read abjurations and they abjured solemnly as is contained in Flesshor's abjuration.

After they had sworn to perform the penance to be enjoined upon them, and upon each one of them, the bishop absolved [...].

The same penance as for Flesshor was enjoined upon Silkeby, Clerc, Wryxham, and Abell [...], namely to be done on 5 December and on the Sunday following that day [...]. The rest of their penance is deferred until the bishop's coming to Coventry.

The other five[b] men – namely Bradeley, Spenser, Longhold,[c] and Hawkyns – shall perform the penance with faggots on the following Friday. Banbrooke shall be present at the cross in the marketplace with a faggot; and when the procession arrives, he will move with the others to St Michael's parish church.

All of them are forbidden meanwhile to practice their occupations openly in their shops or in other places, or to enter a church until after the Sunday, or to converse with one another.

On the Sunday they must be present at the sermon in the aforesaid parish church with Sylkeby and the others, but without faggots.

And[d] he heard his mother reading in the vernacular language this gospel, 'Fear not, little flock'.[125] He submitted himself at last to the Church's judgement. He read the abjuration etc., as above; and he has the penance as is contained [...].[e]

---

community, and Blyth's register records that Villers abjured with the others named here (see above, p. 189). Another record of his abjuration (below, p. 220) suggests that he abjured about 3 December.

[a] breaks off here, presumably infra implied.
[b] five [sic]: note that Banbrook's name has been deleted (see following note).
[c] Banbrooke deleted.
[d] See above p. 205n.
[e] breaks off here, presumably above implied.

Late November or early December 1511

Thomasina Bradeley

[LCB, fo. 11v. Undated. Late November to early December, dating conjectured due to placement in MS following others appearing in late November (see pp. 192, 194– 199), and placement in proximity to others who abjured 3 December 1511 (see following entries and below, p. 220). Examination continued 26 January 1512 (below, p. 243).]

Thomasina, uxor Ricardi Bradley.

Iurata et examinata, et primum an mater sua eam unquam informavit in opinionibus hereticis, negat.

Et dicit quod audivit^a sponsum suum in quodam libro, quem Silkby in domum suam adduxit, legentem.^{b} Et ille liber erat de mandatis in Anglic'.

Fatetur etiam se novisse quod Silkeby erat diffamatus et suspectus super crimine heretice pravitatis.

Interrogatus an audivit Londesdale legentem et cetera, negat deposita per Lodge.^{126}

Et petit ut probationes introducantur contra eam; quod si iuridice probari possit, offert se exponendam extremo periculo mortis.

[English translation]

Thomasina, wife of Richard Bradley.

Sworn and examined, and first whether her mother ever taught her heretical opinions, she denies this.

She says she heard her husband reading in a book which Silkby brought into their house.^{c} The book was of the Commandments in English.

She admits she knew that Silkeby was defamed and suspected of the crime of heresy.

Asked whether he heard Londesdale reading etc., she denies the statements made by Lodge.^{126}

She asks for proofs to be brought against her. If there is juridical proof, she offers to expose herself to the pain of death.

---

^{a} sor *deleted*.
^{b} ex deposicione mariti *in margin*.
^{c} From the deposition of her husband *in margin*.

Margaret Landesdale

[LCB, fo. 11v. Undated. Late November to early December, dating conjectured due to placement in MS following others appearing in late November (see pp. 192, 194–199), and abjuration dated 3 December 1511 (below, p. 219).]

Margereta, uxor Londesdale et cetera.

Iurata et examinata, fatetur quod Silkby bis vel ter accessit ad domum suam, quem communicantem cum viro suo audivit.

Insuper dicit quod[a] vidit[b] libros per Johannam, uxorem Smyth, sponso suo traditos. Et novit locum ubi occultati erant.

Et fatebatur se in heresim incidisse, informacione viri sui. Et eas opiniones hereticas tenuisse quas maritus suus tenuit, videlicet contra sacramentum altaris et cetera.

Dicit quod circiter viii vel ix[m] annos preteritos mater Thome Villers unacum filia sua, nunc uxor Bradeley, intraverunt in domum istius et manserunt ibidem a meridie usque ad vi[tam]. Et dicta[c] mater, iacente marito istius valitudinario in lecto suo, legit in quodam magno libro, presente dicta filia sua et eam audiente.

Et[d] ad quinque annos elapsos uxor Bradeley predicta accessit ad domum istius et cum viro suo communicavit. Effectum tamen huiusmodi communicationis non novit.

[English translation]

Margaret, wife of Londesdale, etc.

Sworn and examined, she admits that Silkby came two or three times to her house and she heard him conversing with her husband.

She says she saw books brought to her husband by Joan, Smyth's wife. She knew the place where they were hidden.

She admitted she had fallen into heresy, through her husband's instruction. She held the same heretical opinions as her husband, namely against the sacrament of the altar etc.

She says that, about eight or nine years ago, the mother of Thomas Villers together with her daughter, now Bradeley's wife, came to her home and remained there from midday until the sixth hour. While the deponent's husband lay ill in bed, the said mother read in a large book while the said daughter listened to her.

[a]   [...] et *deleted.*
[b]   qu' *deleted.*
[c]   mot *deleted.*
[d]   Interrogat' Londesdale *in margin.*

Five years ago,[a] the aforesaid wife of Bradeley came to the deponent's home and communicated with her husband. She does not know the result of this communication.

Alice Lye

[LCB, fo. 11v. Undated. Late November to early December, dating conjectured due to placement in MS following others appearing in late November (see pp. 192, 194–199), and placement in proximity to others who abjured 3 December 1511 (see previous and following entries, and below, p. 220).]

Alicia, uxor Roberti Lye, et cetera.

Iurata et examinata, negat conversacionem cum supranominatis aut opinionum hereticarum noticiam.

Differtur in adventum domini et cetera.

[English translation]

Alice, wife of Robert Lye, etc.

Sworn and examined, she denies conversing with the above named persons or knowledge of heretical opinions.

She is deferred until the bishop's coming etc.

Thomas Kylyngworth

[LCB, fo. 12r. Undated. Late November to early December, dating conjectured due to placement in MS following others appearing in late November (see pp. 192, 194–199), and placement in proximity to others who abjured 3 December 1511 (see previous and following entries, and below, p. 220). Kylyngworth appeared again in January or February (below, p. 247).]

Thomas Kylyngworth civitatis cooper.[b]

Iuratus et cetera, negat conversacionem scienter cum hereticis, quorum opinionibus nunquam favuit, ut asserit.

Dominus, ex consilio sibi assistentium, remisit eum domum, decernens ulterius inquirendum esse contra eum.

[a] Ask Londesdale *in margin*.
[b] civitatis cooper *sic*.

[English translation]

Thomas Kylyngworth of the city, cooper.

Sworn etc., he denies knowingly conversing with heretics and he never favoured their opinions, he says.

The bishop, following the advice of those assisting him, sent him back home, deciding there should be further enquiry against him.

Hugh Parrek

[LCB, fo. 12r. Undated. Late November to early December, dating conjectured due to placement in MS following others appearing in late November (see pp. 192, 194–199), and abjuration dated 3 December 1511 (below, p. 221). See below, p. 273, for the abjuration he signed.]

Hugo Parrek civitatis Coventr', wyerdrawer.

Iuratus et examinatus, dicit quod bis vel ter[a] interfuit[b] Londesdale et audivit eum legentem et communicantem contra sacramentum altaris, peregrinationes et cetera. Et dicit se confessum esse proprio curato in hac parte. Nichilominus quia male credidit in hac parte, submisit se correctioni domini et iudicio ecclesie.

Fatebatur se credidisse quemadmodum Londesdale, Lyeff et Longhold crediderunt et tenuerunt et cetera. Et dicit quod Robertus Hachet eum primo induxit in huiusmodi hereses.

Submisit se correctioni et cetera. Abiuracionem legit et cetera, signum crucis fecit. Habet penitenciam peragendam in die Veneris et Dominica proximis quemadmodum Bradeley, Spenser, Longhold et Hawkyns habent.[c] Absolucione prima.

[English translation]

Hugh Parrek of Coventry, wiredrawer.

Sworn and examined, he says he was with Londesdale two or three times and heard him reading and speaking against the sacrament of the altar, pilgrimages etc. He says he confessed to his own curate in

---

[a] vel ter *interlined.*
[b] in domo *deleted.*
[c] et *deleted.*

the matter. Nevertheless, because he believed ill in this matter, he submitted himself to the bishop's correction and the Church's judgement.

He admitted he had believed as Londesdale, Lyeff, and Longhold believed and held etc. He says that Robert Hachet first drew him into these heresies.

He submitted himself to correction etc. He read the abjuration and he wrote the sign of the cross. He must perform the penance on the following Friday and Sunday: the same penance as for Bradeley, Spenser, Longhold, and Hawkyns. Absolution first.

William Revis

[LCB, fo. 12r. Undated. Late November to early December, dating conjectured due to placement in MS following others appearing in late November (see pp. 194–199), and resumption of his examination on 3 December (below, p. 219).]

Willelmus Revys civitatis Coventr', skynner.

Iuratus et cetera, an unquam habuit huiusmodi verba, videlicet quod Londesdale est vir bonus et dolendum est de vexacione sua, negat prorsus.

Et negat conversacionem cum supranominatis.

Nec vult fateri quod unquam erat opinionis heretice aut fautor pravitatis heretice scienter. Scilicet negat penitus.

[English translation]

William Revys of Coventry, skinner.

Sworn etc., whether he ever said that Londesdale was a good man and it was a pity about his ill treatment, he wholly denies this.

He denies conversing with the above named persons.

Nor is he willing to admit that he ever held an heretical opinion, or was knowingly a supporter of heresy. In other words, he denies everything.

John Cropwell

[LCB, fo. 12v. Undated. Late November to early December, dating conjectured due to placement in MS following others appearing in late November (see pp. 194– 199), and placement in proximity to others who abjured 3 December 1511 (see previous and following entries, and below, p. 220).]

Johannes Cropwell civitatis Coventr', wyerdrawer.

Iuratus et cetera, dicit quod habuit communicationem cum Lyeff, qui dixit sibi[a] de peregrinacionibus.

Et cum iste quondam oblaciones faceret ymagini sancte Marie de Turri, Hachet allocutus est eum, dicendo sibi: 'Quid hic agis, Johannes?' Et respondente isti, 'Offero ymagini beate Marie'. Dixit Hachet, 'A, God help the,[b] thow arte a foole'.

Fatetur quod audivit Landesdale in presentia Lyeff communicacionem habuisse,[c] verba cuius communicacionis non recolit.

Fatetur tunc quod novit eo tempore dictum Londesdale habuisse malum nomen.

Et dicit quod bis in domo Landesdale fuit infra quarterium anni.

Fatetur se audivisse Landesdale et alios dogmatisantes contra sacramentum altaris et cetera.

Et credidit dictis eorum contra peregrinaciones et ymaginum veneraciones, non tamen contra sacramentum altaris.

Differtur ulterior processus in adventum domini ad Coventriam, de consilio sibi assistentium.

[English translation]

John Cropwell of Coventry, wiredrawer.

Sworn etc., he says he communicated with Lyeff, who told him about pilgrimages.

When he was once making an offering to the image of St Mary of the Tower, Hachet spoke to him, saying: 'What are you doing here, John?' He replied, 'I am offering to an image of Blessed Mary'. Hachet said, 'Ah, God help thee, thou art a fool'.

He admits he heard Landesdale speaking in Lyeff's presence; he does not remember the words spoken.

He admits he knew at that time that the said Landesdale had a bad name.

[a] quod non erat *deleted.*
[b] forle *deleted.*
[c] qu' *deleted.*

He says he was in Landesdale's house twice within the last three months.

He admits he heard Landesdale and others teaching against the sacrament of the altar etc.

He believed what they said against pilgrimages and the veneration of images, not, however, against the sacrament of the altar.

Further proceedings are deferred until the bishop's coming to Coventry, on the advice of those assisting him.

Thomas Bown and Roger Landesdale

[LCB, fo. 1v. Undated. Follows in MS entry dated 29 November 1511. John Hebbis was examined in late November or early December (see following entry).]

Bown et Londesdale dicunt quod Hebbis sepe fuit in communicacione cum eis super opinionibus eorum hereticis et cetera. Et sepius petivit consorcium illorum quam ipsi eius consorcium, et cetera.

[English translation]

Bown and Londesdale say that Hebbis often communicated with them about their heretical opinions etc. He more often sought their company than they sought his, etc.

John Hebbis

[LCB, fo. 12v. Undated. Late November to early December, dating conjectured due to placement in MS following others appearing in late November (see pp. 194–199), and placement in proximity to others who abjured 3 December 1511 (see previous and following entries, and below, p. 220). Note that reference is made in his examination to accusations made by Landesdale and Bown (see previous entry).]

Johannes Hebbis civitatis Coventr', sherman.

Iuratus et cetera, negat conversacionem cum Londesdale et Bown, qui eum accusaverunt.[127]

Et tandem fatetur quod audivit eos dogmatisantes contra ymagines et peregrinaciones.

Et parum, ut asseruit, habuit fidem dictis illorum et sepius conversatus est cum eisdem.

Eisdem tunc opinionbius hereticis et ceteris omnibus paratum se optulit renunciare. Et dominus, ex consilio sibi assistentium, distulit abiuracionem suam admittere et ulteriorem processum, ut supra, facere et cetera.

[English translation]

John Hebbis of Coventry, sherman.

Sworn etc., he denies conversing with Londesdale and Bown, who accused him.[127]

At last, he admits he heard them teaching against images and pilgrimages.

And, likewise, as he said, he believed what they said and often spoke with them.

He said he was prepared to renounce these heretical opinions and all others. But the bishop, on the advice of those assisting him, deferred the admission of his abjuration and the further process, as above, etc.

David Clerc

[LCB, fo. 13r. Undated. Late November to early December, dating conjectured due to placement in MS following others appearing in late November (see pp. 194–199), and abjuration dated 3 December 1511 (below, p. 221).]

David Clerc civitatis Coventr' coryar, natus ibidem, etatis xl annorum et ultra.

Iuratus et examinatus, fatebatur quod quater interfuit in consortio[a] Bown, Hachet et Londesdale et Silkby seipse.[b] Et audivit eos communicantes contra peregrinaciones, sacramentum altaris et ymaginum veneraciones, sed non per duos annos, et non credidit dictis illorum contra sacramentum.[c]

Et fatetur quod audivit eos communicantes contra peregrinacionem sancte Marie de Turri.

Dicit insuper quod novit eos fuisse suspectos. Et eo tempore habuit fidem dictis illorum et opinionibus suis tunc favebat.

Submisit se tamen iudicio sancte matris ecclesie.

---

[a]   Silkby *deleted.*
[b]   et Silkby seipse *interlined.*
[c]   contra sacramentum *interlined.*

[English translation]

David Clerc of Coventry, currier, born there, aged forty and more.

Sworn and examined, he admitted he was four times in the company of Bown, Hachet, and Londesdale and Silkby. He heard them speaking against pilgrimages, the sacrament of the altar and the veneration of images, but not for two years, and he did not believe what they said against the sacrament.

He admits he heard them speaking against pilgrimage to St Mary of the Tower.

He says he knew they were suspected. And at that time he trusted what they said and then favoured their opinions.

He submitted himself to the judgement of Holy Mother Church.

John Bull

[LCB, fo. 13r. Undated. Late November to early December, dating conjectured due to placement in MS following others appearing in late November (see pp. 192, 194–199), and abjuration dated 3 December 1511 (below, p. 221).]

Johannes Bull, serviens Thome Villers,[a] natus in Menevia,[128] etatis xvii annorum.[b]

Iuratus et cetera, dicit quod avunculus suus Johannes Blumston, alias vocatus magister John Phisicion, instruxit eum contra[c] sacramentum altaris, ut acciperet illud in signum passionis Christi et non crederet ibi esse verum corpus dominicum.

Et fatetur se dixisse Wrixham quod voluit discedere quando novit de deprehensione Londesdale et aliorum.

Et ulterius fatetur quod opiniones hereticas a nono sue etatis anno[d] tenuit.

[English translation]

John Bull, servant of Thomas Villers, born in St David's,[128] aged seventeen.

Sworn etc., he says that his uncle, John Blumston, otherwise called

---

[a] C *deleted.*
[b] etatis xvii annorum *interlined.*
[c] p' *deleted.*
[d] tenuisse *deleted.*

Master John Physician, taught him against the sacrament of the altar, that he should accept it as a sign of Christ's passion and not believe that the true body of the Lord was there.

He admits he said to Wrixham that he wanted to leave when he heard of the arrest of Londesdale and others.

He admits he held heretical opinions from the ninth year of his life.

Thomas Lyeff

[LCB, fo. 13r. Undated. Late November to early December, dating conjectured due to placement in MS following others appearing in late November (see pp. 194–199), and abjuration dated 3 December 1511 (below, p. 221).]

Thomas Lieff civitatis Coventr' sherman, natus in Carleton,[129] etatis xxx annorum.

Iuratus et cetera, fatebatur se audivisse Londesdale bina vice legentem et verba habentem contra peregrinaciones et cetera. Et fatetur se semel in consorcio fuisse cum Bown. Et quod audivit ab eis dictum quod non est attendendum ymagini quia est nisi truncus mortuus, sed habendum est animus ad Deum et sanctum representatum per ymaginem et cetera.

Ipsis tunc opinionibus quas contra sanam ecclesie doctrinam tenuit prorsus renunciavit, se submittendo ecclesie et correctioni domini et cetera.

Dictorum illorum: 'May we drynke all of a cupp'.[a]

[English translation]

Thomas Lieff of Coventry, sherman, born in Carlton,[129] aged thirty.

Sworn etc., he admitted he twice heard Londesdale reading and speaking against pilgrimages etc. He admits he was once in Bown's company. And that he heard from them that attention should not be given to an image, because it is only a dead log, but rather the mind should focus on God and the saint represented by the image etc.

Then he renounced wholly these opinions which he has held against the Church's sound teaching, submitting himself to the Church and to the bishop's correction etc.

Of their sayings: 'May we drink all of a cup'.[b]

[a] Dictorum [...] cupp' *at the foot of the page; it probably does not specifically refer to Thomas Lieff.*

[b] Of their [...] cup' *at the foot of the page; see previous note.*

Elizabeth Gest

[LCB, fo. 14r. Undated. Late November to early December, dating conjectured due to placement in MS following others appearing in late November (see pp. 194–199), and placement in proximity to others who abjured 3 December 1511 (see previous and following entries, and below, p. 220).]

Elizabeth, uxor Willelmi Gest textoris Coventr'.

Iurata et examinata et cetera, negat.

Et dominus decrevit ulterius inquirere contra eam. Et distulit in adventum suum ad Coventr' et cetera.

———————————

[English translation]

Elizabeth, wife of William Gest, weaver of Coventry.

Sworn and examined etc., she denies.

The bishop decided to enquire further against her, and he deferred this until his coming to Coventry etc.

Julian Yong

[LCB, fo. 14r. Undated. Late November to early December, dating conjectured due to placement in MS following others appearing in late November (see pp. 192, 194–199), and abjuration dated 3 December 1511 (below, p. 221).]

Juliana, filia Agnetis Yong, etatis xx^ti annorum, natus Coventr'.[a]

Iurata et examinata, interrogata an scivit legere, negat. Tandem, affirmante Silkeby in facie sua quod perfecte novit legere, fatebatur.

Et dixit quod audivit Aliciam Rowley communicantem contra peregrinaciones, ymaginum veneraciones et sacramentum altaris, dicendo quod illud quod oblatum erat, erat nil aliud nisi panis et vinum. Quibus dictis credidit ista, ut asseruit.

Interrogata[b] de libro quem ab Alicia Rowley habuit, negat se huiusmodi librum habere, affirmando eum librum traditum fuisse dicte Alicie Rowley. Et dicit quod apportavit dictum librum[c] in domum prenominate Alicie et eundem, unacum libro de mandatis,[d] posuit in

---

[a] etatis [...] Coventr' *interlined.*
[b] Interrogat' *in margin.*
[c] et liber huiusmodi postea ibi erat occultus *in margin.*
[d] unacum [...] mandatis *interlined.*

lecto sub culcitra infra the chapell chambre. Quod,[a] ut asseruit, intimavit dicte Alicie. Dicit insuper quod hoc ideo fecit quia Silkeby aggressus est matrem suam, eam admonendo ut si quos libros haberet, eosdem occultaret ne fortassis in custodia sua deprehendantur.

Fatetur preterea quod in festo nativitatis Domini ultimo preterito, Alicia Rowley legit in domo sua[b] in quodam libro cooperto tegimine rubro. Fatetur quod Alicia Rowley precepit ei et sub iuramento artavit quod non detegeret consilium et secreta[c] eius.[d]

Et dicit quod ad decem annos elapsos dicta Alicia venit in domum matris sue cum libro in sinu suo et eam tunc instruxit in huiusmodi opinionibus hereticis et precipue contra sacramentum altaris. A quo tempore credidit opinionibus suis, ut supra.

[English translation]

Julian, daughter of Agnes Yong, aged twenty, born in Coventry.

Sworn and examined. Asked whether she can read, she says no. When, however, Silkeby affirmed in her presence that she could read perfectly, she finally admitted it.

She said she heard Alice Rowley speaking against pilgrimages, the veneration of images, and the sacrament of the altar, saying that what was offered was nothing but bread and wine. She believed these statements, she said.

Asked about a book which she had from Alice Rowley, she denies she has this book, saying it had been given to the said Alice Rowley. She says she brought the book[e] into the said Alice's house and placed it, together with a book of the Commandments, under a mattress on a bed in the chapel chamber. She told this, she said, to the said Alice. She says she did this because Silkeby approached her mother and warned her to hide any books she had lest perhaps they be found in her keeping.

She admits that, last Christmas, Alice Rowley read in her house a book with a red covering. She admits that Alice Rowley ordered her and bound her under oath not to reveal her counsel and secrets.

She says that, ten years ago, the said Alice came to her mother's house with a book in her sleeve and instructed the deponent in these heretical opinions and especially against the sacrament of the altar. From this time the deponent believed her opinions, as above.

---

[a] quod *interlined; two illegible words deleted.*
[b] in domo sua *interlined.*
[c] eorum *deleted.*
[d] eius *interlined.*
[e] and afterwards this book was hidden there *in margin.*

Wednesday, 3 December 1511

Margaret Landesdale

[LCB, fo. 11v. Continued from late November to early December 1511 (above, p. 208). This entry is dated in the margin. See also below, p. 221, for record in Blyth's register, and p. 273 for the abjuration she signed.]

Submisit[a] se correctioni et cetera. Abiuracionem legit et crucis signum et cetera fecit. Absoluta.

Fatebatur quod Alicia Rowley vigesies accessit ad domum suam et cetera.

Habet penitenciam cum Hugone Parrek.

Reliqua pars differtur in adventum domini.

[English translation]

She[b] submitted herself to correction etc. She read the abjuration and she wrote a sign of the cross etc. Absolved.

She admits that Alice Rowley came to her house on twenty occasions etc.

She has penance with Hugh Parrek.

The rest is deferred until the coming of the bishop.

William Revis

[LCB, fo. 12r. Continued from late November to early December 1511 (above, p. 211). Dated 3rd day of month; December conjectured as appropriate month due to proximity in MS to other entries apparently dating from late November to early December (pp. 192–218). Revis appeared again in January or February (below, p. 245).]

Deinde[c] iii° die mensis et anni supradictorum idem Willelmus, in virtute iuramenti per eum prestiti examinatus de et super singulis premissis,

---

[a] 3° Decembris *in margin.*
[b] 3rd December *in margin.*
[c] idem Willelmus *deleted.*

negat noticiam heretice pravitatis aut conversaciones scienter cum hereticis.[a] Et ulterius negat penitus.

Dominus, ex consilio assistentium sibi, remisit eum domum, decernens ulterius inquirendum esse contra eum.

[English translation]

Then on the 3rd day of the aforesaid month and year the same William, examined about each of the aforesaid matters in virtue of the oath taken by him, denies knowledge of heresy or knowingly conversing with heretics. Again he wholly denies it.

The bishop, on the advice of those assisting him, sent him home, deciding that there should be further enquiry against him.

John Bull, Julian Yong, David Clerc, Thomas Lyeff, Thomas Villers

[LCB, fo. 14r. Undated. Dated by the following entry, which similarly records the abjurations of four of the five accused listed here. See below, p. 270, for the abjuration they signed.]

Johannes Bull et Juliana filia Agnetis Yong – abiurata per eos primitus omni heretica pravitate et absoluti prima – habent penitenciam consimilem cum Silkeby.

Et David Clerc, Thomas Lyeff et Thomas Villers, similiter abiurati et absoluti, habent penitenciam[b] in die Dominica cum dicto Silkeby et aliis et cetera.

[English translation]

John Bull and Julian daughter of Agnes Yong – after they have abjured every heresy and have been absolved – have the same penance as Silkeby.

And David Clerc, Thomas Lyeff, and Thomas Villers, likewise after they have abjured and been absolved, have their penance on Sunday with the said Silkeby and others etc.

[a] Aut *deleted.*
[b] cum Bradeley et aliis simili modo *deleted.*

Hugh Parrek, Margaret Landesdale, David Clerc, John Bull, Thomas Lyeff, and Julian Yong

[Reg. Blyth, fo. 99r. See below, pp. 270 and 273, for the abjurations they signed.]

Tercio die mensis Decembris anno Domini suprascripto apud Maxstock predicta, Hugo Parreck, Margareta uxor Rogeri Landesdale, David Clerc, Johannes Bull, Thomas Lyeff, Juliana Yong filia Agnetis Yong, civitatis Coventr', detecti ut supra, confessi sunt ut supra continetur.

Et abiuraverunt, se submittentes.

Et absolutione prima a sentencia excommunicationis, habent penitenciam consimilem cum Sylkeby et aliis.

[English translation]

On the third day of December in the above mentioned year of the Lord, in Maxstoke, Hugh Parreck, Margaret the wife of Roger Landesdale, David Clerc, John Bull, Thomas Lyeff, Julian Yong the daughter of Agnes Yong, of the city of Coventry, detected as above, confessed as is stated above.

And they abjured, submitting themselves.

After they are absolved from the sentence of excommunication, they have the same penance as Sylkeby and others.

Friday, 16 January 1512

Rose Furnour

[LCB, fo. 14v. The examination continues later the same day after an interval (see below, p. 227).]

xvi Januarii anno supradicto.[a]

Rosa Furnour etatis xxiiii[or] annorum, nata apud Atherston, nuper famula Hachet.

Iurata et cetera, dicit quod litle moder Agnes et Johanna Warde eam instruxerunt in opinionibus hereticis, videlicet contra sacramentum

----

[a] xvi [...] supradicto *is the heading of the page.*

altaris et cetera. Et dicit quod litle moder Agnes optime novit legere; non tamen legit in presencia sua. Nec ista habuit fidem dictis suis. Sed, ut asserit, postquam intellexit huiusmodi dicta fuisse contra fidem catholicam, confitebatur erratum suum[a] cuidam fratri Preston[130] in xl[ma] preterita.

Et[b] dicit ulterius quod Willelmus Revis et uxor sua sepius accesserunt ad domum Hachet ubi communicationem privatam habuerunt, presentibus Abell et Bown. Addit preterea quod Abell infestus est presbiteris.

Et[c] Spon frequentem communicationem habuit[d] cum Hachet in domo eiusdem Hachet de peregrinacionibus. Dicit, concordando cum ceteris, affirmans quod Hachet et ceteri non habuerunt magis complacentiam quam in huiusmodi communicationibus contra fidem.

Addit[e] insuper quod uxor Trussell sepenumero conversabatur cum Johanna Warde.

Audivit[f] Hachet dicentem quod Derlyng erat vir bonus.

Et dicit quod penes Landesdale, uxorem suam, Bown et alios supranominatos opinatur se esse diffamatam. Verumptamen preciso affirmat se nunquam tenuisse aut favisse opinionibus hereticis.

Quare dominus decrevit ulterius inquirere contra eam et remisit eam et cetera.

[English translation]

16 January in the aforesaid year.

Rose Furnour, aged twenty-four, born in Atherstone, recently servant of Hachet.

Sworn etc., she says that Little Mother Agnes and Joan Warde instructed her in heretical opinions, namely against the sacrament of the altar etc. She says that Little Mother Agnes knows how to read very well, although she did not read in her presence. Nor did she believe what Little Mother Agnes said. Rather, as she says, after she understood that the sayings were contrary to the Catholic faith, she confessed her error to a certain Friar Preston,[130] in the last Lent.

She says that William Revis and his wife often came to Hachet's house and conversed privately there in the presence of Abell and Bown. She adds that Abell is hostile to priests.

[a]   suum *interlined.*
[b]   Revis et uxor *in margin.*
[c]   Spon *in margin.*
[d]   b *deleted.*
[e]   uxor Trussell *in margin.*
[f]   Derlyng *in margin.*

And Spon often conversed with Hachet in Hachet's house concerning pilgrimages. She says and affirms, agreeing with others, that Hachet and others had no greater pleasure than in speaking against the faith.

She adds that Trussell's wife often conversed with Joan Warde.

She heard Hachet saying that Derlyng was a good man.

She says that Landesdale, his wife, Bown, and others named above think she is defamed. She affirms specifically, however, that she has never held or favoured heretical opinions.

Therefore the bishop decided to enquire further against her and remanded her etc.

John Jonson

[LCB, fos 14v–15r; Reg. Blyth, fo. 99v. The LCB entry is dated 'the aforesaid day'; it follows in the MS Rose Furnour's examination dated 16 January 1512 (see previous entry). The entry in Blyth's register is dated. Jonson was previously questioned at the end of October (above, pp. 105 and 109). See below, p. 270, for the abjuration he signed.]

[fo. 14v] Prefatis die et loco.[a]

Johannes Jonson de Byrmyngham, cutler, et cetera.

Ulterius examinatus, dicit quod quidam Robertus Qwyck, ville Brystollie parochie sancti Thome in diocesi Bathon',[131] carpet maker, frequentem communicationem habuit cum isto Bouway seniore[132] wever,[b] Henrico Tuck wyer drawer in Brodemede,[c, 33] et Henrico Padwell in parochia sancti Philippi,[134] cutler, et Laurentio Capper in Brodemede atque Karolo Villers parochie sancti Nicholai,[d, 33] mercatore, in cellis [...] contra ymaginum veneraciones et peregrinaciones atque, ut[e] recolit, contra sacramentum altaris. Hoc addendo, quod ista habuerunt verba, 'that the sacrament of the alter is not the very body of our Lorde but materiall brede'.

Et iste communicationes fuerunt presente Bouway seniore circa vi annos elapsos. Et a tempore abiuracionis dicti Bouway junioris, tunc Bouway, ut asserit, nunquam conversabatur cum eisdem[f] eo tempore.

Thomas [...],[g] botell maker, dwelling as a man goith to the temple[136] in seynt Thomas paresh, et Johannes Nayler eiusdem parochie, dwelling

[a] Prefatis die et loco *is the heading.*
[b] seniore wever *interlined.*
[c] wyer drawer in Brodemede *interlined and inserted from margin.*
[d] parochie sancti Nicholai *interlined.*
[e] credit *deleted.*
[f] a tempore *deleted.*
[g] *blank in MS.*

apon the bridge, have been also present at such communicacions with the persons above named. Et huiusmodi communicationes habuerunt non solum in domibus verum etiam in campis, spaciando usque capellam sancti Vincentii.[137]

Tuck et Qwyck pessimos reputat. Tuck scit Apocalipsim totaliter et memoriter.

Karolus tamen Villers non spaciabatur cum eisdem, sed supranominati accessum habuerunt ad domum suam ubi communicaverunt de et super premissis, presente uxore dicti Karoli et audiente.

Et est mala suspicio de uxoribus Padwell, Capper et botell maker, in quorum domibus huiusmodi communicationes habuerunt, uxoribus presentibus.

Et[a] dicit quod Acton erat familiaris cum Rogero Brown et Johanne Phisico.

Et[b] Thomas Archer de Coventr'[c] unacum uxore sua frequentem accessum habuerunt ad domum dicti Johannis Phisici, ubi audiverunt ipsum Johannem dogmatizantem contra peregrinationes et ymaginum venerationes.

Holbache[d] familaris fuit cum Silkby.

[fo. 15r] Johannes[e] Clerc conversabatur cum supranominatis Johanne Phisico et Rogero Brown. Et audivit eosdem dogmatizantes contra peregrinaciones et ymaginum veneraciones.

Verum quin prenominatus Johannes Jonson male sentiebat contra sacramentum altaris et cetera, asserens se velle ad ecclesie unitatem redire, seque submittens iudicio sancte matris ecclesie, omnem hereticam pravitatem sponte abiuravit ut supra, signum crucis subscribens. Qua abiuracione perlecta – in presentiis venerabilium virorum dompni Willelmi Dykens, prioris de Maxstoc,[f] magistrorum Radulphi Cantrell, Thome Orton, decretorum doctorum, Willelmi Skelton, Willelmi Wilton, artium magistrorum, necnon Willelmi Palden, Johannis Blyth, in decretis bacallariorum, dominorum Ricardi Hayes, Johannis Pursell, capellanorum, et nonnullorum aliorum – dominus eundem Johannem, iuratum de perimplendo penitenciam et cetera, a sentencia excommunicationis absolvit.

Et dominus iniunxit penitenciam publicam eidem peragendam cum fasciculo et cetera in die Dominica proxime[g] coram processione in

---

[a]   Acton *in margin.*
[b]   Archer et uxor *in margin.*
[c]   de Coventr' *interlined.*
[d]   Holbache *in margin.*
[e]   Johannes Clerc *in margin.*
[f]   prioris de Maxstoc *interlined.*
[g]   proxime *sic and interlined.*

ecclesia parochiali de Aston iuxta Brymyngham,[138] et in foro apud Coventr' in die Veneris, videlicet penultimo die eiusdem mensis Januarii, quemadmodum Flesshour.

[Reg. Blyth, fo. 99v] xvi^mo die mensis Januarii anno Domini suprascripto apud Maxstock predicta, Johannes Jonson parochie de Aston iuxta Brymyngham, detectus, comparuit.

Et tandem post magnam deliberacionem gravi difficultate, satis aperte recognoscens quod reatum suum in ea parte non posset celare, confessus est seque submisit ut supra cum aliis abiuratis. Itaque eum, et oneratum iuramento de perimplendo penitenciam et cetera, dominus absolvit ab excommunicationis sentencia.

Et quia diu continuavit dampnabiliter in opinionibus suis hereticis suprascriptis et cum multis hereticis variis in locis conversacionem habuit, idcirco dominus iniunxit eidem penitenciam subscriptam. Videlicet, quod die Dominica extunc proxima sequente, precedendo processionem in ecclesia parochiali de Aston Brymyngham,[a] deferat fasciculum lignorum, more penitentis. Similiter faciat die Veneris extunc proximo sequente, eundo coram processione apud Coventr' circa forum et cetera.

[English translation]

The day and the place as given above.

John Jonson of Birmingham, cutler, etc.

Examined further, he says that Robert Qwyck of St Thomas's parish in Bristol in Bath diocese,[131] carpet-maker, often conversed with Bouway senior, weaver,[132] Henry Tuck, wiredrawer in Broadmead,[133] and Henry Padwell in St Philip's parish,[134] cutler, and Laurence Capper in Broadmead, and Charles Villers of St Nicholas's parish,[135] merchant, in rooms [...] against the veneration of images and pilgrimages and, as he recalls, against the sacrament of the altar. He adds that they said the following, 'that the sacrament of the altar is not the very body of our Lord but material bread'.

These communications took place in the presence of Bouway senior about six years ago. From the time of the abjuration of the said Bouway junior, Bouway, as he says, never thereafter conversed with these same people.

Thomas [...],[b] bottle-maker, dwelling as a man goes to the temple[136] in St Thomas's parish, and John Nayler of the same parish, dwelling

---

[a]   defererat *deleted.*
[b]   *blank space in MS.*

upon the bridge, have been also present at such communications with the persons above named. They had these conversations not only in homes but also in fields, walking to St Vincent's chapel.[137]

He considers Tuck and Qwyck to be wicked. Tuck knows by heart all of the Apocalypse.

Charles Villers, however, did not walk with these same people but they came to his house and communicated there about the above matters, with Charles's wife present and listening.

There is a bad suspicion concerning the wives of Padwell, Capper, and the bottle-maker, in whose homes communications of this kind have taken place, in the presence of their wives.

He says that Acton was familiar with Roger Brown and John Physician.

Thomas Archer of Coventry, together with his wife, often came to the said John Physician's home and they listened there to the said John teaching against pilgrimages and the veneration of images.

Holbache was familiar with Silkby.

[fo. 15r] John Clerc conversed with the above named John Physician and Roger Brown, and he heard them teaching against pilgrimages and the veneration of images.

The said John Jonson had thought wrongly against the sacrament of the altar etc. Saying, however, that he wanted to return to the Church's unity, and submitting himself to the judgement of Holy Mother Church, he spontaneously abjured every heresy as above, and he wrote underneath a sign of the cross. After the abjuration had been read – in the presence of the venerable men, Lord William Dykens, Prior of Maxstoke, Masters Ralph Cantrell, Thomas Orton, doctors of decrees, William Skelton, William Wilton, masters of arts, William Palden, John Blyth, bachelors in decrees, Sir Richard Hayes, John Pursell, chaplains, and several others – the bishop absolved the said John, after he had sworn to perform the penance etc., from the sentence of excommunication.

And the bishop enjoined upon him public penance to be performed with a faggot etc. on the following Sunday, in front of the procession in the parish church of Aston near Birmingham,[138] and in the market-place at Coventry on Friday, that is the penultimate day of January, just like Flesshour.

[Reg. Blyth, fo. 99r] On 16 January in the aforesaid year of the Lord, in Maxstoke, John Jonson of Aston parish near Birmingham, detected, appeared.

At last, after much deliberation and with great difficulty, recognizing sufficiently openly that he could not conceal his guilt in this matter, he confessed, and he submitted himself as above with the other abjurers. Therefore, after he had sworn to perform the penance etc., the bishop absolved him from the sentence of excommunication.

Because he continued for a long time, to his damnation, in his above mentioned heretical opinions and conversed with many heretics in various places, the bishop enjoined upon him the following penance. Namely, that on the next Sunday he carry a faggot of wood as a penitent in front of the procession in the parish church of Aston, Birmingham. And likewise on the following Friday, in front of the procession in Coventry around the marketplace etc.

Rose Furnour

[LCB, fos 14v, 15r; Reg. Blyth, fo. 99r. The first entry, from the LCB, is a continuation from an examination earlier the same day (John Jonson's testimony probably intervened). The second entry, from Blyth's register, is dated by analogy with the LCB. See below, p. 273, for the abjuration she signed.]

Tandem dicta Rosa post meridiem eiusdem diei, comparens coram domino, fatebatur se sollicitacionibus Hachet incidisse in heresim et promisisse eidem Hachet quod nunquam detegeret consilia eorum. Et dicit quod sepe locutus est de[a] evangelio: 'Noli timere, pusillus grex'.[139]

Dicta tunc Rosa volens, ut asseruit, ad unitatem ecclesie redire et huiusmodi erroribus prorsus renunciare, submisit se iudicio[b] *[fo. 15r]* sancte matris ecclesie et abiuracionem legit ut supra, signumque crucis subscripsit, in presentiis venerabilium virorum superius nominatorum,[c] magistro Cantrell solummodo excepto.

Et eandem, de perimplendo penitenciam sibi iniungendam corporali iuramento oneratam, et de parendo iuri, dominus absolvit. Et penitenciam subscriptam eidem iniunxit,[d] videlicet quod qualibet vigilia Assumptionis beate Marie virginis per septennium futurum ieiunabit in pane et aqua.[140]

[Reg. Blyth, fo. 99r] Rosa Furnour puella etatis xxiiii[or] annorum, nuper famula Hachet, confessa est omnes et singulos articulos suprascriptos.

Humiliter tunc se submittens et renuncians opinionibus et cetera ut supra, abiuravit.

---

[a] de *repeated in MS.*

[b] *An insertion mark follows. The passage continues at the bottom of fo. 15r, indicated in the margin by a similar insertion mark.*

[c] Virorum superius nominatorum: *this probably refers to the men named in the entry for Jonson (above).*

[d] *two illegible words deleted.*

Absoluta itaque a sentencia excommunicationis, habet penitenciam subscriptam propterea quod sponte et incontenti confessa est, maximo ducta dolore, ut apparuit, et contritione: videlicet quod qualibet vigilia assumptionis beate Marie virginis per septennium futurum in pane et aqua ieiunet.

[English translation]

Eventually, after midday on the same day, the said Rose, appearing before the bishop, admitted that she had fallen into heresy, at the prompting of Hachet, and that she had promised Hachet she would never reveal their counsels. She says he often spoke about the Gospel, 'Fear not, little flock'.[139]

The said Rose, wishing, as she said, to return to the Church's unity and to renounce wholly these errors, submitted herself to the judgement[a] *[fo. 15r]* of Holy Mother Church and she read the abjuration, as above, and wrote underneath a sign of the cross, in the presence of the venerable men named above[b] with the single exception of Master Cantrell.

After she had sworn to perform the penance to be imposed and to obey the law, the bishop absolved her, and he imposed upon her the following penance, namely on each vigil of the Assumption of the Blessed Virgin Mary for the next seven years she will fast on bread and water.[140]

[Reg. Blyth, fo. 99r] Rose Furnour, a young woman aged twenty-four, recently the servant of Hachet, confessed each and every one of the above written articles.

Then, humbly submitting herself and renouncing the opinions etc. as above, she abjured.

After she had been absolved from the sentence of excommunication, therefore, she has the following penance because she confessed spontaneously and immediately with much sorrow, as it appeared, and contrition: namely, that on each vigil of the Assumption of the Blessed Virgin Mary for the next seven years she shall fast on bread and water.

---

[a] *An insertion mark follows. The passage continues at the bottom of fo. 15r, indicated in the margin by a similar insertion mark.*

[b] men named above: *this probably refers to the men named in the entry for Jonson (above).*

John Clerc

[LCB, fo. 26r; Reg. Blyth, fo. 99v. The first entry, from the LCB, is undated; it may have occurred several days before the entry in Blyth's register, which appears in the same paragraph as the record regarding John Jonson (above, p. 225), dated 16 January 1512.]

Johannes Cle[rc] civitatis Coventr'.

Iuratus et examinatus, negat prorsus. Quare d[ominus de] consilio et cetera, decrevit ut supra.

[Reg. Blyth, fo. 99v] Consimilem penitenciam dominus iniunxit Johanni Clerc, peragendam eodem die Veneris apud Coventr': abiuracione sua primitus prima unacum absolutione et caucione de huiusmodi perimplendo penitenciam.

[English translation]

John Cle[rc] of Coventry.

Sworn and examined, he denies everything. Therefore the bishop, on the advice etc., decided as above.

[Reg. Blyth, fo. 99v] The bishop enjoined the same penance on John Clerc, to be performed on the same Friday in Coventry: first his abjuration, together with absolution and the guarantee to perform this penance.

John Davy

[Reg. Blyth, fo. 99v. This appears in Blyth's register in the same paragraph as the entry regarding John Jonson (above, p. 225), dated 16 January 1512. See below, p. 266, for the abjuration he signed.]

Johannes Davy similem habet penitenciam cum Johannem Clerc: abiuracione, absolucione et cautionis prestatione de observantia, penitencia et cetera iniungenda prius in ea parte primis.

[English translation]

John Davy has the same penance with John Clerc: first his abjuration, absolution and guarantee of observance, enjoining of the penance etc.

Alice Rowley

[LCB, fo. 15r. Dated 'aforesaid day'; follows Rose Furnour's and John Jonson's examinations, dated 16 January 1512 (above, pp. 221 and 223).]

Prefatis die et loco, Alicia Rowley,[a] comparens coram domino, fatebatur se dogmatisasse, asseruisse et tenuisse a tempore purgationis sue contra sacramentum altaris et peregrinaciones. Et credidit hostiam oblatam nihil aliud fuisse quam panem materialem ante tempus quo ultimo deprehensa erat, videlicet heri ad xi^{cem} septimanas elapsas,[141] ut asserit.

Et dicit ulterius quod Acton non credidit in sacramento altaris et quod uxor eius audivit sepe communicationes eorundem contra sacramentum et cetera et est eiusdem opinionis.

[English translation]

On the day and in the place given above, Alice Rowley, appearing before the bishop, confessed that, from the time of her purgation, she taught, asserted, and held against the sacrament of the altar and pilgrimages. And before the time that she was last arrested, that is to say eleven weeks ago yesterday,[141] she believed that the host offered was nothing but material bread.

She says, furthermore, that Acton did not believe in the sacrament of the altar, and that his wife often heard their communications against the sacrament etc. and is of the same opinion.

[a] Rowley *interlined.*

Thursday, 22 January 1512

John Cropwell

[LCB, fo. 15v. Cropwell previously appeared late November or early December 1511 (above, p. 212), and his interrogation resumes 4 February 1512 (below, p. 249).]

Apud Coventr' xxii^{do} die Januarii anno Domini supradicto.[a]

Johannes Cropwell supranominatus.

Denuo comparens coram domino, fatebatur se audivisse Hachet, Bown, Londesdale et Silkeby ter seu quater communicantes contra venerationes ymaginum et aliquando contra sacramentum altaris. Non tamen, ut asseruit, credidit dictis eorundem, presertim contra sacramentum altaris, sed solummodo opinatus est eos[b] bene dixisse contra ymaginum veneraciones.

Et fatetur se novisse quod supranominatus Hachet male sentiebat de sacramento altaris et quod celavit consilia eorum in huiusmodi opinionibus hereticis.

Et dicit quod Johanna Smyth eum primo instruxit in huiusmodi opinionibus et cetera, famulam cuius iste duxit in uxorem. Et eadem Johanna sepe dogmatisavit isti contra presbiteros et cetera.

Interrogatus quotiens audivit Hachet huiusmodi communicacionem habentem, dicit quod semel vel bis; Bown ter vel quater; Silkeby totidem ferme; et Londesdale ter vel quater.

[English translation]

In Coventry on 22 January in the aforesaid year of the Lord.

The above named John Cropwell.

Appearing again before the bishop, he admitted he heard Hachet, Bown, Londesdale, and Silkeby three or four times speaking against the veneration of images and sometimes against the sacrament of the altar. He says, however, that he did not believe what they said, especially against the sacrament of the altar, but only thought they spoke well against the veneration of images.

He admits he knew that the above named Hachet thought ill of the sacrament of the altar, and that he concealed their counsels regarding these heretical opinions.

[a] Apud [...] supradicto *is the heading of the page.*
[b] eos *interlined.*

He says that Joan Smyth, whose servant he married, first instructed him in these opinions etc. The same Joan often instructed him against priests etc.

Asked how often he heard Hachet communicating in this way, he says once or twice; Bown three or four times; Silkeby almost as often; and Londesdale three or four times.

Katherine Hachet

[LCB, fo. 15v. Undated; follows previous entry dated 22 January 1512.]

Katherina, uxor Hachet, et cetera.

Comparens coram domino et iuramento corporali et cetera, fatebatur se instructionibus viri sui inductam in opinionibus hereticis, videlicet contra peregrinaciones, ymaginum veneraciones.

Verumptamen nunquam male[a] sentiebat de sacramento altaris.

Et fatetur quod murmurabat contra frequentem viri sui accessum ad Bown, Sylkeby et alios.

[English translation]

Katherine, wife of Hachet, etc.

Appearing before the bishop and under oath etc., she admitted that, through the instruction of her husband, she was led into heretical opinions, namely against pilgrimages and the veneration of images.

She, however, never thought ill of the sacrament of the altar.

She admits she murmured against her husband's frequent visits to Bown, Sylkeby, and others.

Agnes Jonson, Agnes Yong, and Agnes de Bakehouse

[LCB, fo. 16v. Undated. Dated by analogy with record of abjurations in Blyth's register (see p. 236), since the examinations were probably on the same day or closely preceding the abjurations. See below, p. 270, for the abjuration they signed.]

Agnes Jonson civitatis Coventr'.

Iurata et examinata et cetera, fatebatur primum quod quendam

[a] confi *deleted.*

librum habuit, effectum cuius non novit, ut asseruit. Quem librum tradidit cuidam Johanne Blacburn civitatis London'.

Et postea, affirmante Alicia Rowley in facie sua quod ipsa tenuit, astruit et credidit contra sacramentum altaris, peregrinationes et ymaginum veneraciones, fatebatur quod tenuit et cetera contra peregrinaciones et ymaginum veneraciones, non tamen contra sacramentum altaris.

Preterea fatebatur quod habuit librum de Thobia. Et librum de mandatis negat se habuisse. Dicit tamen quod filia sua[142] huiusmodi librum habet de Thobia.

Agnes Yong civitatis Coventr', iurata atque examinata et cetera.

Fatetur quod tenuit, credidit et dogmatisavit contra sacramentum altaris, peregrinaciones et ymaginum veneraciones.

Et quod sepius in domo Alicie Rowley interfuit huiusmodi communicationibus.

Et dicit quod Agnes de Bakehouse interfuit sepenumero huiusmodi communicationibus et cetera.

Agnes de Bakehouse civitatis Coventr', iurata et[a] cetera.

Fatetur quod opinionem tenuit contra peregrinaciones et ymaginum veneraciones.

Et fatetur quod[b] audivit Silkeby et alios sepe communicantes contra sacramentum altaris.

Interrogata quotiens interfuit huiusmodi communicacioni, dicit quod quater et nescit ulterius.

Die et loco supradictis, iste tres mulieres supranominate submiserunt se iudicio sancte matris ecclesie et cetera. Et abiuracionem legerunt, signum crucis sub nomine suo subscribentes.

Et habent penitenciam solempnem peragendam ante processionem in ecclesia sancti Michaelis et cetera, cum fasciculis, die Dominica: videlicet primo die Februarii proximi.

[English translation]

Agnes Jonson of Coventry.

Sworn and examined etc., she admitted first that she had a certain book, of whose contents she was ignorant, as she said. She passed the book to a certain Joan Blacburn of London.

[a] et *repeated in MS.*
[b] *illegible word deleted.*

Afterwards, when Alice Rowley affirmed in her presence that she held, taught, and believed against the sacrament of the altar, pilgrimages, and the veneration of images, she admitted that she held etc. against pilgrimages and the veneration of images, not, however, against the sacrament of the altar.

She admitted she had a Book of Tobit. She denies she had a book of the Commandments. She says, however, that her daughter[142] has the Book of Tobit.

Agnes Yong of Coventry, sworn and examined etc.

She admits she held, believed, and taught against the sacrament of the altar, pilgrimages, and the veneration of images.

And that she was often present at communications of this kind in Alice Rowley's home.

She says that Agnes de Bakehouse often took part in these communications etc.

Agnes de Bakehouse of Coventry, sworn etc.

She admits she held an opinion against pilgrimages and the veneration of images.

She admits she heard Silkeby, and others, often speaking against the sacrament of the altar.

Asked how often she was present at this communication, she says four times and she does not know more.

On the day and in the place given above, these three women named above submitted themselves to the judgement of Holy Mother Church etc. They read the abjuration and wrote a sign of the cross under their name.

They must perform solemn penance in front of the procession in St Michael's church etc., with faggots, on Sunday, namely on the first day of February next.

Agnes Corby

[LCB, fo. 17v. Date illegible. Dated by analogy with record of abjuration in Blyth's register (see p. 236), since the examination was probably on the same day or closely preceding the abjuration. The gaps result from holes in the MS.]

Agnes Corby.

Iurata et examinata ut supra, negat.

[...] mensis [...] supradict', coram commissariis domini subscriptis, in loco inferius descripto, comparens supranominata Agnes Corby et onerata iuramento corporali ad fideliter respondendum.

Primo fatebatur quod didicit a Johanna Warde, 'I am the servant of God and in our lorde Jehsus Criste'[143] et cetera.

Negat tamen se fuisse eiusdem secte.

Tandem fatetur quod audivit Aliciam Rowley explanantem evangelium, 'Noli timere pusillus grex'[144] et cetera.

Et de sacramento altaris, fatetur sensum quod est supra expressum, videlicet quod acciperet illud in memoriam passionis Christi.

Et de peregrinacionibus atque ymaginum veneracionibus,[a] ita tenuit ut supra, quod melius applicaretur in usus pauperum pecunia [...] in parte [...].

[English translation]

Agnes Corby.

Sworn and examined as above, she denies.

[...] of the month [...] given above, before the bishop's commissaries named below, in the place described below, appeared the aforesaid Agnes Corby, under oath to reply faithfully.

First she admitted she learnt from Joan Warde, 'I am the servant of God and in our lord Jesus Christ'[143] etc.

She denies, however, that she was of the sect.

At last, she admits that she heard Alice Rowley explaining the Gospel, 'Fear not, little flock',[144] etc.

About the sacrament of the altar, she admits the sense that is expressed above, namely that she would accept it in memory of Christ's passion.

Regarding pilgrimages, and the veneration of images, she believed as above, that the money would be better given to the benefit of the poor [...] in part [...].

Elizabeth Gest and Agnes Corby

[LCB, fo. 26r. Dated by analogy with record of abjurations in Blyth's register (see p. 236), since the examinations were probably on the same day or closely preceding the abjurations. See below, p. 266, for the abjuration they signed.]

Elizabeth Gest.

[a] MS *veneraciones.*

Iurata et cetera ut supra, prorsus negat. Quare dominus de consilio et cetera, decrevit ut supra.

Tandem tam ipsa quam Agnes Corby, saniori ducte consilio, volentes, ut asseruerunt, ad unitatem ecclesie redire, omnem et omnimodam heresim abiuraverunt. Itaque, absolute, habent penitenciam solemnem cum Agnete Jonson et cetera.

[English translation]

Elizabeth Gest.

Sworn etc. as above, she denies everything. Therefore the bishop, on the advice etc., decided as above.

Eventually, both she and Agnes Corby, following better counsel and wishing, as they said, to return to the unity of the Church, abjured each and every heresy. Therefore, having been absolved, they have solemn penance with Agnes Jonson etc.

Agnes Jonson, Agnes de Bakehouse, Agnes Yong, Agnes Corby, Agnes Brown, and Elizabeth Gest

[Reg. Blyth, fo. 99v. Note that the inclusion of Agnes Brown, as having abjured on this day, is likely erroneous, as she is recorded as still contumaciously refusing to admit heresy in February 1512 (below, p. 251). The abjurations the other women signed are below, pp. 266 and 270.]

xxii^{do} die mensis Januarii anno Domini supradicto apud Coventr'.

Agnes Jonson, Agnes de Bakehouse, Agnes Yong, Agnes Corby, Agnes Brown et Elizabeth Gest, detecte et cetera ut supra, comparuerunt.

Quarum tres prime confesse sunt sese incidisse in opinionibus huiusmodi quemadmodum continetur in articulis supraspecificatis.

Relique tres non incontinenti, sed postea commissariis domini – videlicet magistris Radulpho Cantrell, Johanni Wilcock, sacre theologie professori, et aliis, coniunctim et divisim nominatis – offensas et reatus suos in ea parte confesse sunt publice in iudicio, et quod multis annis in huiusmodi opinionibus hereticis dampnabiliter steterunt.

Submittentes itaque sese iudicio sancte matris ecclesie, atque abiuratis per earum quamlibet huiusmodi opinionibus suis hereticis ut supra, habent penitenciam peragendam in ecclesia sancti Michaelis primo die Februarii, videlicet die Dominica extunc proxima sequente, cum fasciculis, more penitentium, in casu consimili et quemadmodum [...] Flesshor fecit et cetera.

[English translation]

22 January in the aforesaid year of the Lord in Coventry.

Agnes Jonson, Agnes de Bakehouse, Agnes Yong, Agnes Corby, Agnes Brown, and Elizabeth Gest, detected etc. as above, appeared.

The first three of them confessed they had fallen into opinions of this kind as is contained in the articles specified above.

The other three not immediately; but afterwards, publicly in court to the bishop's commissaries – namely, Masters Ralph Cantrell, John Wilcock, professor of sacred theology, and others, who were appointed by name both collectively and individually – they confessed their offences and faults in this matter, and that they had damnably remained for many years in these heretical opinions.

Submitting themselves, therefore, to the judgement of Holy Mother Church and having abjured each of their heretical opinions as above, they have their penance to be performed in St Michael's church on 1 February, that is, the Sunday then following, with faggots, as penitents, in the same way and as [...] Flesshor did etc.

Saturday, 24 January 1512

[Robert?] Hachet

[LCB, fo. 15v. Dated 24ᵗʰ of month; follows in MS other entries dated January 1512 (above, pp. 221–231).]

Apud Coventr' xxiiiiᵗᵒ die mensis et anni.ᵃ

Hachetts, interrogatus an aliquid sinistre opinionis novit vel audivit de Pysford, vel filia sua iam maritata Wiggeston,[145] dicit, in virtute iuramenti per eum prestiti, quod non et cetera.

ᵃ Apud [...] anni *is the heading.*

[English translation]

In Coventry on the 24th day of the month and year.

Hachetts, asked whether he knew or heard any bad opinion of Pysford or his daughter, now married to Wiggeston,[145] says, in virtue of the oath he took, no, etc.

Joan Wasshingburn *alias* Warde

[LCB, fo. 16r. Undated. Follows in MS previous entry dated 24 January 1512 and was likely to have been around that time.]

Johanna[a] Wasshingburn alias Warde[b] prenominata.

Comparens coram domino et iurata et cetera, primum fatebatur quod circiter xx[ti] annos elapsos inducta erat in hereses, videlicet contra sacramentum altaris et cetera, mediis et dogmatisacionibus Alicie Rowley.

Et postea, metu Willelmi Rowley, recessit a Coventr' ad Northampton',[146] Roberto Bastell duce sibi. Ibique moram traxit cum quodam Ose alutario per xx[ti] septimanas et ultra.

A Northamptonia contulit se ad London', ubi cum quodam Blacburn, bedder, mansit a nativitate sancti Johannis Baptiste ad festum sancti Martini in yeme.[147] Et dicit quod uxor dicti Blacburn fuit heretica. Ulterius fatebatur quod mediis cuiusdam Myldener et Briam, hereticorum,[c] nupta fuit cuidam Thome Wasshingburn, sutori, heretico.[148] Cum quo mansit in London' per spacium trium annorum et cetera.

Et tandem ipsa cum viro suo prenominato[d] accessit ad Maydeston,[149] ubi moram traxit. Et tam vir suus quam ipsa unacum aliis ad numerum xv[cem] personarum[e] – videlicet Bukmar et uxor, Lockyn et uxor, aliorum nomina non recolit – deprehensi erant et conventi de et super heretica pravitate, et abiurati, necnon signati in lena maxilla cum littera H.[150]

Interrogata de qua heresi erat abiurata et ob quam causam,[f] dicit quod propter opiniones hereticas,[g] videlicet[h] quia tenuit et credidit[i] contra peregrinaciones, ymaginum veneraciones et propterea quod

---

[a] Warde *deleted.*
[b] Wasshingburn alias Warde *interlined.*
[c] hereticorum *interlined.*
[d] *MS.* prenominata.
[e] annorum *deleted;* personarum *interlined.*
[f] *illegible word deleted.*
[g] opiniones *deleted.*
[h] quod *deleted.*
[i] quia tenuit et credidit *interlined.*

ecclesiam sinagogam appellavit. Ideo abiurata erat confessione sua prima et iudicialiter emissa coram magistro doctore Cambreton[151] et cetera.

Deinde, obiecto et articulato eidem Johanne Wasshingburn quod ipsa a tempore abiuracionis sue huiusmodi relapsa erat et est in huiusmodi dampnatas hereses, et easdem dogmatisavit, astruit, tenuit et credidit, fatebatur publice. Et ulterius confessa est quod communicacionem habuit contra sacramentum altaris, peregrinaciones et ymaginum veneraciones cum Alicia Rowley, Roberto Sylkeby, litle moder Agnes et aliis a tempore abiuracionis sue huiusmodi et cetera.

[English translation]

Joan Wasshingburn *alias* Warde, named above.

Appearing before the bishop and sworn etc., first, she admitted that about twenty years ago she was led into heresies, namely against the sacrament of the altar etc., by means of and through the teachings of Alice Rowley.

Later, from fear of William Rowley, she withdrew from Coventry to Northampton,[146] Robert Bastell leading her. She remained there with a certain Ose, tawyer, for twenty weeks and more.

From Northampton she went to London, where she stayed with a certain Blacburn, bedder, from the nativity of St John the Baptist to the feast of St Martin in winter.[147] She says Blacburn's wife was a heretic. She says that through a certain Myldener and Briam, heretics, she was married to a certain Thomas Wasshingburn, shoemaker, heretic.[148] She remained with him in London for three years etc.

Then she went with her husband to Maidstone,[149] where she lived. And both her husband and she, together with fifteen other persons – namely Bukmar and wife, Lockyn and wife, and the other names she does not remember – were arrested and summoned for heresy. They abjured and were branded with the letter H on their jaw.[150]

Asked about the heresy she abjured and why, she says on account of heretical opinions, namely because she held and believed against pilgrimages, the veneration of images, and because she called the church a synagogue. Thus, she had abjured with her first confession which was made judicially before Master Doctor Cambreton[151] etc.

Then, when it was objected and proposed to the same Joan Wasshingburn that since her abjuration she had relapsed into these condemned heresies and had taught, held, and believed the same, she publicly admitted this. She also confessed that, since her abjuration, she had spoken against the sacrament of the altar, pilgrimages, and the veneration of images with Alice Rowley, Robert Sylkeby, Little Mother Agnes and others.

John Olyver

[LCB, fo. 1r]

xxiiii^to die mensis Januarii anno Domini supradicto apud Coventr', quidam^a Johannes Olyver, parochie de Maxstock, comparuit coram domino.

Et^b idem, oneratus iuramento corporali ad dicendum veritatem de inquirendis et cetera, dicit quod Alicia Rowley habuit hec verba sibi, presente uxore sua, in castro de Maxstock die Martis in prima septimana Adventus Domini^152 ultimi preteriti: 'My^c beleve is better than thers save that we dar not speke it. And why shuld God geve us greate goods more than other men hath^d but bicause of our good stedefaste beleve and good books.'

Et asserenti isto quod hec verba denunciaret domino, dixit illa: 'I care not, thow can not hurte me^e; my Lorde knoweth my mynde all redy.'

[English translation]

On 24 January in the aforesaid year of the Lord in Coventry, John Olyver of Maxstoke parish appeared before the bishop.

Having sworn to tell the truth regarding the questions etc., he says that Alice Rowley^f spoke these words, in the presence of his wife, in the castle of Maxstoke on Tuesday in the first week of Advent last year:^152 'My belief is better than theirs save that we dare not speak it. And why should God give us great goods more than other men have but because of our good steadfast belief and good books.'

When the deponent said he would denounce these words to the bishop, she said: 'I care not, thou cannot hurt me; my Lord knoweth my mind already.'

^a   Oliverus *deleted.*
^b   D *deleted.*
^c   contra Rowley *in margin.*
^d   More [...] hath *inserted from the margin.*
^e   Thow [...] me *interlined.*
^f   Against Rowley *in margin.*

Alice Rowley

*[LCB, fo. 17r; Reg. Blyth, fo. 99v. The first entry, from LCB, dated 'said day';
24 January is the last date recorded in MS, at fo. 15v (above, p. 237). The second
entry, from Blyth's register, is dated '24th of abovewritten month', following other
entries dated January. Reference is made here to Joan Warde alias Wasshingburn's
burning, although she had not yet been officially sentenced (this would occur in
March, below, pp. 252–258); the bishop had clearly decided already that this would
be her fate and probably waited only for confirmation from Canterbury of her
previous abjuration. For Rowley's abjuration, see below, p. 273.]*

[fo. 17r] Dictis die et loco, Alicia Rowley prenominata comparuit coram
domino.

Et fatebatur quod, ex quo purgavit se quod non credidit, tenuit
neque dogmatisavit contra sacramentum altaris, peregrinaciones et
ymaginum veneraciones – the which purgacion, as she saide, she made
for an excuse and untruly – she hathe fallen into heresy ageinst the
sacrament of the alter et cetera ut supra.

Et fatetur quod litle moder Agnes hath had communicacion with
her et cetera. And she, Agnes,[a] had a booke of Thoby and another of
commaundements in English. And this communicacion was had in her
house, otherwhile Agnes Yong being present.

Habet penitenciam ut deferat fasciculum ligneum toto tempore quo
cremata fuerit Johanna Wassingburn, eumque postea deportet ad
ymaginem dive Marie de Turre, ubi offerat xiid.

[Reg. Blyth, fo. 99v] xxiiii^{to} die mensis et anni atque loco suprascriptis,
Alicia Rowley civitatis Coventr' comparuit coram dicto reverendo
patre.

Et tandem recognoscens dampnabiles errores suos quos diu tenuit,
astruit et dogmatisavit, eisdem omnibus et singulis renunciavit, se
submittendo iudicio sancte matris ecclesie. Abiuracionemque legit ut
supra. Cautionemque iuratoriam de perimplendo penitenciam eidem
iniungendam prestitit.

Absoluta itaque a sentencia excommunicationis, habet penitenciam
subscriptam: videlicet quod toto tempore quo Johanna Wasshingburn
luat penas relapsorum quousque in cineres ignita fuerit supra summitatem dolii, deferendo fasciculum lignorum humeris suis continuo
fiet. Et post hec, immediate deportet eundem fasciculum ad ymaginem
dive Marie de Turre, ubi summam xii d. offerat et cetera.

---

[a] Agnes *interlined*.

[English translation]

On the day and in the place given above, the above named Alice Rowley appeared before the bishop.

She admitted that, although she purged herself to the effect that she did not believe, hold, or teach against the sacrament of the altar, pilgrimages, and the veneration of images – the which purgation, as she said, she made for an excuse and untruly – she has fallen into heresy against the sacrament of the altar etc. as above.

She admits that Little Mother Agnes has had communication with her etc. And she, Agnes, had a Book of Tobit, and another of Commandments in English. And this communication was had in her house, all the while Agnes Yong being present.

She has the penance of carrying a faggot of wood all the time while Joan Wasshingburn is being burnt, and afterwards she shall carry it to the image of Blessed Mary of the Tower, where she shall offer 12 pence.

[Reg. Blyth, fo. 99v] On the above written 24th day of the month and year and in the above written place, Alice Rowley of Coventry appeared before the said reverend father.

At last acknowledging her damnable errors which she held, instructed, and taught for a long time, she renounced each and every one of them, submitting herself to the judgement of Holy Mother Church. She read the abjuration as above, and she guaranteed under oath to perform the penance to be imposed on her.

Having, therefore, been absolved from the sentence of excommunication, she has the following penance: namely that throughout the time that Joan Wasshingburn is paying the penalties of the relapsed, until she is burnt to ashes at the top of the place of public punishment,[a] she shall continuously carry a faggot of wood on her shoulders. And afterwards she shall immediately carry the faggot to the image of Blessed Mary of the Tower, where she shall offer the sum of 12 pence etc.

---

[a] *MS:* supra summitatem dolii: *here* dolium *is translated as* place of public punishment *by analogy with London's use of the term* dolium *(literally cask or tun) to denote the place where offenders were put in the stocks, next to the London prison known as the Tun (apparently called after its barrel shape). See Latham s.v.* dolium.

Monday, 26 January 1512

Thomasina Bradley

[LCB, fo. 11v. Examination resumed from late November to early December 1512 (above, p. 207).]

Postea, videlicet xxvi^{to} die mensis Januarii anno Domini supradicto, dicta Thomasina in domo capitulari prioratus Coventr' comparuit coram domino et negavit ut supra.

Quare dominus, ex consilio sibi assisentium, decrevit ulterius inquirendum esse contra eam et cetera.

[English translation]

Subsequently, namely on 26 January in the aforesaid year of the Lord, the said Thomasina appeared before the bishop in the chapter house of Coventry Priory and she denied as above.

Therefore the bishop, on the advice of those assisting him, decided to enquire further against her etc.

Mid-January to mid-February 1512

Richard Rise

[LCB, fo. 17r; p. iii. The surname in the first entry is illegible due to a hole in the MS. Richard Rise, a shoemaker, abjured 4 February 1512, and so this examination is tentatively assigned to him. It is undated, but other entries in proximity to it in the MS date from January or February 1512. The gaps result from holes in the MS. The second entry, undated, where only the surname is legible, comes from a much damaged page of the MS. Both entries presumably predate Rise's recorded abjuration on 4 February (below, p. 250).]

Ricardus [...] civitatis Coventr', sutor.

Iuratus et examinatus,[a] negat omnino se [...] docuisse aut affirmasse aliquid contra doctrinam ecclesie.

Fatetur [...][b] in presentia cuiusdam extranei, Hachet loquen' contra [...] dictis tamen suis nullam habuit fidem.

Dominus de consilio sibi assistentium decrevit ulterius inquirere contra eum.

[p. iii] [...] Ryse[c] C[...] tenuisse [...] quod audi[...] peregrinaciones [...] assistentium [...].

[English translation]

Richard [...] of Coventry, shoemaker.

Sworn and examined, he wholly denies that [...] taught or affirmed anything against the Church's teaching.

He admits [...] in the presence of a certain foreigner, Hachet speaking against [...], however, he had no faith in what was said.

The bishop, on the advice of those assisting him, decided to enquire further against him.

[p. iii] [...] Ryse C[...] to have held [...] that [...] pilgrimages [...] of those assisting [...].

Alice Acton

[LCB, fo. 17r. The entry is undated, but other entries in proximity to it in the MS date from January or February 1512.]

Alicia[d] relicta Thome Acton nuper defuncti civitatis Coventr'.

Negat, ut supra in proximo.

Quare dominus, de consilio sibi assistentium, decrevit ulterius inquirere contra eam.

---

[a] et *deleted.*
[b] eos *deleted.*
[c] *possibly* Ryfe.
[d] uxor *deleted.*

[English translation]

Alice, widow of the recently deceased Thomas Acton of Coventry.
 She denies, as immediately above.
 Therefore the bishop, on the advice of those assisting him, decided
to enquire further against her.

Constance Clerc

*[LCB, fo. 17r. The entry is undated, but other entries in proximity to it in the MS
date from January or February 1512.]*

Constantia, uxor Thome Clerc.
 Iurata et examinata, dicit quod nunquam novit aliquid mali de libro
quem vir suus habuit, donec advenerunt Bown[a] et Johannes Archer
consulentes eidem viro suo ut absconderet ipsum librum.
 Dominus, de consilio sibi assistentium, decrevit ut supra.

[English translation]

Constance, wife of Thomas Clerc.
 Sworn and examined, she says she never knew anything bad about
the book her husband had, until Bown and John Archer came advising
him to hide it.
 The bishop, on the advice of those assisting him, decided as above.

William Revis

*[LCB, fo. 17v. The entry is undated, but other entries in proximity to it in the MS
date from January or February 1512. Revis had previously appeared in late November
to early December (above, pp. 211 and 219).]*

Willelmus Revis, comparens et cetera, negat ut prius. Quare dominus,
de consilio et cetera, decrevit ut supra.

---

[a] Archer *in margin.*

[English translation]

William Revis, appearing etc., denies as before. Therefore the bishop, on the advice etc. decided as above.

Katherine Baker

[LCB, fo. 17v. The entry is undated, but other entries in proximity to it in the MS date from January or February 1512.]

Katherina, uxor Edmundi Baker.
  Iurata et cetera ut supra, negat.

[English translation]

Katherine, wife of Edmund Baker.
  Sworn etc. as above, she denies.

Margaret Grey

[LCB, fo. 17v. The entry is undated, but other entries in proximity to it in the MS date from January or February 1512.]

Margareta Grey.
  Iurata et cetera, negat omnino. Quare dominus, de consilio et cetera, decrevit ut supra.

[English translation]

Margaret Grey.
  Sworn etc., she denies everything. Therefore the bishop, on the advice etc., decided as above.

Thomas Kylyngworth

[LCB, fo. 26r. The entry is undated, but other entries in proximity to it in the MS date from January or February 1512. Kylyngworth previously appeared in late November or early December (above, p. 209).]

Thomas Kylyngworth ut supra comparens, negat ut supra. Dominus, de consilio sibi assistencium, decrevit ut supra.

[English translation]

Thomas Kylyngworth, as above, appearing, denies as above. The bishop, on the advice of those assisting him, decided as above.

Agnes Brown

[LCB, fo. 26r. The entry is undated, but other entries in proximity to it in the MS date from January or February 1512. This examination must precede its resumption on 13 February 1512 (below, p. 251).]

Agnes Brown. Iurata et cetera, negat omnino. Quare dominus et cetera decrevit.

[English translation]

Agnes Brown. Sworn etc., denies everything. Therefore the bishop etc. decided.

John Archer

[LCB, fo. 26v. The entry is undated, but other entries in proximity to it in the MS date from January or February 1512. Archer abjured on 4 February 1512 (below, p. 250).]

Johannes Archer civitatis Coventr' sutor.
Iuratus et cetera, dicit quod audivit Thomam Clerc legentem ter vel quater in libro suo pessimo.

Negat se locutum fuisse Thome Clerc de libri absconsione.

Fatetur tamen quod audivit Hachet et alios communicantes contra peregrinaciones, ymaginum veneraciones. Nescit quotiens.

Habet [...] coram commissariis domini hic die Veneris proximo futuro.

[English translation]

John Archer of Coventry, shoemaker.

Sworn etc., he says he heard Thomas Clerc reading on three or four occasions in his wicked book.

He denies he spoke to Thomas Clerc about hiding the book.

He admits, however, that he heard Hachet and others speaking against pilgrimages, and the veneration of images. He does not know how often.

He has [...] before the bishop's commissaries here on next Friday.

Isabel Trussell

[LCB, fo. 26v. The entry is undated, but other entries in proximity to it in the MS date from January or February 1512. The gaps are due to a large hole on the right side of the folio.]

Isabella, uxor Thome Trussell hosyer [...] dicit se librum pessimum habuisse et eundem librum exempl[...] eundem librum ad confessorem suum et sic ostendit ipsum [...] confitebitur. Negat consensum aut favorem [...] se purgaturam et cetera. Quare dominus decrevit ulterius [...].

[English translation]

Isabel, wife of Thomas Trussell hosier, [...] says she had a wicked book and the same book copied [...] the same book to her confessor and so she showed it [...] will confess. She denies consent or favour [...] will purge herself etc. Therefore the bishop decided further [...].

Administrative note

[LCB, fo. 26v. This follows after Isabel Trussell's examination above (she being the Isabel in question here), but refers to all those who have not confessed to heresy.]

Et notandum quod, inquisitione habita, non potuit constare dictam Isabellam et alios, preter eos qui abiuraverunt et cetera, fuisse atque esse suspectos de et super crimine heretice pravitatis.

[English translation]

Note that after the enquiry it was impossible to be certain that the said Isabel and the others – except those who had abjured etc. – had been, and were, suspected of heresy.

Wednesday, 4 February 1512

John Cropwell

[LCB, fo. 15v. Examination resumed from 22 January 1512 (above, p. 231). Dated by reference to abjuration in Blyth's register (see following entry). See also p. 277 for the abjuration Cropwell signed.]

Tandem[a] tamen saniori ductus consilio, submisit se iudicio sancte matris ecclesie. Renuncians et cetera, abiuravit ut supra, signumque crucis sub nomine suo scripsit.

[English translation]

Eventually, however, following wiser counsel, he submitted himself to the judgement of Holy Mother Church. Renouncing etc., he abjured as above and he wrote a sign of the cross under his name.

[a] Tandem [...] scripsit *in a different hand from the passage preceding it on fo. 15v, dated 22 January 1512.*

John Holywod, John Cropwell, John Spon, John Archer, John Holbache, Roger Toft, Robert Haghmond, and Richard Rise

[Reg. Blyth, fo. 99v. See p. 277 for the abjuration signed by Holywod, Cropwell, Toft, and Haghmond. The others, for whom signed abjurations do not survive, may well have signed in the same place – the surviving folio is only a fragment.]

Et notandum quod iiii[to] Februarii anno Domini suprascripto in domo capitulari ecclesie cathedralis Coventr', commissarii domini – videlicet magistri Johannes Immpingham supprior dicte ecclesie, Robertus Caulyn legum doctor, et alii in commissione sua nominati – subscriptos, videlicet Johannem Holywod, Johannem Cropwell, Johannem Spon, Johannem Archer, Johannem Holbache, Rogerum Toft, Robertum Haghmond et Ricardum Ryse, qui variis temporibus cum Silkeby et aliis interfuerunt, non tamen opinionibus eorum crediderunt, sed partim vacillaverunt, presertim de venerationibus ymaginum et per-egrinacione,[a] ut asseruerunt, ad purgandum se super aliis articulis[b] monuerunt viva voce. Qui vero humiliter sese submittentes, optulerunt se et eorum quemlibet paratos fore ad abiurandum et cetera.

Quare dicti commissarii eorum abiurationes tunc ibidem receperunt, prout continetur in abiuracione Flesshor. Et factis signis crucis per eorum quemlibet, prestitaque caucione de perimplendo penitenciam, absoluti sunt et cetera. Differturque penitencia in adventum domini.

[English translation]

Note that on 4 February in the above written year of the Lord, in the chapter house of the Cathedral church of Coventry, the bishop's commissaries – namely Masters John Immpingham, subprior of the said church, Robert Caulyn, doctor of laws, and others named in his commission – orally warned the following – namely John Holywod, John Cropwell, John Spon, John Archer, John Holbache, Roger Toft, Robert Haghmond, and Richard Ryse, who were present with Silkeby and others on various occasions, but did not believe their opinions, but partly vacillated, especially regarding the veneration of images and pilgrimages, as they said – to purge themselves regarding other articles. Humbly submitting themselves, they offered themselves, and each one of them, as ready to abjure etc.

Therefore, the said commissaries received their abjurations then and there, as is contained in Flesshor's abjuration. After each of them had

[a] qu' *deleted.*
[b] iniunxerunt per *deleted.*

made a sign of the cross, and after they had guaranteed to perform the penance, they were absolved etc. The penance is deferred until the bishop comes.

Note of enquiry

[Reg. Blyth, fo. 99v. Undated; follows previous entry dated 4 February 1512.]

Notandum insuper quod dictus reverendus pater monuit de qualibet custodia ii viros fidedignos infra civitatem Coventr'. Eosque iuramento corporali oneravit ad diligenter inquirendum de et super aliis qui-buscumqe super heretica pravitate qualitercumque suspectis atque ad fideliter rectificandum in premissis.

Qui vero onerati, ut prefertur, neminem culpabilem in ea parte repererunt, quamadmodum ex certificatoriis ipsorum pluries liquet.

Nomina huiusmodi inquisitorum servuntur.

[English translation]

Note further that the said reverend father warned two trustworthy men within Coventry about any concealment. He bound them under oath to enquire diligently about any other persons suspected in any way of heresy and to report back faithfully in the matter.

The men, under oath, as stated above, found nobody blameworthy in the matter, as appears more clearly from their certifications.

The names of these inquisitors are reserved.

Friday, 13 February 1512

Agnes Brown

[LCB, fo. 26r. Continued from mid-January to mid-February 1512 (see above, p. 247).]

Et postea, xiii° die mensis Februarii, Agnes supranominata comparens in ecclesia parochiali sancte Trinitatis civitatis Coventr' coram magistris

Roberto Caulyn et ceter', dompno Johanne Ympingham suppriore ecclesie cathedralis Coventr', et aliis commissariis domini in hac parte sufficienter et legitime deputatis et cetera.

Iurata, negabat omnes articulos ut supra.

Hec mulier doctori Wilkocks[153] secrete confessa est heresim et opiniones suprascriptas se tenuisse. Nondum tamen abiurata.

[English translation]

Afterwards, on 13 February, the above named Agnes appeared in Holy Trinity parish church in Coventry before Masters Robert Caulyn etc., Lord John Ympingham, subprior of the Cathedral church of Coventry, and other commissaries of the bishop sufficiently and legitimately deputed etc. in the matter.

Sworn, she denies all the articles as above.

This woman secretly confessed to Doctor Wilcocks[153] that she held heresy and the above written opinions. Not yet, however, abjured.

Thursday, 11 March 1512

Joan Warde *alias* Wasshingburn

[Reg. Blyth, fo. 100r. Process continued on 12 March 1511 (see following entry).]

Acta habita in ecclesia conventuali et cathedrali Coventr' xi^{mo} die mensis Martii anno Domini secundum computacionem ecclesie Anglicane[a] millesimo quingentesimo xi^{mo} supradicto, in negocio heretice pravitatis et relapsus contra Johannam Warde alias Wasshingburn in ea parte detecta, denunciata et accusata coram venerabilibus viris magistris Roberto Caulyn, Johanne Wilcocks et Thoma Orton, legum, sacre theologie et decretorum doctoribus, necnon Johanne Ympingham, suppriore dicte ecclesie, ac Willelmo Palden, in decretis bacallario, reverendissimi patris antedicti cum illa clausula, 'Quatenus vos vel duo vestrum', commissariis[b] sufficienter et legitime deputatis, tunc ibidem presentibus.

---

[a] xi^{mo} *deleted.*

[b] Clausula [...] commissariis: *might also be read* clausula quatenus vos vel duo vestrum commissariis.

Quo die, lecta commissione et cetera, ministrati erant articuli sub-scripti eidem Johanne, iuramento corporali ad fideliter respondendum eisdem in forma iuris onerate. Quibus respondebat prout sequitur.

In primis objicimus et articulamur tibi Johanne Warde alias Was-shingburn quod tu mense Augusti anno Domini millesimo CCCC nonagesimo quinto, seu ante vel citra illud tempus, in villa de Maydeston coram magistro Roberto Cambreton, sacre theologie professore, rev-erendissimi in Christo patris et domini domini Johannis tunc Can-tuariensis archiepiscopi in ea parte commissario speciali, de et super variis opinionibus hereticis – videlicet de opinionibus contra sac-ramentum altaris, ymaginum venerationes, peregrinationes aliosque errores dampnabiles et detestabiles – detecta, denunciata et tandem convicta fuisti.[154] Fatetur.

Item, objicimus et articulamur tibi ut supra quod tu easdem hereses in specie et omnes alias in genere in villa de Maydeston predicta anno Domini supradicto coram supranominato commissario palam, publice et solemniter abiurasti. Fatetur.

Item, quod tu penitenciam publicam et solemnem in ea parte canonice tibi iniunctam in villis de Maydeston, Cantuaria[155] et London' propter huiusmodi hereses, more abiuratorum, peregisti. Fatetur.

Item, quod tu cum littera H in lena maxilla tua apud Maydeston predicta in signum heretice abiurate signata fuisti. Fatetur.

Item, quod tu post et citra [tempus] abiurationis tue huiusmodi in prefatas hereses et alias dampnabiliter reincidisti, illas easdem animo indurato et pertinaci defendendo, dogmatizando, astruendo et tenendo palam et publice. Fatetur.

Item, quod tu communicationem contra sacramentum altaris, per-egrinationes et ymaginum venerationes in civitate Coventr' cum Alicia Rowley, Rogero Landesdale, Roberto Sylkeby et nonnullis aliis post et citra illud abiurationis tue tempus sepenumero habuisti. Fatetur.

Qua confessione facta, iudex monuit eandem Johannam tunc pre-sentem ad comparandum coram eo et aliis loco prescripto die sequenti, hora viii[ta] ante meridiem, ad allegandum causam rationabilem quare pro relapsa ac relapsorum pena puniri non debeat et ad audiendum sententiam.

[English translation]

Proceedings in the conventual and Cathedral church of Coventry on 11 March, in the year of the Lord 1511/1512 according to the reckoning of the English Church, in the matter of heresy and relapse against Joan Warde *alias* Wasshingburn, detected, denounced, and accused in the matter, before the venerable men, Masters Robert Caulyn, John Wilcocks and Thomas Orton, doctors of laws, of sacred theology and of decrees, and John Ympingham, subprior of the said church, and William Palden, bachelor in decrees, commissaries of the aforesaid reverend father sufficiently and legitimately deputed with the clause 'Inasmuch as you or two of you', present then and there.

On which day, after the commission had been read etc., the articles written below were proposed to the same Joan, who was put under oath in legal form to reply faithfully to them. She replied to them as follows.

First, we accuse and charge you Joan Warde *alias* Wasshingburn, that in August 1495, or before or since that time, in the town of Maidstone, before Master Robert Cambreton, professor of sacred theology, special commissary in this matter of the most Reverend Father and Lord in Christ, Lord John, then Archbishop of Canterbury, you were detected, denounced, and finally convicted regarding various heretical opinions, namely opinions against the sacrament of the altar, the veneration of images, pilgrimages, and other damnable and detestable errors.[54] She admits this.

Also, we accuse and charge you, as above, that in the aforesaid town of Maidstone, in the aforesaid year of the Lord, before the above named commissary, you openly, publicly, and solemnly abjured the same heresies in particular and all others in general. She admits this.

Also, that you, in the manner of abjurers, did public and solemn penance, canonically enjoined upon you in this matter for these heresies, in the towns of Maidstone, Canterbury,[55] and London. She admits this.

Also, that in Maidstone you were branded on your jaw with the letter H as a sign of the heresy abjured. She admits this.

Also, that after and since the time of your abjuration you damnably fell again into the aforesaid and other heresies, openly and publicly, with a hardened and obstinate mind, defending, teaching, and holding them. She admits this.

Also, that after and since the time of your abjuration you often communicated in Coventry with Alice Rowley, Roger Landesdale, Robert Sylkeby, and others against the sacrament of the altar, pilgrimages, and the veneration of images. She admits this.

After she had made this confession, the judge admonished the same Joan who was then present to appear before him and others in the above written place on the following day, at the 8th hour in the morning, to give a reason why she should not be punished as a relapsed person with the penalty of the relapsed and to hear her sentence.

Friday, 12 March 1512

Joan Warde *alias* Wasshingburn

[Reg. Blyth, fo. 100r. Process continued from 11 March 1512 (see previous entry) and resumed again 15 March 1512 (see following entry).]

Quibus die et hora advenientibus, dicta Johanna comparuit. Nichilque pro se allegare prorsus voluit. Sed se submisit divine misericordie. Quare iudex tulit sententiam in scriptis prout sequitur.

In Dei nomine, Amen. Nos, Robertus Caulin, legum doctor, reverendi in Christo patris et domini, domini Galfridi permissione divina Coventr' et Lich' episcopi, in causa heretice pravitatis et relapsus contra te Johannam Warde alias Wasshingburn unacum aliis, cum illa clausula 'Coniunctim et divisim et quatenus[a] vos vel duo eorum', commissarius[b] sufficienter et legitime deputatus.

Auditis, visis et intellectis ac plenarie discussis per nos commissarium atque alios collegas nostros meritis et circumstantiis eiusdem cause; rimatoque toto et integro processu contra te Johannam antedictam coram prenominato reverendo patre in hac parte habito et facto ac diligenter recensito; servatis de iure in hac parte servandis ad nostre sententie diffinitive in huiusmodi causa prolationem; sic duximus procedendum et in hunc qui sequitur procedimus modum.

Quia per acta inactitata, deducta, proposita, inquisita ac per te tam[c] coram memorato reverendo patre quam nobis recognita et confessata, invenimus te – postquam diversas hereses, errores et opiniones dampnatas, videlicet contra sacramentum altaris, peregrinationes, ymaginum venerationes ac contra ecclesiam, appellando ipsam synagogam, atque alias dampnabiles hereses[d] tam in specie quam in genere publice et solemniter in villa de Maydeston Cantuar' diocesis coram ordinario ibidem abiuraveras – in eosdem errores, hereses et opiniones dampnatas alias per te ut premittitur, abiuratos animo pertinaci notorie reincidisse, atque eas ipsas hereses et errores diversis in locis post abiuracionem tuam, ut prefertur, factam animo indurato et deliberato infra Coventr' et Lich' diocesim publice astruisse, tenuisse, docuisse et credidisse.

Idcirco nos commissarius antedictus, Christi nomine primitus memorato, ac ipsum solum Deum oculis nostris proponentes, iudicialiter et

---

[a] d *deleted.*
[b] Clausula [...] commissarius: *might also be read* cum illa clausula coniunctim et divisim et quatenus vos vel duo eorum, commissarius
[c] tam *interlined.*
[d] *MS.* aliis dampnabilibus heresibus.

pro tribunali sedentes, volentes huiusmodi causam fine debito terminare, de consilio solemne, maturo et digesto nonnullorum venerabilium virorum tam in sacra theologia quam in decretis et legibus doctoribus atque graduatorum aliorumque iurisperitorum nobis assistentium cum quibus mature in hac parte communicavimus, te Johannam Warde alias Wasshingburn antedictam in hereses abiuratas et relapsam manifeste fuisse et esse ac relapsorum pena puniendum fore pronunciamus, decernimus et declaramus per hanc nostram sententiam difinitivam, quam ferimus et promulgamus in his scriptis.

Et cum ecclesia non habeat ultra quod faciat, te excommunicatam et maioris excommunicationis sententiam [...] premissorum ipso iure ligatam et innodatam et fuisse et esse declaramus et coram presenti multitudine [...] pronunciamus: relinquentes te exnunc tanquam hereticam relapsam brachio seculari puniendam, rogantes et sincere affectantes quatenus exemplo contra te fiendo citra mortis periculum moderetur ut non sit rigor regula nec mansuetudo dissolvitur sed tamen ad Dei laudem,[a] catholicorum gloriam, anime tue salutem atque salvacionem, multorumque aliorum perversorum metum et terrorem, aliorum premissorum metum et terrorem et causam huiusmodi errores et opiniones dampnatas deferendi.

Qua sententia lecta, vicecomites civitatis Coventr' tunc presentes eam in custodiam suam acceperunt.

[English translation]

When the day and the hour arrived, the said Joan appeared. She refused to say anything on her behalf, rather she submitted herself to the divine mercy. Therefore the judge pronounced the sentence in writing as follows.

In the name of God, Amen. We, Robert Caulin, doctor of laws, commissary of the Reverend Father and Lord in Christ, Lord Geoffrey, by divine permission Bishop of Coventry and Lichfield, sufficiently and legitimately deputed with the clause 'Collectively and individually and inasmuch as you or two of them', together with others, in the case of heresy and relapse against you, Joan Warde *alias* Wasshingburn.

The merits and circumstances of the case have been heard, seen, and understood and fully discussed by us, the commissary, and our other colleagues. The whole process against you, Joan, which was held and made and carefully considered before the above named reverend father, has been examined. What should be observed in the law, for

---

[a] anime *deleted*.

the promulgation of our definitive sentence in this case, has been observed. We have, thus, decided to proceed and we do proceed in the following manner.

Because of the things done, deduced, proposed, enquired, and recognised and confessed by you before both the said reverend father and us, we found that, after you abjured various heresies, errors, and condemned opinions – namely against the sacrament of the altar, pilgrimages, the veneration of images, and against the church, calling it a synagogue, and other damnable heresies – both in particular and in general, publicly and solemnly, in the town of Maidstone in Canterbury diocese, before the ordinary there, you fell again, notoriously and with an obstinate mind, into the same condemned errors, heresies, and opinions that you had otherwise abjured, as stated above, and with a hardened and deliberate mind you publicly instructed, held, taught, and believed, within the diocese of Coventry and Lichfield, these same heresies and errors, in various places, after your abjuration had been made, as stated above.

We, therefore, the aforesaid commissary, mindful first of the name of Christ, and having God alone before our eyes, sitting judicially and in court, wishing to bring this case to its proper conclusion, on the solemn, mature, and considered advice of various venerable men, doctors and graduates both in sacred theology and in decrees and laws, and others expert in the law, assisting us, with whom we have communicated at the proper time in this matter, we pronounce, decide, and declare by this our definitive sentence, which we bear and promulgate in this document, that you, Joan Warde *alias* Wasshingburn, have manifestly relapsed into and remain in the heresies that you abjured, and that you shall receive the punishment of the relapsed.

Since the Church can do no more, we declare and we pronounce before the present multitude [...] that you have been and are excommunicated, and [...] the sentence of major excommunication and bound and constrained by the law itself. We relinquish you henceforth as a relapsed heretic to the secular arm for punishment, asking and sincerely hoping that, by the example that is to be made against you, the trial of death may be moderated in such a way that rigour is not the rule and gentleness is not abandoned, and yet so that the result may be the praise of God, the glory of Catholics, the health and salvation of your soul, the fear and terror of many other perverse people, the fear and terror of the persons mentioned above, and the cause of removing these condemned errors and opinions.

After the sentence had been read, the sheriffs of the city of Coventry, who were then present, took her into their custody.

Monday, 15 March 1512

Joan Warde *alias* Wasshingburn

[Reg. Blyth, fo. 100r. Continued from 12 March 1512 (see previous entry).]

Et die Lune[a] extunc sequente penam tradiderunt.

[English translation]

On the following Monday they carried out the punishment.

[a] et *deleted.*

ABJURATIONS, 1511–1512

[Five abjurations survive in full, nos. 1–5 below. They are virtually identical with each other, with only minor differences in wording and variations in spellings. Four of them appear to be the original abjurations. The exception is no. 2, which appears to be a copy of no. 1 written into the bishop's register.

The first accused to abjure heresy was Thomas Flesshor, whose abjuration was dated 3 November (no. 1). (Margery Locock confessed and submitted herself to the bishop on 31 October, but the bishop chose not to require her to make a formal abjuration for fear that her husband would repudiate her; see above, p. 122.) Only in the case of Flesshor was the name of the abjurer specifically recorded in the text of the abjuration; in the other three original abjurations, which are undated, blank spaces were left for the names of the abjurers. At the end of each of the original abjurations (including Flesshor's) there are names, with crosses underneath or alongside most of them. In most cases, the names are fairly neatly written and appear to be in hands similar to the rest of the MS, whereas the crosses are almost invariably rough in form, indicating that scribes wrote the names of individuals after they abjured and crosses were added by the abjurers in person. In some cases, judging by less practised handwriting evident in some of the signatures, men apparently signed their own names (indicated in the textual notes). Each of the abjurations (with the exception of the fragment no. 6) was used over a period of some weeks or months, in most cases from early November 1511 to January 1512, with names and crosses presumably being added as each suspect abjured. Although the records indicate that the suspects read their abjurations − 'legit abiuracionem' is the usual phrase − in most or all cases this presumably meant a notary or other court official reading out the abjuration on behalf of the abjurer. These abjurations are likely a relatively complete record of those who abjured in 1511–1512. Of those indicated elsewhere in the LCB or Blyth's register as having abjured, only the names of John Clerc, John Holbache, John Archer, John Spon, Richard Rise, and Agnes Brown are missing; given the damaged state of some of the folios in question, it is surprising that more lacunae are not found. In the cases of Holbache, Archer, Spon, and Rise, the missing suspects were recorded as having abjured together on 4 February 1512, and their names probably originally appeared on the same abjuration as that signed by the others who abjured with them that day − the damaged fragment recorded below in no. 6. In Brown's case, it appears that Blyth's register is mistaken about her abjuration dated 22 January 1512, since she still obdurately refused to admit heresy in mid-February (see pp. 236, 247, and 251).

No. 6 is a fragment with names and crosses only. It seems likely that originally there was the text of an abjuration above the names and crosses.]

3 November to 29 November 1511

1. Thomas Flesshor, Robert Silkby, Thomas Wrixham, Thomas Abell, Thomas Clerc, Richard Bradeley, Thomas Spenser, John Longhold, Thomas Banbrooke, and William Hawkyns

[LCB, fo. 25r. The abjuration is in the name of Thomas Flesshor, dated 3 November, and the first cross under the abjuration is presumably his. Silkby, Wrixham, Abell, Clerc, Bradeley, Spenser, Longhold, Banbrooke, and Hawkyns abjured on 25 or 29 November 1511 (pp. 189 and 205).]

In the name of God, Amen. Byfore you reverend fadre in God and lorde Lorde Geffrey by the grace of God busshop of Coventr' and Lich', I Thomas Flesshor, smythe of the citie of Coventr' in your diocese of the seid Coventr' and Lich' detected, denounced and noised to your seid reverend faderhod heretofore to have been suspected of heresy, erroures and other articles evill sowneng, being in dome and jugement afore you.

Felyng and understonding, knoweng and well perceiveng that afore this howr I the foreseid Thomas Flesshour have[a] spoken, affermed and holden divers articles,[b] opynyons and erroures ageinst the feithe of all holy church and contrarie to the determynation of the same, to the evill sowding of the eres[c] of well disposed cristen men, and especially ageinste the sacrament of the alter, wurshipping of ymages and pil-grimages, with divers other, and witholding and conceling books of heresy, favouring also such as I have knowen suspect in this bihalfe, not denownseng them unto your reverend fadrehod ne ony your officers, but rather, being conversante with them and hering[d] often tymes such dampnable lectures as they redde and approbating ther rytes, did concele such ther redinges and rites.

Wherefor I the forseid Thomas Flesshour, truly and feithfully enfour-med, knowleage and knowe well that the articles above rehersed with other concerneng them been[e] erroures and ageynst the true bileve, feith and determynation of all holy church and right evill sownding to the eres of well disposed cristen men. Willing with pure hert and free

---

[a]   seid *deleted.*
[b]   and *deleted.*
[c]   h *of* heres *deleted.*
[d]   of the *deleted.*
[e]   age *deleted.*

will to forsake those erroures and articles and all other errowres, heresies and erronyous opynyons being ageinst the feith and determynation of the seid church and to bileve from hensforward aftir the teching of all holy church and turn to the unytie and determynacion of the seid church, the same erroures, heresies and erroneous opynyons with all other contrary to the true feith and determynacion of all holy churche, I uttrely forsake, renownce and abjure and swere apon this booke that aftir this howr I shall never openly ne prively holde, declare or teche heresy, erroures ne ony maner of doctryne ageinst the feythe or determynation of all holy church. Ne I shall receive, favour and cownsell ne defende, succour ne supporte by myselfe or ony other person or persons prively or openly them that holdeth, techeth or maynteyneth ony such false doctryne, ne yet felisshipp with them[a] witingly, comforte them ne receive them ne give them mete ne drinke,[b] clothe ne money ne ony other weis[c] succour them.

Furthermore I swer that if I may knowe ony person or persones, men or women, suspect of errours or heresies or fautours, cownselers, comforters, defensours, receiptours or that ony privey conventicles contrary to the commen doctryne of holy church, I shall denownce them to you the forseid reverend fadre, your successours or officers or to ther ordynaryes as soon as I goodly may.

So helpe me God and the holy dome. In witnes wherof I with my hand make a cros undrenethe this my solempne abjuracion.

+

Robertus Silkeby	Thomas Wrixham	Thomas Abell
+	+	+
Thomas Clerk[d]	Rechard Bradeley[e]	Thomas Spensare
Johannes Longhold	Thomas Banbroke	Willelmus Hawkyns
+		+

[English translation]

In the name of God, Amen. Before you Reverend Father in God and Lord, Lord Geoffrey, by the grace of God Bishop of Coventry and

[a] witi'l *deleted.*
[b] cho *deleted.*
[c] su' *deleted.*
[d] *probably signed in his own hand.*
[e] *probably signed in his own hand.*

Lichfield, I, Thomas Flesshor, smith of the city of Coventry in your diocese of the said Coventry and Lichfield, detected, denounced, and noised to your said reverend fatherhood heretofore to have been suspected of heresy, errors, and other articles evil sounding, being in doom and judgement before you.

Feeling and understanding, knowing, and well perceiving that before this hour I the foresaid Thomas Flesshour have spoken, affirmed, and held divers articles, opinions, and errors against the faith of all Holy Church and contrary to the determination of the same, to the evil sounding of the ears of well disposed Christian men, and especially against the sacrament of the altar, worshipping of images and pilgrimages, with divers other, and withholding and concealing books of heresy, favouring also such as I have known suspect in this behalf, not denouncing them unto your reverend fatherhood nor any of your officers, but rather, being conversant with them and hearing often times such damnable lectures as they read and approving their rites, did conceal such their readings and rites.

Wherefore, I the foresaid Thomas Flesshour, truly and faithfully informed, acknowledge and know well that the articles above rehearsed with others concerning them were errors and against the true belief, faith, and determination of all Holy Church, and right evil sounding to the ears of well disposed Christian men. Willing with pure heart and free will to forsake those errors and articles and all other errors, heresies, and erroneous opinions being against the faith and determination of the said Church, and to believe from henceforward after the teaching of all Holy Church, and turn to the unity and determination of the said Church, the same errors, heresies, and erroneous opinions with all others contrary to the true faith and determination of all Holy Church, I utterly forsake, renounce, and abjure, and swear upon this book that after this hour I shall never openly nor privily hold, declare, or teach heresy, errors, nor any manner of doctrine against the faith or determination of all Holy Church. Nor shall I receive, favour, and counsel, nor defend, succour, nor support by myself or any other person or persons, privily or openly those that hold, teach, or maintain any such false doctrine, nor yet fellowship with them wittingly, comfort them, nor receive them, nor give them meat nor drink, clothes nor money, nor any other ways succour them.

Furthermore, I swear that if I may know any person or persons, men or women, suspect of errors or heresies or favourers, counsellors, comforters, defenders, receivers, or any privy conventicles contrary to the common doctrine of Holy Church, I shall denounce them to you the foresaid reverend father, your successors, or officers or to their ordinaries as soon as I goodly may.

So help me God and the holy doom. In witness whereof I with my hand make a cross underneath this my solemn abjuration.

+

Robert Silkeby	Thomas Wrixham	Thomas Abell
+	+	+
Thomas Clerk[a]	Rechard Bradeley[b]	Thomas Spensare
John Longhold	Thomas Banbroke	William Hawkyns
+		+

3 November 1511

2. Thomas Flesshor

[Reg. Blyth, fos 98rv. The abjuration is dated 3 November. It is almost identical with – and was probably a copy of – Flesshor's abjuration in LCB (see previous entry), except there is no cross (drawn by Flesshor) at the end of the abjuration and the names and crosses of the other defendants are missing. It apparently served as a model for all subsequent abjurations, since frequently Blyth's register records that suspects abjured 'as in Flesshor's abjuration' (e.g. pp. 169, 190, 205).]

Thomas Flecher

In the name of God, Amen. Byfore you reverend fadre in God and lorde Lorde Geffrey by the grace of God busshop of Coventry and Lichfeld, I Thomas Flesshor, smyth of the citie of Coventry in your diocese of the said Coventry and Lichfeld, detectyd, denounced and noysed to your said reverend fadrehodde hertofore to have byn suspectyd of heresy, erroures and other articuls evill sounynge, being in dome and jugement afore you.

Felyng and understanding, knowyng and well perceyving that afore this houre I the forsaid Thomas Fleshor have spoken, affermed and holden divers articles, opynyons and errours againste the feith of all hooly churche and contrary to the determinacyon of the same to the evyll sowndyng of the eyres of well disposyd crysten men, and especially againste[c] the sacrament of the alter, wurshippyng of ymages and pylgrimages, with divers other, and witholding and conceylyng bokes

---

[a] *probably signed in his own hand.*
[b] *probably signed in his own hand.*
[c] agayn *deleted.*

of heresy, favouryng also such as I have knoen suspect in this behalfe, not denounsyng them unto your reverend fadrehodde ne any your [fo. 98v] officer but rather beyng conversaunte with them and heryng oftyme suche damnable lectures as tho they reede and, approbatyng their rytes,[a] dyd conceul such ther redinges and rites.

Wherefore I the forsaid Thomas Fleshor, truly and feithfully enformed, knoledge and knowe well that the articuls above rehersyd with other concernyng them ben errors and against the true bileve, feith and determinacyon of all holy church and right evyll soundyng to the eyres of wele disposed cristen men. Willing with pure herte and fre wyll to forsake those errours and articles and all odre errors, heresies and erroneous opynyons being against the feith and determinacion of the said churche and to byleve from hensforward aftre the teching of all hoolly churche and turne to the unyte and determinacyon of the said churche, the same erroures, heresies and erroneous opynyons with all other contrary to the true faith and determinacion of all holly churche I utterly forsake, renounce and abjure and swere apon this boke that aftre this houre I shall nyver openly ne prively holde, declare or teiche heresy, errours ne any maner of doctrine against the feith or determinacion of all holy churche. Ne I shall receive, favor, eyd, councell ne defend, succur ne supporte by myself or any other person or persons prively or openly them that holdeth, techeth or maynteneth any such false doctrine, ne yet felyshipp with them wittingly, comforte them ne receive them ne gyve them meyte ne drynke, clothe ne money ne any other weys succur them.

Furthermore I swere that if I may knowe any person or persons, men or women, suspect of errors or heresies or fautors, councellors, comfortors, defensors, receptors or that any privey conventicles contrary to the comyn doctrine of all hooly churche, I shall denounce them to you the forsaid reverend fadre, your successors or officers or to their ordinaries as sone as I goodly may.

So helpe me God and the holy dome. In wytnes whereof I with my hand make a cross undreneath this my solempne abjuration.[b]

Lecta fuit presens abjuracio per sepefatum Thomam Fleshor in prioratu de Maxstocke, Coventr' et Lich' diocesis, tercio die mensis Novembris anno Domini retroscripto. Presentibus tunc ibidem vener-abilibus viris dompno Willelmo Pollesworthe ecclesie cathedralis Cov-entr', et Willelmo Dykons prioratus de Maxstocke, prioribus, necnon magistris Radulpho Cantrell, decretorum doctore, Willelmo Skelton et Willelmo Wilton, artium magistris, Thoma Barker et Johanne Blyth, in

---

[a] and counsell' *deleted*.
[b] *there is no cross underneath the abjuration.*

decretis bacallariis, necnon Thoma[a] Danyelle et David Jacobi, fratribus Observantibus, cum nonnullis aliis.

[English translation]

Thomas Flecher

In the name of God, Amen. Before you Reverend Father in God and Lord, Lord Geoffrey, by the grace of God Bishop of Coventry and Lichfield, I, Thomas Flesshor, smith of the city of Coventry in your diocese of the said Coventry and Lichfield, detected, denounced, and noised to your said reverend fatherhood heretofore to have been suspected of heresy, errors, and other articles evil sounding, being in doom and judgement before you.

Feeling and understanding, knowing, and well perceiving that before this hour, I, the foresaid Thomas Fleshor have spoken, affirmed, and held divers articles, opinions, and errors against the faith of all Holy Church and contrary to the determination of the same, to the evil sounding of the ears of well disposed Christian men, and especially against the sacrament of the altar, worshipping of images, and pilgrimages, with divers other, and withholding and concealing books of heresy, favouring also such as I have known suspect in this behalf, not denouncing them unto your reverend fatherhood nor any of your *[fo. 98v]* officers but rather being conversant with them and hearing oftentimes such damnable lectures as those they read and, approving their rites, did conceal such their readings and rites.

Wherefore, I, the foresaid Thomas Fleshor, truly and faithfully informed, acknowledge and know well that the articles above rehearsed with others concerning them were errors and against the true belief, faith, and determination of all Holy Church, and right evil sounding to the ears of well disposed Christian men. Willing with pure heart and free will to forsake those errors and articles and all other errors, heresies, and erroneous opinions being against the faith and determination of the said Church, and to believe from henceforward after the teaching of all Holy Church, and turn to the unity and determination of the said church, the same errors, heresies, and erroneous opinions with all other contrary to the true faith and determination of all Holy Church I utterly forsake, renounce, and abjure, and swear upon this book that after this hour I shall never openly nor privily hold, declare, or teach heresy, errors, nor any manner of doctrine against the faith or determination of all Holy Church. Nor I shall receive, favour, aid,

---

[a] David *deleted.*

counsel, nor defend, succour, nor support by myself or any other person or persons, privily or openly, them that hold, teach, or maintain any such false doctrine, nor yet fellowship with them wittingly, comfort them, nor receive them, nor give them meat nor drink, clothes nor money, nor any other ways succour them.

Furthermore, I swear that if I may know any person or persons, men or women, suspect of errors, or heresies, or favourers, counsellors, comforters, defenders, receivers, or any privy conventicles contrary to the common doctrine of all Holy Church, I shall denounce them to you the foresaid reverend father, your successors, or officers or to their ordinaries as soon as I goodly may.

So help me God and the holy doom. In witness whereof I with my hand make a cross underneath this my solemn abjuration.[a]

This abjuration was read by the often-mentioned Thomas Fleshor in Maxstoke Priory, of the diocese of Coventry and Lichfield, on 3 November in the year of the Lord written above. Present then and there were the venerable men, Lord William Pollesworth of Coventry Cathedral church and William Dykons of Maxstoke Priory, priors, and Masters Ralph Cantrell, doctor of decrees, William Skelton and William Wilton, masters of arts, Thomas Barker and John Blyth, bachelors in decrees, Thomas Danyelle and David Jacob, Observant friars, with several others.

5 November 1511 to 22 January 1512

3. Roger Landesdale, Thomas Bown, Robert Hachet, John Atkynson, John Davy, Thomas Acton, Matthew Markelond, Agnes Corby, John Gest, Joan Gest, Elizabeth Gest

[LCB, fo. 18r. The abjuration is undated. Landesdale, Bown, Hachet, Atkynson, Acton, and Markelond are recorded as abjuring and making a cross under their name, on 5 and 6 November 1511 (pp. 166 and 169); John Davy abjured on 16 January 1512 (p. 229); while Agnes Corby and Elizabeth Gest abjured on 22 January 1512 (p. 236).]

In the name of God, Amen. Before you, reverend fadre in God and lorde Lorde Geffrey by the grace of God busshopp' of Coventr' and

---

[a] *there is no cross underneath the abjuration.*

Lich', I [...]^a of the citie of Coventr' in your diocese, detected, denounced and noised to your seide reverend fadrehod heretofore to have been suspected of heresy, erroures and other articles evyll soundeng, being in dome and jugement afore you.

Felyng and undrestanding, knoweng and well perceiveng that afore this houre I the foresaid [...]^b have spoken, affermed and holden diverse articles, opinions and erroures ageinst the feith of all holy church and contrary to the determination of the same, to the evyll sounding of the eres of well disposed cristen men, and especially ageinst the sacrament of the alter, pilgremages and wurshipping of ymages, with divers other, and conceling of books of heresy, favouring also such as I have knowen suspect in this behalfe, not denounceng them to your reverend fadrehold ne any other ordinarie in that bihalfe, but rather being conversaunt with them and hering often tymes such dampnable lectures as they did rede and approbating ther rites, did concele such ther redinges and rites.

Wherfor I the forseid [...],^c truly and feithfully enfourmed, knowleage and knowe well that the articles above rehersed with other concerneng them been erroures and agenst the true bileve, feith and determination of all holy churche and right evyll soundeng to the eres of well disposed cristen men. Willing with pure hert and free will to forsake tose erroures and articles and all other erroures, heresies and erroneous opynyons being agenst the feithe and determination of the seide holy churche, and to bileve from hensforthe aftre the teching of all holy churche and turn to the unyte and determination of the seid churche, the same erroures, heresies and erroneous opynyons with all other contrary to the true feith and determination of all holy churche, I uttrely forsake, renounce and abjure and swer upon this booke that aftre this hour I shall never openly ne prively holde, declare or teche heresy, erroures ne ony maner of doctrine agenst the feith or determination of all holy church. Ne I shall receive, favour, aide, counsell ne defend, succour ne support by my selfe or ony other person or personnes prively or openly them that holdeth, techeth or maynteyneth ony suche false doctrine, ne yet felashipp with them, witingle comforte them ne receive them ne geve them mete ne drinke, clothe ne money ne ony other wais succour them.

Furthermore I swere that if I may knowe ony person or personnes, men or women, suspect of errour or heresies or fautours, counsellours, comforters, defensoures, receiptours or ony privy conventicles contrary to the common doctrine of holy church, I shall denounce them to you

^a *blank space in MS.*
^b *blank space in MS.*
^c *blank space in MS.*

the forseid reverend fadre, your successours or officers or to ther ordynaries as soon as I goodly may.

Soo helpe me God and the holy dome. In witnes wherof, I with my hand:

per me Roger   Thomas Bown   Robert Hachetts Johannes Atkynson
  Landysdale[a]   +   +   +

    Johannes Davy   Thomas Acton   Matheus[b] Markelond
       +   +   +

      Agnes Corby   Johannes Gest   Johanna Gest
        +   +   +

      Elizabeth Gest
        +

[English translation]

In the name of God, Amen. Before you, Reverend Father in God and Lord, Lord Geoffrey, by the grace of God Bishop of Coventry and Lichfield, I, [...][c] of the city of Coventry in your diocese, detected, denounced, and noised to your said reverend fatherhood heretofore to have been suspected of heresy, errors, and other articles evil sounding, being in doom and judgement before you.

Feeling and understanding, knowing, and well perceiving that before this hour, I, the aforesaid [...][d] have spoken, affirmed and held diverse articles, opinions, and errors against the faith of all Holy Church, and contrary to the determination of the same, to the evil sounding of the ears of well disposed Christian men, and especially against the sacrament of the altar, pilgrimages, and worshipping of images, with divers other, and concealing of books of heresy, favouring also such as I have known suspect in this behalf, not denouncing them to your reverend fatherhood, nor any other ordinary in that behalf, but rather being conversant with them and hearing often times such damnable lectures as they did read and approving their rites, did conceal such their readings and rites.

Wherefore I the aforesaid [...],[e] truly and faithfully informed, acknowledge, and know well that the articles above rehearsed with other concerning them been errors and against the true belief, faith, and

   [a] *signed in his own hand.*
   [b] Robertus *deleted.*
   [c] *blank space in MS.*
   [d] *blank space in MS.*
   [e] *blank space in MS.*

determination of all Holy Church, and right evil sounding to the ears of well disposed Christian men. Willing with pure heart and free will to forsake those errors and articles and all other errors, heresies, and erroneous opinions being against the faith and determination of the said Holy Church, and to believe from henceforth after the teaching of all Holy Church, and turn to the unity and determination of the said Church, the same errors, heresies, and erroneous opinions with all other contrary to the true faith and determination of all Holy Church, I utterly forsake, renounce, and abjure, and swear upon this book that after this hour I shall never openly nor privily hold, declare, or teach heresy, errors, nor any manner of doctrine against the faith or determination of all Holy Church. Nor I shall receive, favour, aid, counsel nor defend, succour nor support, by myself or any other person or persons, privily or openly, those that hold, teach, or maintain any such false doctrine, nor yet fellowship with them, wittingly comfort them, nor receive them, nor give them meat nor drink, clothes nor money, nor any other ways succour them.

Furthermore I swear that if I may know any person or persons, men or women, suspect of error or heresies, or favourers, counsellors, comforters, defenders, receivers, or any privy conventicles contrary to the common doctrine of Holy Church, I shall denounce them to you the foresaid reverend father, your successors or officers, or to their ordinaries as soon as I goodly may.

So help me God and the holy doom. In witness whereof, I with my hand:

by me Roger Landysdale[a]	Thomas Bown +	Robert Hachetts +	John Atkynson +
John Davy +	Thomas Acton +	Matthew[b] Markelond +	
Agnes Corby +	John Gest +	Joan Gest +	
Elizabeth Gest +			

[a] *signed in his own hand.*
[b] Robert *deleted.*

5 November 1511 to 22 January 1512

4. Joan Smyth, Thomas Villers, Thomas Lyeff, John Bull, Julian Yong, David Clerc, John Jonson, Agnes Yong, Agnes Jonson, and Agnes de Bakehouse

[LCB, fo. 23r. The abjuration is undated. Joan Smyth read and signed her abjuration on 5 November (p. 162); Thomas Villers likely abjured on 3 December, or possibly a few days earlier (pp. 189, 205 and 220); Thomas Lieff, John Bull, Julian Yong, and David Clerc on 3 December (p. 220); John Jonson on 16 January 1512 (p. 224); and Agnes Yong, Agnes Jonson, and Agnes de Bakehouse on 22 January 1512 (p. 236).]

In the name of God, Amen. Before you reverend[a] fadre in God and lorde Lorde Geffrey by the grace of God busshopp of Coventr' and Lich', I [...][b] of the citie of Coventr' in your diocese detected, denounced and noised to your said reverend fadrehod hertofore to have been suspected of heresy, erroures and evyll sounding articles, being in dome and jugement afore you.

Feling and undrestonding, knoweng and well perceiving that afor this hour I the forseid [...][c] have spoken, affermed and holden dyverse articles, opynyons and erroures ageinst the feith of all holy church and contrary to the determination of the same, to the evill sounding of the eres of well disposed cristen men, and especially ageinst the sacrament of the alter, pilgremages and wurshipping of ymages, with dyverse other, and conceling books of heresy, favoureng also such as I have knowen suspect in this behalfe, not denounceng them to your reverend fadrehod ne ony other ordynary in that behalfe, but rather, being conversaunt with them and hering often tymes such dampnable lectures as they did rede and approbating ther rites, did concele such ther redinges and rites.

Wherfor I the forseid [...],[d] truly and feithfully enfourmed, knowleage and knowe well that the articles above rehersed with other concernyng them been erroures and ageinst the true bileve, feithe and determination of all holy church and right evyll soundeng to the eres of well disposed cristen men. Willing with pure hert and free will to forsake those erroures and articles and all other erroures, heresies and erroneous

---

[a] *MS* rereverend.
[b] *blank space in MS.*
[c] *blank space in MS.*
[d] *blank space in MS.*

opynyons being ageinst the feithe and determinacion of the said holy church, and to bileve from hensforthe aftre the teching of all holy churche and turne to the unyte and determination of the seid church, the same erroures, heresies and erroneous opynyons with all other contrary to the true feith and determinacion of all holy church, I uttrely forsake, renounce and abjure and swere apon this booke that aftre this houre I shall never openly ne privyly hold, declare or teche heresy, erroures ne ony maner doctrine ageinst the feith or determination of all holy church. Ne I shall receive, favour, aide, counsell ne defend, succour ne supporte by myselfe or ony other person or personnes privyly or openly them that holdeth, techeth or maynteyneth any such false doctrine, ne yet felisshipp with them wetingly, comforte them ne receive them ne geve them mete ne drinke, clothe ne money ne ony other wais succour them.

Furthermore I swere that if I may know ony person or personnes, men or women, suspect of errour or heresies or fautours, counsellours, comfortours, defensours, receiptours or ony privy conventicles contrary to the commen doctryne of holy church, I shall denounce them to you the forseid reverend fadre, your successoures or officers or to other ordynaries as soon as I goodly may.

Soo helpe me God and the holy dome. In witnes wherof I:

Johanna, uxor Ricardi Smyth Coventr'

Thomas Vyllers[a]   Thomas Lyeff
                                                      +

John Bull[b]   Davy Clerc
                                                      +

Juliana Yong   +
        +   John Jonson, cutler

Agnes Yong   Agnes Jonson
        +   +

                    Agnes de Bakehouse
                              +

---

[a] *probably signed in his own hand.*
[b] *probably signed in his own hand.*

[English translation]

In the name of God, Amen. Before you Reverend Father in God and Lord, Lord Geoffrey, by the grace of God Bishop of Coventry and Lichfield, I, [...][a] of the city of Coventry in your diocese, detected, denounced, and noised to your said reverend fatherhood heretofore to have been suspected of heresy, errors, and evil sounding articles, being in doom and judgement before you.

Feeling and understanding, knowing, and well perceiving that before this hour, I, the foresaid [...][b] have spoken, affirmed, and held diverse articles, opinions, and errors against the faith of all Holy Church and contrary to the determination of the same, to the evil sounding of the ears of well disposed Christian men, and especially against the sacrament of the altar, pilgrimages, and worshipping of images, with diverse other, and concealing books of heresy, favouring also such as I have known suspect in this behalf, not denouncing them to your reverend fatherhood nor any other ordinary in that behalf, but rather, being conversant with them and hearing often times such damnable lectures as they did read and approving their rites, did conceal such their readings and rites.

Wherefore, I, the aforesaid [...],[c] truly and faithfully informed, acknowledge, and know well that the articles above rehearsed with others concerning them were errors and against the true belief, faith, and determination of all Holy Church, and right evil sounding to the ears of well disposed Christian men. Willing with pure heart and free will to forsake those errors and articles and all other errors, heresies, and erroneous opinions being against the faith and determination of the said Holy Church, and to believe from henceforth after the teaching of all Holy Church and turn to the unity and determination of the said Church, the same errors, heresies, and erroneous opinions with all other contrary to the true faith and determination of all Holy Church, I utterly forsake, renounce, and abjure, and swear upon this book that after this hour I shall never openly nor privily hold, declare, or teach heresy, errors, nor any manner of doctrine against the faith or determination of all Holy Church. Nor I shall receive, favour, aid, counsel, nor defend, succour, nor support by myself or any other person or persons, privily or openly, those that hold, teach, or maintain any such false doctrine, nor yet fellowship with them wittingly, comfort them, nor receive them, nor give them meat nor drink, clothes nor money, nor any other ways succour them.

[a] *blank space in MS.*
[b] *blank space in MS.*
[c] *blank space in MS.*

Furthermore I swear that if I may know any person or persons, men or women, suspect of error or heresies or favourers, counsellors, comforters, defenders, receivers or any privy conventicles contrary to the common doctrine of Holy Church, I shall denounce them to you the foresaid reverend father, your successors or officers, or to other ordinaries as soon as I goodly may.

So help me God and the holy doom. In witness whereof I:

Joan, wife of Richard Smyth of
Coventry

Thomas Vyllers[a]   Thomas Lyeff
                                                                        +

John Bull[b]   Davy Clerc
                                                                        +

Juliana Yong   +
        +   John Jonson, cutler

Agnes Yong   Agnes Jonson
        +   +

                    Agnes de Bakehouse
                                +

6 *November 1511 to 24 January 1512*

5. Balthasar Shugborow, Robert Peg, Ralph Lye, Thomas Warde, Hugh Parrek, [...] Pygstappe, Rose Furnour, Margaret Landesdale, and Alice Rowley

[LCB, fo. 22r. The abjuration is undated. Balthasar Shugborow, Robert Peg, and Ralph Lye signed abjurations on 6 November (pp. 171, 176 and 177); Thomas Warde on 25 or 29 November (pp. 190 and 205); Hugh Parrek and Margaret Landesdale on 3 December (p. 221); Rose Furnour on 16 January 1512 (above, p. 227); Alice Rowley on 24 January (p. 241). This abjuration is the only evidence for Pygstappe, who does not otherwise appear in any of the records.]

---

[a] *probably signed in his own hand.*
[b] *probably signed in his own hand.*

In the name of God, Amen. Before you reverend fadre in God and lorde Lorde Geffrey by the grace of God busshopp of Coventr' and Lich', I [...]ᵃ of the citie of Coventr' in your diocese, detected, denownsed and noised to your seid reverend fadrehod heretofore to have been suspected of heresy, erroures and other articles evill sowneng, being in dome and jugement afor you.ᵇ

Feling and undrestonding, knoweng and well perceiveng that afore this howr I the forseid [...]ᶜ have spoken, affermed and holden diverse articles, opinions and erroures ageinst the feith of all holy church and contrary to the determynacion of the same, to the evyll sounding of the eris of wel disposed cristen men, and especially agenst the sacrament of the alter, pilgremages and worshipping of ymages, with divers others, and conceling books of heresy, favouring also such as I have known suspect in this behalfe, not denownceng them to your reverend fadrehod ne ony other ordinarie in this behalfe, but rather, being conversaunt with them and hering often tymes such dampnable lectures as they did rede and approbating ther rites, did concele such ther redinges and rites.

Wherfor I the forseid [...],ᵈ truly and feithfully enformed, knowleage and know well that the articles above reheresed with other concernyng them been errours and ageinst the true bileve, feith and determynation of all holy church and right evill soundeng to the eres of well disposed cristen men. Willing with pure hert and free will to forsake those erroures and articles and all other erroures, heresies and erroneous opynyons being agenst the feith and determynacion of the seid holy church, and to beleve from hensforth aftre the teching of all holy church and turn to the unite and determynacion of the said church, the same erroures, heresies and erroneous opynyons with all other contrary to the same feith and determynacion of all holy church, I utterly forsake, renounce and abjure and swere upon this booke that aftre this houre I shall nevyr openly ne privily hold, declare or teche heresy, erroures ne ony maner of doctrine ageinst the feith or determynation of all holy church. Ne I shall receive, favour, aide, counsell ne defend, succour ne supporte by my selfe ne ony other person or personnes privily or openly them that holdeth, techeth or mayneteyneth ony suche false doctrine, ne yet felasshipp with them witingly, comforte them ne receive them, ne geve them mete ne drinke, clothe ne money, ne ony other wais succour them.

Furthermore, I swere that if I may knowe ony person or persones,

---

ᵃ *blank space in MS.*
ᵇ you *interlined.*
ᶜ *blank space in MS.*
ᵈ *blank space in MS.*

men or women, suspect of erroures or heresies or fautors, counsellors, comfortours, defensours, receiptors or ony prive conventicles contrary to the common doctryne of holy church, I shall denounce them to you the forsaid reverend fadre, your successours or officers or to ther ordinaries as soon as I goodly may.

So helpe me God and the holy dome. In witnes whereof, I with my hand:

[...] Shukburgh[a]   Robertus Pegge   Ranulphus Lye
                                                  +

Hugo Parret   +
      +   Thomas Warde

                  [...] Pygstappe[b]   Rosa Furnour
                                             +

Margareta Londesdale   Alicia Rowley
          +   +

[English translation]

In the name of God, Amen. Before you reverend father in God and Lord, Lord Geoffrey, by the grace of God Bishop of Coventry and Lichfield, I, [...][c] of the city of Coventry in your diocese, detected, denounced, and noised to your said reverend fatherhood heretofore to have been suspected of heresy, errors, and other articles evil sounding, being in doom and judgement before you.

Feeling and understanding, knowing, and well perceiving that before this hour I the foresaid [...][d] have spoken, affirmed, and held divers articles, opinions, and errors against the faith of all Holy Church and contrary to the determination of the same, to the evil sounding of the ears of well disposed Christian men, and especially against the sacrament of the altar, pilgrimages, and worshipping of images, with divers other, and concealing books of heresy, favouring also such as I have known suspect in this behalf, not denouncing them to your reverend fatherhood nor any other ordinary in that behalf, but rather, being conversant with them and hearing often times such damnable lectures as they did read and approving their rites, did conceal such their readings and rites.

[a] *probably signed in his own hand.*
[b] *probably signed in his or her own hand.*
[c] *blank space in MS.*
[d] *blank space in MS.*

Wherefore I the aforesaid [...],[a] truly and faithfully informed, acknowledge, and know well that the articles above rehearsed with others concerning them were errors and against the true belief, faith, and determination of all Holy Church, and right evil sounding to the ears of well disposed Christian men. Willing with pure heart and free will to forsake those errors and articles and all other errors, heresies, and erroneous opinions being against the faith and determination of the said Holy Church, and to believe from henceforth after the teaching of all Holy Church, and turn to the unity and determination of the said Church, the same errors, heresies, and erroneous opinions with all other contrary to the same faith and determination of all Holy Church, I utterly forsake, renounce, and abjure, and swear upon this book that after this hour I shall never openly nor privily hold, declare, or teach heresy, errors, nor any manner of doctrine against the faith or determination of all Holy Church. Nor I shall receive, favour, aid, counsel nor defend, succour, nor support by myself or any other person or persons, privily or openly, those that hold, teach, or maintain any such false doctrine, nor yet fellowship with them wittingly, comfort them, nor receive them nor give them meat nor drink, clothes nor money nor any other ways succour them.

Furthermore, I swear that if I may know any person or persons, men or women, suspect of error or heresies, or favourers, counsellors, comforters, defenders, receivers, or any privy conventicles contrary to the common doctrine of Holy Church, I shall denounce them to you the foresaid reverend father, your successors or officers, or to other ordinaries as soon as I goodly may.

So help me God and the holy doom. In witness whereof I with my hand:

[...] Shukburgh[b]   Robert Pegge   Ralph Lye
                                                    +

    Hugh Parret   +
         +   Thomas Warde

                          [...] Pygstappe[c]   Rose Furnour
                                                    +

    Margaret Londesdale   Alice Rowley
            +   +

[a] *blank space in MS.*
[b] *probably signed in his own hand.*
[c] *probably signed in his or her own hand.*

4 February 1512

6. John Holywod, John Cropwell, John [...], Roger Toft, and Robert Hagmond

[LCB, p. iii. The fragment is undated but all the identifiable persons are recorded as abjuring, and making a cross under their name, on 4 February 1512 (p. 250).]

Johannes Holywod   Johannes [Cro]pwell   Johannes [...]

+

R[ogerus] Toft   Robertus Hagmond
+

[English translation]

John Holywod   John [Cro]pwell   John [...]
+

R[oger] Toft   Robert Hagmond
+

[LCB, p. i. Only a few fragments of this page survive and only the following words are legible.]

[...] sacramentum altaris [...] verba [...]

[English translation]

[...] sacrament of the altar [...] words [...]

[LCB, p. ii. Only a few fragments of this page survive and only one word is legible.]

[...] omnibus [...]

[English translation]

[...] all [...]

[LCB, p. iii. On this page are mounted three fragments, each possibly originally from separate folios. There is no indication of dates. The other two fragments are transcribed above: the second is included with other material related to Richard Rise, above, p. 244; the third fragment is Abjuration no. 6, above, p. 277.]

In Dei nomine, Amen. Nos Galfridus [...] legittime procedentes. Quia invenimus [...] dixisse et tenuisse seu saltem libr' [...] ad sanam ecclesie doctrinam et eccl[...] omni heretica pravitate ac prestita' [...] quam ea occasione incidisti [...] restituimus.

[English translation]

In the name of God, Amen. We, Geoffrey [...] legitimately proceeding. Because we have found [...] to have said and held or at least [...] to the sound teaching of the Church [...] every heretical deformity and sworn [...] which on that occasion you have fallen [...] we restore.

[LCB, fos 26r–27v]

[...] ut supra iurat' negat. Quare dominus ex consilio [...] ut supra.

Johannes [...]

[...] Coventr', iurat' et cetera [...] eo animo [...] dominus [...] et [...] ut supra.
[...] apud Coventriam [...] coram suppriore doctore [...] domin' secrete abiurat' [...].

———————————————

[English translation]

[...] as above, denies. Therefore the lord on the advice [...] as above.

John [...]

[...] Coventry, sworn etc. [...] that mind [...] the lord [...] and [...] as above.
[...] in Coventry [...] before the subprior, doctor [...] the lord, secretly abjured [...].

Tuesday, 22 May 1515

William Borodall

[Blyth's Visitation Book, Lichfield Record Office, MS B/V/1/1, p. 99. Also transcribed in Peter Heath (ed.) Bishop Geoffrey Blythe's Visitations c. 1515–1525, Collections for a History of Staffordshire, Staffordshire Record Society, 4ᵗʰ series, 7 (1973), p. 101.]

xxii Maii anno domini 1515.ᵃ

Willelmus Borodall, etatis circiter xxi annorum,ᵇ parochie sancte Trinitiatis, serviens cum Johanne Vicars, hatmaker, coram Magistro Thoma Fitzherbert, Magistro Thoma Orton et Magistro Thoma Clement.

Fatebatur quod in xlⁱⁱ ad biennium elapse quodᶜ Nicholaus Boradall et Margareta uxor eius sporiar parochie sancti Michaelisᵈ persuaserunt et induxerunt eum ut nonᵉ crederet in sacramentum altaris nec reciperet at ne quidem confiteretur peccata sua, quia deus non erat in sacramento illo. Et dicit preterea quod consiliis eorum recepit communionem confessione nulla prima.

Postea tamen penitentia ductus accessit ad fratrem quemdam de ordine minorum qui recusavit eius confessionem audire. Et sic tandem aggressus est Magistrum Thomam Orton et verba prescripta in ordine eidem rettulit extra confessione coram Magistro Clement et aliis.ᶠ

Dicit insuper patrem suum mansisse cum Rogero Sporyer et cetera.

ᵃ xxii Maii [...] 1515 *is the heading of the page.*
ᵇ etatis [...] annorum *interlined.*
ᶜ Quod [...] quod: *[sic] in MS.*
ᵈ Parochie [...] Michaelis *interlined.*
ᵉ reciperet *deleted.*
ᶠ Extra [...] et aliis *interlined.*

Fatetur preterea patrem suum ad viii annos elapsos[a] dedisse ei in mandatis ut accederet ad Landesdale propter cibaria[b] et ad Hachet[c] pro calceis.

Dicit tandem quod pretextu receptionis communionis sic ut premittitur per eum facte[d] laborante eo infirmitate et exclamante atque vociferante contra parentes tanquam demone, vocante eos hereticos, parentes sui predicti eum deserverint.

Dicit insuper patrem suum conversatus fuisse sepius cum Hachet et Banbroke, cum quo quidem Banbroke mater sua serviens erat.

[English translation]

22 May 1515.

William Borodall, aged about twenty-one, of Holy Trinity parish, servant with John Vicars, hatmaker, before Master Thomas Fitzherbert, Master Thomas Orton, and Master Thomas Clement.

He admitted that in Lent two years ago Nicholas Boradall and Margaret his wife, spurrier of St Michael's parish, persuaded and induced him not to believe in or receive the sacrament of the altar, nor to confess his sins, because God was not in that sacrament. He says that following their advice he received communion without confession beforehand.

Afterwards, however, brought to repentance, he came to a friar of the order of Minorites who refused to hear his confession. And so he approached Master Thomas Orton and told him the above words in order, outside confession in the presence of Master Clement and others.

He says his father stayed with Roger Sporyer etc. He admits that seven years ago his father told him to go to Landesdale for food and Hachet for shoes.

He eventually says that on account of the communion he received, as stated above, he has become ill and shouts against his parents like a demon, calling them heretics, and as a result they have disowned him.

He says his father often conversed with Hachet and Banbroke; his mother was a servant with Banbroke.

---

[a] ad viii annos elapsos *interlined.*
[b] victum *deleted;* cibaria *interlined.*
[c] Landesdale *deleted;* Hachet *interlined.*
[d] Pretextu [...] eum facte *interlined.*

Ralph Lowe

[Blyth's Visitations, Lichfield Record Office, MS B/V/1/1, p. 99. The left side of the page is damaged. Also transcribed in Peter Heath (ed.) Bishop Geoffrey Blythe's Visitations c. 1515–1525, Collections for a History of Staffordshire, Staffordshire Record Society, 4th series, 7 (1973), pp. 101–102.]

Radulphus Lowe serviens cum Rowley[156] vicecomite nuper Coventr', vidit Johannam Smyth exeuntem a domo Landesdale et [...] quam ex precepto domini sui insecutus est ut videret quemadmodum et qualis esset. Ipsa tamen tunc [...] animadvertente insequentem finxit se alio transire ubi advenit domum propriam. Et continuo [...] ingressus est aulam gaole. Tum evestigio ipsa perspiciens necnon [...] ad ostium domus proprie et moram aliquantulam ibidem faciens vidit [...] exeuntem aulam gaole predicte quem incontinenti secuta est vociferans [...] Ac ipse dissimulans se non audisse nullum responsum dedit quousque dixit [...] 'servant M. Shireffis servant For the passion of criste thinke [...]' Quo respondente, 'quedam causa est ob quam ego male conquerem de vobis' dixit [...] 'saw me cum owte[a] of my brodres howse For I had suche [...] deth that I went to my sistre for to have ease of my payn'.

[English translation]

Ralph Lowe, servant with Rowley,[156] recently Sheriff of Coventry, saw Joan Smyth leaving Landesdale's house and [...] whom he followed on his master's instructions in order to see who and what kind of person she was. She, however, [...] noticing that he was following, pretended to go elsewhere when she arrived at her home. Straightaway, [...] he went into the hall of the gaol. Then from the footsteps she, noticing also [...] to the door of her own house and, delaying some time there, she saw [...] him leaving the hall of the said gaol and she immediately followed him, calling out [...]. He, pretending that he had not heard, did not reply until she said [...] 'servant M. Sheriffs servant, for the passion of Christe think [...]'. He replied 'there is a reason why I think ill of you', [...] 'saw me come out of my brother's house. For I had suche [...] death that I went to my sister for to have ease of my pain'.

---

[a] from *deleted;* owte *interlined.*

Monday, 21 December 1521 or Monday, 13 January 1522

Robert Silkby

[LCB, fo. 9r. Undated. Silkby's execution is recorded in the Coventry Civic Annals as having taken place on the Monday before Christmas 1521 (i.e. 23 December; see below, pp. 315–317), while John Foxe dated it to 13 January 1522 (see below, pp. 298 and 311). For Silkby's abjuration in 1511, see above, p. 260.]

In Dei nomine, Amen. Nos, Thomas Fitzherbert, sacrorum canonun professor, reverendi in Christo patris et domini domini Galfridi Dei gracia Coventr' et Lich' episcopi vicarius in spiritualibus generalis atque in causa heretice pravitatis et reincidencie in hereses abiuratas et relapsus – unacum honorando in Christo patre et domino domino Johanne Dei benignitate ecclesie cathedralis Coventr' priore,[157] ac aliis venerabilibus et egregiis viris in litteris commissionum eiusdem reverendi patris cum illa clausula, 'coniunctim et divisim', nominatis – commissarius sufficienter et legitime deputatus, legittime procedentes.

Quia per acta inactitata, deducta, proposita, inquisita atque per te Robertum Silkeby alias Dumbleby coram nobis in iudicio publice recognita et confessata – meritis huiusmodi cause heretice pravitatis et relapsus per nos auditis, intellectis, recognitis, recensitis ac plenarie discussis, servatisque de iure in hac parte servandis – intuemus[a] te Robertum Sylkeby alias Dumbleby, postquam diversos errores et opiniones dampnatos – videlicet contra sacramentum altaris, peregrinaciones, imaginum veneraciones unacum aliis heresibus tam in specie quam in genere, in prioratu de Maxstocke coram prefato reverendo patre publice et solemniter abiurandas, in easdem hereses, errores et opiniones dampnatas et per te abiuratas notorie et animo pertinaci reincidisse, easque variis in locis huius Coventr' et Lich' diocesis animo indurato et deliberato astruisse, tenuisse, docuisse et credidisse.

Idcirco nos Thomas Fitzherbert commissarius antedictus, Christi nomine primitus invocato atque ipsum solum Deum omnibus nostris proponentes, iudicialiter et pro tribunali sedentes, volentes huiusmodi causam sive negotium fame debito terminare, de consilio nonnullorum venerabilium atque egregiorum virorum tum sacre theologie quam canonum professorum atque aliorum iuris utriusque peritorum nobis assistentium, cum quibus mature in hac parte communicavimus: te Robertum Sylkeby alias Dumbleby in hereses per te abiuratas fuisse et

---

[a] *illegible word deleted.*

esse manifeste relapsum, penaque relapsorum in heresim puniendum fore, pronunciamus et decernimus atque declaramus per hanc nostram sentenciam difinitivam, quam ferrimus et promulgamus in his scriptis.

Teque, cum ecclesia non habeat[a] ultra quid faciat, maioris sentencia excommunicacionis ligatum[b] atque ea innodatum et involutum fuisse et esse premissorum pretextu, coram presenti multitudine, pronunciamus et declaramus. Relinquentes te tanquam hereticum relapsum brachio seculari[c] puniendum, rogantes ut executio contra te fienda citra mortis articulum moderetur, ut non sit rigor rigidus nec mansuetudo dissoluta sed tantum ad Dei laudem, catholicorum gloriam, animeque tue salutem et salvacionem, aliorumque nonnullorum metum et terrorem, atque huiusmodi hereses et errores dampnatos deserendi causam.

Clausula[d] inserenda in sententia cum quis sit [...] ac eo pretextu merito degradand' et ab omni ordine [...] debere [...] sacros canones in hac parte [...] declaramus [...] et cetera.[e]

[English translation]

In the name of God, Amen. We, Thomas Fitzherbert, professor of the sacred canons, vicar general in spirituals of the Reverend Father and Lord in Christ, Lord Geoffrey, by the grace of God Bishop of Coventry and Lichfield, and commissary, sufficiently and legitimately deputed, in the case of heresy and relapse into abjured heresies – together with the Honourable Father and Lord in Christ, Lord John, by the grace of God Prior of Coventry Cathedral church,[157] and other venerable and distinguished men, named in the same reverend father's letter of commission with the clause 'collectively and individually' – legitimately proceeding.

Because of the things done, deduced, proposed, enquired and publicly acknowledged and confessed by you, Robert Silkeby *alias* Dumbleby, before us in court – the merits of this case of heresy and relapse having been heard, understood, reviewed, examined, and fully discussed by us, and following the observance in law of what ought to be observed in this matter – we find that you, Robert Sylkeby *alias* Dumbleby, after you had publicly and solemnly abjured in Maxstoke Priory, before the said reverend father, various condemned errors and opinions – namely against the sacrament of the altar, pilgrimages, the veneration of images,

[a] ult' *deleted.*
[b] ligatum *interlined.*
[c] p' *deleted.*
[d] cu' *deleted.*
[e] Clausula [...] declaramus *in a different hand, separated by a gap from the previous text.*

and other heresies, both in particular and in general – have fallen again notoriously and with an obstinate mind into the same condemned heresies, errors, and opinions that you abjured, and have instructed, held, taught, and believed them with a hardened and deliberate mind in various places in this diocese of Coventry and Lichfield.

Therefore we, Thomas Fitzherbert, the aforesaid commissary – having first invoked Christ's name and keeping before our eyes God alone, sitting judicially and in court, wishing to bring this case to its proper conclusion, on the advice of various venerable and distinguished men, professors both of sacred theology and of the canons, and of other experts in both laws, assisting us, with whom we have communicated at the proper time in this matter – pronounce and decide and declare by this our definitive sentence, which we bear and promulgate in this document, that you, Robert Sylkeby *alias* Dumbleby, have manifestly relapsed into and remain in the heresies that you abjured, and that you shall receive the punishment of those who relapse into heresy.

Since the church can do no more, we pronounce and declare before the present multitude that you have been and are, on account of the matters mentioned above, bound by the sentence of major excommunication, tied and restrained by it. We relinquish you as a relapsed heretic to the secular arm for punishment, asking that the sentence to be carried out against you may be moderated regarding the trial of death, in such a way that rigour is not inflexible nor gentleness abandoned, and yet so that the result may be only the praise of God, the glory of Catholics, the health and salvation of your soul, the fear and terror of others, and the cause of removing these condemned errors and heresies.

The clause to be inserted in the sentence since [...] and for that reason deservedly to be degraded and from every order [...] ought [...] sacred canons in this matter [...] we declare [...] etc.

EXPLANATORY NOTES

[1] The parish church of St Michael, Coventry.

[2] These refer respectively to the shrines of Mary at Doncaster, Walsingham, and in the Carmelite friary of Coventry. See above, p. 16.

[3] The Shrine of the Blood of Christ at Hailes, Gloucestershire. See above, p. 16.

[4] i.e. *quadragesima*, Lent.

[5] Cf. Latham: *vaccineus*, of a cow.

[6] 10 March 1486.

[7] 12 March 1486.

[8] 9 March 1486.

[9] The Bishop of Coventry and Lichfield's manor at Beaudesert, Warwickshire, south-west of Coventry.

[10] Ashbourne, Derbyshire.

[11] i.e. the Saturday before Pentecost, or 24 May 1488.

[12] i.e. Coventry.

[13] Bolton, Lancashire (now Greater Manchester).

[14] John Holywod's deposition, which was likely to have been made very early in the proceedings, does not survive. He appeared on 4 February 1512 to receive penance (see p. 250).

[15] Here and below (p. 106) the editors have punctuated this to indicate that two persons are meant by 'Rogerum' and 'Hachet' (i.e. Roger Landesdale and Robert Hachet). It is also possible that 'Roger' was a scribal error for 'Robert', or that there was a separate person named Roger Hachet.

[16] Bristol, Gloucestershire. See Thomson, *Later Lollards*, pp. 46–47, regarding John Bouway, Sr and John Bouway, Jr, who abjured before the Bishop of Bath and Wells c. 1499.

[17] Mill Lane outside the New Gate, Coventry. The illegible words probably refer to Mother Margaret, who lived in Mylne Lane (see below, p. 148).

[18] John Alcock, D.C.L., rector of Ibstock, Leicestershire (see Introduction, p. 41).

[19] William Kent, M.A., rector of Stoney Stanton, Leicestershire (see Introduction, p. 40).

[20] Preston, in Amounderness Hundred, Lancashire.

[21] Also known as John Atkynson, painter.

[22] Also known as John Davy, painter.

[23] See above n. 15.

[24] The Book of Tobit, a deutero-canonical book of the Old Testament (not considered fully authentic in some versions of the Christian scriptures today, but canonical in the Middle Ages).

[25] Ralph and William Kent of Stoney Stanton, Leicestershire (see Introduction, p. 40).

[26] Skelton, York.

[27] Seacoal Lane, near the Fleet Prison, London.

[28] Maidstone, Kent.

[29] Gloucester, Gloucestershire.

[30] See above, p. 5.

[31] Redcliff Street, Bristol. For maps and street names of medieval Bristol, see *The Atlas of Historic Towns*, II, *Bristol*.

[32] See above n. 16.

[33] Taunton, Somerset.

[34] Perhaps Brittany, France.

[35] Perhaps Bordeaux, France.

[36] Holborn Cross, City of London.

[37] Garstang, Lancashire, near the Premonstratensian Abbey of Cockersand (see Knowles and Hadcock, *Medieval Religious Houses*, p. 164).

[38] See the introduction, p. 28, n. 104, for a discussion of this passage.

[39] Allesley, Warwickshire (three or four miles west-north-west of Coventry). Ralph Lye, a weaver, lived in Allesley and he is presumably meant here.

[40] Thomas Bayly was active in Coventry civic life from 1481 to 1510, including acting as Justice of the Peace and Master of the Guild of the Holy Trinity in 1494. *Coventry Leet Book*, pp. 481–628.

[41] Little Park Street, Coventry.

[42] Presumably an inn or a tavern in Coventry called The Crown; unidentified.

[43] This suggests that (Thomas) Bown was present during Landesdale's testimony. But see below n. 48.

[44] Fleet Street, Coventry.

[45] i.e. Matthew Markelond.

[46] John 1.1.

[47] Gosford Street, Coventry.

[48] It is unclear what Hachet means by saying that Bown has now fled; it is possible that he was present in custody on the same day as Hachet's deposition, as is suggested in Landesdale's testimony (above p. 118). He was certainly in custody by 3 November when he made his own deposition (below p. 130).

[49] Jordan Well was the name both of a street and of a ward in Coventry.

[50] John Alcock, D.C.L., rector of Ibstock, Leicestershire (see Introduction, p. 41).

[51] According to the marginal note, vicar of Corby (Northamptonshire, or possibly Corby Glen, Lincolnshire); otherwise unidentified.

[52] Warwick, Warwickshire.

[53] Possibly Thomas Latimer, OP, D.Th. 1501, prior of Warwick Convent in 1495; *BRUO*, II, p. 1106.

[54] Stivichall, West Midlands, just outside Coventry.

[55] Possibly an inn or tavern in Coventry called The Angel; there was an inn by this name in 1600 (*REED Coventry*, p. 356).

[56] NB: William Grevis appears to be identical with William Revis.

[57] This may have been a printed German Bible; unlike England, Germany saw many editions of vernacular Bibles come off the printing presses in the pre-Reformation period. See Bernd Moeller, 'Piety in Germany around 1500',

in Steven E. Ozment (ed.) *The Reformation in Medieval Perspective* (Chicago IL, 1971), pp. 58–59.

[58] See below, n. 112.

[59] Perhaps Charlbury, Oxfordshire (just north-west of Woodstock), although fifteen to twenty miles from Banbury.

[60] John Hales, Bishop of Coventry and Lichfield 1459–1490; Richard Weston is unidentified.

[61] Thomas Bowd, vicar of Holy Trinity, Coventry c. 1504–1508 (among many other ecclesiastical offices); see *BRUC*, p. 82.

[62] Note that Blyth chose, in the end, to 'convict' John Davy himself; Davy abjured heresy before Blyth on 16 January 1512 (below pp. 229 and 266), although there is no record of his having been questioned.

[63] See Introduction, p. 40.

[64] William Smith, Bishop of Lincoln 1496–1514.

[65] Unidentified; possibly an episcopal official.

[66] Northfield, Worcestershire (about six miles south-south-west of Birmingham).

[67] Matthew 18.7.

[68] Napton, Warwickshire (see Introduction, p. 26).

[69] Earl Street, Coventry.

[70] Ralph Lye, weaver, of Allesley.

[71] Evidence of this prosecution at Leicester does not survive other than this and another allusion in the Lichfield Court Book (see below p. 157).

[72] Hachet seems to be present at Silkby's examination, and is confirming some of his statements.

[73] Gosford Street, Coventry.

[74] This may be Thomas Forde, or possibly his brother William. Thomas Forde was active in Coventry civic life from 1461 to 1516 and William from 1474 to 1508, including the mayoralty in 1497. *Coventry Leet Book*, pp. 313–647 *passim*.

[75] Chester, Cheshire.

[76] Unidentified. Presumably not the same as James Preston, D.Th., vicar of St Michael's, Coventry (see above p. 29), who was not a Franciscan friar and who was dead by 1507 (reference is made below, p. 222, to Friar Preston hearing confession in 1511).

[77] Devizes, Wiltshire, sometimes known as 'Vies' or 'The Vies'; see Lucy Toulmin Smith (ed.) *The Itinerary of John Leland*, 5 vols (London: Centaur Press, 1964), V, pp. 81–82. Our thanks to John A.W. Lock for this suggestion.

[78] Possibly Hatton, Derbyshire or Haughton, Staffordshire.

[79] i.e. during the episcopate of John Hales, Bishop of Coventry and Lichfield, 1459–1490.

[80] i.e. the abjurations of John Smyth and the others in 1486.

[81] Abbots Bromley, Staffordshire.

[82] Napton, Warwickshire.

[83] This sentence appears to be a note relating to the interrogation of John Gest, Jr rather than Joan Gest, his wife.

[84] 1 Corinthians 13, and Matthew 4.1–11.

[85] The three women Alice Rowley names here were probably the wives of

prominent men on the Coventry civic scene, commensurate with Rowley's own status as the widow of a former mayor. The wife of Duddesbury could have been the wife of John Duddesbury, active in civic affairs from 1477 until 1523, chamberlain in 1484, sheriff in 1487, mayor in 1505, and Master of the Holy Trinity Guild in 1508. *Coventry Leet Book*, pp. 422–684, especially 518, 532, 603, 621. The wife of Haddon may have been the wife of John Haddon, active in civic affairs from 1480 until 1519, warden in 1488, sheriff in 1492, bailiff in 1493, and mayor in 1500. *Coventry Leet Book*, pp. 432–665, especially 533, 544, 547, 599. The wife of Butler may have been the wife of John Butler, steward and town clerk from 1481 until at least 1504, and coroner from 1509–1521. *Coventry Leet Book*, pp. 474–603, 624–76. See Phythian-Adams, *Desolation*, pp. 90–91, about the role of the mayoress and other women of the oligarchy.

[86] The Bishop of Coventry and Lichfield's manor at Beaudesert, Warwickshire. It is not clear when Alice Rowley was at Beaudesert (which had been the site of Margery Goyte's trial in 1488, above, p. 87); it is possible that it was during Rowley's earlier encounter with the bishop about 1506, referred to just above, although the allusion to handing over books to Master Longland implies a more recent past (see p. 142).

[87] Unidentified; possibly an episcopal official.

[88] New Gate, one of the gates to the city of Coventry.

[89] Probably Thomas Bayly; see above, n. 40.

[90] See above, n. 71.

[91] This could be Roger Landesdale, 'scissor', usually translated as tailor, but sometimes meaning cutler.

[92] Banbury, Oxfordshire. No other evidence survives regarding this burning.

[93] James Preston, D.Th. (1479–1480), who was admitted as vicar of St Michael's parish, Coventry, in 1488 and died by 1507. See above, p. 29.

[94] The Franciscan friary on the south-west side of Coventry (then surrounded by a field or garden).

[95] See Introduction, p. 29.

[96] Possibly John Derlyng or Darlyng, active in Coventry civic life; see p. 31.

[97] Greyfriars Lane, Coventry.

[98] i.e. fo. 23r; see below, p. 270.

[99] Although there is no direct evidence for proceedings against and execution of a Lollard named Christopher, this man is possibly the same as the Christopher Shoemaker of Great Missenden (Buckinghamshire), whom Foxe reports to have been burned at Newbury in 1518 (Foxe could have been mistaken about the date). Foxe, *A&M* (1570), p. 945; *A&M* (1843), IV, pp. 217, 229.

[100] The record of this prosecution in Maidstone (Kent) c. 1495 does not survive.

[101] Spon Street was a street and a city ward on the western edge of Coventry; a cawsey was 'a mound, embankment or dam, to retain the water of a river or pond' (*OED*, s.v. 'causey'), and thus Spon Cawsey may be the same as the Spate Dam on the River Sherbourne running through Spon Street ward.

[102] Atherstone, Warwickshire, fourteen miles north of Coventry.

[103] Note that Robert Hachet appears to have been present at Warde's examination and corroborates this statement.

[104] Possibly Weston-under-Lizard, Staffordshire.

[105] Gosford Street, Coventry.

[106] Unidentified.

[107] St Werburgh's Abbey, Chester.

[108] Caernarvon, Gwyned, Wales.

[109] Stafford, Staffordshire.

[110] Holt Castle, Holt, Clwyd, Wales.

[111] Wrexham, Clwyd, Wales.

[112] The Wigston and Pysford families were wealthy and politically powerful, both in Coventry and in Leicester. William Pysford the Elder was active in Coventry civic politics from 1486 to 1518 and held the position of mayor in 1501. His son, Henry Pysford, was very wealthy, being evaluated as possessing £400 in the 1524 subsidy. The Wigstons made their chief home in Leicester, but John Wigston held prominent civic offices in Coventry, including the mayoralty and the Mastership of the Holy Trinity Guild. A William Wigston (either John's son or nephew) was also referred to in the *Coventry Leet Book* from 1491 to 1509. In Leicester, William Wigston the Younger was by far the wealthiest man in the city by 1523, and he and his brothers and cousins held a number of important political positions. The families intermarried; see below, p. 237. See McSheffrey, *Gender*, p. 180, n. 102 for references.

[113] Master Bayly is likely Thomas Bayly (see above, n. 40); Robert Bayly does not appear in the *Coventry Leet Book*.

[114] William Banwell, mercer, was active in Coventry civic life from 1501 to 1531. See *Coventry Leet Book*, pp. 601–706.

[115] Probably Hardingstone, Northamptonshire.

[116] See Introduction, p. 29.

[117] Kingswinford, West Midlands.

[118] Mirfield, near Wakefield, Yorkshire.

[119] Winchcombe, Gloucestershire.

[120] The church now known as Throapham St John's, near Laughton-en-le-Morthen, South Yorkshire.

[121] This likely refers to John Bull, nephew of John Physician and servant of Thomas Villers (see below p. 215).

[122] Unidentified; possibly *Here begynneth a lytell treatyse of a dyenge creature enfected with sykenes* (London, 1507; STC 6034), an orthodox devotional treatise in the 'art of dying' genre. See Introduction, p. 42.

[123] The county of Rutland.

[124] Probably Penkridge, Staffordshire.

[125] Luke 12.32.

[126] See above, p. 200.

[127] Following this is a scribal doodle, implying that the scribe may have had to wait for some time while the witness was questioned further and then finally admitted that he had heard Bown and Landesdale teaching.

[128] St David's, Dyfed, Wales.

[129] Possibly Carlton-on-Trent, Nottinghamshire.

[130] See above n. 76.

[131] The parish of St Thomas in Bristol, diocese of Bath.

[132] See above n. 16.

[133] Broadmead, Bristol.

134 The parish of Sts Philip and James, Bristol.

135 The parish of St Nicholas, Bristol.

136 The Temple Church, Bristol.

137 Chapel unidentified; it may have been in the Bristol suburb of Clifton, where there were a number of streets bearing the name St Vincent. See *The Atlas of Historic Towns*, II, *Bristol, Cambridge, Coventry, Norwich*.

138 Aston, Warwickshire (north-north-west of Birmingham).

139 Luke 12.32.

140 Note that the section on fo. 15r (and the penance enjoined on Rose Furnour) was mistakenly thought to refer to Alice Rowley in McSheffrey, *Gender*, p. 123.

141 i.e. 30 October 1511.

142 Margaret Grey.

143 May be a quotation, but not apparently scriptural.

144 Luke 12.32.

145 Presumably Agnes Wigston, wife of William Wigston, and her father, William Pysford Sr. In her later life, at least, Agnes Wigston was an orthodox Catholic, even conservatively so: in 1536, as a widow, she appeared before Bishop Longland of Lincoln and took a vow of widowed chastity. PRO, PCC Prob. 11/19 (9 Ayloffe), fos 67r–68v, 70r, Will of William Pysford of Coventry, 1518; *Lincoln Diocese Documents, 1450–1544*, ed. Andrew Clark, EETS, o.s., 149 (1914), 209–210.

146 Northampton, Northamptonshire.

147 Between 24 June and 11 November, the feasts of St John the Baptist and St Martin in winter (*hyeme* – i.e. St Martin of Tours).

148 Thomas Wasshingburn had previously abjured heresy in London in 1482. See Introduction, p. 39.

149 Maidstone, Kent.

150 See Introduction, p. 40, on branding.

151 Possibly John Camberton, D.Th. from Cambridge; he was Vice-Chancellor of Cambridge University 1489–1490, and Master of Maidstone College from 1495 until his death in 1505 or 1506; *BRUC*, p. 188. The record of these trials does not survive.

152 2 December 1511.

153 John Wilcocks, D.Th.; see Appendix 3.

154 See above n. 151. The Archbishop of Canterbury in question was John Morton.

155 Canterbury, Kent.

156 Thomas Rowley, Sheriff of Coventry 1513–1514 (*Coventry Leet Book*, p. 637) and son of Alice Rowley. See above p. 27.

157 John Webbe; see Appendix 3.

PROSECUTION OF THE COVENTRY LOLLARDS IN FOXE'S MARTYROLOGIES AND IN THE COVENTRY CIVIC ANNALS

PROSECUTION OF THE COVENTRY LOLLARDS IN FOXE'S MARTYROLOGIES AND IN THE COVENTRY CIVIC ANNALS

The Coventry Lollards in John Foxe's *Rerum in ecclesia gestarum*

[John Foxe, Rerum in ecclesia gestarum *(Basel, 1559), pp. 116–117.]*

[p. 116]   Uxor D. Smytthi, cum sex aliis Couentriae exustis[a]

Svbit hic mihi, in hoc praestantissimarum mulierum ordine, memoria foeminae cuiusdam Couentriensis, ignoto quidem nomine: nisi quod uir illius, praefecturam aliquando in ea urbe gerens, Smythus diceretur. Haec igitur Smythi uxor, circa haec tempora,[1] aut non multo secus, cum sex alijs eiusdem martyrij sodalibus, extra urbis moenia, in cauam fossam perducta, quę in hunc diem tracto ab ipsis nomine, Puteus haereticorum dicitur,[2] incendio data est. His autem *[p. 117]* septem Machabaeis haud aliud exitio fuisse dicitur, quam quod scripturis in suam uersis linguam, operam interdum dare deprehenderentur. Poterat tamen ea, ut ferebat fama, ex illo emergere periculo: nisi schedula forte quaedam a ductore per manicata brachij redimicula, quae orationem Dominicam uernaculo idiomate contineret, perspecta, in odium primum episcopi & theologorum, deinde in condemnationem eam retraxisset. Erat praeterea ciuium ac opificum numerus eadem hac tempestate non exiguus, cateruatim in puteos suburbanos confluentium, ad uerbi Domini sacram auscultationem: in quos vario suppliciorum genere desaeuitum est. Alij enim impositis ad publicam ignominiam fasciculis ostentui producebantur. Multi auribus pendebant in publico foro, ad machinam affixis: maxime qui spreta pontificij ieiunij indictione, per quadragesimam minus abstineret a carnibus. Tanta erat uel horum inscitia temporum, uel hominum saeuitia.

---

[a] Uxor [...] exustis *is the heading.*

[English translation]

[p. 116]   The Wife of Sir Smyth, with six others of Coventry, burned

Coming to mind here, in this series of most excellent women, is the memory of a certain woman of Coventry whose name, however, is unknown: except that her husband, who at one time governed that town, was called Smyth. This wife of Smyth thus, around that time or not long after,[1] along with six other comrades of her martyrdom, was led outside the city walls into a hollow ditch, which nowadays – taking its name from them – is called Heretics' Hollow,[2] and was given up to the fire. It is said, however, that for these seven Maccabees there could not have been any other possible outcome, than that they would at some point be arrested because of their writings translated into their own tongue. But as rumour had it, she could have escaped that danger, except for a certain document, containing the Lord's Prayer in the vernacular idiom, which was perceived by the one who was leading her on, holding her by the sleeves, and he brought her back, first into the enmity of the bishop and theologians, and then to condemnation. There was, moreover, a considerable number of citizens and craftsmen at that time, converging in groups in the various ditches of the suburbs, to hear the holy word of the Lord: they were treated cruelly by various kinds of punishments. Others also were openly displayed in public ignominy with faggots. Many were hanged in the public market, their ears nailed to the gallows: especially those who despising the pontifical order concerning fasting had not abstained from meat during Lent. Such was either the ignorance of the times, or the cruelty of men.

The Coventry Lollards in John Foxe's *Acts and Monuments*

The 1563 edition

[From John Foxe, Actes & monuments of these latter & perillous dayes, *touching matters of the church (London: J. Daye, 1563; STC 11222), pp. 420–421, 1738–1740. The first section detailed the history of the 'seven godly martyrs' of Coventry who were executed in 1520. The latter section, part of an appendix of material Foxe acquired as the printing of his work was already underway, involved the prosecutions of 1486–1488. Foxe meant this account to be inserted before the story of the 1520 executions, as he indicates by a marginal note. In 1570, he placed the 1486–1488 material along with other material from the*

reign of Henry VII; as the 1570 version is almost identical to the 1563 account (apart from the opening and closing paragraphs), the material drawn from the register has been transcribed here only once, with significant variants recorded in the textual notes (distinguished by date – 1563 for the earlier version, 1570 for the later).]

[p. 420] Maistres Smith widdowe of Couentry with sixe other men burned[a]

Vpon[b] Ashewednisday in this year of our Lord God. 1519. In the City of Couentry, John Bond then being Maier, Thomas Dod and Thomas Crampe Shrives. Their was taken for heresie (as they call it) by the said shriues officers, and one Symond Mourton then being somner, sixe men and one gentlewoman, at which time also one Robert Silkeb fled away and escaped vntaken. The names of them that were apprehended were these. Robert Hatchetes, a shoemaker, one Archer a shomaker, one Haukins a shomaker, Thomas Bound shomaker, one Wrigsham a glouer, one Landsdall a hosyer, & one maistres Smith a widow.[3] The only cause of ther apprehension was for that thei taught in their houses their children & family, the Lordes praier, the articles of the christian faith, and the x commaundements in English, for the which they were put in prison. Some in places vnder the ground and some in chambers and other places thereaboutes vntill the next Friday following. Upon which day, they were sent from the fornamed places to a monastery called Mackstocke Abbey, sixe miles distant from the said City of Couentry. Wheare they wer prisoned in like maner as before, during which time of ther imprisonment, they being at the said abbey, their childern were sent for to the grayfriers in Couentry, before one frier Stafford with others, which frier Stafford then was warden of y[e] said gray friers.[4] Who straightly examining their babes of their beliefe, and what heresy their fathers had taught them, charged them vpon payne of such death as ther fathers should suffer, y[t] they in no wise shuld meddle w[t] y[e] Lordes prayer, the articles of the christian faith, and the x commaundements in english, which (said they) is abhominable heresie and therfor in no wise to be knowen. Now after that done the children departed thence home again. And on palme sonday following, which was y[e] sonday next before Easter, the fathers of these children were brought back again from the said Abbey, to the City of Couentry. In which place they had borne (a fower yeares before or more) faggots in their churches and market sted. Now the weke followinge, being the weke before Easter, the Bishop and doctours called before them the fornamed persones, and the said gentilwoman,

---

[a] Maistres [...] burned *is the heading of the page.*
[b] 1519 *in left margin.*

saieng vnto them that they should were faggotes portured in their clothes, to signifie to the people that they wer heretickes. Than Robert Hatchetes hearinge that, said vnto the byshop these wordes. Why my Lorde (saieth he) we desyre no more but the Lordes praier, the articles of the christian faythe, & the commaundements in Englishe, which I thynke [p. 421] suerly euery christian man ought to haue, and wyll you punyshe vs for that? Unto this one doctour aunswered and sayd. Lo my Lorde you may see, what fellowes would these be if they might raigne? At the which woordes, the byshop cried away with them, & so gaue iudgement on them all to be burned, except the sayd meistres Smith wyddow, which at that time was pardoned & admitted to libertie, and because it was in ye euening, she shold go home, her sight being somewhat dime to see her way. The said Simon Mourton the somner offered himself to go home w^t her. Nowe as he was leading her home, he hard ratling of a skrol which was in the sleue of the same arme he lede her by. Then when he harde it rattle he said: Yea? What haue ye here, and so with that he tooke it from her, lokinge therine he espied that it was the Lords praier, ye articles of ye faith, & x commaundements in English. Now when he saw it was so he saide, ah serra come, it is as good nowe as another time, and so brought her backe again to ye bishop, wher as she was immediately condempned, & so burned with the vi men before named, the iiii of Aprill next folowyng, in a place there by, called the litle parke.

After this the sayd Robert Silkeb, that fled away when the other were taken, about 2 yeares after, was aprehended in Kent, and brought againe to the saide citie of Couentre, where he was also burned, the morrowe after he came thether, whiche was about twenty daies after Christmas, An. 1521. Thus when they were dispatched and gone, immediately the shryues went home to their houses, and toke all their goodes & cattell to their own vse, not leauing their wyfes and children any parcell therof to helpe them withal, and moste cruelly toke all away as couetouse Cormorantes hauing no mercie. Now when ye simple people perceiuing this, & considring what the parties were that thus were executed, they grudged there at very sore, & said it was great pitie they were put to death. For that they were men of good life, true dealing, & honest conuersation. But suche is the fruite of these vnmercifull Tyrantes & blodie papistes, that al thinges may be suffred to be done & practised, sauing y^t which maketh to the glory of God, & the keping of a good conscience. Yet these cruel hangmen were ashamed of their doing, & therfore to cloke their shameful murthir & cruel mischief withal, they sente abroade their Skollianes, their slaues, their reteiners, & those whome thei had set in their fearmes and dayres, to brute abrode that they wer not burned for hauing the Lordes prayer the articles of our faith, & the x commaundementes in English, but because they did eate fleshe on frydaies & other fasting daies. Which thinges as they could neuer proue, neither before their death nor after: So was that no part of those matters they were charged with in the tyme of their examinacions. But that viperous generation wil neuer be without their old practise to couer their shame withall. The Lorde turne the hartes of them al.

[p. 1738] A note of certain accused and examined at Couentrye.[a]

Moreouer,[b] forsomuche as our cauilling aduersaries bee wont to obiect against vs the newnes of Christes olde and auncient religion, *[p. 1739]* to thentent they may see the doctrine thereof not to be so new as they report. I would they would consyder the tyme and articles here obiected against these Couentry men, as foloweth here to be seen, if it shal please them a lytle to reade and perpend the same.

The yeare of oure Lorde, 1485, March. ix, amongste diuers and sondrye other good men in Couentry, partly mentioned before, theise nine[c] here vnder named were examined before John bishop of Couentry and Lichfield, in sainct Michaels churche, vpon these articles, folowyng in order.

Firste,[d] John Blumston is openlye and publikly infamed, accused, reported and appeached that he was and is a very heretike, because he hathe preached, taughte, holden, and affirmed, that the power attributed to S. Peter in the churche of God, by oure sauiour Jesus Christ, immediatly did not flit, or pas from him, to remain with his successours.

Item, that there was as much vertue in an herbe as in the blessed Virgin Mary.[e]

Item, that praier and almes auayle not the dead. For incontinent after death, he goeth either to heauen or hel, wherupon he concludeth there is no Purgatory.[f]

Item,[g] that it was folishnes to go on pilgrimage to the Images of oure lady of Dancaster, Walsingham or of the Toure of the City of Couentry, for a man might as well worship the blessed virgin by the fyer syde in the kechin as in the forsaid places, and as wel might a man worship the blessed virgin, when he see his mother or sister as in visiting the Images, because they bee no more but dead stockes and stones.

Item, that he said in english with a frowning countenance, as it

---

[a] *1563:* A note [...] Couentrye *is the heading.*

[b] *1563:* Refer this to the page 420,b *in margin.*

[c] *1563 and 1570:* nine *[sic].*

[d] *1563 and 1570:* John Blumston *in margin; 1570:* The power of Peter flytteth not to his soccessours *in margin.*

[e] *1563:* in an herbe as in the blessed Virgin Mary; *1570:* in an herbe as in the Image of the Virgine Mary.

[f] *1570:* Purgatory denyed *in margin, following this item.*

[g] *1570:* Images not to be worshipped *in margin.*

appeared: A vengeance on all such horson priests, for they haue great enuy that a poore man should get hys lyuing among them.

Firste,[a] Richard Hegham of the same Citye is accused etc. that he is a very heretike, because he holdeth that a christen man being at the poynt of deathe shoulde renounce all his owne works good and ill,[b] and submit him to the mercy of god.

Item, that it is fondnes to worship the Images of oure Lady oth Toure in the forsaid citye, or of other sainctes, for they are but stockes and stones.[c]

Item, that if the image of our lady oth Toure wer put into the fier, it would make a good fier.

Item, that it were better to deale money unto poore folkes then to offer to the Images of Christe and other sainctes, which are but deade stockes and stones.

Firste,[d] Robert Crowther of the same Citie is accused, yat he is an heretike because he holdeth that whoso receyueth the sacrament of the alter in dedly synne or oute of charitie, receyueth nothyng but breade and wyne.

Item, that neither bishop, nor priestes or curates of churches, haue power in the market of penaunce to bynde and louse.

Item,[e] that the pilgrimage to thimage of oure lady oth Toure is folyshnes, for it is but a stock or a stone.

First,[f] John Smith is accused that he is a very heretike, because he holdeth that euery man is bound to know[g] the Lords prayer and the crede in englishe, if he might for these false priestes.

Item, that whoso beleueth as the church beleueth, beleueth ill: and that he hathe nede to frequent the scholes a yere,[h] ere that he can attayne to the knowledge of the true and ryght fayth.

Item, that no priest hathe power to assoyle a man in the market of penance from his sinnes.

Roger[i] Broun of the same citie, is accused to be an heretike because he holdeth, no man ought to worship thimage of our lady of Walsingham nor the bloud of christ at Hailes, but rather god almightie, who would geue him what soeuer he woulde aske.[j]

[a] *1563 and 1570:* Richarde Hegham *in margin.*
[b] *1570:* Merites condemned *in margin.*
[c] *1570:* Images seru rather to be burned then to be worshipped *in margin.*
[d] *1563 and 1570:* Roberte Crowther *in margin.*
[e] *1570:* Agaynst pilgrymage *in margin.*
[f] *1563 and 1570:* John Smithe *in margin*
[g] *1570:* The Lords prayer to be in Englyshe *in margin.*
[h] *1563:* a yere; *1570:* a good while.
[i] *1563 and 1570:* Roger Brown *in margin.*
[j] *1570:* Agaynst pilgrymage *in margin.*

Item, that he holdeth not vp his hands, nor looketh at the eleuation of the eucharist.

Item, he promised one to shew him certayn bookes of heresye, if he woulde sweare that he would not vtter them, and if he wold credit them.

Item,[a] that he did eate fleshe in lent, and was taken with the maner.

Item,[b] if any man were not shriuen, his hole lyfe longe, and in the poynt of death woulde be confessed and could not, if he had no more but contricyon only, he should pas to ioye without purgatory. And if he were confessed of any syn, and were enioyned only to say for penaunce one Pater noster, if he thought he should haue any punishment in purgatorye for that sinne, he would neuer be confessed again for any syn.

Item,[c] he saith al is lost that is geuen to priests.

Item, that there was no purgatory, and that God would pardon all sinnes withoute confession and satisfaction.

Thomas[d] Butler of the same Citye, is openly accused to be a very heretike, because he holdeth there are but two wayes, that is to saye, to heauen and to hell.

Item,[e] that no faithfull man shoulde abide any payne after the deathe of Christ for any sinne, because Christe died for oure sinnes.

Item, that there was no purgatory, for euery man immediatly after death passeth either to heauen or hell.

Item,[f] that whosoeuer departeth in the fayth of Christe and the churche, howsoeuer he hathe lyued, shalbe saued.

Item, that praiers and pilgrimages ar nothing worth, and auaile not to purchase heauen.

John[g] Falkes is accused to be a very heretik, because he holdeth that it is a folysh thing to offer to the Image of our Ladye, saying, her head shalbe hoare[h] or I offer to her, what is it but a blocke? If it could speake to me, I woulde geue it an halpenyworth of ale.

Item, that when the priest carieth to the sicke the bodye of Christe, why carieth he not also the bloud of Christ?

Item, that he eate kowe milke vpon the firste sonday of this Lente.

Item, that as concerning the sacrament of penance and absolution,

---

[a] *1570:* Flesh eatyng in Lent *in margin.*
[b] *1570:* Agaynst purgatory and confession auricular *in margin.*
[c] *1570:* Agaynst confession and satisfaction *in margin.*
[d] *1563 and 1570:* Thomas Butler *in margin.*
[e] *1570:* Agaynst purgatory *in margin.*
[f] *1570:* Agaynst merites *in margin.*
[g] *1563 and 1570:* John Falkes *in margin.*
[h] *1570:* Agaynste Images *in margin.*

no priest hath power to assoyle any man from hys sinnes, when as he can not make one heare of his head.

Item,[a] that the Image of our Lady was but a stone or a blocke.

Rychard[b] Hilmin is accused that he is a very heretike, because he holdeth it better to depart with money to the poore, then to geue tythes to priestes or to offer to the images of oure Ladye, and that it were better to offer to images made by God, then to the images of God painted.

Item,[c] that he had the Lordes prayer and the salutation of the angell and the crede in english, and an other booke did he see and had, which conteyned the Epistles and gospels in english, and [p. 1740] according to them would he liue, and therby beleued he to be saued.

Item, that no priest speaketh better in the pulpit then that booke.

Item, that the sacramente of the altar is but breade, and that the priestes make it to blind the people.

Item, that a priest whiles he is at mas is a pryest, and after one mas done, til the beginning of an other mas, he is no more then a lay man and hath no more power then a mere lay man.

After[d] they were enforced to recant, they wer assoyled, and put to penance.

The accusation of Margery Goyt, wyfe of James Goyt of Asburn, the 8[e] of Aprill, 1488, before the said John, bishop of Couentrye and Lychefylde.[f]

Fyrst,[g] that she sayd, that which the priestes lift ouer their heades at mas,[h] is not the true and very body of Chryst. For if it wer so, the priestes could not break it so lyghtly into iiii parts, and swalow it as they doo: for the Lordes body hath fleshe and bones. So hathe not that whiche the priestes receyue.

Item, that priestes bying xl cakes for a halfpeny, and shewing them to the people and saying, that of euery of them they make the body of christ, doo nothing but deceyue the people and enriche them selue.

Item, seyng God in the beginning did create and make man, how can it be that man should be able to make God?

This[i] woman also, was constrayned to recant, and so was she assoyled and did penance.

---

[a] *1570:* It is heresy to say a stone is a stone, and a blocke is a blocke *in margin.*
[b] *1563 and 1570:* Richarde Hilmin *in margin.*
[c] *1570:* Scripture in English *in margin.*
[d] *1563: A pointing hand precedes this paragraph; 1570: this paragraph in italics.*
[e] *1563:* 8; *1570:* iii.
[f] *1563:* The accusation [...] Lychefylde *is the heading.*
[g] *1563 and 1570:* Margerye Goyt *in margin.*
[h] *1570:* Against the Sacrament of the Altar *in margin.*
[i] *1563: A pointing hand precedes this paragraph; 1570: this paragraph in italics.*

[English translation]

[p. 420] Mistress Smith widow of Coventry with six other men burned.[a]

Upon[b] Ash Wednesday in the year of our Lord God 1519. In the City of Coventry, John Bond then being Mayor, Thomas Dod and Thomas Crampe, Sheriffs. There were taken for heresy (as they call it) by the said sheriffs' officers, and one Simon Mourton, then being summoner, six men and one gentlewoman, at which time also one Robert Silkeb fled away and escaped untaken. The names of those who were apprehended were these: Robert Hatchetes, a shoemaker; one Archer, a shoemaker; one Haukins, a shoemaker; Thomas Bound, shoemaker; one Wrigsham, a glover; one Landsdail, a hosier; and one mistress Smith, a widow.[3] The only cause of their apprehension was that they taught in their houses to their children and family the Lord's Prayer, the articles of the Christian faith, and the Ten Commandments in English, for the which they were put in prison, some in places underground and some in chambers and other places thereabouts until the next Friday following. Upon which day, they were sent from the forenamed places to a monastery called Maxstoke Abbey, six miles distant from the said City of Coventry, where they were imprisoned in like manner as before. During the time of their imprisonment at the said abbey, their children were summoned to the Grey Friars in Coventry, before one Friar Stafford with others, which Friar Stafford then was Warden of the said Grey Friars.[4] He, straightly examining their babes of their belief and what heresy their fathers had taught them, charged them upon pain of such death as their fathers would suffer, that they in no wise should meddle with the Lord's Prayer, the articles of the Christian faith and the Ten Commandments in English, which (said they) is abominable heresy and therefore in no wise to be known. Now after that was done the children departed thence home again. And on Palm Sunday following, which was the Sunday next before Easter, the fathers of these children were brought back again from the said abbey to the City of Coventry. In which place they had borne (a four years before or more) faggots in their churches and market place. Now the week following, being the week before Easter, the bishop and doctors called before them the forenamed persons and the said gentlewoman, saying unto them that they should wear faggots painted on their clothes, to signify to the people that they were heretics. Then Robert Hatchetes, hearing that, said unto the bishop these words: 'Why my Lord', sayeth he, 'we desire no more but the Lord's Prayer,

---

[a] Mistress [...] burned *is the heading of the page.*
[b] 1519 *in left margin.*

the articles of the Christian faith and the commandments in English, which I think [*p. 421*] surely every Christian man ought to have, and will you punish us for that?' Unto this, one doctor answered and said, 'Lo, my Lord, you may see what fellows would these be if they might reign?' At the which words, the bishop cried, 'Away with them', and so gave judgement on them all to be burned, except the said Mistress Smith, widow, who at that time was pardoned and admitted to liberty. And because it was in the evening she should go home, her sight being somewhat dim to see her way, the said summoner, Simon Morton, offered himself to go home with her. Now as he was leading her home, he heard the rattling of a scroll which was in the sleeve of the same arm he led her by. Then when he heard it rattle he said, 'Yea? What have ye here?' and so with that he took it from her. Looking therein, he espied that it was the Lord's Prayer, the articles of the faith and Ten Commandments in English. Now when he saw it was so he said, 'Ah, sirrah, come, it is as good now as another time', and so brought her back again to the bishop, where she was immediately condemned, and so burned with the six men before named, the fourth of April next following, in a place thereby, called the Little Park.

After this the said Robert Silkeb, who fled away when the others were taken, about two years after was apprehended in Kent, and brought again to the said city of Coventry, where he was also burned, the morrow after he came thither, which was about twenty days after Christmas in the year 1521. Thus when they were dispatched and gone, immediately the sheriffs went home to their houses and took all their goods and chattels to their own use, not leaving their wives and children any parcel thereof to help them and so on and most cruelly took all away, as covetous cormorants having no mercy. Now when the simple people perceiving this, and considering what the parties were that thus were executed, they grudged thereat very sore, and said it was a great pity they were put to death, for that they were men of good life, true dealing and honest conversation. But such is the fruit of these unmerciful tyrants and bloody papists, that all things may be suffered to be done and practised, saving that which makes to the glory of God and the keeping of a good conscience. Yet these cruel hangmen were ashamed of their doing, and therefore to cloak their shameful murder and cruel mischief and so on, they sent abroad their menial servants, their retainers and those whom they had set in their farms and dairies, to bruit abroad that they were not burned for having the Lord's Prayer, the articles of our faith and the Ten Commandments in English, but because they did eat flesh on Fridays and other fasting days. These things they could never prove, neither before their death nor after: so that it was no part of those matters they were charged with in the time of their examinations. But that viperous generation will never be without their old practice to cover their shame notwithstanding. The Lord turn the hearts of them all.

[p. 1738]   A note of certain accused and examined at Coventry.

Moreover, forasmuch as our cavilling adversaries are wont to object against us the newness of Christ's old and ancient religion, *[p. 1739]* so that they may see the doctrine thereof not to be as new as they report, I would that they consider the time and articles here objected against these Coventry men, as follows here to be seen, if it shall please them a little to read and ponder the same.

The year of our Lord 1485, March 9, amongst divers and sundry other good men in Coventry, partly mentioned before, these nine here undernamed were examined before John, Bishop of Coventry and Lichfield, in St Michael's church, upon these articles, following in order.

First,[a] John Blumston is openly and publicly defamed, accused, reported and impeached that he was and is a true heretic, because he has preached, taught, held and affirmed that the power attributed to St Peter in the church of God, by our saviour Jesus Christ, immediately did not flit, or pass from him, to remain with his successors.

Item, that there was as much virtue in an herb as in the blessed Virgin Mary.[b]

Item, that prayer and alms avail not the dead, for incontinent after death, he goes either to heaven or hell, whereupon he concludes there is no purgatory.[c]

Item,[d] that it was foolishness to go on pilgrimage to the images of Our Lady of Doncaster, Walsingham, or of the Tower of the City of Coventry: for a man might as well worship the Blessed Virgin by the fireside in the kitchen as in the foresaid places, and as well might a man worship the Blessed Virgin, when he sees his mother or sister as in visiting the images, because they are no more than dead sticks and stones.

Item, that he said in English with a frowning countenaunce, as it appeared: a vengeance on all such whoreson priests, for they have great envy that a poor man should get his living among them.

First, Richard[e] Hegham of the same city is accused, etc., that he is a true heretic, because he holds that a Christian man being at the

---

[a] *1563 and 1570:* John Blumston; *1570:* The power of Peter flits not to his successors *in margin.*

[b] *1563:* in an herb as in the blessed Virgin Mary; *1570:* in an herb as in the image of the Virgin Mary.

[c] *1570:* Purgatory denied *in margin, following this item.*

[d] *1570:* Images not to be worshipped *in margin.*

[e] *1563 and 1570:* Richard Hegham *in margin.*

point of death should renounce all his own works good and ill,[a] and
submit himself to the mercy of God.

Item, that it is foolishness to worship the images of Our Lady of the
Tower in the foresaid city, or of other saints, for they are but sticks
and stones.[b]

Item, that if the image of Our Lady of the Tower were put into the
fire, it would make a good fire.

Item, that it would be better to deal money unto poor folks than to
offer to the images of Christ and other saints, which are but dead sticks
and stones.

First, Robert[c] Crowther of the same city is accused, that he is a
heretic because he holds that whoever receives the sacrament of the
altar in deadly sin or outside charity, receives nothing but bread and
wine.

Item, that neither bishop nor priests or curates of churches have
power in the market of penance to bind and loose.

Item,[d] that pilgrimage to the image of Our Lady of the Tower is
foolishness, for it is but a stick or a stone.

First, John[e] Smith is accused that he is a true heretic, because he
holds that every man is bound to know[f] the Lord's Prayer and the
Creed in English, if he might for these false priests.

Item, that whoever believes as the church believes, believes ill: and
that he has need to frequent the schools a year[g] before he can attain
to the knowledge of the true and right faith.

Item, that no priest has power to absolve a man in the market of
penance from his sins.

Roger[h] Browne of the same City, is accused to be a heretic because
he holds that no man ought to worship the image of Our Lady of
Walsingham, nor the blood of Christ at Hailes, but rather God almighty,
who would give him whatsoever he would ask.[i]

Item, that he does not hold up his hands nor looks at the elevation
of the Eucharist.

Item, that he promised a man to show him certain books of heresy,
if he would swear that he would not betray them and if he would
believe in them.

---

[a] *1570:* Merits condemned *in margin.*
[b] *1570:* Images serve rather to be burned than to be worshipped *in margin.*
[c] *1563 and 1570:* Robert Crowther *in margin.*
[d] *1570:* Against pilgrimage *in margin.*
[e] *1563 and 1570:* John Smith *in margin.*
[f] *1570:* The Lord's prayer to be in English *in margin.*
[g] *1563:* a year; *1570:* a good while.
[h] *1563 and 1570:* Roger Brown *in margin.*
[i] *1570:* Against pilgrymage *in margin.*

Item,[a] that he ate flesh in Lent and was taken with the manner.

Item,[b] if any man were not shriven his whole life long, and at the point of death wanted to confess and could not, if he had nothing but contrition, he should pass to joy without purgatory. And if he were confessed of any sin and were enjoined only to say for penance one *Pater noster*, if he thought he should have any punishment in purgatory for that sin, he would never be confessed for any sin.

Item,[c] says all is lost that is given to priests.

Item, that there was no purgatory, and that God would pardon all sins without confession and satisfaction.

Thomas[d] Butler of the same city is openly accused to be a true heretic, because he holds that there are but two ways, that is to say, to heaven and to hell.

Item,[e] that no faithful man should abide any pain after the death of Christ for any sin, because Christ died for our sins.

Item, that there was no purgatory, for every man immediately after death passes either to heaven or hell.

Item,[f] that whoever departs in the faith of Christ and the Church, however he has lived, shall be saved.

Item, that prayers and pilgrimages are worth nothing and avail not to purchase heaven.

John[g] Falkes is accused to be a true heretic, because he holds that it is a foolish thing to offer to the image of Our Lady, saying, her head shall be old and grey[h] before I offer to her: what is it but a block? If it could speak to me, I would give it a halfpennyworth of ale.

Item, that when the priest carries to the sick the body of Christ, why does he not carry also the blood of Christ?

Item, that he did eat cow's milk upon the first Sunday of Lent.

Item, that as concerning the sacrament of penance and absolution, no priest has power to absolve any man from his sins, since he cannot make one hair of his head.

Item,[i] that the image of Our Lady was but a stone or a block.

Richard[j] Hilmin is accused that he is a true heretic, because he holds that it is better to give money to the poor than to give tithes to priests or to offer to the images of Our Lady, and that it was better to offer

---

[a] *1570:* Flesh eating in Lent *in margin.*
[b] *1570:* Against purgatory and confession auricular *in margin.*
[c] *1570:* Against confession and satisfaction *in margin.*
[d] *1563 and 1570:* Thomas Butler *in margin.*
[e] *1570:* Against purgatory *in margin.*
[f] *1570:* Against merites *in margin.*
[g] *1563 and 1570:* John Falkes *in margin.*
[h] *1570:* Against Images *in margin;* old and grey: *original* hoare.
[i] *1570:* It is heresy to say a stone is a stone, and a block is a block *in margin.*
[j] *1563 and 1570:* Richard Hilmin *in margin.*

to images made by God than to the images of God painted.

Item,[a] that he had the Lord's Prayer and the Salutation of the Angel and the Creed in English, and he saw and had another book which contained the Epistles and Gospels in English, and [p. 1740] according to them he would live and by doing so he believed he would be saved.

Item, that no priest speaks better in the pulpit than that book.

Item, that the sacrament of the altar is but bread, and that the priests make it to blind the people.

Item, that a priest while he is at Mass is a priest, and after one Mass done until the beginning of another Mass he is no more than a layman, and has no more power then a mere layman.

After they were forced to recant, they were absolved and put to penance.[b]

The accusation of Margery Goyt, wife of James Goyt of Ashbourne, the eighth[c] of April 1488, before the said John, Bishop of Coventry and Lichfield.

First,[d] that she said, that which the priests lift over their heads at Mass[e] is not the true and real body of Christ, for if it were so, the priests could not break it so lightly into four parts, and swallow it as they do, for the Lord's body has flesh and bones, but that which the priests receive has not.

Item, that priests buying forty cakes for a halfpenny, and showing them to the people and saying that of every of them they make the body of Christ, do nothing but deceive the people and enrich themselves.

Item, saying God in the beginning did create and make man, how can it be that man should be able to make God?

This[f] woman was also constrained to recant, and so she was absolved and did penance.

The 1570 edition

[From John Foxe, The first (second) volume of the ecclesiasticall history contaynyng the Actes and Monumentes, newly recognised and inlarged, *2 vols. continuously paginated (London, 1570; STC 11223), pp. 921–922 and 1107. The 1570 version of the 1486–1488 prosecutions (pp. 921–922), drawn from the register of Bishop John Hales, is almost identical to that presented in 1563, and*

[a] *1570:* Scripture in English *in margin.*

[b] *1563: a pointing hand precedes this paragraph; 1570: this paragraph is in italics.*

[c] *1563:* eighth; *1570:* third.

[d] *1563 and 1570:* Margery Goyte *in margin.*

[e] *1570:* Against the Sacrament of the Altar *in margin.*

[f] *1563: a pointing hand precedes this paragraph; 1570: this paragraph in italics.*

so only the introductory and concluding paragraphs are included here. Refer to the textual notes for the preceding section for the few significant variants (differences in spelling and verb tense are not recorded). In the cases both of the 1486–1488 prosecutions and the 'seven godly martyrs' of 1520, much the same text, with modernized spelling, is found in Foxe, Acts and Monuments, *Townsend, ed. (1843), IV, pp. 133–135, 556–558.]*

[p. 921] Among[a] many other thynges incident in the reigne of this kyng Henry vii I haue ouerpassed the hystory of certeine godly persons persecuted in the dioces of Couentry and Lychefield, as we finde them in the Registers of the dioces recorded, here folowing.

The yeare of our Lord. 1485. March ix amongest diuers and sondry other good men in Couentry, these ix[b] here vnder named were examined before Iohn, Byshop of Couentry and Lichfield, in S. Michaels Churche, vpon these Articles, folowyng in order.

[...] *[see the previous section for the text derived from the register]*

[p. 922] Thus much I thought here good to inserte, touchyng these foresayd men of Couentry, especially for this purpose, because our cauilling aduersaries be wont to obiect agaynst vs the newnes of Christes old and auncient Religion. To y[c] entent therfore they may see this doctrine not to be so new as they reporte, I wyshe they would consider both the tyme and Articles here obiected agaynste these foresayd persons, as is aboue premised.

[p. 1107] The eight booke continuyng the history of Englishe matters apperteinyng to both the states, a well ecclesiasticall, as ciuill and temporall.[c]

Persecuters[d]	*Martyrs*	*The causes*
	Maistres Smith, widow.	The principall cause of y[e] apprehension of these
	Rob. Hatchets, a shomaker.	persons, was for teachyng theyr children, & familie, the
Simon Mourton the Byshops Somner.	Archer, a shomaker.	Lordes prayer, & x Commaundementes in
	Hawkyns, a Shomaker.	Englishe: for whiche they were vppon Ashewedensday,

[a] Couentry men persecuted *in right margin.*

[b] ix *[sic].*

[c] The eight [...] temporall *heading for the page. Running header:* Henry 8 Vij. Martyrs of Couentrie. M. Patricke Hamelton, Martyr.

[d] Martyrs of Couentrie. Maistres Smyth. Rob. Hatchets. Archer. Haukins. Thomas Bond. Wrigham. Lansdale. Martyrs *in left margin.*

The Byshop of
Couentry.

Frier Stafford,
Warden.

Thomas Bond,
Shomaker.
Wrigham, a
Glouer.
Landsdale, an
Hosier
At Couentrie.
an. 1519.

taken and put in prison, some
in places vnder the ground,
some in Chambers, & other
places about, till Friday
folowyng. Then they were
sent to a Monasterie called
Mackstocke Abbey 6 Myles
from Couentry. During
whiche tyme, their children
were sent for to the
Grayfriers in Couentry,
before the warden of the sayd
Friers, called Frier Stafford:
who straitly examinyng them
of their beliefe, & what
heresie their fathers
had taught them, charged them vpon payne of suffering such death, as
their fathers should, in no wise to medle any more with ye Lordes
prayer,[a] the Crede, and commaundements in English, &c. Whiche
done, vpon Palmesonday, the fathers of these children were brought
backe agayne to Couentrie, and there, the weeke next before Easter,
were condemned for relapse (because most of them had borne fagottes
in the same Citie before) to be burned.

Only Maistres Smith was dimissed for that present, & sent away.
And because it was in ye euening being Somewhat darke, as she should
go home, the foresayd Simon Mourton the Somner offered him selfe
to go home with her. Now as he was leadyng her by the arme, and
heard the rattelyng of a scrole within her sleue: yea (sayth hee)[b] what
haue ye here? And so tooke it from her, and espyed that it was the
Lordes prayer, the Articles of the faith, & x Commaundementes in
Englishe. Whiche when the wretched Somner vnderstode, ah serrha
(sayd he) come, as good now as an other tyme, & so brought her backe
agayne[c] to the Byshop, where she was immediatly condemned, and so
burned with the vi men before named, the fourth of Aprill, in a place
thereby called the litle parke. an. 1519.

Persecuters	Martyrs	The causes
		In^d the same number of these
		Couentrie men aboue

---

[a] The Lords Prayer in Englishe, forbidden by the Papistes *in left margin.*
[b] *after this is inserted a woodcut labelled* vii godly Martyrs of Couentrie, burned.
[c] Maistres Smyth condemned for hauing the Lords prayer in Englishe *in right margin.*
[d] An. 1521; Rob. Silkeb, Martyr *in right margin.*

Robert Silkeb.

At Couentrie.
an. 1521.

rehearsed, was also Robert Silkeb, who at the apprehension of these, as is aboue recited, fled away, and for that tyme, escaped: But about ii yeares after, hee was taken agayne, and brought to the said Citie of Couentrie, where he was also burned the morow after hee came thether, whiche was about the xiii day of January, an. 1521.

Thus, when these were dispatched, immediately ye Shriffes went to their houses, and toke all their goods & cattel to their own vse, not leauyng their wiues and children any parcell therof to helpe themselues with all. And for so much as the people began to grudge somewhat, at the crueltie shewed, and at the uniust death of these innocent Martyrs, the Byshop, with his officers & priestes, caused it to be noysed abroad, by their tenauntes, seruauntes, and fermers, that they were not burned for hauyng the Lordes prayer and Commaundementes in Englishe, but because they did eate fleshe on Fridayes and other fastyng dayes. which neither could be proued, either before their death, or after, nor yet was any such matter greatly obiected to them in their examinations. The[a] witnesses of this historie be yet alyue, which both saw them and knew them. Of whom one is by name mother Halle, dwellyng now in Bagington ii myles from Couentrie. By whom also this is testified of them, that they aboue all other in Couentrie pretended most shew of worship and deuotion, at the holdyng vp of the Sacrament, whether to colour the matter, or no, it is not knowen. This is certeine, that in godlynes of life they differed from all the rest of the Citie: Neither in their occupying they would vse any othe: nor could abyde it in them that occupyed with them.

---

[a] Testimonie of thys storye. Note, howe these Martyrs holding with the popishe sacramentes, yet were burned of the Papistes, onely for a fewe Scriptures in Englishe *in right margin.*

[English translation]

[p. 921] Among[a] many other things incident in the reign of this king Henry VII, I have overpassed the history of certain godly persons persecuted in the diocese of Coventry and Lichfield, as we find them in the registers of the diocese recorded, here following.

The year of our Lord 1485, March 9, amongst divers and sundry other good men in Coventry, these nine here undernamed were examined before John, Bishop of Coventry and Lichfield, in St Michael's church, upon these articles, following in order.

[...] *[see the previous section for the text derived from the register]*

[p. 922] Thus much I thought here good to insert, touching these foresaid men of Coventry, especially for this purpose, because our cavilling adversaries are wont to object against us the newness of Christ's old and ancient religion. To the intent therefore they may see this doctrine not to be so new as they report, I wish they would consider both the time and articles here objected against these foresaid persons, as is above premised.

[p. 1107] The eighth book continuing the history of English matters appertaining to both the states, as well ecclesiastical, as civil and temporal.

Persecutors[b]	Martyrs	The causes
	Mistress Smith, widow.	The principal cause of the apprehension of these
	Rob. Hatchets, a shoemaker.	persons was for teaching their children and family the
Simon Mourton the Bishop's Summoner.	Archer, a shoemaker.	Lord's Prayer and Ten Commandments in English:
	Hawkyns, a shoemaker.	for which they were upon Ash Wednesday taken and put in
	Thomas Bond, shoemaker.	prison, some in places under the ground, some in
The Bishop of Coventry.	Wrigham, a glover.	chambers, and other places about, till Friday following.
	Landsdale, a hosier.	Then they were sent to a monastery called Maxstoke
Friar Stafford, Warden.	At Coventry. In the year 1519.	Abbey six miles from Coventry. During which

[a] Coventry men persecuted *in right margin.*

[b] Martyrs of Coventry. Mistress Smyth. Rob. Hatchets. Archer. Haukins. Thomas Bond. Wrigham. Lansdale. Martyrs *in left margin.*

time, their children were
summoned to the Grey Friars
in Coventry, before the
Warden of the said Friars,
called Friar Stafford: who
strictly examining them of
their belief, and what heresy
their fathers had taught
them, charged them
upon pain of suffering such death as their fathers should, in no wise to
meddle any more with the Lord's Prayer,[a] the Creed, and commandments in English, etc. Which done, upon Palm Sunday, the fathers
of these children were brought back again to Coventry, and there, the
week next before Easter, were condemned for relapse (because most of
them had borne faggots in the same City before) to be burned.

Only Mistress Smith was dismissed for the time being and sent away.
And because it was in the evening, being somewhat dark as she should
go home, the foresaid Simon Mourton the Summoner offered himself
to go home with her. Now as he was leading her by the arm, and
heard the rattling of a scroll within her sleeve: 'Yea', (says he)[b] 'what
have ye here?' And so took it from her, and espied that it was the
Lord's Prayer, the articles of the faith and Ten Commandments in
English. Which when the wretched Summoner understood, 'Ah sirrah',
(said he), 'come, as good now as another time', and so brought her
back again[c] to the bishop, where she was immediately condemned and
so burned with the six men before named, the fourth of April, in a
place thereby called the little park, in the year 1519.

Persecutors	Martyrs	The causes
		In[d] the same number of these Coventry men above rehearsed, was also Robert
	Robert Silkeb.	Silkeb, who at the apprehension of these, as is above recited, fled away and for that time, escaped. But about two years after, he was taken again, and brought to
	At Coventry.	the said city of Coventry,

[a] The Lord's Prayer in English, forbidden by the Papists *in left margin.*
[b] *after this is inserted a woodcut labelled* Seven godly Martyrs of Coventry, burned.
[c] Mistress Smyth condemned for having the Lord's prayer in English *in right margin.*
[d] In the year 1521; Rob. Silkeb, Martyr *in right margin.*

In the year 1521/22.

where he was also burned the morrow after he came thither, which was about the thirteenth day of January, in the year 1521/22.

Thus, when these were dispatched, immediately the Sheriffs went to their houses, and took all their goods and chattel to their own use, not leaving their wives and children any parcel thereof to help themselves and so on. And for so much as the people began to grudge somewhat at the cruelty shown and at the unjust death of these innocent martyrs, the bishop, with his officers and priests, caused it to be noised abroad, by their tenants, servants and farmers, that they were not burned for having the Lord's Prayer and Commandments in English, but because they ate flesh on Fridays and other fasting days. Which neither could be proved, either before their death, or after, nor yet was any such matter greatly objected to them in their examinations. The[a] witnesses of this history are yet alive, which both saw them and knew them. Of whom one is by name Mother Halle, dwelling now in Bagington, two miles from Coventry. By whom also this is testified of them, that they above all other in Coventry pretended most show of worship and devotion, at the holding up of the Sacrament, whether to colour the matter, or no, it is not known. This is certain, that in godliness of life they differed from all the rest of the city. Neither in their occupying they would use any oath: nor could abide it in them that occupied with them.

---

[a] Testimony of this story. Note, how these Martyrs holding with the popish sacraments, yet were burned of the Papists, only for a few Scriptures in English. *in right margin.*

Coventry civic annals

The Bodleian annal

[A List of ye Mayors & Sheriffs &c. of Coventrey with Historical & memorable Events touching ye Antiquity of ye Auncient Citty & Corporation from ye Year 1344 to ye Year 1686, *Oxford Bodl. Library MS 31431 (Top. Warw. d. 4).*]

[fo. 12v] Richard Cooke maior 1485 and ended in 1486 [...] In his yeare came the bisshop of Chester to Coventrey. Before him was brought diuers persons suspect of heresy, whom he appoynted to beare faggotts about the Citty on the Markett day.

[fo. 13r] William Rowley, draper, maior 1491 and ended in 1492. Then was St Michaell's church suspended.[5]

[fo. 15r] John Stronge, mercer, maior 1510 and ended in 1511. In his yeare King Henry 8th came to Coventrey wth the Queene [...] Then were certaine persons peched of heresy, whereof some bare fagotts before the procession on the markett day. The principall was mistris Rowley and Jone Warde.

Richard^a Harsall, draper, maior 1511 and ended in 1512. In his year vii persons were burned in the little parke and another did pennance one a pipe head while the others were burning, holding a fagot on his shoulder. One of them that was burned was Jone Warde. Then was the crosse taken downe and new made.

[fo. 16r] John Bond, draper, maior 1519 and ended in 1520. Then the Bishopp came to Coventrey to examine certain persons of heresy. Vii were condemned, videlicet Mistress Lansdail alias (Smith), Thomas Lansdail her brother in Law, hosier,[6] Hawkins the skinner, Wrixam a glover, Robart Hochet, Orchard and Bonde. These vii were burnt in the little parke, but one Silkesbe fled. There heresy was because they had the lord's praier, the Creed and the ten Commandements in English.

William Wixam, draper, maior 1520 and ended in 1521. In his year, Robart Silkesbe was taken and burnt the Munday before Christmas for holding opinion against the Sacrament.

---

^a 7 persons burned in the little park for heresy *in margin*.

[English translation]

[fo. 12v] Richard Cooke mayor 1485 and ended in 1486 [...] In his year came the Bishop of Chester to Coventry. Before him were brought divers persons suspect of heresy, whom he appointed to bear faggots about the city on the market day.

[fo. 13r] William Rowley, draper, mayor 1491 and ended in 1492. Then was St Michael's church suspended.[5]

[fo. 15r] John Stronge, mercer, mayor 1510 and ended in 1511. In his year King Henry VIII came to Coventry with the Queen [...]. Then were certain persons impeached of heresy, whereof some bore faggots before the procession on the market day. The principal were Mistress Rowley and Joan Ward.

Richard[a] Harsall mayor 1511 and ended in 1512. In his year seven persons were burned in the Little Park and another did penance on a pipe head while the others were burning, holding a faggot on his shoulder. One of them that was burned was Joan Warde. Then was the cross taken down and new made.

[fo. 16r] John Bond, draper, mayor 1519 and ended in 1520. Then the bishop came to Coventry to examine certain persons of heresy. Seven were condemned, that is Mistress Lansdail *alias* (Smith), Thomas Lansdail, her brother-in-law, hosier,[6] Hawkins the skinner, Wrixam a glover, Robert Hochet, Orchard, and Bonde. These seven were burnt in the Little Park, but one Silkesbe fled. Their heresy was because they had the Lord's Prayer, the Creed, and the Ten Commandments in English.

William Wixam, draper, mayor 1520 and ended in 1521. In his year, Robert Silkesbe was taken and burnt the Monday before Christmas for holding an opinion against the Sacrament.

The Birmingham annal

[Birmingham City Archive, MS 273978[IIR 42], 'Coventry City Annals'.]

[fo. 5r] In ye year 1486, Richard Cooke Mayor. In January King Henry 7th marryed the Lady Elizabeth, eldest daughter of King Edward ye 4th, by which means ye two familyes of Yorke and Lancaster was united. The Bishop of Chester came to Coventry and divers persons

---

[a] 7 persons burned in the little park for heresy *in margin.*

for herisye were appoynted to bear fagotts about the Citty on the markett day.

[fo. 5v] In yᵉ year 1511 John Strong Mercer Mayor, the King and Queen came to Coventry where was 3 pageants, one att Jorden Well and one att Broadgate and one att Crosse Cheaping, by which they passed the Mayor bearing yᵉ sword before the King to yᵉ priory. There were certain persons suspected of herisy, some of which bare fagotts, 2 of which was one Mistress Rowlys and Mistress Jone Ward.

[fo. 5v] In yᵉ year 1512 Richard Hartshall Draper Mayor, 7 persons was burned in yᵉ Little Parke and one did pennance on a pipe head while the other burned. [...]

[fo. 6r] In yᵉ year 1520 John Bond Draper Mayor, the Bishop Came to Coventry to examine certain persons for herisie. Hee condemned 7.

[fo. 6r] In yᵉ year 1521 William Wickam Draper Mayor [...] This year Robert Silkesby was burnt the Monday before Christmas for holding an opinion that Christ was not bodily in the Sacrament.

[English translation]

[fo. 5r] In the year 1486, Richard Cooke, Mayor. In January King Henry VII married the Lady Elizabeth, eldest daughter of King Edward IV, by which means the two families of York and Lancaster were united. The Bishop of Chester came to Coventry and divers persons for heresy were appointed to bear faggots about the city on the market day.

[fo. 5v] In the year 1511 John Strong, mercer, Mayor. The King and Queen came to Coventry where there were three pageants, one at Jordan Well, one at Broadgate, and one at Crosse Cheaping, by which they passed the mayor bearing the sword before the King to the priory. There were certain persons suspected of heresy, some of whom bore faggots, two of which were one Mistress Rowlys and Mistress Joan Ward.

[fo. 5v] In the year 1512 Richard Hartshall, draper, Mayor. Seven persons were burned in the Little Park and one did penance on a pipe head while the others burned.

[fo. 6r] In the year 1520 John Bond, Draper, Mayor. The Bishop came

to Coventry to examine certain persons for heresy. He condemned seven.

[fo. 6r] In the year 1521 William Wickam, draper, Mayor [...]. This year Robert Silkesby was burnt the Monday before Christmas for holding an opinion that Christ was not bodily in the sacrament.

EXPLANATORY NOTES

[1] The previous entry, which deals briefly with the burning of the mother of Lady Yonge (wife of a former Lord Mayor of London), is dated 1490, so Foxe is here mistaken by about thirty years.

[2] While we have identified no 'Heretics' Hollow [or Ditch or Well]', it is possible that this refers to Park Hollow (an old stone quarry) in the Little Park (where the civic annals locate the execution; see below p. 315). See Lobel, *Atlas of Historic Towns*, II.

[3] Only 'Robert Hatchetes', 'Thomas Bound', and 'Robert Silkeb' are given first names in Foxe's narrative, the others being identified only by their surnames. There is some question about whether the 'Landsdail, hosier' mentioned by Foxe is the same man as the Roger Landesdale, tailor, who was a leading member of the Lollard community in 1511. Foxe's source for this story was apparently inaccurate regarding the precise trades of some of the other men executed: Foxe called both Hachet, a tawyer, and Hawkyns, a skinner, shoemakers. One of the other sources also suggests doubt about the executed man's name: the Bodleian Annal names the man burned in 1520 as 'Thomas Lansdail', the brother-in-law of Joan Smyth (see below, p. 315). It has nonetheless been assumed here that it was Roger (also Joan Smyth's brother-in-law) who was relapsed and burned in 1520, since there is no record of a Thomas Landesdale having been previously prosecuted (nor any other mention of a Thomas Landesdale) although, of course, it always remains possible that another member of the Landesdale family was involved in heresy.

[4] John Stafford; see Appendix 3.

[5] William Rowley was Alice Rowley's husband, but apparently not a Lollard (see above, p. 28). It is unclear what the suspension of St Michael's church means.

[6] See above, n. 3.

APPENDIX 1
Suspects named in the Coventry heresy prosecutions, 1486–1522

This table includes all who were prosecuted for heresy in Coventry between 1486 and 1522 and all who were named as suspect or possibly suspect of heresy, according to the records of prosecution presented in this volume. Individuals who were mentioned in passing, with no reference to heresy (such as the name of a person to whom a man had been apprenticed in his youth), are not recorded here. Although in some cases the editors suspect that a given person may have been known by two different names, unless it is fairly clear both names are included in the list, with a note.

An (A) beside a date in the 'Date(s) of appearance' column indicates the date on which the person in question abjured heresy. In cases where two dates are indicated, it seems unlikely that there were two abjurations but rather a slight discrepancy in the dates given in two different sources.

Name	City	Sex	Age	Occupation	Marital status	Name of spouse(s)	Date(s) of appearance	Notes
Abell, Thomas	Coventry	M	42	Shoemaker			22 November 1511 25 November 1511 (A) 29 November 1511 (A)	
Acton, Alice	Coventry	F			Widowed	Thomas Acton	Mid-January to mid-February 1512	
Acton, Thomas	Coventry	M	50	Purser	Married	Alice Acton	5 November 1511 (A) 6 November 1511 (A)	Apparently dies between his abjuration and 24 January 1512, when his wife is described as 'relicta Thome Acton nuper defuncti'.
Alcock, John	Ibstock (Leicestershire.)	M		Priest	Cleric			
Annesty, ('pseudo-prophet')		M						
Archer, John	Coventry	M		Shoemaker			Mid-January to mid-February 1512 4 February 1512 (A) 4 April 1520 (executed)	
Archer, Thomas	Coventry	M			Married	(Wife of Thomas Archer)		

Name	Place	Sex	Age	Occupation	Marital status	Spouse/Relation	Dates	Notes
Archer, [Unknown]	Coventry	F			Married	Thomas Archer		
Atkynson, *alias* Peyntour Jr, John	Coventry	M	22	Painter			29 October 1511 / 30 October 1511 / 2 November 1511 / 5 November. 1511 (A) / 6 November 1511 (A)	
Bakehouse, Agnes de	Coventry	F					22 January 1512 (A)	
Baker, Katherine	Coventry	F			Married	Edmund Baker	Mid-January to mid-February 1512	
Banbrooke, [Unknown]	Coventry	F			Married	Thomas Banbrooke		Although named as suspect by some, her husband and other deponents deny her involvement.
Banbrooke, Thomas	Coventry	M	52	Brewer	Married	(Wife of Thomas Banbrooke)	25 November 1511 (A?) / 29 November 1511 (A)	
Banwell, William	Coventry	M		Mercer				
Bastell, Robert	Coventry	M						
Bayly, Robert	Coventry	M						
Bayly, Thomas	Coventry	M						

Name	City	Sex	Age	Occupation	Marital status	Name of spouse(s)	Date(s) of appearance	Notes
Blacburn, [Unknown]	London	M		Bedder	Married	Joan Blacburn		May not have been a heretic (although his wife was).
Blacburn, Joan	London	F			Married	Blacburn, a bedder		
Bluet, [Unknown]	Coventry	F			Married	Bluet		Sister of John Harris
Blumston, *alias* Phisicion, John	Coventry	M		Physician			9 March 1486 (A) Between 12 March and 26 April 1486	Uncle of John Bull
Borodall, Margaret	Coventry	F		Servant	Married	Nicholas Borodall		
Borodall, Nicholas	Coventry	M		Spurrier	Married	Margaret Borodall		
Borodall, William	Coventry	M	21	Servant			22 May 1515	Son of Nicholas and Margaret Borodall
Bouway Jr., John	Bristol	M		Weaver				
Bouway Sr., John	Bristol	M						

Name	Place	Sex	Age	Occupation	Marital status	Relation	Dates	Notes
Bown, Thomas	Coventry	M	40	Shoemaker			3 November 1511; 5 November 1511 (A); 6 November 1511 (A); Late November to early December 1511; 4 April 1520 (executed)	
Bradeley, Richard	Coventry	M	34	Mercer	Married	Thomasina Bradeley	25 November 1511 (A?); Before 28 November 1511; 28 November 1511; 29 November 1511 (A)	
Bradeley, Thomasina	Coventry	F			Married	Richard Bradeley	Late November to early December 1511; 26 January 1512	
Briam, [Unknown]	London	M						
Bromley, [Unknown]	Coventry	F		Servant	Widowed	Roger Bromley, bedder		
Bromley, Roger	Coventry	M		Bedder; spurrier	Married	(Wife of Roger Bromley)		
Brown, Agnes	Coventry	F			Widowed	Thomas Brown	22 January 1512 (A?); Mid-January to mid-February 1512; 13 February 1512	Mother of the wife of Dawney. Although noted as having abjured 22 January, this is likely an error since she is said still to be denying heresy 13 February.

Name	City	Sex	Age	Occupation	Marital status	Name of spouse(s)	Date(s) of appearance	Notes
Brown, Richard	Coventry	M						Possibly a scribal error for Roger Brown
Brown, Roger	Coventry	M					9 March 1486 (A) Between 12 March and 26 April 1486	Brother of Thomas Brown?
Brown, Thomas	Coventry	M			Married	Agnes Brown		Brother of Roger Brown?
Bukmar, [Unknown]	Maidstone (Kent)	F			Married	Bukmar		
Bukmar, [Unknown]	Maidstone (Kent)	M			Married	(Wife of Bukmar)		
Bull, John	Coventry	M	17	Servant			Late November to early December 1511 3 December 1511 (A)	Nephew of John Blumstone
Butler, Thomas	Coventry	M					9 March 1486 (A) Between 12 March and 26 April 1486	
Capper, [Unknown]	Bristol	F			Married	Laurence Capper		
Capper, Laurence	Bristol	M		Merchant	Married	(Wife of Laurence Capper)		

Name	Place	Sex	Age	Occupation	Marital status	Associated person	Dates	Notes
Clerc, Constance or Christian	Coventry	F			Married	Thomas Clerc	Mid-January to mid-February 1512	She and her husband deny her involvement.
Clerc, David	Coventry	M	40	Currier			Late November to early December 1511; 3 December 1511 (A)	
Clerc, John	Coventry	M		Hosier			16 January 1512 (A)	
Clerc, Thomas	Coventry	M	50	Hosier	Married	Constance or Christian Clerc	25 November 1511 (A?); 29 November 1511 (A)	
Clerke, *alias* Teylour, Robert	Coventry	M		Tailor?			27 February 1490 (A)	Likely not a Lollard.
Cooke, Mistress [Jane]	Coventry	F			Married	Richard Cooke		
Cooke, Richard	Coventry	M			Married	Mistress [Jane] Cooke		
Corby, Agnes	Coventry	F			Widowed?		22 January 1512 (A)	Mother of Elizabeth Gest
Cropwell, John	Coventry	M		Wiredrawer		(Servant of Joan Smyth)	Late November to early December 1511; 22 January 1512; 4 February 1512 (A)	
Crowther, Robert	Coventry	M					9 March 1486 (A); Between 12 March and 26 April 1486	

Name	City	Sex	Age	Occupation	Marital status	Name of spouse(s)	Date(s) of appearance	Notes
Cutler, Roger	Coventry	M						Possibly to be identified with Roger Landesdale, 'scissor', usually translated as tailor, but sometimes meaning cutler.
Davy, [Unknown]	Leicester	M		Painter				Brother of John Davy *alias* Peyntour Sr.
Davy, *alias* Peyntour Sr., John	Leicester	M		Painter			16 January 1512 (A)	
Dawney, [Unknown]	Coventry	F			Married	Dawney		Daughter of Agnes Brown
Dawson, Laurence		M						Possibly the 'known man' who stayed with Thomas Acton (see below under 'Unknown').
Derlyng, [Unknown]	Coventry	M						Possibly John Derlyng

Name	Place	Sex	Age	Painter	Betrothed?	(Betrothed to Julian Yong?)		Notes
Dowcheman, Richard	Leicester	M						Either Dutch or German by origin.
Duke, Tuke, or Tuck, Henry	Bristol	M						'Duke' or 'Tuke', tentatively identified with Henry Tuck, wiredrawer of Bristol.
Falk, John	Coventry	M					9 March 1486 (A) Between 12 March and 26 April 1486	
Flaxrell, Alice	Coventry	F						
Flesshor, Thomas	Coventry	M	67	Smith			28 October 1511 3 November 1511 (A)	
Forde, (Master)	Coventry	M						
Frayne, Stephen	Unknown	M						
Furnour, Rose	Atherstone (Warwickshire)	F	24	Servant			16 January 1512 (A)	
Garton, Katherine	Coventry	F						
Gest, [Unknown]	Birmingham	F			Married	John Smyth; Richard Gest		
Gest, Elizabeth	Coventry	F			Married	William Gest, weaver	Late November to early December 1511 22 January 1512 (A)	Daughter of Agnes Corby

Name	City	Sex	Age	Occupation	Marital status	Name of spouse(s)	Date(s) of appearance	Notes
Gest, Joan	Birmingham	F	40	Servant	Married	John Gest	5 November 1511 (A) 6 November 1511 (A)	
Gest, John	Birmingham	M	30	Shoemaker	Married	Joan Gest	5 November 1511 (A) 6 November 1511 (A)	Son of Richard Gest and brother of Thomas Gest
Gest, Richard	Birmingham	M	60		Married	(widow of John Smyth)	4 November 1511	Father of John and Thomas Gest
Gest, Thomas	Unknown	M		Chaplain	Cleric			Son of Richard Gest and brother of John Gest; unclear whether he sympathizes with the Lollard leanings of his family.
Gilmyn, Richard	Coventry	M					9 March 1486 (A) Between 12 March and 26 April 1486	
Goyte, Margery	Ashbourne (Derbyshire)	F			Married	James Goyte	8 April 1488 (A)	
Grey, Margaret	Coventry	F			Married	William Grey	Mid-January to mid-February 1512	Daughter of Agnes Jonson

Name	Place	Sex	Age	Occupation	Marital status	Spouse	Dates	Notes
Hachet, Katherine	Coventry	F			Married	Robert Hachet	22 January 1512	Although named as suspect by Landesdale, denied by her husband and partially by her.
Hachet, Robert	Coventry	M	60	Tawyer (Foxe: shoemaker)	Married	Katherine Hachet	31 October 1511 5 November 1511 (A) 6 November 1511 (A) 24 January 1512 4 April 1520 (executed)	
Haghmond, Robert	Coventry	M					4 February 1512 (A)	
Harris, John	Coventry	M						Brother of Bluet's wife
Hawkyns, William	Coventry	M	48	Skinner (Foxe: shoemaker)			25 November 1511 (A?) 29 November 1511 (A) 4 April 1520 (executed)	
Hebbis, John	Coventry	M		Sherman			Late November to early December 1511	
Hegham, Richard	Coventry	M					9 March 1486 (A) Between 12 March and 26 April 1486	
Heywod, William	Coventry	M						
Holbache, [Unknown]	Coventry	F			Married	John Holbache		

Name	City	Sex	Age	Occupation	Marital status	Name of spouse(s)	Date(s) of appearance	Notes
Holbache, John	Coventry	M			Married	(Wife of John Holbache)	4 February 1512 (A)	
Holywod, John	Coventry	M					Unknown, some time before 28 October 1511 4 February 1512 (A)	Two references made to his deposition (by John Jonson and Robert Silkby), but it does not survive.
Hyde, Richard	Unknown	M					5 November 1511	Likely not a Lollard.
Jonson, John	Aston, near Birmingham	M	37	Cutler			Before 28 October 1511 28 October 1511 16 January 1512 (A)	
Jonson, Agnes, *alias* 'litle moder Agnes'	Coventry	F			Widowed?		22 January 1512 (A)	Mother of Margaret Grey
Kent, Ralph	Lincoln diocese	M		Priest	Cleric			Nephew of William Kent
Kent, William	Stoney Stanton (Leicestershire.)	M		Priest (rector of Stoney Stanton)	Cleric			Uncle of Ralph Kent
Kylyngworth, Thomas	Coventry	M		Cooper			Late November to early December 1511 Mid-January to mid-February 1512	

Name	Place	Sex	Age	Occupation	Status	Spouse/Relation	Dates	Notes
Landesdale, Margaret	Coventry	F			Married	Roger Landesdale	Late November to early December 1511; 3 December 1511 (A)	
Landesdale, Richard	Coventry	M			Married	Joan (later Smyth)		Likely brother of Roger Landesdale
Landesdale, Roger	Coventry	M	63	tailor (Foxe: hosier)	Married	Margaret Landesdale	29 October 1511; 31 October 1511; 5 November 1511 (A); 6 November 1511 (A); Late November to early December 1511; 4 April 1520 (executed?)	Likely brother of Richard Landesdale. To be identified with 'Thomas' Landesdale named in civic annal?
Landesdale?, [Unknown]	Coventry	F						Daughter of Joan Smyth, possibly daughter of Richard Landesdale
Lockyn, [Unknown]	Maidstone (Kent)	F			Married	Lockyn		
Lockyn, [Unknown]	Maidstone (Kent)	M			Married	(Wife of Lockyn)		
Locock, Margery	Coventry	F			Married	Hugh Stubbe; Henry Locock, girdler	31 October 1511	

Name	City	Sex	Age	Occupation	Marital status	Name of spouse(s)	Date(s) of appearance	Notes
Lodge, William	Coventry	M	25	Mercer			29 November 1511	Son of Alice Lye. May not have been suspect of Lollardy; acts as 'witness for the prosecution' and not forced to abjure.
Longhold, John	Coventry	M	34	Sherman			25 November 1511 (A?) 29 November 1511 (A)	
Lye, Alice	Coventry	F			Married	Robert Lye; Lodge, cutler	Late November to early December 1511	Mother of William Lodge
Lye, Ralph	Allesley (Warws.)	M	50	Weaver			6 November 1511 (A)	
Lye, Robert	Coventry	M			Married	Alice Lye		
Lyeff, Thomas	Coventry	M	30	Sherman	Married	Daughter of Margaret Landesdale	Late November to early December 1511 3 December 1511 (A)	
Markelond or Maclyn, Matthew	Coventry	M	58	Fuller			5 November 1511 6 November 1511 (A)	
Myldener, [Unknown]	London	M						
Nayler, John	Bristol	M						

Name	Place	Sex	Age	Occupation	Status	Spouse/Relation	Date	Notes
Northopp, [Unknown]	Coventry	F			Married	Richard Northopp		Daughter of Joan Smyth and possibly daughter of Richard Landesdale. Although named as suspect by some, her husband denies her involvement.
Northopp, Richard	Coventry	M	31	Mercer	Married	(Daughter of Joan Smyth)	29 November 1511	
Ose, [Unknown]	Northampton	M		Tawyer				
Padwell, [Unknown]	Bristol	F			Married	Henry Padwell		
Padwell, Henry	Bristol	M		Cutler	Married	(wife of Henry Padwell)		
Parek, Hugh	Coventry	M		Wiredrawer			Late November to early December 1511; 3 December 1511 (A)	
Peg, Robert	Coventry	M	30	Painter			5 November 1511 (A); 6 November 1511 (A)	
Preston, James	Coventry	M		Priest (vicar)	Cleric			

Name	City	Sex	Age	Occupation	Marital status	Name of spouse(s)	Date(s) of appearance	Notes
Pygstappe, [Unknown]	Unknown	?					Unknown, some time 1511–1512 (A)	
Pysford, [William Sr.]	Coventry	M						Although named as suspect by some, denied by Hachet.
Qwyck, Robert	Bristol	M		Carpet-maker				
Revis, Katherine	Coventry	F		Piemaker	Married	William Revis		
Revis, William	Coventry	M		Skinner	Married	Katherine Revis	Late November to early December 1511 3 December 1511 Mid-January to mid-February 1512	
Rise, Richard	Coventry	M		Shoemaker			Mid-January to mid-February 1512 4 February 1512 (A)	
Rowley, Alice	Coventry	F			Widowed	William Rowley, merchant	31 October 1511 5 November 1511 16 January 1512 24 January 1512 (A)	
Sheperde, John	Bolton on the Moors, Lancashire	M					13 November 1503 (A)	

Name	Place	Sex	Age	Occupation	Status	Relation/Spouse	Dates	Notes
Shor, Ralph	Unknown	M		Cleric	Cleric			
Shugborow, Balthasar	Napton (Warwickshire)	M	50	Gentleman			4 November 1511; 6 November 1511 (A)	
Silkby *alias* Dumbleby, Robert	Coventry	M	40	Shoemaker			Before 28 October 1511; 28 October 1511; 5 November 1511; 25 November 1511 (A?); 29 November 1511 (A); 23 December 1521 or 13 January 1522 (executed)	
Smyth, Joan	Coventry	F	50		Married	Richard Landesdale; John Padland, capper; Richard Smyth, mercer	4 November 1511; 5 November 1511 (A); 4 April 1520 (executed)	Mother of Richard Northopp's wife; mother of another unnamed daughter (Landesdale?)
Smyth, John	Coventry	M		Tailor	Married	(Now wife of Richard Gest)	9 March 1486 (A); Between 12 March and 26 April 1486	To be identified with John Tailiour?
Spenser, [Unknown]	Coventry	M						Father of Thomas Spenser
Spenser, Thomas	Coventry	M	31	Mercer			25 November 1511 (A?); 29 November 1511 (A)	
Spon, John	Coventry	M	40	Butcher			3 November 1511; 4 February 1512 (A)	

Name	City	Sex	Age	Occupation	Marital status	Name of spouse(s)	Date(s) of appearance	Notes
Tailiour, John	Coventry	M						Possibly to be identified with John Smyth, tailor
Toft, Roger	Coventry	M					4 February 1512 (A)	
Trussell, Isabel	Coventry	F			Married	Thomas Trussell, hosier	Mid-January to mid-February 1512	
Villers, [Unknown]	Bristol	F			Married	Charles Villers		
Villers, [Unknown]	Coventry and Leicester	F			Widowed	Charles Villers of Bristol?		Mother of Thomas Villers, Thomasina Bradeley, and the wife of Thomas Banbrooke
Villers, Charles	Bristol	M		Merchant	Married	(Wife of Charles Villers)		
Villers, Thomas	Coventry	M	27	Spicer	Married	Daughter of Thomas Redhell of Birmingham	25 November 1511 (A?) 27 November 1511 28 November 1511 29 November 1511 3 December 1511 (A)	Son of Widow Villers, brother of Thomasina Bradeley, and wife of Thomas Banbrooke
Warde, Thomas	Coventry	M	63	Barker			25 November 1511 (A?) 29 November 1511 (A)	

Name	Place	Sex	Age	Occupation	Marital status	Spouse/relation	Dates	Notes
Warde *alias* Wasshingburn, Joan	Coventry	F	60		Widowed?	Thomas Wasshingburn	17 November 1511 24 January 1512 11 March 1512 12 March 1512 15 March 1512 (executed)	
Wasshingburn, Thomas	London	M		Shoemaker	Married	Joan Warde *alias* Wasshingburn		
Weston, Richard	Coventry	M						
White, Agnes or Margaret	Coventry	F		Servant				
Wigston, [Agnes]	Coventry	F			Married	William Wigston Jr		When questioned about her, Hachet denies her involvement.
Wigston, [Unknown] William Jr?	Coventry	M						
Wrixham, Thomas	Coventry	M	40	Glover			25 November 1511 (A?) 29 November 1511 (A) 4 April 1520 (executed)	
Yong, Agnes	Coventry	F		Spinster	Widowed	(A tailor)	22 January 1512 (A)	Mother of Julian Yong

Name	City	Sex	Age	Occupation	Marital status	Name of spouse(s)	Date(s) of appearance	Notes
Yong, Julian	Coventry	F	20		Betrothed?	(Betrothed to Richard Dowcheman?)	Late November to early December 1511; 3 December 1511 (A)	Daughter of Agnes Yong
[Unknown], Christopher	Devizes, Wiltshire	M		Shoemaker				Same as Christopher Shoemaker of Great Missenden, Buckinghamshire?
[Unknown], Katherine	Coventry	F			Married	(A miller in Gosford Street)		
[Unknown], Margaret, *alias* Mother Margaret	Coventry	F			Widowed			
[Unknown], Thomas	Bristol	M		Bottlemaker	Married	(wife of Thomas, bottlemaker)		
[Unknown], [Unknown]	Bristol	F			Married	Thomas, bottlemaker		
[Unknown], [Unknown]	Unknown	F			Married	(A certain foreigner)		

[Unknown], [Unknown]	Unknown	M	Married	(Wife of a certain foreigner)	Thomas Flesshour reported that a foreigner (extraneus) and his wife were present while Rowley, Landesdale, and John Peyntour Jr had communication against priests; Richard the shoemaker (likely Richard Rise) said that Hachet spoke in the presence of a certain foreigner.
[Unknown], [Unknown]	Unknown	M			A 'knowen man' visited Coventry for a few days, staying with Thomas Acton (20r).

Totals

Note: these totals can only be rough estimates. A number of suspects may have been counted twice; and some counted here may have been falsely accused, at the same time as others involved in Coventry heresy escaped detection, at least in surviving documents.

Total number implicated in heresy, 1486–1522	158
Number of defendants 1486–1522	79
Number of defendants 1511–1512	67
Number abjured 1486–1522	61
Number abjured 1511–1512	49
Total number of men implicated	107*
Total number of women implicated	50*

*Note that the total number implicated (158) includes one person whose sex is not clear.

APPENDIX 2

Books named in records of Coventry heresy
prosecutions, 1486–1512

Note that many books were simply referred to as 'books containing heresy' – whether this is how the deponents designated them or whether the clerk translated whatever the deponents said to '*libros continentes heresim*' is impossible to discern at this remove. Page references are to the Latin text.

Scriptural

Old Testament (pp. 116, 118, 125, 132).

The Commandments (pp. 106, 117, 128, 146, 155, 158, 179, 194, 207, 217, 241): these could easily be commentaries on the decalogue, of which there were both Lollard and (much more plentifully) orthodox versions available in the first decades of the sixteenth century.

Psalter (p. 155).

Vita Thobie (*Book of Tobit*) (pp. 106, 116, 233, 241).

New Testament (*Nova Lege*) (pp. 117, 157).

Gospels (pp. 103, 106, 152, 156, 157, 173).

Gospel of St Matthew (pp. 117, 146).

Gospel of St John (pp. 118, 146).

Gospels and Epistles (pp. 72, 146, 182).

Acts of the Apostles (p. 117).

Epistles of Paul (pp. 116, 117, 130, 133, 147, 173, 197, 200).

Epistle of James (p. 155).

The Apocalypse (*Book of Revelation*) (pp. 146, 150).

(Orthodox) devotional works

Lives of saints (p. 133); likely to be one of the many editions in English of the *Legenda aurea* printed before 1511.

Book of the passion of Christ and Adam (p. 142).

A primer in English (p. 145).

A book 'on the dying or sick man' (pp. 147, 179, 202); possibly *Here begynneth a lytell treatyse of the dyenge creature enfected with sykenes* (London, 1507; STC 6034).

Possible Lollard tracts

A book against the sacrament of the altar (p. 115).

A book of 'heretical depravity' which began, 'At the begynnyng whan God man' (p. 118) – but was possibly *Genesis* (see Introduction, p. 42, n. 106).

Other

Richard Dowcheman had a book in his own vernacular, presumably Dutch or German (p. 128). This may have been a printed German Bible (see p. 287, n. 57).

APPENDIX 3
Clerics and others present at Coventry heresy prosecutions, 1486–1522

B.Cn.L. = Bachelor of Canon Law
B.Cn. & C.L. = Bachelor of Canon and Civil Law
B.Th. = Bachelor of Theology
D.C.L. = Doctor of Civil Law
D.Cn.L. = Doctor of Canon Law
D.Th. = Doctor of Theology
M.A. = Master of Arts

Page references are to the Latin text.

Clerics

Alcock, John, D.Cn.L. See *BRUC*, p. 6. Present on 9 March 1486 (p. 74). Later suspect of heresy; see pp. 41, 103, 125.

Barker, Thomas, B.Cn.L. Present on 5 and 6 November 1511 (pp. 166, 170, 176, 264).

Blyth, Geoffrey, D.Th. Bishop of Coventry and Lichfield 1503–1531. See *BRUC*, pp. 67–68; *DNB*, V, p. 277. Presiding at all trials from October 1511 to 26 January 1512.

Blyth, John, B.Cn.L. Chancellor of Lichfield Cathedral, 1509–1512; Archdeacon of Coventry, 1512. See Le Neve, *Cov. & Lich.*, pp. 10, 16. Present on 3, 5, and 6 November 1511, and 16 January 1512 (pp. 135, 166, 170, 176, 224, 264).

Cantrell, Ralph, D.Cn.L. Canon of Lichfield Cathedral, 1509–1531. See *BRUC*, p. 121; Le Neve, *Cov. and Lich.*, p. 59. Present on 3, 5, and 6 November 1511, and 16 January 1512 (pp. 135, 166, 170, 176, 224, 264); commisary of the bishop 22 January 1512 (p. 236); recorded as *not* present at another abjuration, 16 January 1512 (p. 227).

Caulin (Caulyn), Robert, D.C.L. Rector of Holy Trinity, Chester, 1507–1513. See *BRUC*, p. 127, under Robert Caudylyn. Commissary of the bishop on 4 and 13 February, 11 and 12 March 1512 (pp. 250, 252, 255).

Clement, Thomas, M.A.? (styled '*magister*'). Commissary of the bishop on 22 May 1515 (p. 280).

Clone, David, B.Cn. & C.L. See *BRUC*, p. 143, under David Clun. Present on 9 March 1486 (p. 74).

Coventry, Richard [*alias* Share, Shaw, Shawe], D.Th. Prior of the Benedictine cathedral priory of Coventry, 1481–1501. See Greatrex, p. 351; Le Neve, *Cov. & Lich.*, p. 5. Present on 9 March 1486 (p. 73).

Danyell, Thomas. Observant Franciscan friar. Present on 3, 5, and 6 November 1511 (pp. 166, 170, 176, 265).

Dykons (Dykans, Dykens), William. Prior of Maxstoke Priory of Augustinian canons, 1505–1538. See *VCH Warws.*, II, p. 94. Present on 3, 5, and 6 November 1511 and 16 January 1512 (pp. 135, 166, 170, 176, 224, 264).

Eliot, Henry. Sub-prior of Maxstoke Priory of Augustinian canons. Present on 3 November 1511 (p. 135).

Fitzherbert, Thomas, D.Cn.L. Bishop Blyth's vicar-general in spirituals 1515–1524. See *Bishop Blyth's Visitations*, p. xiv; *BRUC*, p. 231. Commissary of the bishop May 1515 and December 1521 or January 1522 (pp. 280, 283).

Frysby, John, D.Th. (Bologna?). Canon of Lichfield Cathedral, 1465–1489. See *BRUO to 1500*, II, p. 729 under John Frisby; Le Neve, *Cov. & Lich.*, p. 44. Present on 9 March 1486 (p. 73).

Garstange, Thomas, D.Th. Present on 9 March 1486 (p. 73).

Gerarde, William, B.Th. Present on 9 March 1486 (p. 74).

Hale, Edmund, B.Cn.L. Archdeacon of Shrewsbury, 1486; Archdeacon of Derby, 1485–?1499; kinsman of Bishop John Hales. See *BRUO to 1500*, II, p. 856, under Edmund Halse; Le Neve, *Cov. & Lich.*, p. 17, under Hals. Present on 9 March 1486 (p. 74).

Hales, John, D.Th.. Bishop of Coventry and Lichfield 1459–1490. See *BRUO to 1500*, II, pp. 856–857. Presiding at all trials 1486–1490.

Hawardyn, Humphrey, D.C.L. Canon of Lichfield Cathedral, 1482–?; vicar-general in spirituals to Bishop Hales, c. 1485; Dean of Arches and official principal of the court of Canterbury, 1504–15. See *BRUO to 1500*, II, pp. 887–888. Present on 9 March 1486 (p. 73).

Hayes, Richard. Chaplain. Present on 16 January 1512 (p. 224).

Immpingham (Ympingham), John. Sub-prior of the Benedictine cathedral priory of Coventry, later prior (1516–1517). See Greatrex, p. 359. Commissary of the bishop on 4 and 13 February and 11 March 1512 (pp. 250, 252).

Jacob or Jacobi, David. Observant Franciscan friar. Present 3 and 5 November 1511 (pp. 166, 170, 176, 265).

John, Prior – see under Webbe, John.

Lehe, Hugh, M.A. Canon of St Chad's, Shrewsbury, 1479–?; canon of

Lichfield Cathedral, 1488–?. See *BRUO to 1500*, II, pp. 1127–1128, under Hugh Lehee. Present 9 March 1486 and 8 April 1488 (pp. 74, 88).

Lewys, Henry, M.A. See *BRUC*, p. 365, under Henry Lewes (?). Present on 9 March 1486 (p. 74).

Leylonde, Richard, D.Th. Warden of two chantries in Holy Trinity, Coventry, c. 1484–1491. See *BRUO to 1500*, II, p. 1143. Present on 9 March 1486 (p. 73); see also p. 80.

Mourton, Simon. Summoner. According to Foxe, present April 1520 (pp. 298, 309).

Orton, Thomas, D.Cn.L. Vicar of Holy Trinity parish, Coventry, 1508–1524/25; canon of Lichfield Cathedral 1510–1524/25. See *BRUO to 1500*, II, p. 405. Present on 16 January 1512 and commissary of the bishop on 11 March 1512, and 22 May 1515 (pp. 224, 252, 280).

Palden, William, B.Cn.L. Vicar of Honington, Warwickshire, c. 1507. See *BRUO to 1500*, III, p. 1420. Present on 16 January 1512 and commissary of the bishop on 11 March 1512 (pp. 224, 252).

Pollesworthe, William. Prior of the Benedictine cathedral priory of Coventry, 1501–1516. See Greatrex, pp. 366–367; Le Neve, *Cov. & Lich.*, p. 5. Present on 3 and 6 November 1511 (pp. 169, 176, 264).

Pratt, Robert, B.Cn. & C.L. See *BRUO to 1500*, III, p. 1514. Present on 8 April 1488 (p. 88). Possibly the same as Robert Pratt, notary (see below).

Preston, John, D.Th. Present on 9 March 1486 (p. 73).

Pursell, John. Chaplain. Present on 16 January 1512 (p. 224).

Salter, Richard, D.Cn.L. Canon of Salisbury, 1483–?; canon of Lichfield, 1489–1501. See *BRUO to 1500*, III, p. 1653. Present on 8 April 1488 (p. 88).

Sharpe, John, B.Cn.L. Canon of Lichfield, 1486–1492. See *BRUO to 1500*, III, p. 1681. Present on 9 March 1486 and 8 April 1488 (pp. 74, 88).

Skelton, William, M.A. Vicar of Ashby-de-la-Zouche, Leicestershire, 1510–1535. See *BRUC*, p. 530. Present on 3, 5, and 6 November 1511, and 16 January 1512 (pp. 135, 166, 170, 176, 224, 264).

Stafford, John. Warden of Franciscan friary, Coventry, up to 1538. See *Valor Ecclesiasticus tempore Henrici VIII*, 6 vols, John Caley (ed.) (London, 1810–1834), III, p. 57; A.G. Little, *Studies in English Franciscan History* (Manchester, 1917), p. 46. According to Foxe, present April 1520 (pp. 297, 310).

Strangeweys, George, D.Th. Canon of Lichfield Cathedral, 1486–1512; later

Archdeacon of Coventry, 1505–1512. See *BRUO to 1500*, III, pp. 1795–1796, under George Strangways; Le Neve, *Cov. &. Lich.*, p. 15. Present on 8 April 1488 and commissary of the bishop 13 November 1503 (pp. 88, 97).

Webbe, John. Prior of the Benedictine cathedral priory of Coventry, 1517–1527. See Greatrex, p. 373; Le Neve, *Cov. & Lich.*, p. 5. Commissary of the bishop in 1522 (p. 283).

Wilcocks, John, D.Cn.L. of Turin. Rector of Cranford, Northamptonshire, 1510 to December 1512. See *BRUC*, p. 639. Commissary of the bishop 22 January and 11 March 1512 (pp. 236 and 252); see also 13 February 1512 for reference (p. 252).

Wilton, William, M.A. Rector of Doveridge, Derbyshire, 1510–1521. See *BRUC*, p. 658, under William Wylton (?). Present on 3, 5, and 6 November 1511, and 16 January 1512 (pp. 135, 166, 170, 176, 224, 264).

Ympingham – see under *Immpingham.*

Yotton, John, D.Th. Dean of Lichfield Cathedral, 1493–1512. See *BRUC*, p. 667; Le Neve, *Cov. & Lich.*, p. 6. Commissary of the bishop 13 November 1503 (p. 97).

Others present

Big, Henry. Present on 3 November 1511 (p. 135).

Dawes, Hugh, draper, Sheriff of Coventry. See *Coventry Leet Book,* p. 633. Present on 12 March 1512 (p. 256).

Formewerke, Thomas. Notary. Present on 9 March 1486 and 8 April 1488 (pp. 74, 88).

Pratt, Robert. Notary. Present on 9 March 1486 (p. 74). Possibly the same as Robert Pratt, B.Cn. & C.L (see above).

Sheriffs of Coventry – see under *Dawes, Hugh*; and *Turner, Thomas.*

Turner, Thomas, grazier, Sheriff of Coventry. See *Coventry Leet Book,* p. 633. Present on 12 March 1512 (p. 256).

INDEX

Bold numbers indicate appearance or examination of that person before the bishops or their commissaries.

References to explanatory notes are given in brackets.

Abandonment of heresy prior to prosecution 13, 47, 150, 151, 152, 153, 203

Abbots Bromley (Staffordshire) 153

Abell, Thomas 21, 37, 44, 58, 59, 128, 129, 131, 132, 157, 160, 179, 181, **182–184**, 185, 186, 188, **189–191**, 203, 204, **205–206**, 222, **260–263**, 322

Abjuration of heresy 20, 122, 123, 259–260
  record that suspect abjured 95, 96, 135–136, 137–138, 162, 163, 164, 165, 166, 167, 169, 170, 171, 172, 173, 174, 175, 176, 177, 178, 183, 184, 185, 187, 188, 189, 190, 191, 194, 195, 196, 197, 198, 199, 203, 204, 205, 206, 210, 211, 219, 220, 221, 224, 225, 226–227, 227, 228, 229, 230, 233, 234, 236, 237, 241, 242, 249, 250, 278, 279
  reference to previous abjuration 178, 180, 238, 239, 253, 254, 255, 256, 283, 284
  texts of abjurations 74–75, 77–78, 89, 92–93, 97–98, 99–100, 260–263, 263–266, 266–269, 270–273, 273–276, 277

Acton, Alice 60, 125, 127, 156, 157, 159, 160, 188, 189, 230, 244, 245, 322

Acton, Thomas 13, 39, 42, 58, 116, 119, 125, 126, 127, 128, 129–130, 131, 132, 146, 148, **150–151**, 155, 156, 157, 159, 160, **165–168**, **169–170**, 173, 188, 189, 224, 226, 230, 244, 245, **266–269**, 322, 328, 341

Acts of the Apostles, book containing the 42, 117, 120, 343

Acts and Monuments, by John Foxe (*see* Foxe, John)

Agnes, Little Mother (*see* Jonson, Agnes)

Alcock, John 41, 44, 73–74, 77, 103, 104, 125, 127, 322, 345

Alen, William 155, 159

Allesley (Warwickshire) 117, 120, 131, 132, 133, 146, 148, 174, 175, 177, 178, 334

Amounderness Hundred (Lancashire) 105, 107

Angel, sign of the, Coventry 128, 129

Annals, Coventry civic 23, 53, 55–56, 315–318

Annesty, pseudo-prophet 185, 186, 322

Anticlericalism 17, 30, 31, 64, 65, 67, 68, 69, 70, 72, 73, 87, 91, 95, 96, 103, 104, 106, 107, 110, 112, 154, 157, 161, 173, 174, 185, 186, 222, 231, 232, 299–300, 301, 302, 305, 306, 307, 308

Apocalypse (Revelation of St John)
  book containing the 42, 146, 148, 150, 151, 343
  memorization of 45, 224, 226

Archer, John 9, 60, 245, **247–248**, **250–251**, 259, **297–298**, **303–304**, **309–310**, **312–313**, 315, 316, 322

Archer, Thomas 186, 187, 224, 226, 322, 323

Archer, wife of Thomas 224, 226, 323

Arrests on suspicion of heresy 46, 180, 182, 184, 186, 215, 216, 230, 295, 296, 297, 298, 303, 304, 310, 311, 312, 313

Ars moriendi, books in the tradition of the 42, 290n (122)

Articles of faith (*see* Creed)

Arundel, John, Bishop of Coventry and Lichfield (1496–1502) 4

Ashbourne (Derbyshire) 7, 18, 87, 90, 91, 94, 302, 308, 330

Aston (Warwickshire) 225, 226, 227, 332

Atherstone (Warwickshire) 179, 181, 221, 222, 329

Atkynson *alias* Peyntour Jr, John 12, 35, 36, 41, 57, 58, 102, 103, 106, 107, **113–114**, **115**, 116, 119, **127–130**, **165–168**, **169–170**, **266–269**, 286n (21), 323, 341

Ave Maria (*see* Hail Mary)

Baginton (Warwickshire) 54, 311, 314

Bakehouse, Agnes de 37, 59, 60, 158, 161, 179, 181, **232–234**, 233, 234, **236–237**, **270–273**, 323

Baker, Edmund 246, 323

Baker, Katherine 60, **246**, 323

Banbrooke or Bambrooke, Thomas 8, 13, 33, 37, 42, 58, 59, 111, 113, 118, 121, 156, 157, 160, 179, 184, 185, 186, 187, **189–191**, 192, 194, **195–196**, 200, 201, 202, 203, 204, **205–206**, **260–263**, 281, 323, 338

Banbrooke or Bambrooke, wife of Thomas 33–34, 111, 113, 156, 160, 185, 187, 191, 192, 195, 196, 323, 338

Banbury (Oxfordshire) 39, 130, 131, 157, 160

Banwell, William 185, 187, 188, 189, 323

Baptism 19, 88, 91

Barker, Thomas 6, 166, 168, 170, 176, 177, 264, 266, 345

Bastell, Robert 39, 46, 110, 112, 130–131, 132, 157, 160, 238, 239, 323

Bayly, Master 156, 159, 180, 181, 323

Bayly, Robert 185, 186, 323

Bayly, Thomas 117, 120, 287n (40), 323

Beaudesert, episcopal manor at 3, 87, 91, 155, 159, 289n (85)

Bentham, master of Bluet's wife 158, 161

Bentham, Thomas 54

Bentham, wife of 148, 149

Bible
  discussion of 39, 150, 151
  translations of 14–15, 30, 31–32, 41–42, 287–288n (57), 311n, 314n, 343, 344
  (*see also* Acts of the Apostles; Apocalypse; Commandments; Epistles; Gospels; New Testament; Old Testament; Psalter; Tobit)

Big, Henry 135, 138, 348

Birell, Master 184, 186

Birmingham (West Midlands) 24, 39, 105, 110, 112, 131, 132, 143, 144, 153, 154, 166, 167, 169, 170, 223, 224, 225, 226, 329, 330, 332

Bishops' registers 48–51
  Geoffrey Blyth's register 15–16, 47, 49
  John Hales's register 15, 47, 49, 53–54

Blackburn or Blacburn, husband of Joan 39, 238, 239, 324

Blackburn or Blacburn, Joan 39, 233, 238, 239, 324

Blessings by bishops, attitudes towards 188, 189

Bluet, wife of 148, 149, 158, 161, 324, 338

Blumston *alias* Phisicion, John 5, 17, 18, 21, 32, 57, **63**, **64–65**, **73–80**, **80–87**, 109, 111, 158, 161, 195, 196, 200, 201, 215–216, 224, 226, **299–300**, **305**, 324, 326

Blyth, Geoffrey, Bishop of Coventry and Lichfield (1503–1531) 2, 3, 4, 5, 9, 10, 11–12, 15, 16, 19, 22, 23, 30, 31, 32, 40, 41, 43, 47, 48, 97, 99, 100, 255, 256, 257, 260, 261–262, 266–267, 268, 270, 272, 274, 275, 278, 279, 283, 284, 345
  presiding over 1511–1512 and 1520–1522 heresy prosecutions 102–249, 297–298, 303–304, 309–314

Blyth, John 6, 135, 138, 166, 168, 170, 176, 177, 224, 226, 264, 266, 345

Blyth's Visitation Book 47, 48, 49

Bolton (Lancashire) 97, 99, 336

Bond, John 297, 303, 315, 316, 317

Bond, Thomas (*see* Bown)

Books 17–18, 30, 31, 41–45, 68, 69, 72, 73, 343–344
  copying 43, 117, 118, 120, 121, 248
  destruction 106, 107, 126, 127, 152, 153, 157, 160, 185, 187, 188, 189
  hiding 208, 217–218, 245, 248, 260, 262, 263–264, 265, 267, 268, 270, 272, 274, 275
  possession or reading, as evidence for heresy 30, 31, 32, 34–35, 40, 41, 53n (207), 68, 69, 103, 104, 106, 107, 108, 109, 110–111, 112, 114, 115, 116–117, 118, 119–120, 121, 122, 123, 124, 125, 126, 127, 128, 129, 130, 132, 133, 135, 136, 137, 138, 139, 140, 141, 142, 143, 144, 148, 149, 150, 155, 156, 157, 159, 160, 162, 163, 164, 165, 166, 167, 176, 177, 179, 180, 181, 184, 185, 186, 187, 188, 189, 191, 192, 193, 197, 198, 201, 202, 203, 208, 218, 233, 245, 247–248, 248, 295, 296, 301, 306, 315, 316
  surrendering to bishop or other ecclesiastical official 106, 107, 142, 143, 155, 156, 159, 184, 185, 186, 187, 248
  trading and exchange 41–43, 106, 107, 110–111, 112, 116–118, 119–121, 130, 131, 141, 142, 147, 149, 150, 151, 155, 156, 157, 159, 160, 161, 179, 181, 183, 184, 197–198, 200, 201, 207, 208, 217, 218, 233
  (*see also* Bible, translations of; Gatherings, reading at; Literacy; Lollard or Wycliffite texts; Memorization; Orthodox devotional works)

Bordeaux (France) 110, 112

Borodall, Margaret 11, 33, 280, 281, 324

Borodall, Nicholas 11, 33, 280, 281, 324

Borodall, William 11, 26, 33, 60, **280–281**, 324

Bottlemaker of Bristol, Thomas (*see* Thomas, bottlemaker of Bristol)

Bouway, John 103, 104,

Bouway, John Jr 109, 112, 223, 225, 286n (16), 324

Bouway, John Sr 109, 112, 223, 225, 286n (16), 324

Bowd or Bowde, Thomas 132–133

Bown, Bownd, or Bond, Thomas 9, 13, 21, 24, 26, 32–33, 37, 44, 46, 57, 58, 59, 102, 104, 106, 107, 110, 112, 116, 118, 119, 121, 125, 126, 128, 129, **130–132**, 143, 144, 150, 151, 152, 156, 157, 158, 159, 160, 161, **165–168, 169–170**, 173, 174, 175, 178, 179, 180, 181, 182, 183, 185, 186, 197, 203, **213**, 214, 215, 216, 222, 223, 231, 232, 245, **266–269,** 287nn (43, 48), **297–298, 303–304, 309–310, 312–313**, 315, 316, 325

Bradeley, Richard 12, 13, 14, 25, 34, 38, 42, 44, 58, 59, 111, 113, 118, 121, 147, 149, 156–157, 160, 184, 186, 185, 187, **189–191, 192–193**, 197, 198, 200, 201, 202, **205–206**, 207, 210, 211, **260–263,** 325

Bradeley, Thomasina 12, 13–14, 33, 34, 38, 42, 44, 45, 59, 60, 111, 113, 118, 121, 147, 149, 156, 160, 191, 192, 194, 195, 200, 201, **207**, 208, 209, 243, **243**, 325, 338

Branding (*see* Penances, branding)

Briam, of London 238, 239, 325

Bristol (Gloucestershire) 24, 34, 39, 103, 104, 109–110, 111–112, 126, 127, 147, 149, 190, 191, 223–224, 225–226, 324, 326, 329, 334, 335, 336, 338, 340

Brittany (France) 110, 112

Broadmead, Bristol 223, 225

Bromley, Roger 106, 107, 148, 149, 158, 161, 325

Bromley, wife of Roger 12, 36, 148, 149, 158, 161, 325

Brown, Agnes 46, 60, 158, 161, 179, 181, **236–237, 247, 251–252**, 259, 325, 326, 328

Brown, Richard 147, 149, 326

Brown , Roger 5, 16, 17, 18, 19, 32, 37, 57, **63, 68–69, 73–80, 80–87**, 106, 107, 109, 110, 111, 112, 114, 203, 204, 224, 226, **300–301, 306–307**, 326

Brown, Thomas 158, 161, 179, 181, 325, 326

Bukmar, of Maidstone 238, 239, 326

Bukmar, wife of 238, 239, 326

Bull, John 44, 46, 59, 200, 201, **215–216, 220, 221, 270–273**, 290n (121), 324, 326

Burning of heretics in other prosecutions, references to 9, 40, 157, 160, 173, 174 (*see also* Penances, execution by burning)

Butler, John 289n (85)

Butler, Thomas 16, 57, **63, 69–71, 73–80, 80–87, 301, 307**, 326

Butler, wife of 29, 155, 159, 289n (85)

Caernarvon (Gwynned) 182, 183

Cambreton, Robert or John 239, 253, 254, 291n (151)

Canterbury (Kent) 253, 254

Cantrell, Ralph 6, 135, 138, 166, 168, 170, 176, 177, 224, 226, 227, 228, 236, 237, 264, 266, 345

Capper, Laurence 223, 224, 225, 226, 326

Capper, wife of Laurence 225, 226, 326

Carleton (Carlton-on-Trent, Nottinghamshire?) 216

Carmelite friary, Coventry (*see* Tower, Our Lady of the)

Caulyn, Robert 250, 252, 254, 255, 256, 345

Charlbury (Oxfordshire) 130, 131

Chester (Cheshire) 150, 151, 174, 175, 182, 183

Christ's Passion and Adam, book of 42, 142, 143, 344

Christopher, shoemaker of Devizes 173, 174, 340

Church, suspects' attitudes towards 17, 22, 68, 110, 112, 119, 121, 145, 157, 161, 238, 239, 255, 256, 300, 306

Clement, Thomas 280, 281, 345

Clerc, Constance or Christian 37, 60, 180, 181, 188, 189, **245**, 327

Clerc, David 59, 119, 121, 147, 149, 158, 161, **214–215, 220, 221, 270–273,** 327

Clerc, John 59, 122, 145, 146–147, 149, 187, 189, 224, 226, **229**, 259, 327

Clerc, Thomas 37, 44, 58, 59, 126, 127, 131, 132, 145, 146, 147, 148, 149, 180, 181, 186, 187, **187–189, 189–191**, 203, **205–206**, 245, 247–248, **260–263**, 327

Clerke *alias* Teylour, Robert 7, 19, 57, **94–97**, 327

Clone, David 74, 77, 345

Cokersand, Premonstratensian Abbey of 113

Commandments 22, 297–298, 303–304, 309, 310, 312, 313
  book or scroll of 10, 42, 106, 107, 117, 120, 128, 130, 146, 148, 155, 158, 159, 161, 179, 181, 194, 195, 207, 217, 218, 233, 234, 241, 242, 298, 304, 310, 311, 313, 314, 315, 316, 343
  commentaries on 42, 343
Commentarii rerum in ecclesia gestarum (*see* Foxe, John)
Compurgation 4, 29, 123, 124, 155, 159, 230, 241, 242, 250
Concealing (*see* Books, hiding; Receiving or concealing suspect persons as element of heresy)
Confession (*see* Penance, sacrament of)
Confession of heresy prior to prosecution 45–46, 203, 210, 222, 248, 280, 281
Cook or Coke, Joan 29, 157, 160, 188, 189, 327
Cook or Coke, Richard 29, 188, 189, 315, 316, 317, 327
Coor, William 128, 129
Corby, Agnes 60, 156, 158, 159, 161, 179, 181, 180, 182, **234–235**, **235–236**, **236–237**, **266–269**, 327, 329
Corby (Northamptonshire or Lincolnshire) 128n, 129n
Court books, as records of prosecution of heresy 47–51
Coventry, Richard 73, 77, 346
Coventry cathedral priory
  heretical discussions in church or cloister 37, 158, 161
  penitential procession in 171, 172, 173
  proceedings in church 5, 252, 253
  proceedings in chapter house 5, 243, 250
Coventry heretical community
  age of suspects 24–25
  civic elite's participation 29–32, 117, 120, 125, 126, 128, 129, 156, 157, 158, 159, 160, 161, 180, 181, 185, 186, 187, 189, 222, 223, 237, 238
  economic ties between suspects 27, 111, 113, 156, 159, 160, 179, 181, 203, 281
  gender ratio among suspects 24, 342
  social status of suspects 26–32
  ties to heretical groups elsewhere 39–40
  visitors to 20, 39, 42–43, 106, 107, 150, 151, 179, 181, 244
  (*see also* Gatherings)
Crampe, Thomas 297, 303

Creed 17, 18, 22, 66, 67, 68, 95, 96, 168, 297–298, 300, 303–304, 306, 310, 313
  scroll or book containing 10, 72, 73, 298, 302, 304, 308, 310, 313, 315, 316
Cropwell, John 22, 36, 59, 60, 119, 121, 158, 161, 188, 189, **212–213**, **231–232**, **249**, **250–251**, **277**, 327
Cropwell, wife of John 231, 232, 327
Crown, sign of the, Coventry 118, 121
Crowther, Robert 17, 18, 57, **63**, **66–67**, **73–80**, **80–87**, **300**, **306**, 327
Cult of saints 14–15, 16, 35, 130, 131, 133, 151, 152
  (*see also* Hailes, Holy Blood of; Images, pilgrimages and shrines; Mary, Virgin; Prayer as intercession)
Cutler, John (*see* Jonson, *alias* Cutler, John)
Cutler, Roger 157, 160, 328

Danyell, Thomas 6, 166, 168, 170, 176, 177, 265, 266, 346
Davy, brother of John 116, 119, 139, 140, 328
Davy *alias* Peyntour Sr, John 35, 59, 102, 103, 104, 106, 107, 116, 118, 119, 121, 127, 128, 129, 139, 140, 146, 148, 185, 186, **229–230**, **266–269**, 286n (22), 288n (62), 328
Dawes, Hugh 348
Dawney, wife of 158, 161, 325, 328
Dawson, Lawrence 10, 39, 42, 43, 157, 160, 179, 181, 328
De heretico comburendo (statute 1401) 10
Denial of involvement in heresy 13–14, 33–34, 35, 45, 46, 123, 124, 133, 134, 184, 186, 192, 193, 194, 195, 196, 197, 201, 202, 207, 209, 210, 211, 213, 214, 217, 219–220, 222, 223, 229, 235, 236, 243, 244, 245, 246, 247, 249, 252, 279
Derlyng, of Coventry 31, 119, 121, 157, 161, 185, 186, 187, 189, 222, 223, 328
Derlyng, John 31, 328
Devizes (Wiltshire) 13, 151, 152, 173, 174, 340
Dikons, William (*see* Dykons, William)
Divinity of Christ 19, 88, 91
Dod, Thomas 297, 303
Doncaster, Our Lady of 16, 64, 65, 299, 305
Dowcheman or Ducheman, Richard 44, 118, 121, 124, 126, 128, 129, 139, 140, 147, 149, 329, 340, 344
Duddesbury, John 289n (85)
Duddesbury, wife of 29, 155, 159, 289n (85)

Duke, Tuck, or Tuke 39, 45, 46, 157, 160, 180, 182, 329
(*see also* Tuck, Henry)
Dumbleby (*see* Silkby, *alias* Dumbleby)
Dunham, cutler 109, 111
Durdant family, of Middlesex 27
Dykons or Dikons, William 6, 135, 138, 166, 168, 170, 176, 177, 224, 226, 264, 266, 346

Earl Street, Coventry 145
Eliot, Henry 135, 138, 346
Epistle of James, book containing 42, 155, 159
Epistles, discussion of 150, 151, 154, 155
(*see also* Gospels and Epistles)
Epistles of Paul
book containing 42, 116, 117, 119, 120, 130, 131, 133, 134, 147, 149, 173, 174, 197, 200, 343
memorization of 45, 154, 200, 201
Eucharist, attitudes towards 14–15, 17, 18–19, 20, 21, 22, 23, 34, 35, 36, 41, 66, 67, 68, 69, 71, 72, 73, 87–88, 91, 102, 103, 103–104, 106, 107, 108, 110, 111, 112, 113, 115, 116–117, 119, 120, 121, 124, 126, 128, 129, 130, 131–132, 133, 134, 135, 136, 137, 138, 139, 140, 141, 142, 143, 144, 145, 148, 149, 150, 151, 151, 152, 153–154, 155, 156, 159, 162, 163, 164, 165, 167, 174, 175, 176, 177, 178, 180, 180, 182, 183, 184, 186, 195, 196, 200, 201, 208, 210, 212, 213, 214, 215, 216, 217, 218, 221–222, 223, 224, 225, 226, 230, 231, 232, 233, 234, 235, 238, 239, 241, 242, 253, 254, 255, 256, 260, 262, 263, 265, 267, 268, 270, 272, 274, 275, 278, 280, 281, 283, 284, 300, 301, 302, 306, 307, 308, 311, 314, 315, 316, 317, 318
Excommunication, attitudes towards 22, 118, 121
Excommunication, fulmination of sentence of before proceedings in 1511 45–46, 132, 133
Execution (*see* Burning of heretics; Penances, execution by burning)

Falk or Falkys, John 16, 17, 57, **63**, **71–72**, **73–80**, **80–87**, **301–302**, **307**, 329
Fasting, attitudes towards 22, 68, 69, 71, 295, 296, 299, 301, 304, 306, 307, 311, 314
(*see also* Penances, fasting)

Fitzherbert, Thomas 6, 48, 280, 281, 283, 284, 285, 346
Flaxrell, Alice 147, 149, 329
Fleet Street, Coventry 119, 121
Flemmyng, Master 180, 182
Flemyng, Henry 182, 183
Flesshor or Flesshour, Thomas 7–8, 11, 27, 35, 36, 49, 57, 102, 103, 104, **105–107**, 115, **134–139**, 155, 159, 163, 165, 166, 167, 169, 170, 180, 181, 190, 191, 205, 206, 236, 237, 250, 259, **260–263**, **263–266**, 329, 341
Flight of suspects 6–7, 10, 46, 125, 126, 215, 216, 298, 303, 304, 311, 313–314, 315, 316
Forde, Master 148, 149, 158, 161, 329
Forde, Thomas 125, 126, 288n (74)
Forde, William 288n (74)
Formewerke, Thomas 74, 77, 88, 92, 348
Foxe, John 6, 10, 44, 47, 50, 51–52, 54, 296
accuracy of 22–23, 54–55
historians' use of 52
use of oral history 52, 311, 314
Acts and Monuments 22, 51–52
1563 edition 51, 53–54, 296–308, 309
1570 edition 52, 54, 296–297, 308–314
Commentarii rerum in ecclesia gestarum (1554) 51
Rerum in ecclesia gestarum [...] commentarii (1559) 51, 52–53, 295–296
Franciscan friary, Coventry 37, 157, 160, 297, 303, 310, 313
Frayne, Stephen 174, 175, 329
Frysby, John 73, 77, 346
Furnour, Rose 8, 26, 35, 37, 45, 59, 179, 181, **221–223**, **227–228**, 230, **273–276**, 329

Garstang (Lancashire) 113
Garstange, Thomas 73, 77, 346
Garton, Katherine 156, 159, 329
Gatherings 27, 35–38, 41, 102, 103–104, 106, 107, 108, 109–110, 111–112, 116–119, 119–121, 122, 123, 125, 124, 126, 128, 129, 135, 136, 137, 138, 142, 143, 144, 147, 148, 149, 150, 151, 156, 157, 158, 159, 160, 161, 162, 163, 164, 165, 167, 175, 176, 179, 181, 182, 183, 185, 186, 187, 189, 193, 194, 197, 198, 199, 200, 201, 202, 203, 207, 208, 209, 210, 212, 213, 214, 215, 216, 217, 218, 219, 222, 223–224, 225–226, 231, 232, 233, 234, 241, 242, 248, 260, 262, 264, 265, 267, 268, 270, 272, 274, 275

Gatherings – *contd*
at ecclesiastical sites 37, 147, 149, 157, 158, 160, 161, 202
grouping by sex and marital status 37–38
in private homes 35–36
reading at 20, 34–36, 38, 41, 43, 44–45, 103, 104, 106, 107, 111, 113, 116–118, 119–121, 122, 123, 125, 126, 128, 129, 132, 133, 135, 136, 137, 138, 142, 143, 147, 149, 156, 157, 159, 160, 165, 167, 175, 176, 179, 181, 182, 183, 186, 187, 189, 193, 197, 198, 200, 201, 202, 203, 207, 208, 210, 216, 248, 260, 262, 264, 265, 267, 268, 270, 272, 274, 275
walking out of doors 36, 115, 118, 121, 131, 132, 185, 187, 188, 189, 198, 199, 224, 226, 295, 296
Gentry participation in Lollardy 26–27
(*see also* Shugborow, Balthasar)
Gerarde, William 74, 77, 346
Gest, Elizabeth 59, 60, 158, 161, 180, 182, **217**, **235–236**, **236–237**, **266–269**, 327, 329
Gest, Joan 8, 58, 110, 112, 125, 127, **153–154**, 154, **165–168**, **169–170**, **266–269**, 288n (83), 330
Gest, John (Gest Jr) 45, 58, 110, 112, 117, 120, 125, 127, 144, 153, 154, **154–155**, **165–168**, **169–170**, **266–269**, 288n (83), 330
Gest, Richard (Gest Sr) 35, 42, 58, 110, 112, 117–118, 120, 125, 127, 131, 132, 133, **143–144**, 146, 148, 329, 330
Gest, Thomas 118, 120, 125, 127, 143, 144, 330
Gest, wife of Richard 102, 104, 125, 127, 131, 132, 329, 330, 337
Gilbert, Robert 109, 111
Gilmyn, Gylmyn, or Hilmin, Richard 57, **63**, **72–73**, **73–80**, **80–87**, **302**, **307–308**, 330
Gloucester (Gloucestershire) 109, 111
Gosford Street, Coventry 124, 126, 147, 149, 180, 182
Gospel of St John
book containing 45, 118, 121, 146, 148, 343
memorization of 124, 126
Gospel of St Luke, discussion of 21, 205, 206, 227, 228, 235
Gospel of St Matthew
book containing 117, 120, 146, 149, 343

Gospel of St Matthew – *contd*
memorization of 154
discussion of 143, 144
Gospels
book containing 42, 103, 104, 106, 107, 152, 153, 156, 157, 159, 160, 173, 174, 343
discussion of 36, 102, 104, 150, 151, 154, 155
Gospels and Epistles, book containing 72, 73, 146, 148, 182, 183, 302, 308, 343
Goyte, James 87, 91, 302, 308, 330
Goyte, Margery 7, 8, 18–19, 57, **87–94**, **302**, **308**, 330
Grevis, William (*see* Revis, William)
Grey, Margaret (daughter of Agnes Jonson) 37, 60, 180, 182, 233, 234, **236**, 330, 332
Grey, William 180, 182, 330
Grey Friars Lane, Coventry 158, 161

Hachet, Katherine 26, 59, 116, 119, 125, 127, **232**, 331
Hachet or Hachetts, Robert 9–10, 13, 21, 22, 24, 26, 30, 32, 37, 41, 44, 46, 54, 57, 58, 59, 60, 102, 104, 106, 107, 110, 112, 116, 117, 119, 120, **124–127**, 130, 131, 132, 143, 144, 147, 149, 151, 152, 156, 159, **165–168**, **169–170**, 174, 175, 178, 179, 180, 181, 182, 183, 187, 189, 203, 204, 210, 211, 212, 214, 215, 221, 222, 223, 227, 228, 231, 232, 237, 244, 248, **266–269**, 281, 286n (15), **297–298**, **303–304**, **309–310**, **312–313**, 315, 316, 331, 336, 339, 341
Haddon, wife of 29, 155, 159, 289n (85)
Haddon, John 289n (85)
Haghmond, Roger 60, **250–251**, **277**, 331
Hail Mary (*Ave Maria*) 18, 19, 67, 68, 95, 96, 168
scroll or book containing 72, 73, 302, 308
Hailes, Holy Blood of 16, 68, 69, 300, 306
Hale, Edmund 74, 77, 346
Hales, John, Bishop of Coventry and Lichfield (1459–1490) 2, 3, 10, 13, 15, 16, 17, 32, 33, 41, 47, 130, 131, 152, 153, 315, 316, 317, 346
presides over 1486–1490 heresy prosecutions 63–97, 299–308, 309, 312
Halle, Mother 22, 53, 54, 311, 314
Hardingstone (Northamptonshire) 187, 188

Harris, John 158, 161, 324, 331
Harshall or Hartshall, Richard 315, 316, 317
Hawardyn, Humphrey 73, 77, 346
Hawkyns, William 9, 37, 58, 59, 118, 121, 147, 149, 156, 157, 158, 159, 160, 161, 180, 182, 185, 186, 188, **189–191, 204, 205–206**, 210, 211, **260–263, 297– 298, 303–304, 309–310, 312–313,** 315, 316, 331
Hayes, Richard 224, 226, 346
Hebbis, John 13, 59, 158, 161, 213, **213– 214**, 331
Hegham, Richard 16, 57, **63, 65–66, 73– 80, 80–87, 300, 305–306,** 331
Here begynneth a lytell treatyse of a dyenge creature enfected with sykenes 290n (122), 344
Heretics' Hollow (*Puteus haereticorum*), Coventry 295, 296, 319n (2)
Heywod, William 187, 188, 189, 331
Hilmin, Richard (*see* Gilmyn, Richard)
Holbache, John 60, 118, 121, 185, 187, 224, 226, **250–251**, 259, 331, 332
Holbache, wife of 118, 121, 331, 332
Holborn Cross, London 110, 112
Holt Castle (Clwyd) 184, 186
Holy Blood of Hailes (*see* Hailes, Holy Blood of)
Holy Trinity parish, Coventry 52, 133, 280, 281
    proceedings in church 5, 251, 252
Holywod, John 12, 36, 41, 44, 60, 102, 103, 104, 108, 109, 111, 113, 115, **250–251, 277,** 286n (14), 332
Hyde, Richard 58, **168**, 332

Ibstock (Leicestershire) 41, 103, 104, 125, 127, 322
Images, pilgrimages, and shrines, attitudes towards 16, 17, 20, 21–22, 64, 65, 66, 67, 70, 71, 72, 103, 104, 106, 107, 110, 111, 112, 113, 128, 129, 130, 131, 133, 134, 135, 136, 137, 138, 139, 140, 141, 142, 143, 144, 145, 150, 151, 152, 153, 154, 156, 157, 158, 159, 160, 161, 162, 163, 164, 165, 167, 174, 175, 176, 177, 178, 180, 183, 194, 195, 196, 197, 198, 199, 210, 212, 213, 214, 215, 216, 217, 218, 222, 223, 224, 225, 226, 230, 231, 232, 233, 234, 235, 238, 239, 240, 241, 242, 244, 248, 250, 253, 254, 255, 256, 260, 262, 263, 265, 267, 268, 270, 272, 274, 275, 283, 284, 299, 300, 301, 302, 305, 306, 307–308

Images, pilgrimages, and shrines, attitudes towards – *contd*
    (*see also* Cult of saints; Doncaster, Our Lady of; Hailes, Holy Blood of; Tower, Our Lady of the; Walsingham, Our Lady of)
Immpingham or Ympingham, John 6, 250, 252, 254, 346
Imprisonment of suspects 5, 6, 10–11, 41, 75, 79, 81, 84, 113, 114, 139, 140, 157, 160, 193, 297, 303, 310, 312
Interrogatories for examination of suspects 20, 49, 134–136, 137–138, 162–163, 164–165, 165–166, 167, 175–176, 176– 177, 283–285

Jacob or Jacobi, David 6, 166, 168, 170, 176, 177, 265, 266, 346
Jonson, Agnes, *alias* Little Mother Agnes 37, 38, 44, 59, 60, 158, 161, 179, 180, 181, 182, 188, 189, 221, 222, **232–234, 236–237,** 239, 240, 241, 242, **270– 273,** 330, 332
Jonson, daughter of Agnes (*see* Grey, Margaret)
Jonson *alias* Cutler, John 12, 13, 32, 35, 39, 43, 57, 59, 102, 104, **105, 109–113,** 117, 120, 143, 144, 147, 149, 154, 155, 180, 181, 194, 201, 202, **223–227, 270–273,** 332
Jordan Well, street or ward of Coventry 125, 126

Katherine, wife of a miller in Gosford Street 147, 149, 180, 182, 340
Kent, Ralph 40, 44, 108, 109, 139, 140, 332
Kent, William 40, 44, 103, 104, 108, 109, 139, 140, 332
Kingswinford (West Midlands) 193
'knowen man' 39, 150, 151, 155, 159
Kylyngworth, Thomas 59, 60, 119, 121, **209–210, 247,** 332

Lacock (*see* Locock)
Landesdale or Londesdale, Margaret 28, 59, 110, 112, 116, 119, 122, 123, 179, 181, **208–209, 219, 221,** 222, 223, **273–276,** 282, 333, 334
Landesdale or Londesdale, Richard 27n (101), 28, 141, 142, 197, 198, 333, 334, 337

Landesdale or Londesdale, Roger 9, 12, 13, 21, 22, 24, 26, 27n (101), 28, 32, 34–35, 36, 38, 42, 43, 44, 46, 57, 58, 59, 102, 104, 106, 107, 110, 112, **114, 116–121**, 122, 123, 124, 125, 126, 128, 129, 130, 131, 132, 133, 134, 135, 136, 137, 138, 139, 140, 141, 142, 147, 149, 151, 152, 153, 156, 159, **165–168, 169–170**, 178, 179, 180, 181, 182, 183, 184, 185, 186, 187, 188, 189, 190, 191, 194, 197, 198, 199, 200, 201, 202, 204, 207, 208, 209, 210, 211, 212, **213**, 214, 215, 216, 219, 221, 222, 223, 231, 232, 253, 254, **266–269**, 273, 281, 282, 286n (15), 289n (91), **297–298, 303–304, 309–310, 312–313**, 319n (3), 328, 331, 333, 334, 335, 337, 341

Landesdale or Londesdale, Thomas 9, 24, **297–298, 303–304, 309–310, 312–313**, 315, 316, 319n (3), 333

Landesdale or Londesdale?, daughter of Joan Smyth 156, 160, 197, 198, 333, 337

Latemer, (Thomas?) 128, 129

Latimer, Thomas 287n (53)

Laughton en le Morthen (South Yorkshire) 198, 199

Leadership of heretical community 44

Legenda aurea (Golden Legend) 343
    (*see also* Lives of saints)

Lehe, Hugh 74, 77, 88, 92, 346–347

Leicester (Leicestershire) 24, 25, 33, 39, 48, 102, 103, 116, 117, 118, 121, 124, 126, 139, 140, 146, 147, 148, 149, 157, 160, 185, 186, 288n (71), 290n (112), 328, 329, 338

Letter, Bishop Geoffrey Blyth to Bishop William Smith 48, 139–141

Lever, Thomas 54

Lewys, Henry 74, 77, 347

Leylonde, Richard 73, 77, 80, 84, 347

Lichfield Cathedral, proceedings in 3, 97, 99

Lichfield Court Book 1, 3, 11, 19–20, 47, 48, 49–50

Lichfield episcopal palace, proceedings in 3, 94, 96

Lieff (*see* Lyeff)

Literacy 43–45, 108, 109, 147, 148, 149, 150, 179, 181, 200, 201, 203, 217, 218, 222
    (*see also* Books; Gatherings, reading at; Memorization of religious texts)

Little Mother Agnes (*see* Jonson, Agnes)

Little Park, Coventry 10, 36, 115, 118, 121, 131, 132, 198, 199, 298, 304, 310, 313, 315, 316, 317, 319n (2)

Little Park Street, Coventry 118, 120, 124, 126

Lives of saints, book containing 34, 42, 133, 134, 343

Lockyn, of Maidstone 238, 239, 333

Lockyn, wife of 238, 239, 333

Locock or Lacock, Henry 122, 123, 259, 333

Locock or Lacock, Margery 8, 57, 108, **122–123**, 259, 333

Lodge, former husband of Alice Lye 119n, 121n, 158, 161, 185n, 187n

Lodge, William 12, 13, 25, 34, 59, 109, 111, **199–201**, 201, 202, 207, 334

Lollard books (*see* Books; Lollard or Wycliffite texts)

Lollard or Wycliffite texts 15, 31, 41–42, 115, 118, 121, 345

Londesdale (*see* Landesdale)

London 39, 43, 109, 110, 111, 112, 184, 186, 233, 238, 239, 253, 254, 324, 334, 339

Longhold or Longhald, John 36, 58, 59, 147, 149, 179, 181, 185, 187, 188, **189–191, 198–199, 205–206**, 210, 211, **260–263**, 334

Longland, Master 142, 143, 156, 159

Lord's Prayer (*see* Our Father)

Lowe, Ralph 60, **282**

Lye, Alice 59, 119n, 121n, 158, 161, 185n, 187n, 200, 201, **209**, 334

Lye, Ralph 58, 117, 120, 125, 127, 131, 132, 146, 148, **174–175, 175–177, 177–178, 273–276**, 287n (39), 334

Lye, Robert 200, 201, 209, 334

Lyeff, Thomas 59, 147, 149, 179, 181, 185, 187, 188, 189, 210, 211, 212, **215, 220, 221, 270–273**, 334

Lyeff, wife of Thomas 179, 181, 334

Maclyn (*see* Markelond)

Maidstone (Kent) 40, 109, 111, 178, 180, 238, 239, 253, 254, 255, 256, 326, 333

Margaret, Mother 12, 36, 148, 149, 158, 161, 286n (17), 340

Markelond or Maclyn, Matthew 4, 13, 45, 47, 58, 106, 107, 118, 120–121, 124, 126, 131, 132, 145, 146, 148, **152–153, 169–170, 266–269**, 334

Marketplace, Coventry, penance performed in 76, 79, 82, 85, 190, 191, 205, 206, 225, 226, 227

Mary, Virgin 16–17, 64, 65, 299, 305
  (*see also* Doncaster, Our Lady of; Hail
  Mary; Images, pilgrimages and
  shrines; Parentage of Christ; Tower,
  Our Lady of the; Walsingham, Our
  Lady of)
Maxstoke (Warwickshire) 11, 240
Maxstoke Castle 5, 240
Maxstoke Priory 5, 6, 9, 37, 109, 111, 134,
  135, 137, 138, 140, 162, 164, 166, 168,
  169, 170, 176, 177, 189, 190, 221, 224,
  225, 226, 264, 266, 283, 284, 297, 303,
  310, 312
Memorization of religious texts 45, 124,
  126, 154, 200, 201, 224, 226
Mill Lane, Coventry 103, 104, 148, 149
Mirfield (West Yorkshire) 196
More, Thomas 31
Morton, John, Archbishop of Canterbury
  (1486–1500) 253, 254
Mourton or Morton, Simon 297, 298, 303,
  304, 309–310, 312–313, 347
Myldener, of London 238, 239, 334

Napton (Warwickshire) 26, 145, 153, 154,
  171, 173, 337
Nayler, John 223–224, 225–226, 334
New Gate, Coventry 155, 159
New Testament, book containing 29, 42,
  117–118, 120, 157, 160, 343
Northampton (Northamptonshire) 39, 238,
  239, 335
Northopp, Richard 33, 58, 156, 157, 160,
  185, 186, **196**, 197, 335, 337
Northopp, wife of Richard 156, 157, 160,
  185, 186, 196, 197, 198, 335, 337

Oaths 19, 22, 95, 96, 311, 314
Occupations of suspects 25–26, 33, 322–
  340
Old Testament 35, 42, 116, 118, 119–120,
  121, 125, 126, 132, 133, 343
Olyver, John 11, 60, **240**
Olyver, wife of John 240
Orthodox devotional works 15, 30, 31, 34–
  35, 41–42, 343–344
Orton, Thomas 224, 226, 252, 254, 280,
  281, 347
Ose, tawyer of Northampton 238, 239, 335
Our Father (*Pater noster*) 18, 19, 22, 67, 68,
  95, 96, 124, 126, 168, 297–298, 300,
  301, 303–304, 306, 307, 309, 310, 311,
  312, 313, 314

Our Father (*Pater noster*) – *contd*
  scroll or book containing 10, 53, 54, 72,
  73, 295, 296, 298, 302, 304, 308,
  310, 313, 315, 316
Our Lady of the Tower (*see* Tower, Our
  Lady of the)

Padland, John 27n (101), 28n (103), 106,
  107, 118, 121, 124, 126, 141, 142, 337
Padland, Thomas 28n (103)
Padwell, Henry 109–110, 112, 223, 225,
  335
Padwell, wife of Henry 224, 226, 335
Palden, William 6, 224, 226, 252, 254,
  347
Park (*see* Little Park, Coventry)
Park Hollow, Coventry 319n (2)
Parentage of Christ 18, 19, 66, 67, 68, 69,
  88, 91
Parrek or Parret, Hugh 45, 59, 119, 121,
  122, **210–211**, 219, **221**, **273–276**,
  335
Passion of Christ and Adam (*see* Christ's
  Passion and Adam)
Pater noster (*see* Our Father)
Peg, Robert 13, 58, 116, 119, 124, 126, 130,
  131, 132, 146, 148, **151–152**, **165–168**,
  169–170, **173–174**, **175–177**, **177–
  178**, **273–276**, 335
Penance, sacrament of, attitudes towards
  66, 67, 68, 69, 71–72, 280, 281, 300,
  301–302, 302–303, 306, 307
Penances and sentences 7–11
  badges painted with faggots 10, 298, 303
  branding 40, 238, 239, 253, 254
  execution by burning (relaxation to
    secular arm) 9–10, 36, 40, 49, 56,
    207, 241, 242, 256, 257, 258, 284,
    285, 295, 296, 298, 304, 310, 311,
    313, 314, 315, 316, 317, 318
  fasting 8, 227, 228
  hanging in public market, with ears
    nailed to gallows 295, 296
  imprisonment 10–11, 75–76, 79
  offering at shrine of Our Lady of the
    Tower, Carmelite friary 7, 9, 76,
    79–80, 82, 85–86, 241, 242
  offering before crucifix in parish church
    90, 94
  penitents forbidden to enter church
    certain days 190, 191, 205, 206
  penitents forbidden to work certain days
    8, 190, 191, 205, 206

Penances and sentences – *contd*
  procession in penitential garb, carrying
    faggot 7, 76, 79–80, 82, 85–86, 90,
    94, 95, 97, 134, 136, 137, 138, 171,
    172, 173, 190, 191, 205, 206, 210,
    211, 219, 224–225, 226, 227, 229,
    230, 233, 234, 236, 295, 296, 297,
    303, 310, 313, 315, 316, 317
  same as that of Thomas Flesshor
    (procession with faggot) 163, 165,
    166, 167, 169, 170, 174, 190, 191,
    205, 206, 225, 226, 236, 237
  same as that of Robert Silkby
    (procession with faggot) 177, 178,
    220, 221
  watching execution of another 9, 241,
    242
  women's mitigated 8, 122, 123, 166, 167,
    169, 170
Penkridge (Staffordshire) 204
Peyntour Jr (*see* Atkynson *alias* Peyntour
  Jr)
Peyntour Sr (*see* Davy *alias* Peyntour Sr)
Phisicion (*see* Blumston *alias* Phisicion)
Pilgrimage (*see* Doncaster, Our Lady of;
  Hailes, Holy Blood of; Images, pil-
  grimages and shrines; Tower, Our
  Lady of the; Walsingham, Our Lady
  of)
Pollesworthe, William 6, 169, 170, 176, 177,
  264, 266, 347
Poor, alms and offerings to be given to the
  17, 19, 21, 65, 66, 72, 95, 96, 103, 104,
  150, 151, 157, 160, 199, 235, 300, 302,
  306, 307–308
Pope, attitudes towards 17, 18, 22, 64–65,
  145, 299, 305
Pratt, Robert 74, 77, 88, 92, 347, 348
Prayer as intercession, objections to 64, 65,
  70, 299, 301, 305, 307
Prayer in English, advocacy of 10, 17–18,
  19, 22, 23, 41, 54, 67, 68, 72, 73, 295,
  296, 297–298, 303–304, 309–310, 311,
  312–313, 314, 315, 316
  (*see also* Creed; Hail Mary; Our Father)
Preston, friar 29n (107), 150, 151, 222, 288n
  (76)
Preston, James 29, 157, 160, 288n (76),
  335
Preston, John 73, 77, 347
Preston, Lancashire 105, 107
Primer or book of hours 42, 145, 344
Prophecies 185, 186

Prosecution of heresy
  defendants directly confronted by wit-
    nesses for the prosecution 12–13,
    151, 152, 201, 202, 213, 217, 218, 233
  defendants, number 24, 342
  inquiry into heresy in Coventry by 'two
    trustworthy men' 251
  strategies 11–12, 15–16, 18, 19–20, 23
  suspects, number implicated 24, 342
  use of witnesses from outside heretical
    community 11, 240, 282
Psalter 42, 155, 159, 343
Purgatory 64, 65, 68, 69, 70, 299, 301, 305,
  307
Pursell, John 224, 226, 347
Pygstappe 24, 44, **273–276**, 336
Pysford, Henry 290n (112)
Pysford, Master 32, 128, 129, 185, 186, 290n
  (112)
Pysford, William Sr 30, 237, 238, 290n
  (112), 291n (145), 336

Questionnaires (*see* Interrogatories)
Qwyck, Robert 223, 224, 225, 226, 336

Ralph, weaver (*see* Lye, Ralph)
Randall, Agnes 53
Receiving or concealing of suspect persons
  as element of heresy 20, 74–75, 78, 84,
    89, 93, 98, 100, 106, 107, 135, 136, 137,
    138, 157, 160, 162, 163, 164, 166, 167,
    176, 177, 261, 262, 264, 265, 266, 267,
    269, 271, 272, 273, 274, 275, 276
  (*see also* Coventry heretical community,
    visitors to)
Recruitment to heresy 32–35
Redcliff Street, Bristol 109, 111–112
Redhell, Thomas 191, 192, 338
Relapse into heresy 6–7, 9–10, 40, 164, 178,
  181, 239–240, 241, 242, 252–254, 255–
  257, 283–285, 310, 313
Rerum in ecclesia gestarum [. . .] commentarii (*see*
  Foxe, John)
Revelation of St John (*see* Apocalypse)
Revis, Katherine 25, 37, 157, 160, 180, 181,
  184, 186, 336
Revis, William 12, 59, 60, 119, 121, 128,
  129, 157, 158, 160, 161, 180, 181, 184,
  186, 187, **211**, **219–220**, 222, **245–
  246**, 336
Reynesford, James 128, 129
Rise, Richard 60, 158, 161, 188, 189, **243–
  244**, **250–251**, 259, 336, 341

Rowley, Alice 4, 5n (12), 9, 12, 13, 20, 21, 25, 27–29, 30, 35, 36, 37, 38, 39, 40, 42, 44, 45, 46, 57, 58, 59, 60, 102, 103, 104, 106, 107, 110, 112, 116–117, 119–120, **123–124**, 125, 126, 130–131, 131–132, 142, 143, 145, 146, 148, 149, 150, 151, **155–161**, 178, 179, 180, 181, 182, 194, 217, 218, 219, **230**, 233, 234, 235, 238, 239, 240, **241–242**, 253, 254, **273–276**, 289nn (85–86), 291n (140), 315, 316, 317, 336, 341
Rowley, Thomas 11, 25, 27–28, 282
Rowley, William 25, 27–28, 39, 123, 123–124, 238, 239, 315, 316, 336
Rutland, county 202, 204

St David's, diocese of 215
St John's parish (see Throapham St John's parish)
St Michael's parish, Coventry 29, 80, 84, 94, 96, 280, 281, 315, 316
   proceedings in church 63, 81, 84, 299, 305, 309, 312
   penitential procession from or in 7, 76, 79, 82, 83, 85–86, 134, 136, 137, 138–139, 171, 172, 173, 190, 191, 205, 206, 233, 234, 236, 237
St Nicholas's parish, Bristol 223, 225
St Philip's and St James's parish, Bristol 223, 225
St Thomas's parish, Bristol 223, 225
St Vincent's chapel, near Bristol 224, 226, 291n (137)
St Werburgh's parish, Chester 182, 183
Salter, Richard 88, 92, 347
Salvation through faith, not works 16, 65, 66, 68, 69, 70, 300, 301, 305–306, 307
Schools 67, 68, 300, 306
Seacoal Lane, London 109, 111
Secrecy and secret words within heretical community 29, 36, 45, 68, 69, 108, 110, 112, 117, 120, 125, 127, 142, 143, 156, 157, 160, 194, 195, 197, 198, 201, 202, 216, 218, 222, 227, 228, 231, 301, 306
Sentences (see Penances)
Sharpe, John 74, 77, 88, 92, 347
Sheperde, John 4, 19, 57, **97–101**, 336
Sheriffs of Coventry 256, 257, 258, 282, 348
   (see also Crampe, Thomas; Dawes, Hugh; Dod, Thomas; Rowley, Thomas; Turner, Thomas)

Shoemaker, Christopher 289n (99)
   (see also Christopher, shoemaker)
Shor, Ralph 41, 125, 126, 337
Shrines (see Doncaster, Our Lady of; Hailes, Holy Blood of; Images, pilgrimages and shrines; Tower, Our Lady of the; Walsingham, Our Lady of)
Shugborow, Balthasar 20, 22, 26–27, 30, 35, 37, 43n (171), 44, 58, 102, 103, 104, 106, 107, 108, 113, 114, 118, 120, 124, 126, 135, 136, 137, 138, **144–145**, 158, 161, **171–173**, **175–177**, 197, 198, 200, 201, 203, **273–276**, 337
Shugborow or Shukborowe, Thomas 26n (97)
Shugborow or Shukeborowe, William 26–27n (97)
Silkby, alias Dumbleby, Robert 6–7, 8, 10, 12, 13, 21, 23, 24, 26, 32, 35, 36, 37, 38, 39, 40, 41, 42, 43, 44, 45, 46, 49, 50, 57, 58, 59, 60, **102–104**, 105, 106, 107, **108–109**, 110, 111, 112, 113, 114, 115, 116, 118, 119, 120, 122, 123, 124, 126, 127, 128, 129, 130, 131, 132, 135, 136, 137, 138, 139, 140, **146–150**, 151, 155, 156, 157, 158, 159, 160, 161, 171, 172, 173, 174, 175, 178, 179, 180, 181, 182, 185, 186, 187, **189–191**, 194, 195, 197, 198, 201, 202, 204, **205–206**, 207, 208, 214, 215, 217, 218, 224, 226, 231, 232, 234, 239, 240, 250, 253, 254, **260–263**, **283–285**, 297, **298**, 303, **304**, **311**, **313–314**, 315, 316, 317, 318, 332, 337
Sin, venial and mortal 20–21, 155, 159
Skelton, William 6, 135, 138, 166, 168, 170, 176, 177, 224, 226, 264, 266, 347
Skelton (Yorkshire) 109, 111
Smith, William, Bishop of Lincoln (1495–1514) 48, 139–141
Smyth, daughters of Joan (see Landesdale?, daughter of Joan Smyth; Northopp, wife of Richard)
Smyth, Joan 9–10, 11, 25, 27–29, 30, 38, 43, 44, 46, 52–53, 54, 57, 58, 106, 107, 117, 118, 120, 121, 124, 126, **141–143**, 155, 156, 157, 159, 160, **161–165**, 197, 198, 208, 231, 232, **270–273**, 282, **295–296**, **297–298**, **303–304**, **309–310**, **312–313**, 315, 316, 327, 333, 335, 337
Smyth, John 17, 32, 57, **63**, **67–68**, **73–80**, **80–87**, 109, 111, 125, 127, 145, 152, 153, **300**, **306**, 329, 330, 337, 338

Smyth, Richard 27–28, 106, 107, 117, 118,
    120, 121, 124, 126, 141, 142, 156, 159,
    162, 163, 164, 271, 273, 337
Smyth, wife of John (*see* Gest, wife of
    Richard, formerly wife of John Smyth)
Spenser, father of Thomas 147, 149, 197,
    337
Spenser, Thomas 25, 42, 44, 58, 59, 147,
    149, 156, 157, 160, 171, 172, 185, 186,
    189–191, 194, 195, **197–198**, **205–
    206**, 206, 210, 211, **260–263**, 337
Spon, John 34–35, 37, 45, 57, 60, 110, 112,
    116, 118, 119, 120, 121, 125, 126, 131,
    132, **132–134**, 145, 147, 149, 156, 159,
    203, 222, 223, **250–251**, 259, 337
Sporyer, Roger 280, 281
Stafford, John (friar) 297, 303, 310, 312–
    313, 347
Stafford (Staffordshire) 182, 183
Stivichall (Warwickshire) 128, 129
Stoney Stanton (Leicestershire) 40, 103,
    104, 108, 109, 139, 140, 332
Strangeweys or Strangwais, George 88, 92,
    97–101, 347–348
Stronge, John 315, 316, 317
Stubbe, Hugh 108, 122, 123, 333
Sykeman or *Sikeman, The* 37, 42, 147, 149,
    179, 181, 201, 202, 344
    (*see also Here begynneth a lytell treatyse of a
    dyenge creature enfected with sykenes*)
Symon 11, 57, **122**

Tailiour, John, 158, 161, 337, 338
Taunton (Somerset), 110, 112
Temple church, Bristol, 223, 225
Thomas, bottlemaker of Bristol, 223–224,
    225–226, 340
Thomas, bottlemaker of Bristol, wife of
    224, 226, 340
Throapham St John's parish, near Laugh-
    ton en le Morthen (South Yorkshire)
    198, 199
Tithes 72, 154, 302, 307
Tobit, book containing 42, 106, 107, 116,
    120, 233, 234, 241, 242, 286n (24), 343
    discussion of, 198, 199
Toft, Roger 60, **250–251**, **277**, 338
Tower, Our Lady of the (Carmelite friary,
    Coventry) 7, 9, 16, 21–22, 64, 65, 66,
    67, 76, 79–80, 82, 85, 212, 214, 215,
    241, 242, 299, 300, 305, 306
Transience of suspects' involvement in
    heresy 13, 46–47

Trussell, Isabel 14, 43, 45, 60, 125, 126, 185,
    187, 222, 223, **248**, 249, 338
Trussell, Thomas 125, 126, 248, 338
Tuck, Henry 223, 224, 225, 226, 328
    (*see also* Duke, Tuke, or Tuck)
Tuke (*see* Duke, Tuck, or Tuke; Tuck,
    Henry)

Vernacular prayer (*see* Prayer in English)
Vernacular scripture (*see* Bible, translations
    of)
Vicars, John 280, 281
Villers, Charles 223, 224, 226, 225, 338
Villers, mother of Thomas Villers,
    Thomasina Bradeley, and the wife of
    Banbrooke 12, 33, 44, 146, 148, 201,
    202, 205n, 207, 208, 338
Villers, Thomas 12–13, 25, 33, 34, 37, 44,
    45, 58, 59, 111, 113, 146, 147, 148, 149,
    156, 160, 184, 186, **189–191**, **191–
    192**, **193**, 194, 195, 199, 200, **201–
    202**, **205–206**, 208, 215, **220**, 223,
    224, 225, 226, **270–273**, 338
Villers, wife of Charles 224, 226, 338
Villers, wife of Thomas 191, 192, 338
Virgin Mary (*see* Mary, Virgin)
Visitation Book (*see* Blyth's Visitation Book)

Walsingham, Our Lady of 16, 17, 65, 68,
    69, 299, 300, 305, 306, 64, 65, 299,
    300, 305, 306
Warde, *alias* Wasshingburn, Joan 9, 24, 25,
    28, 36, 37, 38, 39, 40, 44, 49, 56, 58,
    60, 158, 161, **178–182**, 183, 184, 221,
    222, 223, 234, **238–240**, 241, 242,
    252–254, **255–257**, **258**, 315, 316,
    317, 339
Warde, Thomas 4, 27, 35, 37, 42, 43–44,
    47, 58, 59, 147, 149, 171, 172, 179,
    181, 185, 186, 187, **189–191**, **202–
    204**, **205–206**, **273–276**, 338
Warham, William, Archbishop of Can-
    terbury (1503–1532) 8, 9
Warwick (Warwickshire) 128, 129
Wasshingburn, Joan (*see* Warde *alias* Wass-
    hingburn, Joan)
Wasshingburn, Thomas 39, 40, 238, 239,
    291n (148), 339
Webbe, John 6, 283, 284, 348
Weston, Richard 33, 130, 131, 339
White, Agnes Margaret 179, 181, 339
Wickam or Wixam, William 315, 316, 317,
    318

Wigston, [Agnes] 30, 237, 238, 291n (145), 339
Wigston, John 290n (112)
Wigston, Master 32, 185, 186, 290n (112)
Wigston, [William] 30, 237, 238, 290n (112), 291n (145), 339
Wilcocks, John 46, 236, 237, 252, 254, 348
Wilcocks, Richard 109, 111
Wills and bequests as evidence for heresy 29–30
Wilton or Wylton, William 6, 135, 138, 166, 168, 170, 176, 177, 224, 226, 264, 266, 348
Winchcombe (Gloucestershire) 197
Witnesses (see Prosecution)
Wixam (see Wickam)
Women among heresy suspects 29, 38, 44 (see also Coventry heretical community, gender ratio among suspects; Penances, women's mitigated)

Wrexham (Clwyd) 184, 186
Wrixham, Thomas 8, 9, 12, 32, 34, 58, 59, 118, 121, 131, 132, 146, 148, **184–187**, **189–191**, **205–206**, 215, 216, **260–263**, **297–298**, **303–304**, **309–310**, **312–313**, 315, 316, 339
Wyclif, John 1, 14, 21, 36, 182, 183
Wylton (see Wilton)

Yate, tailor of Coventry 179, 181
Ympingham (see Immpingham)
Yong, Agnes 36, 59, 60, 146, 148, 149, 155, 159, 217, 218, **232–234**, **236–237**, 241, 242, **270–273**, 339, 340
Yong, Julian 36, 44, 45, 46, 59, 147, 148, 149, 150, **217–218**, **220**, **221**, **270–273**, 329, 339, 340
Yonge, Joan 319n (1)
Yotton, John 97–101, 348